CATHOLIC RECORD SOCIETY
PUBLICATIONS

MONOGRAPH SERIES
VOLUME 9

Editor for the Catholic Record Society

Paul Arblaster

The Editorial Committee

Caroline Bowden
Judith Champ
Peter Doyle

A Youth Disco Cruise on a Mersey ferry during the National Pastoral Congress, Liverpool, 1980. Liverpool Archdiocesan Archives.

Lay Catholic Societies in Twentieth-Century Britain

Edited by
MARIA POWER AND JONATHAN BUSH

PUBLISHED FOR
THE CATHOLIC RECORD SOCIETY
BY
THE BOYDELL PRESS
2025

© The Catholic Record Society 2025
Registered Charity No. 313529

All rights reserved. Except as permitted under current legislation
no part of this work may be photocopied, stored in a retrieval system,
published, performed in public, adapted, broadcast,
transmitted, recorded or reproduced in any form or by any means,
without the prior permission of the copyright owner

First published 2025

ISBN 978-0-902832-36-7

A Catholic Record Society publication
published by The Boydell Press
an imprint of Boydell & Brewer Ltd
PO Box 9, Woodbridge, Suffolk IP12 3DF, UK
and of Boydell & Brewer Inc.
668 Mt Hope Avenue, Rochester, NY 14620–2731, USA
website: www.boydellandbrewer.com

A CIP catalogue record for this book is available
from the British Library

The publisher has no responsibility for the continued existence or accuracy
of URLs for external or third-party internet websites referred to in this book,
and does not guarantee that any content on such websites is, or will remain,
accurate or appropriate

Printed and bound in Great Britain by
TJ Books Limited, Padstow, Cornwall

This collection of essays is dedicated to our parents,
Alice and Eric Power
and
Edna and Nigel Bush
who gave us the gift of education.

CONTENTS

List of Contributors   xi
List of Abbreviations   xiv
Editors' Introduction   1

1. Lay Catholic Societies in the Twentieth Century: Historiographical Trends   3
   Maria Power

2. A Middle-Class Convert's *Crucible*: Margaret Fletcher and the Origins of the Catholic Women's League   20
   Kathryn Lamontagne

3. 'In the interests of justice, morality and religion': St Joan's Social and Political Alliance, 1920s–1930s   40
   Carmen M. Mangion

4. 'Its Achievements and its Hopes': The Catholic Evidence Guild between the Two World Wars   59
   Richard Finn O.P.

5. Catholic Action in Scotland: The Early Years of the Guild of Catholic Teachers   76
   Leonardo Franchi

6. The Newman Association and Lay Catholic Support for Exiled Polish Intellectuals in Britain, 1942–1962   94
   Jonathan Bush

7. 'Be proud to be a worker girl, like Christ your worker king': The Transformative Impact of the Young Christian Workers on Working-Class Catholic Girls and Young Women in the Long 1950s   113
   Pat Jones

8. 'Something more than a mere Catholic dining club'? English Catholic Masculinities, Religious Sociability and a Century of the Catenian Association   132
   Alana Harris

9. The British Catholic Worker Movement and Its Influence on Lay Social Catholicism   159
   Anna Blackman

10	'Today it is not the great saint who is thundering forth': The Laity and Catholic Charismatic Renewal in England *John Maiden*	180
11	HIV and AIDS in England and Wales: How Lay People Led the Catholic Response *Vincent Manning*	198

Bibliography 227
Index 243

CONTRIBUTORS

Anna Blackman is a Lecturer in Catholic Religious Education at the University of Glasgow. Prior to her time at Glasgow, she lectured at the universities of Roehampton, Durham, Newcastle and Tubingen, as well as working as a Research Associate in the area of Catholic social thought and practice at the Centre for Social Concerns at the University of Notre Dame. She serves on the Columban Missionaries in Britain's Justice, Peace and Integrity of Creation Committee and co-chairs the Catholic Theological Ethics in the World Church's roundtable on nonviolence and just peace. Anna has also worked with the London, Glasgow and South Bend, IN, Catholic Workers. Her previous publications on the Catholic Worker movement include the articles 'Nourishing Nonviolence: Dorothy Day as Exemplar and Educator', *Journal of Catholic Social Thought*, 20/2 (2023), pp. 305–26; and 'Holy Disobedience: Political Resistance in the London Catholic Worker Community', *Implicit Religion*, 21/2 (2018), pp. 122–41.

Dr Jonathan Bush is a qualified archivist working at Durham University. Prior to his current role as University Archivist, he spent ten years developing the Catholic collections of Durham University and at Ushaw College. This included acquiring, cataloguing and making publicly available a number of Catholic lay society collections, including the Newman Association, the National Board of Catholic Women, and Catholics for a Changing Church. He is currently the Chair of the Catholic Archives Society, an organisation that provides guidance to Catholic archives on managing their collections. He specialises in nineteenth- and twentieth-century Catholic history and is the author of *'Papists' and Prejudice: Popular Anti-Catholicism and Anglo-Irish Conflict in the North-East of England, 1845–70* (Newcastle, 2013).

Rev. Dr Richard Finn is a Dominican Friar and Director of the Las Casas Institute for Social Justice at Blackfriars Hall in the University of Oxford, where he is a member of the Faculties of Classics, and Theology and Religion. He is the author of *Almsgiving in the Later Roman Empire* (Oxford University Press, 2006), *Asceticism in the Greco-Roman World* (Cambridge University Press, 2009), and *The Dominicans in the British Isles and Beyond* (Cambridge University Press, 2023).

Dr Leonardo Franchi is an academic in the University of Glasgow (School of Education) and the University of Notre Dame Australia (School of Philosophy and Theology). His scholarly interests include religious education, teacher formation, and the potential of the liberal arts to shape higher education. Leonardo has published widely in these areas. He is currently a series editor for *Catholic Education Globally – Challenges and Opportunities*, published by Springer, and *Education and Integral Human Development*, published by Catholic University of America Press. He sits on the Executive of the Association of Catholic Institutes of Education (a sectorial body of the International Federation of Catholic Universities) and has since September 2024 been co-convenor of the Scottish Catholic Historical Association.

Dr Alana Harris is a Reader in Modern British Social, Cultural, and Gender History at King's College London, having previously acted as the Director of Liberal Arts and taught as a Fellow at Lincoln College, University of Oxford. She has authored eight books, including the pathbreaking *Faith in the Family: A Lived Religious History of English Catholicism, 1945–1982* (Manchester University Press, 2013) and her most recent publication as editor of *The Oxford History of British and Irish Catholicism, 1914–2021* (Oxford University Press, 2023).

Dr Pat Jones is a post-doctoral research associate in the Centre for Catholic Studies at Durham University. Her doctorate explored experiences of Catholic social mission in relation to Catholic social teaching. Previously she was a senior manager for Depaul International and deputy director of CAFOD. Earlier, she was the first lay female assistant general secretary to the Catholic Bishops' Conference and director of adult formation for many years in her home diocese of Liverpool.

Dr Kathryn Lamontagne is Senior Lecturer in Social Sciences and History at Boston University, USA. She is a social and cultural historian who works in areas of gender, sexuality and faith in the British Atlantic world. Educated in the US at Jesuit and Dominican institutions, she is the author of *Reconsidering Lay Catholic Women: Pious Transgressors in Late Nineteenth and Early Twentieth Century England* (Routledge, 2024) and appears regularly in the US media as an authority on the monarchy.

Dr John Maiden is Head of Department and Senior Lecturer in Religious Studies at The Open University. He has authored widely on global evangelicalism, Protestant and Catholic charismatic movements, and anti-Catholicism in the twentieth century. His latest book is *Age of the Spirit: Charismatic Renewal, the Anglo-World and Global Christianity, 1945–1980* (Oxford University Press, 2022). He is also Director of the Evangelical Studies Programme at Baylor University, Texas.

Dr Carmen M. Mangion teaches modern British history at Birkbeck University of London. Her research examines the cultural and social history of gender and religion in nineteenth- and twentieth-century Britain, relating to how religious identities were formed, imagined and lived during times of social change. Her most recent edited volume, co-edited with Susan O'Brien, *Oxford History of British and Irish Catholicism, Volume 4, Building Identity, 1830–1913* (Oxford University Press, 2023) examines the Catholic revival in Britain and Ireland. Her current research has two strands: examining religious life in the inner city after 1970, and interrogating the decline of the lay sisters state of religious life, 1880s–1960.

Dr Vincent Manning is Director of Catholics for AIDS Prevention and Support (CAPS) C.I.O. which supports people living with HIV in the UK and Ireland. He has been involved in HIV activism since the late 1980s. His PhD research explored the theological meaning and spiritual significance of HIV for Christians diagnosed with HIV and living in the UK.

Dr Maria Power is a Senior Research Fellow at the Las Casas Institute for Social Justice, Blackfriars Hall, University of Oxford. Her work focuses mainly on peacebuilding within divided communities in Northern Ireland. Her most recent publications include *Catholic Social Teaching and Theologies of Peace in Northern Ireland: Cardinal Cahal Daly and the Pursuit of the Peaceable Kingdom* (Routledge, 2021) and *Violence and Peace in Sacred Texts* (Palgrave, 2023). She is currently writing a monograph exploring the role of the Bible in the conflict in Northern Ireland, which will be published by Routledge in 2025.

ABBREVIATIONS

ACTU	Association of Catholic Trade Unionists
CAGO	Catholic Action Girls Organisation
CAL	Catholic AIDS Link
CAPS	Catholics for AIDS Prevention and Support
CCRSC	Catholic Charismatic Renewal Services Committee
CDF	Congregation for the Doctrine of the Faith
C.E.G.	Catholic Evidence Guild
CL	Catholic Life
CLFF	Catholic Life and Family Forum
CMAC	Catholic Marriage Advisory Council
CPA	Catholic Peace Action
CSG	Catholic Social Guild
CW	Catholic Worker
CWFF	Catholic Worker and Family Forum
CWL	Catholic Women's League
CWSS	Catholic Women's Suffrage Society
ICAN	International Christian AIDS Network
IEF	International Ecumenical Fellowship
JOC	Jeunesse ouvrière chrétienne [Young Christian Workers]
LofC	Ladies of Charity
NCAN	National Catholic AIDS Network
N.C.W.C.	National Catholic Welfare Conference
NSC	National Service Committee
THT	Terrence Higgins Trust
YCW	Young Christian Workers

EDITORS' INTRODUCTION

Maria Power and Jonathan Bush

This collection of essays originated from a series of conversations between the editors at Ushaw College, Durham. In 2019, Power was a Holland Fellow researching the Catholic Women's League, and Bush was the archivist of the collection. During these conversations, we noted that notwithstanding the Catholic Church's vibrant history of lay Catholic activity both before and after the Second Vatican Council, and archival material being available, the history of British lay Catholic societies remains largely unwritten. This collection of essays is an attempt to meet that need. It seeks to showcase the scope of existing research and inspire further research into all areas of lay activity in Britain. The fact that this history can be written at all is in no small part due to the greater accessibility of lay society archive collections to researchers, a phenomenon predominantly facilitated by the expanded acquisition policies of various archival repositories. These endeavours have notably focused on rescuing endangered Catholic collections, many of which faced imminent loss. Prominent members of these societies have recognised the pivotal role played by lay societies in the broader context of the twentieth-century Catholic Church. Consequently, they have demonstrated a commendable willingness to entrust their valuable collections to archival repositories, with the stipulation that these resources be made readily available for historical research. Despite these efforts, the proportion of lay society collections in archival repositories remains negligible. Many collections continue to languish in the garages, attics or spare rooms of private houses, posing a genuine risk of neglect or destruction. It is our aspiration, therefore, that the dissemination of this collection of scholarly essays will serve to heighten public awareness regarding the crucial role played by Catholic lay societies and underscore the imperative of preserving these records for the benefit of future generations.

This collection comprises eleven chapters which are organised chronologically. The opening chapter by Power maps the current historiography of lay Catholic societies in twentieth-century Britain. This historiographical review demonstrates the weight placed on pre-Vatican II lay Catholic societies in the literature. It is an emphasis mirrored in this collection, and it reflects the wider landscape of research on the history of the Catholic laity in twentieth-century Britain. Power suggests further avenues for research and the collection of the life histories of the post-Vatican II lay activists who are now reaching old age. This is followed by chapters from Kathryn G. Lamontagne and Carmen M. Mangion, both of whom present the history of women's organisations: the Catholic Women's League and the St Joan's Social and Political Alliance. Both essays focus on the early years of the twentieth century and show how Catholic women organised to improve their social, political and economic positions within society. The next chapter by Richard Finn O.P. explores the history of the Catholic Evidence Guild during the interwar period. In this essay, Finn demonstrates how lay Catholics were trained to promote Catholicism through public speaking and debate. Chapter five turns to Catholic action in Scotland with Leonard Franchi charting the foundation of the Guild of Catholic Teachers. In doing so, he shows how bishops, clergy and laity worked together to create an organisation that emphasised the mission of the laity. In chapter six, Jonathan Bush illustrates the work undertaken by the Newman Association in support of exiled Polish intellectuals. It shows the way in which, in the years immediately following the Second World War, lay societies adopted an outward-facing and globally conscious perspective that was shaped by pan-Europeanism, anti-communism and Catholic social teaching. Pat Jones returns to the theme of lay women with her chapter on the Young Christian Workers during the long 1950s. Here the emphasis is once more on methods of evangelisation with working-class women, the gendered nature of this work, and the women's journeys through the Young Christian Worker Movement. The theme of gender is also explored in Alana Harris's chapter on the Catenian Association, founded in 1908 in Manchester. Harris demonstrates how this middle-class organisation provided Catholic laymen with a wider means of expressing their faith than Mass attendance. In her chapter on the Catholic Worker movement in Britain, Anna Blackman looks at the movement's development, and in particular the publication of the *Catholic Worker*. John Maiden's chapter on the Catholic charismatic renewal or Pentecostalist movement explores its development in the 1970s and 1980s, and its relationship to the movement in the United States. Finally, Vincent Manning's chapter outlines lay Catholic responses to the HIV/AIDS pandemic in the 1980s and 1990s.

The 'twentieth century' in the title of this volume may appear, at first glance, to be a misnomer. Most of the essays concentrate on the period before the Second Vatican Council, with only two venturing into the later years of the century. This is a result of the deliberate choice of the authors to emphasise the importance of a lively and sustained culture of pre-conciliar lay Catholicism, challenging the narrative of 'rupture' often associated with the effects of Vatican II. Although the importance of the Second Vatican Council to lay Catholicism should not be underestimated, most of the essays in this volume demonstrate that lay activism and spirituality existed long before ordinary Catholics were gifted this agency by papal decree.

1

LAY CATHOLIC SOCIETIES IN THE TWENTIETH CENTURY: HISTORIOGRAPHICAL TRENDS

Maria Power

In the introduction to Volume V of the new *Oxford History of British and Irish Catholicism*, the editor, Alana Harris, describes the twentieth century as 'a century of the laity'.[1] Such a characterisation calls attention not only to the increased importance of the laity within the Catholic Church itself, but also to the flourishing of lay societies which 'were established to address pressing moral issues, ameliorate challenging social conditions, and work for the "rechristianisation" of society. Speaking to concerns spanning the "Catholic Family", politics and economics, working-class unrest, and middle-class movement into the professions',[2] these organisations demonstrated the increased confidence of the Catholic community in Britain resulting from social mobility and growth brought about by mass immigration from traditionally Catholic countries such as Ireland, Poland and Italy. Further 'the First World War accelerated public toleration of Catholicism, putting any vestigial suspicions of Catholic disloyalty to rest, and with this heightened sense of being part of the national community came a greater confidence and assertiveness on the part of its leaders'.[3] As early as the turn of the twentieth century,

> a social Catholicism [inspired by papal encyclicals] was developing, distinct from traditional charitable works, and local political involvement, with lay leadership subordinate to clerical leadership. ... New avenues of evangelisation opened up for the laity at national and diocesan levels, while the laity was itself changing through education and the impact of lay converts used to a greater civil and social involvement.[4]

---

[1] Alana Harris, 'Introduction' in *The Oxford History of British and Irish Catholicism, Volume V: Recapturing the Apostolate of the Laity 1914—2021*, edited by Alana Harris (Oxford, 2023), p. 6.
[2] Harris, 'Introduction', p. 1.
[3] Kester Aspden, *Fortress Church: The English Roman Catholic Bishops and Politics, 1903–1963* (Leominster, 2002), p. 9.
[4] Peter Doyle, 'Episcopal Leaders and Leadership', in *The Oxford History of British and Irish Catholicism, Volume IV: Building Identity 1830–1913*, edited by Carmen M. Mangion and Susan O'Brien (Oxford, 2023), pp. 53–4.

However, this history of lay Catholic societies somewhat complicates the traditional picture of Catholicism in twentieth-century Britain. Whilst some conformed to the stereotype of a 'self-contained, distinctive Catholic milieu',[5] others provide a picture of Catholics engaging with the world beyond the walls of their parishes to influence social and political change through the lens of Catholic social teaching. Further, despite popular perceptions of the Second Vatican Council causing a rupture in the church and acting essentially as a second reformation, as this collection of essays demonstrates, it does not act as a hinge point in the history of lay societies. Instead throughout the century there were 'modulations or gradual, non-linear modifications of Catholics' understandings of their identities, beliefs and practices'.[6] This historiographical review seeks to set the scene for the essays on lay societies in twentieth-century Britain that follow. It will show the main themes that have emerged in writing on lay societies, concluding with a reflection on the gaps that still need to be addressed.

Ghetto Catholicism? The nature of the Catholic Church and its influence on lay societies

Writing on the nature of the Catholic Church in Britain during the first half of the twentieth century characterises the Church either as a 'Fortress'[7] or as a 'Ghetto'.[8] In *Roman Catholic Beliefs in England,* sociologist Michael Hornsby-Smith suggests that 'Roman Catholicism in England had something of the character of a ghetto church, at least until the 1950s.'[9] Hugh McLeod, in an influential article supporting this view, argues that there were three trends within the Catholic Church which caused this, summarised by Clifford Williamson as follows:

> First, there was the centralisation (or more accurately remaking of) the Catholic Church in the middle of the nineteenth century culminating in the Vatican Council of 1869–70 which re-established the papacy at the centre of the Catholic world both in doctrinal and organisational terms. Second, there was a revival in the membership and activities of religious orders. Although the reappearance of the Jesuits in particular can be seen as particularly inflammatory to

---

5   Alana Harris, *Faith in the Family: A Lived Religious History of English Catholicism, 1945–1982* (Manchester, 2013), p. 36.
6   Ibid., p. 3.
7   Aspden, *Fortress Church.*
8   Hugh McLeod, 'Building the Catholic "Ghetto": Catholic Organisations, 1870–1914', in *Voluntary Religion: Papers Read at the 1985 Summer Meeting and Winter Meeting of the Ecclesiastical History Society: Studies of Church History*, edited by William J. Sheils and Diana Wood (Oxford, 1986), pp. 411–44.
9   Michael Hornsby-Smith, *Roman Catholic Beliefs in England: Customary Catholicism and Transformation of Religious Authority* (Cambridge, 1991), p. 91.

anti-clericals, there was a practical dimension to this trend. The religious orders often provided key welfare and education services to the growing urban Catholic communities. The third trend was a revival of visible devotion, through the processional and pilgrimage movements associated with a series of Marian apparitions throughout the middle years of the nineteenth century.[10]

Here, McLeod paints a picture of an insular church, turned away from the world, and primarily concerned with ensuring the retention and devotion of its members. Laity, when they are mentioned, are presented as passive recipients of the faith. Post-Second World War Catholicism is presented in a similar fashion by Jay P. Corrin:

> British Catholicism after World War II can best be described as authoritarian and paternalistic in structure, leadership and teaching. The old aristocratic recusant families that had dominated the Church had been obliged to give way to Vatican ultramontane power with the restoration of the hierarchy in 1850, and gentry influence was further compromised by the huge infusion of Irish immigrants seeking employment in England's industrial cities.[11]

The Catholic Church certainly took an interventionist stance towards its adherents, and this influence is evident in some of the literature on lay Catholic societies which presents the parish being expected 'to act as focus for local Catholics'.[12] Indeed, the influence of the parish was believed to be such that it provided the main element of a Catholic's identity and could 'give a man or woman a place in a family society that will stop him from drifting into the hopeless position of a name on a card'.[13] The main aim of lay Catholic societies according to the historiography then was to support the Church in retaining its membership and in the interwar period at least 'the watchword ... was 'defence'. This is demonstrated by the likes of the Catholic Union where the emphasis of the Union was in keeping Catholics out of the way of harm and 'protected' from secular influences.'[14]

It is suggested that much of this behaviour was the result of the minority status of Catholics in British society. In 1921 (the earliest year that figures are available) Roman Catholics constituted approximately six per cent of the British population with this figure reaching a high

---

[10] Clifford Williamson, *The History of Catholic Intellectual Life in Scotland, 1918–1965* (London, 2016), p. 19.
[11] Jay P. Corrin, *Catholic Progressives in England after Vatican II* (South Bend, IN, 2013), p. 9.
[12] Joan Keating, 'Faith and Community Threatened? Roman Catholic Responses to the Welfare State, Materialism and Social Mobility, 1945–62', *Twentieth Century British History*, 9:1 (1998), p. 90.
[13] Morgan V. Sweeney, 'Diocesan Organisation and Administration', in *English Catholics 1850–1950*, edited by George Andrew Beck (London, 1950), p. 149.
[14] Williamson, *The History of Catholic Intellectual Life in Scotland*, p. 148.

of nine per cent in the 1970s and remaining there ever since.[15] Although numerically the Catholic population was characterised by growth and it was the largest Christian denomination after Anglicanism, in the opening years of the twentieth century, its minority status and separateness were emphasised by the suspicion of the majority population of its relationship with Rome and loyalty to the pope. James E. Kelly and John McCafferty state the importance of this thus: 'populist suspicion and the enduring presence of Catholics acted as serious engines of identity and state formation in England during the time of the faith's official proscription, from the reign of Elizabeth I to Catholic Emancipation in 1829'.[16] This suspicion endured until the early twentieth century. This operated in two ways, both of which impacted on the analysis of lay Catholic societies. First, within the Catholic community itself, it accentuated the ghetto mentality, creating a defensive stance towards society and a desire to protect communal interests[17] which will be illustrated later in the discussion of Catholicism and socialism. Secondly, there was the phenomenon of anti-Catholicism which although becoming more latent as the century progressed still impacted upon believers' lives which, with 'its underlying everyday presence, largely invisible to the historical record, no doubt impacted significantly on the lives of individual Catholics, from the Irish poor ... to socially elite converts, who felt themselves ostracised and distrusted by relatives and former friends, and women labelled 'unnatural' for entering religious communities'.[18] This anti-Catholicism was further accentuated by the perceived control that clergy and bishops had on the lives of lay Catholics – a control which is characterised by Michael Hornsby-Smith as a 'rule-bound Catholicism'.[19]

To the outsider looking into the Catholic Church, it certainly seemed as though the laity were under the control of the clergy and bishops. Three examples from the literature illustrate this: David Holmes, in an article influenced by McLeod's thesis, argues that 'The Church's office was to teach its adherents what to believe and what to do, to direct them how to live and regulate the conduct of their lives. It considered the

---

[15] These figures have been calculated from Timothy Kinnear, 'Statistical Appendices' in *Oxford History of British and Irish Catholicism*, vol. V, pp. 357–77. The numbers of Catholics in Britain in the twentieth century were as follows: 2.5 million in 1921; 2.8 million in 1931; 3 million in 1939/40; 3.5 million in 1951; 4.3 million in 1961; 4.8 million in 1970/71; 5 million in 1981; 5 million in 1991; 4.8 million in 2001.
[16] James E. Kelly and John McCafferty, 'Series Introduction', in *Oxford History of British and Irish Catholicism*, vol. V, p. xxii.
[17] Tom Buchanan, 'Great Britain', in *Political Catholicism in Europe, 1918–1965*, edited by Tom Buchanan and Martin Conway (Oxford, 1996), p. 249.
[18] John Wolffe, 'Anti-Catholicism', in *Oxford History of British and Irish Catholicism*, vol. IV, pp. 205–6.
[19] Hornsby-Smith, *Roman Catholic Beliefs in England*, p. 193.

intellectual refinement and social comfort not to be the primary ends of their existence.'[20] Paula M. Kane states that 'Clerical and hierarchical control were an inherent feature of any lay group, particularly in the context of a contemporary theological watershed, the Modernist controversy of 1907.'[21] Peter Doyle offers the following: 'When, for example, members of the Salford Catholic Federation asked how the laity were to know whether a particular issue was vital to Catholic interests or not, the answer was, "when the bishop in his wisdom directs that it is".'[22] But such a view is contested, and the picture of lay–clergy relationships is more nuanced than these illustrations would indicate. Joan Keating, in the work on Catholics and politics which formed the basis of her 1992 doctoral thesis,[23] highlights a gap in the historiography when she says 'there are also suggestions of a degree of compliance by the laity for which there is a distinct lack of evidence'.[24] A close examination of the historiography demonstrates that clerical and episcopal involvement in lay Catholic societies was more supportive than the traditional picture would suggest.[25] Furthermore, 'it has been suggested that [post-Vatican II], clerical forms of domination are being replaced by new forms of domination by the middle-class, articulate, progressive, activist laity.'[26] Indeed Clifford Williamson has argued that this was the case even prior to the Second Vatican Council, stating of the Newman Association that 'it could be argued that although [it] was keen to see the replacement of the clerical elite, it was only replacing it or demanding recognition for yet another elite themselves'.[27] Further research is thus needed to understand the dynamics of the relationship of clergy to the laity and the impact of this upon their social, political and spiritual action, and to understand the role of Catholic intellectual elites in the changing dynamics of this, especially in the light of increased social mobility in the second half of the century. Such an analysis is supported by Keating who argues that 'the postwar people of God were different from their predecessors in

---

[20] David Holmes, 'Catholic Spirit of Association: Catholic Popular Culture, Confraternities, Guilds and a Restored Community in the Industrial Diocese of Late Victorian-Early Edwardian West Riding of Yorkshire', *Northern History*, 57:2 (2020), p. 232.
[21] Paula M. Kane, '"The Willing Captive of Home?": The English Catholic Women's League, 1906–1920', *Church History*, 60/3 (1991), pp. 331–55, 333.
[22] Peter Doyle, 'Episcopal Leaders and Leadership', pp. 53–4.
[23] Joan Keating, 'Roman Catholics, Christian Democracy, and the British Labour Movement, 1910–1960', Unpublished PhD Thesis, University of Manchester, 1992.
[24] Joan Keating, 'The Making of the Catholic Labour Activist: The Catholic Social Guild and Catholic Workers' College, 1909–1939', *Labour History Review*, 59:3 (1994), p. 44.
[25] For example, 'The CWL [Catholic Women's League] was born from a joining of convert zeal and episcopal-clerical support to a tradition of lay initiative among English Catholics.' Kane, 'The Willing Captive of Home?', pp. 331–2.
[26] Hornsby-Smith, *Roman Catholic Beliefs in England*, p. 120.
[27] Williamson, *The History of Catholic Intellectual Life in Scotland*, p. 147.

important ways. No longer were British Catholics, emboldened by security and social mobility, ready to be unthinkingly deferential, but nor did they feel that the Church offered them so little that they were prepared to jettison it.'[28] This leads us to the next question: how far did class divisions within the Catholic community impact upon lay Catholic societies?

The Catholic community in Britain during the first half of the twentieth century – the period covered by most of the writing on lay Catholic societies – consisted of three main groups: Recusants or Old Catholics, Converts, and Irish Catholics who were mostly (or were perceived to be) working class. And 'while the flock was predominantly working-class Irish, bishops were almost exclusively drawn from old English recusant families or upper-middle-class converts'.[29] Holmes argues that the divisions were clear: 'No matter what they may have shared religiously, English and Irish Catholics had completely separate affiliations with the Church and its societies. Indeed, the habits, virtues and attitudes of both cultures would retain sufficient force to be seen as separate traditions.'[30] However, it is uncertain what impact such divisions had upon lay Catholic societies. Much of the vitality of Catholic intellectual life in the first half of the twentieth century certainly came from converts to the faith. Indeed, Hornsby-Smith found that converts were more likely than cradle Catholics to become actively involved in church structures.[31] James R. Lothian argues that most of Catholic intellectual life was concerned with social and political issues,[32] and that involvement in informal Catholic lay networks[33] offered converts succour. For example, when writing of the popularity of Hilaire Belloc's historical analysis Lothian states:

> Many of the writers who were to make up the English Catholic intellectual community were converts to Catholicism. The converts, in many cases, were the ones who agreed most strongly with Belloc's interpretation of English history. Although they did not make this explicit, one might surmise that Bellocian history was a comfort to them, letting them know that just because they were leaving the Church of England for the Church of Rome, they were not abandoning their English heritage.[34]

---

[28] Keating, 'Faith and Community Threatened?', p. 108.
[29] Keating, 'Making of the Catholic Labour Activist', p. 52.
[30] Holmes, 'Catholic Spirit of Association', p. 232.
[31] Valerie Flessati, 'PAX: The History of a Catholic Peace Society in Britain, 1936–1971', unpublished doctoral thesis, University of Bradford, 1991, p. 507; M. P. Hornsby-Smith and R. M. Lee, *Roman Catholic Opinion: A Study of Roman Catholics in England and Wales in the 1970s* (Guildford, University of Surrey, 1979), p. 183.
[32] James R. Lothian, *The Making and Unmaking of the English Catholic Intellectual Community, 1910–1950* (South Bend, IN, 2009), p. 11. See also Jay P. Corrin, *Catholic Intellectuals and the Challenge of Democracy* (South Bend, IN, 2002).
[33] These will not be dealt with in detail in this review, which focuses on formal lay Catholic societies.
[34] Lothian, *Making and Unmaking*, p. 50.

This view is supported by Kathryn Horlock in her work on twentieth-century pilgrimages, which paints a picture of the Catholic Church seeking to display its deep roots in Englishness – particularly in its medieval and early modern forms.[35] The relationships between the classes in British Catholicism by and large played themselves out in the realm of political action, especially in the Catholic Social Guild which sought to empower working-class Catholics, to which we turn next.

Catholics and politics

In common with most other aspects of the history of lay Catholic societies in Britain, the focus on the social or political aspects of their work centres upon the period before 1962. A number of organisations feature in this historiography, including the Catholic Socialist Society,[36] the Catholic Social Guild (CSG),[37] and the Newman Association.[38] Notwithstanding Pius XI's vision of such organisations facilitating 'the participation of the laity in the apostolate of the hierarchy',[39] this aspect of their work is not subjected to scrutiny. Instead, Buchanan defines the character of their activities thus: 'Many social catholic movements of this period [1918–1965] played an undeniably political role, both defensively (teaching the laity to resist socialism) and offensively (projecting a Catholic vision of society).'[40] This characterisation summarises the historiographical arguments made with two sets of analysis emerging: one in which the work of lay Catholic societies to reform society along the lines of Catholic social teaching is examined, and another in which reactions to the threat of socialism and communism are discussed.

In his article on the Catholic Social Guild in Scotland, Piotr Potocki tells us that 'at the turn of the twentieth century ... Catholicism in Britain came under increasing pressures from an elite group within the Church that sought to revitalise Catholic life' and that figures within this 'progressive elite with a principled commitment to social justice' were deeply influenced by Cardinal Manning.[41] This led to the establishment of the Guild, the task of which was 'to make known in Britain the Catholic principles

---

35   Kathryn Hurlock, 'The Guild of Our Lady of Ransom and Pilgrimage in England and Wales, c. 1890–1914', *British Catholic History*, 35:3 (2021), pp. 316–17.
36   Gerry C. Gunnin, *John Wheatley, Catholic Socialism, and Irish Labour in the West of Scotland, 1906–1924* (Abingdon, 1987).
37   Piotr Potocki, 'The Origins of the Catholic Social Guild in Scotland: "We have not attacked the Socialists professedly"', *Innes Review*, 69:2 (2018), pp. 131–46.
38   Williamson, *History of Catholic Intellectual Life in Scotland*.
39   Pius XI cited in Yves Congar, *Lay People in the Church* (London, 1965), p. 364.
40   Buchanan, 'Great Britain', p. 243.
41   Potocki, 'Origins of the Catholic Social Guild in Scotland', p. 131.

applicable to the social and economic problems of the twentieth century'.[42] Its founders 'objected to the insular nature of what some scholars describe as "ghetto Catholicism", in favour of more confident and outward-looking attitudes'.[43] In such an aim, the Catholic Social Guild was joined by the Newman Association, 'an organisation which was expressly formed to keep the Catholic Church in contact with the changing parameters of discussion across all fields of intellectual activity and through active participation in this way, it aimed to maintain a Catholic voice in these areas'.[44] The voice with which the leadership and members of these societies spoke was largely derived from papal encyclicals, most notably *Rerum Novarum*[45] and *Quadragesimo Anno*.[46] In the establishment of such an organisation, 'sections of the laity organised themselves, supported on occasion by a conservative hierarchy, to advance a distinctively Catholic critique of (and an alternative to) British society as they found it'.[47] The history of the Catholic Social Guild raises a number of issues that are common within the historiography of lay Catholic societies which are also evident in the literature on other organisations.

The most prominent of these is class. Whilst these organisations were founded by elites, they soon became a vehicle for social mobility amongst the Catholic working classes by ensuring that they were sufficiently well educated to take their faith out into the world. Thus, the leadership became more working class. As Buchanan argues:

> The CSG was very much a child of its times, given the vogue for social investigation – nor were comparisons with the Fabian society irrelevant, given the personal connections between some Fabians and members of the CSG. Surprisingly, however, the Guild soon developed away from its intellectual and middle-class origins to lay the basis, with support from some parish priests, of a committed working-class following in the years before the First World War.[48]

Keating commends this: 'The uplifting of the workers must be done by themselves. They cannot be dragged up by "superior people" who talk down to them or aspire to lead them from the heights as too many of the workers' leaders aim at doing.'[49]

---

42   J. M. Cleary, *Catholic Social Action in Britain, 1909–1959* (Oxford, 1961), p. 13.
43   Potocki, 'Origins of the Catholic Social Guild in Scotland', p. 133.
44   Williamson, *History of Catholic Intellectual Life in Scotland*, p. 148.
45   Leo XIII, *Rerum Novarum: On Capital and Labour*, 15 May 1891, https://www.vatican.va/content/leo-xiii/en/encyclicals/documents/hf_l-xiii_enc_15051891_rerum-novarum.html, accessed 28 July 2023.
46   Pius XI, *Quadragesimo Anno: On Reconstruction of the Social Order*, 15 May 1931, https://www.vatican.va/content/pius-xi/en/encyclicals/documents/hf_p-xi_enc_19310515_quadragesimo-anno.html, accessed 28 July 2023.
47   Buchanan, 'Great Britain', p. 249.
48   Ibid., p. 262.
49   Keating, 'Making of the Catholic Labour Activist', p. 49.

The defensive nature of Catholic lay societies has received more attention in the literature. In his history of Catholic intellectual life in Scotland, Williamson argues that 'Social Catholicism is a sophisticated phenomenon working on different levels but to attain a single objective, the consolidation of the position of the Catholic Church.'[50] Consequently, the threat of socialism and communism was taken very seriously by the Catholic Church,[51] even though 'in England ... the church exaggerated the threat of socialism among the working class'.[52] Catholic lay societies were at the forefront of this conflict with, for instance, the Legion of Mary being 'created as a means to radicalise and mobilise the laity to challenge the appeal and influence of secular movements, most notably the Communist Party'.[53] In his monograph on the Catholic Socialist Society in Scotland, Gerry Gurrin confirms the offensive nature of some of the work of the Catholic Church, but also demonstrates how this was blended with defensiveness:

> The Church approved the amelioration of working-class conditions, but the anti-Socialist Catholics insisted that a clear distinction be made between social reform and Socialism. When the workers' improvement was articulated in the name of Socialism, the 'emotive meaning' of the world educed a response from Catholic critics which was predictably condemnatory.[54]

Such an attitude was joined by a prolonged debate surrounding the Labour Party, which demonstrates some of the work of Catholic lay societies in countering the threat of socialism. For example, in 1912 the National Confederation of Catholic Trade Unionists was able to persuade Labour to abandon a commitment to secular education.[55] As Keating argues, these issues 'need to be tackled with a clearer understanding of how the British Catholic Church has operated and how socio-religious ideas are transmitted to the laity'.[56]

Spiritual and devotional practices

Some attention is paid in the literature to lay Catholic societies that promoted spiritual and devotional practices. A devotion to Our Lady is one of the key characteristics of modern Catholicism[57] with the Legion of Mary being one of the most famous apostolates in Britain and Ireland. Williamson sums up their importance thus:

---

50 Williamson, *History of Catholic Intellectual Life in Scotland*, p. 82.
51 Gunnin, *John Wheatley*, p. 132.
52 Kane, 'The Willing Captive of Home?', p. 350.
53 Williamson, *History of Catholic Intellectual Life in Scotland*, p. 139.
54 Gunnin, *John Wheatley*, p. 136.
55 Buchanan, 'Great Britain', p. 264.
56 Keating, 'Making of the Catholic Labour Activist', p. 44.
57 Williamson, *History of Catholic Intellectual Life in Scotland*, p. 126.

The Legion [of Mary] can be seen as the first example of the modern lay apostolate, where the laity were the essential element in religious devotion. Its emphasis was on the spirituality of the laity based not on the parish church or chapel but on personal behaviour. This did not exclude the clergy from its traditional role as shepherds to the flock. Clerical influence was very strong though in a different way from before. The lay members of the Legion set the priorities in devotion and piety. It was a devotional society that was built from the laity.[58]

The objective of these societies was to allow participants 'to fulfil the end for which God had made them and work on the salvation of their souls', as well as the souls of others.[59] In the work of the Legion of Mary this involved direct action such as rescuing prostitutes and promoting temperance. This lay activity also took the form of pilgrimages, outward displays 'which allowed Catholics to express their faith in the face of widespread opposition'.[60] Although they were interceding for the conversion of England and Wales in the early part of the twentieth century, in the years immediately after the Second World War they provided veterans with 'a chance [to use] their wartime experiences in the arduous context of pilgrimages' as well as 'atoning for wartime actions'.[61] The theme of devotion and lay spirituality is important to understandings of twentieth-century Catholicism. But again, with the exception of work by Williamson and Hurlock, it is a neglected area deserving attention.

Ecumenism

One activity of lay Catholic societies has been well served in the historiography: ecumenical activity.[62] This lay action has been used to demonstrate Catholic civic engagement and national loyalty, particularly during the Second World War. The most prominent of these organisations was Sword of the Spirit,[63] founded in 1940 as 'a movement for a more united and more intensive Catholic effort in support of the struggle which our country has

---

[58] Ibid., p. 135.
[59] Holmes, 'Catholic Spirit of Association', p. 232.
[60] Hurlock, 'The Guild of Our Lady of Ransom', p. 317.
[61] Kathryn Hurlock, 'Army Style, We Marched: War and Peace in the Cross-Carrying Pilgrimages to Vézelay and Walsingham, 1946–1948', *British Catholic History*, 36:4 (2023), pp. 410–30.
[62] For an overview of this topic see Maria Power, 'Ecumenism and Interfaith Relations', in *Oxford History of British and Irish Catholicism*, vol. V, pp. 229–48.
[63] This organisation was later to become the Catholic Institute for International Relations and subsequently Progressio. Some aspects of its work later in the twentieth century are discussed in Maria Power, 'The Catholic Church and Human Rights: A Case Study of 1980s South Africa', *Catholic Archives*, 41 (2021), pp. 65–77.

been forced to enter'.[64] It has been framed in different ways by historians. Stuart Mews sees it as a 'dramatic demonstration of Catholic loyalty'[65] to the national interest in the atmosphere of mobilisation during the early years of the Second World War; whilst Michael J. Walsh views it as a lay-led movement confident in its ability to reach out to non-Catholics, powered by theories of Catholic Action and Catholic Social Teaching to propel Christian initiatives for social reconstruction.[66] In their analyses both are correct, and the story of the Sword of the Spirit also shows the difficulties inherent in ecumenical contact and social initiatives before the changes initiated by the Second Vatican Council.

The history of this organisation's foundation therefore demonstrates two elements regarding lay Catholic societies in the twentieth century. First, that the Catholic Church was keen to become involved in national life and saw ecumenical cooperation as a means to 'unite on practical measures to defend the inheritance of Christian principles on which our civilisation has been built against the tyranny of Godless or pagan forces that seem to rob us of our heritage'.[67] Secondly, the early history of Sword shows that the laity took a much broader and more proactive approach to ecumenical activity but were frustrated in their attempts by cautious elements within the episcopacy. They therefore had to engage in delicate diplomacy within their own church structures in order to extend the hand of cooperation to other Christians.[68] Throughout its operation, a power struggle emerged regarding the structure of the organisation and particularly the issue of joint prayer, compounded by questions of non-Catholic membership of the movement's committees. However, whilst the early years of ecumenical activity have been the focus of some scholarly engagement, its later iterations have not – again highlighting a gap in post-Vatican II historiography.

Women

The history of Catholic lay societies that operated in the early years of the twentieth century and focused on the concerns of women has been well served in recent years with a good number of studies being published

---

64   Stuart Mews, 'The Sword of the Spirit: A Catholic Cultural Crusade of 1940', *Studies in Church History: The Church and War*, 20 (1983), p. 420.
65   Ibid.
66   Michael J. Walsh. 'Ecumenism in War-Time Britain: The Sword of the Spirit and Religion and Life, 1940–1945 (1)', *Heythrop Journal*, 23:3 (1982), pp. 243–58; 'Ecumenism in War-Time Britain: the Sword of the Spirit and Religion and Life (2)', *Heythrop Journal*, 23:4 (1982), pp. 365–76.
67   Walsh, 'Ecumenism in War-Time Britain (1)', p. 248.
68   Ibid., p. 247.

of individual women[69] as well as of the organisations that they founded, such as the Catholic Women's League and St Joan's Alliance. Serious consideration of lay women's organisations in the Catholic Church did not begin until the twenty-first century. Elaine Clark posits the following reason for this lacuna in our knowledge: 'Anti-Catholic propaganda has so long marginalised Catholic women that it was easy to think of them as absorbed in narrow concerns and too cowed by clerical authority to venture into the political fray.'[70] The history of Catholic women's lay societies in the early twentieth century tells a different story, one of clerical and episcopal cooperation and 'light-touch' involvement rather than control, active participation with secular organisations, and a desire to improve the lives of other women.

The historiography concentrates on only two organisations: the Catholic Women's League, and the Catholic Women's Suffrage Society (later the St Joan's Alliance). The Catholic Women's League was founded in 1906 because Margaret Fletcher believed 'it was necessary for the church to find ways to draw laywomen together outside of convent schools and sisterhoods, in order to overcome the patterns of individualism set by religious, gender, and class distinctions'.[71] She therefore established an organisation that amongst other things professionalised:

> Catholic benevolence by coordinating the existing network of church charities. With respect to women's higher education and employment, the league founded bureaus which created a lecture and debate series, a scholarship fund for women to attend the London School of Economics and the Catholic Worker College, and an Information Office, which served as a women's employment agency for volunteer and salaried labour.[72]

The work of the Catholic Women's Suffrage Society, the first Catholic organisation of its kind in the world, was overtly political and its aim 'to bring Catholic women actively into the suffrage movement and to proclaim a leadership among Catholics in the international suffrage movement created, in the process, a Catholic feminist movement'.[73] These two organisations, which represent female lay Catholic organisations in the

---

[69] Kathryn G. Lamontagne, *Reconsidering Catholic Lay Womanhood: Pious Transgressors in Late Nineteenth and Early Twentieth Century England* (Abingdon, 2024).
[70] Elaine Clark, 'Catholics and the Campaign for Women's Suffrage in England', *Church History*, 73:3 (2004), pp. 648. She also states (p. 635) that 'Narratives about women and religion in Victorian and Edwardian society seldom addressed the world of the Catholic laity, leaving the impression that Catholics were unimportant in English history. ... So commonplace was this particular point of view that it obscured Catholic participation in social causes such as the hard fought campaign for women's suffrage.'
[71] Kane, 'The Willing Captive of Home?', p. 339.
[72] Ibid., p. 344.
[73] Francis M. Mason, 'The Newer Eve: The Catholic Women's Suffrage Society in England, 1911–1923', *Catholic Historical Review*, 72:4 (1986), p. 620.

literature, highlight a number of issues that frame our understandings of lay action in both the offensive and defensive methods suggested by Buchanan, with a desire to improve the lives of women characterising their approaches.

The matter of clerical and episcopal control, so important in maintaining Catholic identity, is prominent in writing on female lay Catholic societies. Whilst Buchanan argues that 'Catholic women continued to encounter a mixture of expectation and condescension from their male leaders throughout this period',[74] it is evident that the level of control suggested here did not materialise. This was true of the Catholic Women's League where 'backing from bishops and clergy was essential to [its] success'.[75] Kane, supporting the idea of the Catholic Women's League as a defensive organisation, argues that this was forthcoming because: 'The central usefulness of the CWL to the church lay in its assisting with the church's self-proclaimed task of keeping middle-class women out of politics and keeping the Catholic working-class Christian, aims far removed from the expansion of women's rights sought by many contemporary women's associations.'[76] Whether this is the reason for Cardinal Francis Bourne's attitude to and support for the League is unclear and is never fully investigated in the existing literature. Although Clark does not support Kane's arguments for the reasons behind clerical and episcopal attitudes, she also suggests that clerical control and episcopal censorship were not a major feature of these organisations, writing of the Catholic Women's Suffrage Society that: 'although many people in the early 1900s identified the Catholic Church with clerical authority, the CWSS encouraged the public to see the church in broader, more inclusionary terms',[77] thus showing that the outward-facing nature of these female-led organisations was the most important aspect of their history.

Writing on the work of these female lay Catholic societies presents a picture of their wider and more complex relationship with British society than Kane's 1992 article on the Catholic Women's League would suggest. Whilst she argues for a 'ghetto-style' Catholic subculture, work by Elaine Clark,[78] Mary V. Newman,[79] Susan L. Tanabaum,[80] and Caitríona

---

74 Buchanan, 'Great Britain', p. 263.
75 Kane, 'The Willing Captive of Home?', p. 335.
76 Ibid., p. 349.
77 Clark, 'Catholics and the Campaign for Women's Suffrage in England', p. 664.
78 Elaine Clark, 'Catholic Men in Support of the Women's Suffrage Movement in England', *The Catholic Historical Review*, 94:1 (2008), pp. 22–44; Idem, 'Catholics and the Campaign for Women's Suffrage in England'.
79 Mary V. Newman, 'The Educational Work of the Catholic Women's League in England, 1906–1923', unpublished PhD thesis, Institute of Education, University of London, 2010.
80 Susan L. Tanabaum, 'Rescue Work: Catholic Care in Britain from the 1880s to 1920s', *Journal of the History of Childhood and Youth*, 12:1 (2019), pp. 45–67, which points out (p.

Beaumont[81] establishes that these were organisations employed in an 'offensive' relationship with secular society, as well as being engaged in vigorous debates about feminism. The main focus of their work was to improve the lives of women. In order to achieve this, both the CWL and the CWSS at times brought Catholic social teaching into secular settings. Beaumont argues of the Catholic Women's League that 'despite the fact that [it appears] to be out of step with the wider women's movement, they succeeded in highlighting a number of major social and welfare concerns facing women at the time'.[82] For example, the CWL devoted its energies to social welfare issues believing that such improvements would prevent the need for divorce, abortion and birth control. Whilst Catholic suffragists 'believed there was an equally pressing need for the active participation of Catholic women in all that concerned women's work and women's emancipation',[83] their behaviour was influenced by debates internal to Catholicism which focused on feminism and the nature of Catholic womanhood. The 'Catholic "social feminists" [of the Catholic Women's League] sought relatively modest goals of extended educational opportunity, protection against workplace abuse, and recognition for women's social potential.'[84] Meanwhile, 'among members [of the CWSS] there was a renewed determination to reform political life and to further the work and usefulness of Catholic women as citizens.'[85]

Lay Catholic societies after the Second Vatican Council (1962–1965)

British Catholicism was unprepared for the changes brought by the Second Vatican Council.[86] In her essay 'The Changing Nature of Catholic Organisations', Mildred Neville tells us that in the years immediately before the opening of the Second Vatican Council by Pope John XXIII in 1962:

> Catholic organisations were not of one mind in their experience of reality and their understanding of the Church. There was a wide divergence of political views. If the Church presented a united front, it was because there was little questioning of the *status quo*. Class analysis within the Church was unheard of and loyal criticism was in its infancy.[87]

---

46) the 'important role Catholics played in professionalising social services and increasing opportunities for women'.
81 Caitriona Beaumont, 'Moral Dilemmas and Women's Rights: The attitude of the Mothers' Union and Catholic Women's League to divorce, birth control and abortion in England, 1928–1939', *Women's History Review*, 16:4 (2007), p. 463.
82 Beaumont, 'Moral Dilemmas and Women's Rights', p. 463.
83 Clark, 'Catholics and the Campaign for Women's Suffrage in England', p. 637.
84 Kane, 'The Willing Captive of Home?', p. 341.
85 Clark, 'Catholics and the Campaign for Women's Suffrage in England', p. 659.
86 Adrian Hastings, *A History of English Christianity, 1920–1990* (London, 1991), p. 529.
87 Mildred Neville, 'The Changing Nature of Catholic Organisations', in *Catholics in England, 1950–2000: Historical and Sociological Perspectives*, edited by Michael Hornsby-Smith (London, 1999), p. 106.

One of the major innovations of the Second Vatican Council was the increased inclusion of lay people in the institutional life of the Church. Lay men and women could now become Eucharistic Ministers and Readers at Mass but as Hornsby-Smith points out 'although there is clearly more lay participation in the Church now than in the pre-war years, in many ways it remains somewhat limited, for example at the parish level as a result of clerical intransigence or lay passivity'.[88] In addition to this, the publication of *Humanae Vitae* caused a crisis of authority within the Catholic Church which has still not been resolved.[89] Neville points out that a consequence of these factors in Britain was that the reforms implemented in Vatican II did not materialise into the model of Church envisaged by the Council Fathers. Instead,

> throughout these years has been, and remains, the apparent gap between the model of Church led by the hierarchy and clergy which we experience at parish and diocesan level, and the model of Church as instanced in the response to the 'joys and hopes, the griefs and anxieties of the world, and especially of those who are poor' (*Gaudium et Spes,* §1) which has been developed by Catholic organisations since Vatican II.[90]

Corrin supports this observation by arguing that there was 'frustration among many Catholics concerning the English episcopate's dilatory response to the progressive messages of Vatican II, especially those that envisaged more actively engaged lay men and women in religious affairs.'[91] The reforms were received in different ways within the British Catholic Churches, with the development of traditionalist and progressive wings who respectively rejected and embraced the changes.[92] But how have these developments affected the progress of lay Catholic societies in Britain? Unfortunately, little has been written on the history of lay Catholic societies post-Vatican II, with what literature there is focusing primarily on the progressive elements within the Church.

Lay Catholic societies operating in the more traditional wing of the Church have received virtually no attention from historians. The Second Vatican Council is mainly known for its liturgical changes, which for many suggested a surrender to Protestantism,[93] and these 'liturgical and disciplinary reforms which emanated from the Second Vatican Council … raised howls of heartfelt protest from fearful traditionalists'.[94] This

---

[88] Hornsby-Smith, *Roman Catholic Beliefs in England,* p. 193.
[89] Alana Harris (ed.), *The Schism of 68: Catholics, Contraception and Humanae Vitae in Europe, 1945–1975* (Basingstoke, 2018).
[90] Neville, 'Changing Nature of Catholic Organisations', p. 99.
[91] Corrin, *Catholic Progressives,* p. 221.
[92] Williamson speaks of 'Frustration at the slow pace of reform after Vatican II' (*The History of Catholic Intellectual Life in Scotland,* p. 162).
[93] Corrin, *Catholic Progressives,* pp. 155–6.
[94] Michael Hornsby-Smith, 'A Transformed Church', in *Catholics in England, 1950–2000,* p. 8.

led, in 1965, to the formation of the Latin Mass Society 'as a platform for loyal dissent to the reforms of Vatican II'.[95]

The writing on progressive lay Catholic societies provides a slightly fuller picture of these organisations in the wake of the Second Vatican Council. It is generally agreed that such movements are a form of contestation:

> Recent examples might include the Charismatic Movement, in so far as it reflected a protest against restrictive forms of spirituality in the Church; the Basic Christian Community movement, reflecting a greater awareness of the social, economic and political concerns of Catholics in their everyday lives; the Justice and Peace Movement, contesting the low priority given to these moral issues in pastoral practice.[96]

Key examples of such organisations include, but are not limited to, Pax Christi, the Catholic Association for Racial Justice, Progressio, the Catholic Women's Network, the Catholic Housing Aid Society, and the Society of St Vincent de Paul. Such lay-led organisations, like Pax, understood the importance of working with other Christian and secular organisations in order to achieve their aims, intersecting with 'the Church in a strategic sense to achieve their goals'.[97] But like their traditionalist or conservative counterparts, the creation and development of organisations has not been the subject of historical study.

Conclusion

This historiographical review of the literature on lay Catholic societies in twentieth-century Britain has shown the paucity of research in this area. Whilst some themes, such as ecumenism and to a certain extent women's organisations, are served well, there are others which are not. We still understand little of the influence of religious orders on organised lay activity, whilst the history of 'third orders' remains unknown. Anecdotal evidence tells us that there is a vast history of lay Catholic activity in Britain which remains unwritten. The 'Vatican II generation' are now in their seventies and eighties, and indeed some of those most closely involved in lay Catholic societies, such as Bruce Kent, have passed away during the production of this collection. It is thus essential that their life histories and experiences are recorded for future generations.[98] Catholicism no longer resides in a ghetto and the form of lay Catholic societies is changing. Lay Catholic societies are now working closely through

---

95 Corrin, *Catholic Progressives*, p. 157.
96 Hornsby-Smith, *Roman Catholic Beliefs*, pp. 145–6.
97 Neville, 'Changing Nature of Catholic Organisations', p. 116.
98 The author is currently undertaking this task for a planned history of progressive lay Catholic societies in the era after the Second Vatican Council.

ecumenical, inter-faith, and secular channels, but whether this evolution is pragmatic or based upon the developing teaching of the Church in this area remains to be seen. It is hoped that this collection will contribute to this historiography and inspire debates around questions of lay Catholic involvement both in the church and in society.

2

A MIDDLE-CLASS CONVERT'S *CRUCIBLE*: MARGARET FLETCHER AND THE ORIGINS OF THE CATHOLIC WOMEN'S LEAGUE

KATHRYN LAMONTAGNE

If we consider figures such as John Henry Newman, Henry Manning and Gerard Manley Hopkins, some of the most publicly identifiable members of the Catholic Church in late-Victorian Britain were converts to the faith. However, the experiences of lay middle-class convert women remain historically enigmatic, despite their contributions to the English Catholic Church. Lay Catholic convert Margaret Fletcher (1862–1943), founder of the Catholic Women's League (CWL) and its mouthpiece *The Crucible*, fought to raise the status of middle-class English Catholic women in the secular world and the Church. She demonstrated the potential of Catholic women's groups and publications in the Edwardian era to provide a space in which non-elite lay women could assert agency and autonomy both in their private and public works.

Fletcher founded *The Crucible* and the CWL over 1905/6 to support converts and 'born' Catholic middle-class lay women, who she felt were raised apart for fear of persecution and consequently lacked a connection with the secular world.[1] A generation earlier, Cardinal Manning had lamented the absence of the Catholic laity from public life, stating that the 'social exile in which they had lived, and their exclusion … from public and private employment, have seriously diminished our capacity for usefulness'.[2] To change this absence into a presence, Fletcher sought to create an organisation through which middle-class professional Catholic lay women could be 'useful' beyond 'convent/ional' expectations. She wrote to the hierarchy in 1906: 'the philanthropic work of Catholic lay women in England, in its present undeveloped and unorganised state,

---

[1] Mary G. Segar, *Margaret Fletcher, 1862–1943* (London, 1945), pp. 13–14; Margaret Fletcher, *O, Call Back Yesterday* (Oxford, 1939), pp. 128–9.
[2] James Pereiro, 'Who Are the Laity?', in *From Without the Flaminian Gate: 150 Years of Roman Catholicism in England and Wales, 1850–2000*, edited by V. Alan McClelland and Michael Hodgetts (London, 1999), p. 169.

may be said to be a weak spot in our social fabric', resulting in 'overlap' and 'isolation'.³ She insisted that an organisation – the CWL – could unite middle-class women, and 'its work would not be destructive of existing work, but constructive and conservative ... [so that the Church may] enlarge its borders'.⁴

Ultimately, Fletcher was very successful in widening the scope of Catholic interests among women of the professional classes. The CWL provided opportunities for lay women to engage with concerns beyond their parochial environment, class and geography. These were to be the first such opportunities occurring nationally across Britain for middle-class lay Catholic women and manifested mostly through social works and newfound fellowship.⁵ With the tacit approval of the hierarchy, the CWL helped provide a generation of middle-class Catholic lay women with a greater sense of agency and autonomy. Due to her status as a middle-class convert, Fletcher's efforts were initially not well received by some elite 'born' Catholic women. In some quarters, she was regarded with suspicion as 'too liberal', a 'socialist', and a 'suffragist'. Some saw her support for women's rights as a possible indication of impiety.⁶ Regardless of what others expected for her and her efforts (as a convert and single woman), Fletcher greatly contributed to a change in expectations for Catholic women in England at the start of the twentieth century. By retracing the founding days of the CWL and *The Crucible*, this chapter will demonstrate how Fletcher helped reinterpret lay Catholicism for middle-class women through the CWL and *The Crucible*, helping to bring them

---

3   Margaret Fletcher, 'Proposals for a League of Catholic Women Workers', offprint from *The Crucible*, September 1906, p. 5; Bourne 1/30 1906–1912, Westminster Diocesan Archives (WDA), p. 1.
4   Ibid., p. 6.
5   For further reading on Catholic Women's Leagues, see Helena Dawes, *Catholic Women's Movements in Liberal and Fascist Italy* (Houndmills, 2014) Mary M. Macken, 'The German Catholic Women's League', *Studies: An Irish Quarterly Review*, 20:80 (1931), pp. 555–69; L. McKenna, 'An Irish Catholic Women's League', *Irish Monthly*, 45:528 (1917), pp. 353–68; Hilary M. Carey, *Truly Feminine, Truly Catholic: A History of the Catholic Women's League in the Archdiocese of Sydney, 1913–87* (Kensington, 1987). For further information on other Catholic women's groups in Britain and their social import, see Virginia M. Crawford, 'The Coming of Age of the CSG (Catholic Social Guild)', *Studies: An Irish Quarterly Review*, 19:75 (1930), pp. 456–66.
6   Fletcher and other converts could find themselves to be the objects of prejudicial views held by those sharing their faith and not just outsiders. Converts were viewed warily in some quarters, especially by 'born' Catholics such as Lady Mary Talbot and the Ladies of Charity, so their work was, early on, regarded with suspicion. Pau ine Adams has argued that English Catholic converts in the mid-nineteenth century particularly faced a great amount of prejudice. Patrick Allitt has shown that this prejudice subsided to some extent in the early twentieth century but was still of issue. Pauline Adams, *English Catholic Converts and the Oxford Movement in Mid 19th Century Britain* (Bethesda, 2010), pp. 137–212; Patrick Allitt, *Catholic Converts* (Ithaca, NY, 2000).

in from the 'fringes' of English society, as well as to bring in Catholic lay women – converts and 'born' – from the fringes of their own faith.

Biographical sketch

Margaret Fletcher was born in Oxford in 1862 to Carteret J. H. Fletcher and Agnes Fletcher. Her father was an outspoken Anglican vicar and, due in part to her father's position, Fletcher had an early consciousness of religion, gender inequalities and class.[7] Educated in Oxford at a progressive non-denominational high school, she later studied art at the Royal Academy in London and the Sorbonne. Similar to other young women of the middle classes, Fletcher was interested in painting, drama, writing and travel.[8] Mirroring the 'typical' New Woman experience, Fletcher travelled in Europe unaccompanied; but notably, she published a book in 1892 on her cultural experiences abroad.[9] Unlike other young people who equated modernity and *fin de siècle* culture with secularism, Fletcher's 'ferment' 'involved no irreparable break with Christian belief'.[10] Fletcher's time on the Continent revealed other ways of life and their possibility for providing agency. From her travels abroad, she grew increasingly uncomfortable with masculine exceptionalist expressions of British Protestantism and Empire, which she felt to be oppressive.

Settling back into Oxford life after her travels, Fletcher continued to question her Anglicanism. Accordingly, in 1896 she began a friendship with an Irish convert from Protestantism, Fr Basil W. Maturin, and eventually she too converted to Catholicism at the Jesuit stronghold of Farm Street on 9 September 1897. The day after being received into the Church she received her first communion in Southwark. She became a communicant at St Aloysius, Oxford, mere steps from the home she shared with her Anglican vicar father and her siblings. The new Catholic

---

[7] The last trial of heresy in Oxford, 1886, was brought against Rev. C. J. H. Fletcher (rector of St Martin's, Carfax) due to his liberal sermons related to Anglo-Catholicism (Segar, *Margaret Fletcher*, pp. 1–5), and in particular his *The Taking Away of the Veil: A Sermon Preached before the University in the Church of St Mary-le-Virgin, Oxford, on Sunday, December 12th, 1886* (Oxford, [1887]); Fletcher *O, Call Back Yesterday*, pp. 20, 26–28, 30.
[8] Fletcher was also a skilled dramatist and artist. See: 'Literary and Other notices', *Jackson's Oxford Journal*, Saturday, 25 May 1895; Rosina Filippi, *Duologues and Scenes from the Novels of Jane Austen, arranged and adapted for drawing room performance. With illustrations by Miss Fletcher* (London, 1895); 'Untitled', *The Pall Mall Gazette*, 22 May 1891; 'Literary and Other Notices', *Jackson's Oxford Journal*, 25 May 1895; 'Romeo and Juliet at Oxford', *The Era*, 19 February 1898; 'Shakespeare at Oxford', *The Standard*, 17 February 1898; 'Banbury', *Jackson's Oxford Journal*, 25 November 1898; 'Notes by an Oxford Lady', *Jackson's Oxford Journal*, 25 November 1899.
[9] Fletcher, *Sketches of Life and Character in Hungary* (London, 1892).
[10] Fletcher, *O, Call Back Yesterday*, p. 80.

dedicated her work to the women of her new faith, but she continued to travel wherever she was needed. Together with her sister, Philippa, Fletcher lived with their father until his death in 1918.[11] Her single status gave her the flexibility to care for her father and maintain her work.[12] After the Great War, Fletcher travelled alone through Czechoslovakia and Poland, visiting Catholics in areas still suffering the devastating effects of the conflict.[13] At the behest of Bishop Keating in Liverpool, she founded the *Catholic Women's Outlook* (1922–30), loosely based on *The Crucible*, to provide a space for lay women's discourse on 'burning questions ... which intimately concerned women' that Keating felt were ignored by the majority of lay women.[14] Fletcher also played an integral role in founding the Catholic Workers' College in 1922, later known as Plater College, in Headington, Oxford, the same year she went to Rome.[15] She died in 1943.

Pinpointing differences and inequalities for middle-class lay women

The founding of *The Crucible* and the CWL pivoted on what Fletcher, after her conversion, perceived as the minority status of middle-class Catholic women. In contrast to other scholars, such as Mary Newman, who champion the role of education as a motivating factor for the founding of the CWL, I argue that Fletcher's true focus – grounded in her own experience – was to create a space for Catholic women to connect through both social works and thoughtful, academic conversation beyond that of purely prayerful sodalities like the Rosary Confraternity (1897).[16] Fletcher wrote of the difficulty in feeling 'separate' from the professional classes as a convert:

> The professional and upper middle-classes were very thinly represented at that time in the Catholic body. Groups of friends could gather together and generate a modicum of Catholic atmosphere, but numbers did not permit of

---

[11] England & Wales, National Probate Calendar (Index of Wills and Administrations), 1858–1966 for Carteret John Halford Fletcher.
[12] For an expanded discussion on this topic and others in the life of Margaret Fletcher, see Kathryn Lamontagne, *Reconsidering Catholic Lay Womanhood: Pious Transgressors in Late Nineteenth and Early Twentieth Century England* (Abingdon. 2024), pp. 56–87.
[13] Fletcher, *O, Call Back Yesterday*, pp. 140–60.
[14] Ibid., pp. 173–75.
[15] Ibid., p. 177; Segar, *Margaret Fletcher*, p. 18.
[16] Mary Newman's dissertation on Fletcher's educational pursuits contains seven helpful short biographical sketches of other women who were early leaders of the CWL. Mary V. Newman, 'The Educational Work of the Catholic Women's League in England, 1906–1923', unpublished PhD dissertation, Institute of Education, University of London, 2010; Olivier Rota, 'Margaret Fletcher and the Roman Catholic Thinking on Women before the First World War: An Idea of Woman and Woman's Higher Education', *Women's History Magazine*, 58 (2008), pp. 34–7; 'The Rosary Month', *The Tablet*, 28 September 1901.

a Catholic society. In one respect convert men were better off than convert women, and still are ... There is no parallel [in fellowship] to this for women ... [Female] converts ... were lacerated by the experiences of transition.[17]

She continues to explain that there 'was no place in [the Catholic world] as yet for new classes', and hence those converts of the middle classes struggled socially.[18] Spiritually, Fletcher believed Catholic women were better off, but that they lacked the worldly advantages of middle-class Protestant women. Education was a way to correct this disparity, but not the only way.[19]

In terms of class, Fletcher's parish of St Aloysius had parishioners from across the social spectrum, not just the elite or upper middle class.[20] In describing the mixed parish faithful she said:

> Socially we were rather a huddled little flock, very thinly recruited from the University, with one or two remnants of old Catholic families, and for the rest drawn from modest commercial and industrial circles.[21]

But, she claims, 'every effort was made by the clergy to draw us together [so] that an atmosphere of brotherhood might keep us warm' despite differences in status.[22] This example underpins vast differences in the Church, but it reveals efforts were being made to bring Catholics together and gain agency. In her efforts to further a shared experience for those who had completed their formal education, Fletcher sought out those like her – professional, middle- and upper-middle-class women – whom she found to be 'very thinly represented' in the Catholic body.[23] As a convert, she missed the conviviality of Anglican and secular societies and sought to create an equivalent experience for lay Catholic women.[24] Fletcher desired a society, not segregation.

Entering the faith, Fletcher knew of few middle-class female Catholics with whom she could meet up for shared purposes, especially those who were similarly educated, and observed a lack of formal opportunities for social engagement.[25] She was newly aware of a model which already

---

[17] Fletcher, *O, Call Back Yesterday*, p. 103.
[18] Ibid., p. 104.
[19] Ibid.
[20] Ibid., p. 106.
[21] Ibid.
[22] Ibid.
[23] Ibid.
[24] Ibid. There is also evidence of this in a number of works on conversion. See Allitt, *Catholic Converts*; Adam Schwartz, *The Third Spring* (Washington, DC, 2005); Frederick S. Roden, 'Michael Field, John Gray, and Marc-Andre Raffalovich: Reinventing Romantic Friendship in Modernity', in *Catholic Figures, Queer Narratives*, edited by Lowell Gallagher, Frederick S. Roden and Patricia Juliana Smith (Basingstoke, 2007), pp. 57–68.
[25] Unfortunately, due to the lack of research in this area, it remains unclear just how many lay women were involved in these areas and to what degree. But, as an example, the Catholic Social Guild was not formed until 1909.

existed to correct this lacuna elsewhere, the German *Frauenbund*. The *Frauenbund* was an umbrella organisation set up by the episcopate to link various Catholic women's groups. Reflecting on the disparity between English Catholic women and those in other countries, Fletcher's sympathies were roused for herself, but also for middle-class 'born Catholic' lay women:

> Tradition and convention and isolation from national life had done their work too well, and that there was a widespread feeling that tranquillity after persecution was so blessed that it was a pity to risk breaking it.[26]

As a convert, Fletcher saw an opportunity to model the activities of Catholic women in Britain on those already existing in Germany and the Northern United States. Consequently, she advocated for an end to isolation, first through a magazine, and then through the creation of a central bureau like the *Frauenbund* to coordinate lay women's efforts.[27] Thus, she was the first English voice to insist on bettering the social lives of lay Catholic women nationally beyond localised sodalities.[28] Yet while middle-class women were isolated, and convert middle-class women further isolated, elite Catholic women did not face the same barriers due to access to institutionalised networks of kinship and/or shared convent educations abroad.

Led by upper-class Catholics like Lady Talbot, members of the elite London-based Ladies of Charity (LofC) or the mixed-gender Catholic Social Union (established around 1895) were involved in philanthropy and often educated abroad in Belgian or French convents.[29] Most middle-class Catholic women did not have much access to these opportunities. Elite, lay Catholic groups focused their social work on small, urban areas and in helping poor or working-class Catholic women, rather than aiding middle-class women to find greater agency.[30] Fletcher felt this did not bode well for the future of Catholic women, because 'not a soul in that particular little flock had been interested in the social questions which had troubled the whole country, much less about women's position'.[31]

---

[26] Fletcher, *O, Call Back Yesterday*, p. 109.
[27] Her suggestion for a national group of women of all classes 'mixing freely in intercourse' and 'not merely assembled in printed lists' to 'extricate a Christian feminism' was what made Fletcher's work distinctly different from the women of the LofC or any other smaller, devotional parochial groups. This is also why the organisation was subject to such debate by aristocratic women. See: Fletcher, *O, Call Back Yesterday*, p. 110.
[28] Other Protestant women who converted to Catholicism and became involved in social issues were Flora Freeman, Alice Meynell, and Ethel Romanes.
[29] Bonnie G. Smith, *Ladies of the Leisure Class* (Princeton, NJ, 1981). Also, J. L. Lilly and Edmund Talbot *Manual of the Ladies of Charity* (London, 1926), p. 192.
[30] Much of what I surmise about the situation of these women has had to have been inferred from *Catholic Directories* of the time.
[31] Fletcher, *O, Call Back Yesterday*, p. 106.

Founding of The Crucible

Meeting two renowned American Catholic lay women, the poet Louise Imogen Guiney and Mary Miller, compelled Fletcher to action. They shared ideas for creating a national forum for middle-class women to discuss educational methods, history, science, religion and literature. Miller spent time on the continent and was acquainted with the *Frauenbund*. This then influenced Fletcher in articulating the progressive image of Catholic womanhood, dedicated to uniting and increasing the opportunities available to middle-class Catholic women and girls.[32] Not all members of the hierarchy initially supported her aspirations, but Archbishop Bourne and Fr Bernard Vaughan S.J. helped make Fletcher's ideas a success. Helpfully, Guiney and Miller believed in this vision and assisted in funding *The Crucible*. The magazine would be integral to showcasing her ideas for a yet unnamed, associated women's group.

The ideas behind *The Crucible* were first iterated publicly by a short pamphlet and talk called the *Light for New Times* given at a small, well-received lecture at Holy Child Convent, Cavendish Square, London, in 1905, a year before the CWL was founded.[33] Consequently, Fletcher decided to expand on this and trial a publication for 'A Catholic Magazine of Higher Education for Women' about Catholic women and girls' education and other matters of consequence.[34] After receiving initial funding, Fletcher was left to her own devices for *The Crucible*, which was published from 1905 until 1913. The magazine was guided by the presupposition that Catholic women would support one another in their good works. It featured articles that promoted an exchange of ideas among isolated Catholic communities in England, with each other and with others on the Continent. Greatly influenced by Catholic social thought, papal encyclicals, and later the worker's movement, *The Crucible* soon also began to have a voice on labour issues, morality, the treatment of women at Oxford, and Catholic history. For her own part, Fletcher wrote articles that drew from her own past concerns within the Anglican Communion and on pieces of interest to 'born' Catholics and converts alike.[35]

---

32 Dawes, *Catholic Women's Movements*; Macken, 'German Catholic Women's League'; McKenna, 'An Irish Catholic Women's League'.
33 Fletcher, *O, Call Back Yesterday*, p. 133; Margaret Fletcher, *Light for New Times* (New York, 1905).
34 Fletcher, 'Proposal: to start a small magazine devoted to the interests of Secondary Education in Catholic Girls' Schools, to consist both of contributions from the Religious Educational Orders, and from minds in the secular world best fitted for the work by experience and mental gifts.' BO 1/30 CWL Heading, 1906–1912, WDA; Fletcher, 'The Catholic Women's League', *The Crucible*, 25 June 1907, p. 4.
35 Fletcher felt High and Low Church Anglican women had lost the connection between suffrage and Christianity and it was necessary for Catholic women to reconnect freedom with religious belief. See *The Crucible*, 20 September 1905, pp. 65–6.

The Crucible confirmed Fletcher's suspicions that there was a need in the Catholic community for a women's magazine concerned with timely issues of substance. Fletcher contributed at least one article per issue and as the editor, her ideas and points of view were disseminated globally. Catholic women from all over the globe subscribed, from places as disparate as Australia, India and America. In 1906, one year after publication of the first volume of the magazine, it had accrued 314 annual subscribers worldwide, nearly a third of those subscriptions wholly subsidised by an anonymous American Catholic benefactress.[36] The following year there were nearly 400 subscribers. Notices in the back of each edition indicate that individual copies were passed around extensively (especially in institutional settings), making the true readership impossible to judge, but it was certainly higher than the actual subscription figures.

Overall, the Church provided Fletcher with an empowering space and context to flex her opinions, granting her influence and agency to further her work for Catholic women. Archbishop Bourne wholeheartedly approved of the production of the magazine, but 'begged' Fletcher not to request the assistance of an official Church censor, 'who would inevitably decide cautiously'.[37] Bourne said lightly, 'we will rap you over the knuckles if you go over the lines', and his tacit approval, and open mind, gave Fletcher an amount of latitude to put across her ideas that may have been controversial.[38] Despite such support from within the hierarchy, other priest friends:

> Were all against the attempt: they said I would fail, no one would read it, that I should make money and make enemies; and they surely felt, but were too kind to put into words, that I would be considered a great impertinence that I should rush in at all.[39]

In this example, the parochialism of the parish priests might be noted. Perhaps they also were (to some extent unconsciously) acknowledging a shift heralding a loss of authority to another body. Further, to sacrifice agency to a convert, a woman, might be a step too far.

Finding agency in The Crucible

The Crucible, as its name suggests, was a 'test', to see how far lay Catholic womanhood could be engaged in secular and religious issues. It showed how public debates could be intertwined with Catholic thought,

---

36 Fletcher, 'Birthday Notes', *The Crucible*, 20 June 1906, pp. 5–6. It would be safe to assume the anonymous American was Guiney.
37 Fletcher, *O, Call Back Yesterday*, p. 109.
38 Ibid., p. 110.
39 Ibid., p. 109.

demonstrating that, given the opportunity for a national (and international) conversation, women could find validation of their Christian feminist ideas from each other and the institutional Church. As part of this work, Fletcher continued her quest to spread her ideas for a more inclusive version of Catholic womanhood in England.

This mouthpiece for Catholic womanhood gave a voice, and with it, implicit agency from the Church to carry out its mission. From the start, the magazine contained articles on a variety of 'women's topics' weighted and differentiated to women from every class, in order to achieve the class mixing Fletcher desired. As a result, the topics covered in *The Crucible* were very broad, including nursing as a profession, salaries of women teachers, moral instruction, and the experiences of female students in higher education.[40] Fletcher sought to engage non-professional working women, middle-class women, and elites, across classes and beyond politics, on the basis of gender and a shared faith.[41]

The Crucible was the first forum in which ideas about women's rights could be aired and discussed in the English Catholic context for a specifically female audience. Fletcher's style of Christian feminism became a locus of empowerment within a patriarchal religion and a space apart from the contentious political debates for women's suffrage which Fletcher felt was far too combative. Equality was an area all could agree on. Women with every kind of interest about issues applicable to Catholic womanhood were invited to contribute articles. Tellingly, most of the articles put forward the uncontested thesis of women's rights, or told historic stories about women, such as Joan of Arc. Alice Abadam, a noted Catholic suffragist, wrote in *The Crucible* about women's lives in medieval Britain as a means of connecting with influential Catholic women of the past.[42] Abadam saw the Middle Ages as a time of powerful Catholic women in Britain, and used this example to encourage contemporary empowerment in the public sphere.

Under Fletcher's stewardship and with the Church's implicit support, lay Catholic women writers in *The Crucible* often wrote in support of Catholic women's equality. Papal documents did not always endorse this idea of equality with the same arguments that Fletcher used. The Vatican officially supported the claims that both men and women were equal and created in Christ's image, but such proclamations came with

---

[40] For example, the 20 December 1906 edition of *The Crucible* included articles by a Dominican priest on 'Impersonal Teaching' and by Alice Gruner on 'Salaries of Women Teachers' *The Crucible*, 20 December 1906, pp. 138–42.
[41] Isabel Clarke, 'The Work of the Girls Protection Society', *The Crucible*, 20 September 1906, pp. 87–92.
[42] Alice Abadam, 'Medieval Women and the Women's Movement', *The Crucible*, 2:8 (1907), pp. 216–25.

reservations. Pius X and Leo XIII argued that women had a particularly inescapable and exceptional duty to fulfil the role of home and family makers (a view shored up by 'incontestable' biology). Papal logic then followed that women should remain in their traditional roles. Therefore, any papal rhetoric that appeared to support equality was ultimately undermined by (if not a smokescreen for) conservatism. Leo XIII expressed his social conscience and concern for the 'wretched' working class, but he also wrote that:

> Women, again, are not suited for certain occupations; a woman is by nature fitted for home-work, and it is that which is best adapted at once to preserve her modesty and to promote the good bringing up of children and the well-being of the family.[43]

In *Arcanum Divinae* (1880), Leo XIII stated that women should be obedient to their husbands, promoting married womanhood as the Catholic ideal.[44] The ultra-conservative Pius X (1903–14), Leo's successor, was even clearer in his opinion of lay women in the public sphere. Speaking to the Italian League of Women in 1909 he said, 'Woman can never be man's equal and cannot therefore enjoy equal rights.'[45] The power of the patriarchy was not, however, an idea advocated for in *The Crucible*, published, lest we forget, with the blessing of the Church. The statements of the pope might be authoritative, yet Fletcher clearly challenged them to some extent and, in the process, reconceptualised Catholic womanhood personally and publicly. Clearly, throughout the pre-war era, Catholicism was reinterpreted in alternate and individual ways regardless of papal declarations.

Combining work and womanhood, lay woman Mabel Willison deterred alarmist thinking that equated professional working women with the breakdown of the family unit, writing in *The Crucible* that, 'women workers do not foreswear the duties of wifehood and motherhood in order to enjoy the independent liberty of a widened sphere of activity ... they are forced to be self-supporting'.[46] Willison contended that 'economics' and 'social conditions' meant that wives needed to undertake work as a

---

43   Leo XIII, *Rerum Novarum* (1891), §42. https://www.vatican.va/content/leo-xiii/en/encyclicals/documents/hf_l-xiii_enc_15051891_rerum-novarum.html.
44   Leo wrote: 'The woman, because she is flesh of his flesh, and bone of his bone, must be subject to her husband and obey him; not, indeed, as a servant, but as a companion, so that her obedience shall be wanting in neither honor nor dignity. Since the husband represents Christ, and since the wife represents the Church, let there always be, both in him who commands and in her who obeys, a heaven-born love guiding both in their respective duties.' *Arcanum Divinae* (1880), §11. https://www.vatican.va/content/leo-xiii/en/encyclicals/documents/hf_l-xiii_enc_10021880_arcanum.html.
45   'Pope is against Women in Politics', *New York Times*, 22 April 1909.
46   Mabel B. Willison, 'Modern Catholic Woman', *The Crucible*, 29 September 1908, pp. 97–102, 98.

matter of 'economic' and 'social conditions'.[47] She explained, 'the old sheltered life, once her sphere and privilege, has gone forever'.[48] Part of the modern condition was that the 'angel' had left the house.[49] In an echo of Fletcher's own arguments about the lack of companionship for educated, middle-class Catholic girls, Willison further states that:

> The position of the Catholic woman works for her own intellectual progress, ... among alien fellow students ... She shares a common study with them, is animated with the same idea, the advancement of the sex through individual attainment; yet on every fundamental principle of the religious and moral structure, her views are all but diametrically opposed to theirs. She is cut off from true companionship by her religion, and this is not because of intentional bigotry on their part, but rather because of a preconceived and rooted idea of theirs that as a Catholic she will be against all such progress.[50]

Perhaps the issue of the modern Catholic woman's place remained unresolved as she may have tried to become more fully assimilated into British society in the Edwardian period. However, papal pronouncements and popular conceptions of Catholic womanhood meant that Catholic women remained enigmatic in English society. Willison reiterated that British (by which she meant Anglican) women were unsure of what Catholic women could contribute to modern society given their 'old' ideas that Catholic women were 'backward' because their faith was perceived as antithetical to the modern world, especially in 1908 at the height of the Modernist movement.

Lay women contributors consistently promoted the progressive work of Catholic women across vocations such as education and the medical professions. In a 1907 piece, 'Roman Catholic Woman's College', Eleanor Warner detailed her efforts to create a Catholic residential college for women at Oxford and Cambridge, as Catholic men already had the same. She asked, '[why] should Catholic women of the present day lag behind their pre-Christian sisters in the strenuous cultivation of their God-given natural powers?'[51] In challenging the 'invisibility' of Catholic women within English society, she queried how it was possible that Catholic women were disallowed a university experience in powerful Imperial Britain:

> Surely the role of a Catholic woman in so vast an Empire as the British, is no mean one, whether her vocation be to the religious life, to motherhood, or to an independent professional or philanthropic life.[52]

---

47 Ibid.
48 Ibid.
49 Ibid.
50 Ibid., p. 99.
51 Eleanor Warner, 'Roman Catholic Woman's College', *The Crucible*, 25 September 1907, pp. 69–79, 77.
52 Ibid. Warner was a physician in Hyderabad and was involved in Roman Catholic medical missionary work. She had an audience with the Pope where he approved a Catholic

Like Fletcher, Warner believed that being a 'good' Catholic woman did not mean being limited to the spheres of motherhood and family. She described Catholic women contributing to the power of the Empire as a means of conferring agency and patriotism on them, reflecting wider thinking in British society of women's citizenship. By claiming British citizenship for Catholic women, Warner implied that lay Catholic women were entitled to the same rights as other Britons. In particular, Warner, along with Maisie Ward, was most interested with advocating for a place for Catholic women in higher education.[53] Her campaign was successful, and Warner gained approval from the Pope for Catholic women to matriculate at universities in Britain.[54] Warner was not the only contributor to advocate for women's inclusion in higher education. Annie Rogers, a longtime secretary of the Association for the Higher Education of Women in Oxford, and founder of the then women's college, St Hilda's, also contributed articles advocating that women had the right to attend and graduate from universities in Britain.[55]

The magazine's contributors were generally lay women, but religious authors and men were also included. In this sense *The Crucible* created an intersection between lay and religious women such as *Fille de Marie* Maude Petre and Missionary Sister of Our Lady of Africa, Mother Marie-Salomé, both of whom wrote for the publication. Petre contributed a touching article in the early days on 'Aids to Beauty from Within', whilst Mother Marie-Salomé, a missionary in Africa, advocated for women's equality.[56] Mother Marie-Salomé asked, 'must a woman, endowed with all the qualifications necessary to make a good physician, be denied the privilege of practice because it is considered unseemly to her sex?'[57] Male writers for *The Crucible* were generally of a more liberal bent. Francis Urquhart, of an old Catholic family (and the first Catholic to be a tutor at Oxford since the 1500s), and Fr C. C. Martindale, a convert and Jesuit from Farm Street and Oxford, contributed articles.[58]

Convert women, such as Fletcher and suffragist Virginia Crawford, tended to write on more progressive, liberal, and even sometimes taboo topics than the women 'born' Catholic, reflecting their educational background and longer engagement with social issues. Crawford, who would

---

residential ladies' college at Cambridge.
53 'Proposed Catholic College for Women at Cambridge', *The Tablet*, 13 July 1907.
54 Fletcher, *O, Call Back Yesterday*, p.116; 'Proposed Catholic College'.
55 'St Anne's College', *A History of the County of Oxford: Volume 3*, edited by H. E. Salter and Mary D. Lobel (London, 1954), pp. 351–3.
56 Maude Petre, 'Aids to Beauty from Within', *The Crucible*, 25 March 1907, pp. 229–32; Mary Salomé, I.M., 'Ad Majorem Dei Gloriam', *The Crucible*, 25 September 1907, pp. 80–4.
57 Mary Salomé, 'Ad Majorem Dei Gloriam', pp. 82–3.
58 'Fr. C. C. Martindale S.J.', *The Tablet*, 30 March 1963.

go on to establish the Catholic Social Guild in 1909, wrote on liberalism and Catholic social thought.[59] In 'The Evolution of the Christian Woman', Fletcher set out to rectify ideas of women's natural equality and correlate them with Church doctrine and papal writings.[60] Her tone was pious and polite in her task of 'spinning' papal writings to better match her own aims.[61]

Not surprisingly, it was in the pages of *The Crucible*, in 1906, that Fletcher first posited the idea for a 'League of Women Workers', planting the seed for the CWL.[62] The potential for non-elite professional and working women to bolster Catholic fellowship through work was a driving force behind *The Crucible*. However, for many, the term 'League of Women Workers' sounded far too proletarian for teachers and nurses. Proletarianism was fearful for elite women, evoking ideas of radical workers and revolutions outside the remit of Fletcher's ideal. She needed other women to understand that work was an issue critical to modern lay Catholic womanhood:

> Catholic women who are forewomen of factories, wardresses of prisons, matrons and nurses in workhouses, hospital nurses, and by no means the least, those remarkable sources the teachers in elementary schools, will prove some of our most valuable members.[63]

Fletcher made no distinction regarding what 'kind' of worker *The Crucible* readership would appeal to, while linking women and worker's rights, whether labourers, working-class women, or professional women, even across religious boundaries. For example, the famous socialist campaigner Clementina Black wrote an article on work and wages in 1906.[64] Black advocated for fair trade and a standard minimum wage for male and female workers in Britain, echoing the words of Cardinal Manning, a strong supporter of labour, and Pope Leo XIII from *Rerum Novarum* (1891): '[a] remedy must be found quickly for the misery and wretchedness pressing so unjustly on the majority of the working class'.[65] Fletcher felt that more Catholic women in work, specifically education, would help the position of all other Catholics in Britain, increasing awareness

---

[59] 'Mrs. Virginia Crawford', *The Tablet*, 30 October 1948; 'Virginia Crawford Remembered', *The Catholic Herald*, 16 November 1962.
[60] Fletcher, 'The Evolution of Christian Woman', *The Crucible*, 1:1 (1905), pp. 47–58.
[61] Ibid.
[62] Fletcher, 'Proposals for a League of Catholic Women Workers', *The Crucible*, 20 September 1906, pp. 67–73.
[63] Fletcher, 'The Catholic Women's League', *The Crucible*, 25 June 1907, p. 6.
[64] Clementina Black, 'Work and Wage', *The Crucible*, 20 December 1906, 160–4. I cannot find any references to Black being a Catholic, but one could presume that she was influenced by the Christian Socialist movement.
[65] Ibid., p. 161; Leo XIII, *Rerum Novarum*.

of women's rights in society by 'bringing [together] the ablest minds into constant touch with one another'.⁶⁶

The Catholic Women's League and the Ladies of Charity

Despite its name, the League of Catholic Women Workers was meant to be a place for lay women of all classes, not just the proletariat, to 'mix freely'.⁶⁷ Fletcher envisioned the new League as a place for lay women to be autonomous and self-governing, building on the ideas posited in *The Crucible*. In many ways, it would be vital to the ongoing but slow transformation of a hierarchical, parochial, or patriarchal Church. This was despite Pius X's *motu proprio* prohibiting women from exercising liturgical office even as choristers.⁶⁸ Fletcher's 1905 proposal for the League was forwarded to Bourne and discussed with Catholic women in London and Brighton, who received it with mixed indifference and distaste, due to its revolutionary schema. In Brighton, at the National Catholic Conference, she faced great hostility:

> I remember finding myself sitting on a stool surrounded by inquirers who wanted to get at what was behind it all in my mind. What axe did I want to grind through such an organization? Was I a Socialist, or a Suffragist, or any other 'ist'? And in all this I saw what was to be the kind of difficulty ahead. Only converts who had lived in touch with England's social evolution, knew the English connotation for terms in use abroad. Knowing myself not to be an 'ist' in either sense, I yet saw that there would have to be much holding of hands over a gulf ...⁶⁹

This moment in Brighton is especially enlightening because it shows that Fletcher, as a convert of only a decade, was still considered an outsider, a reputation that gave her distinctly less agency among women 'born' Catholic, despite all her work for Catholic women. These women were unclear how an organisation linking women across classes could ever be beneficial in the English setting. As a single woman who worked as an art teacher, she remained a curiosity to those elites gathered at the Catholic Conference. This audience was uncertain of and unaware of movements further afield – underlining the isolationist mentality still at work in many aspects of English Catholicism in the early years of the twentieth century.

The Catholic Church might be a place of inclusion or 'universality', as its name signifies, but the exclusive class system of Britain created

---

66   Margaret Fletcher, 'Proposal: to start a small magazine ...' BO 1/30 CWL Heading, 1906–1912, WDA.
67   Fletcher, *O, Call Back Yesterday*, p. 110.
68   Pius X, *Tra Le Sollecitudini: On Sacred Music* (1903).
69   Fletcher, *O, Call Back Yesterday*, p. 111.

an obstacle. One group of elite women present at the Catholic Conference was particularly troubled by Fletcher's new work and her idea for a League of Women Workers. At the time of the founding of the CWL, the pre-eminent Catholic women's group in London, although of French origin, was the Association of the Ladies of Charity of St Vincent de Paul, or the LofC (1900). The LofC was founded in Britain in the spirit of the settlement house movement, along with organisations such as Samuel and Henrietta Barnett's Toynbee Hall and Octavia Hill's Charity Organisation Society. LofC members, unlike other social movements, came from the Catholic aristocracy, with members including the Dowager Duchess of Newcastle, Lady Mary Howard, Viscountess Encombe and Lady Mary Talbot.[70] The Ladies did important philanthropic work for the poor or underemployed Irish Catholics and for the working-class native-born population. The LofC were also concerned with stemming 'leakage', or Catholics leaving the faith, through marriage or lack of Catholic opportunities.[71]

Due to the exalted position the LofC derived from their elite, recusant status, Fletcher was urged to seek their approval before she officially set up the CWL. As a result of federation, the LofC would, theoretically, be under the auspices of the CWL, alongside the much less privileged Southwark Rescue Society (1888) or the Needlework Guild (1885).[72] Fletcher's representative, Miss Lucy Wyatt-Papworth, took an early draft of the aims of the CWL to an LofC meeting in late 1906 to test the waters around linking together.[73] Wyatt-Papworth was a member of both organizations and a well-chosen emissary.

Despite Wyatt-Papworth's efforts, Lady Mary Talbot and the LofC reacted badly to the idea of the League, which they argued sounded socialist and not religious enough, citing tensions between aristocratic recusants and middle-class converts. Talbot angrily wrote to Bourne explaining her reticence over rumours of the new group for Catholic women based on class and geography:

> Great Promoters of the Proposed League have been tactless by talking and saying that the L.O.C. are too spiritual, not up to date, etc. etc. What I thought rather scurious [sic] at the Sub.Com[tee] meeting was that Miss Wyatt-Papworth [a founding member of the CWL] who is a Lady ... [and] feeling has been stirred

---

[70] Lady Edmund Talbot to Archbishop of Westminster, 19 November [1906]. BO 1/30 CWL Heading, 1906–1912, WDA.
[71] Rev. Dean Billington, et al. [Mary Talbot], 'Catholic Truth Society', *The Tablet*, 11 July 1903, pp. 61–2.
[72] 'Southwark Catholic Rescue Society', *The Tablet*, 23 June 1923; 'Catholic Needlework Guild', *The Tablet*, 16 June 1894.
[73] Fletcher, 'Draft suggestions for the Initial Work of organising the Proposed League of Catholic women, to be laid before the Ladies of Charity at their meeting 3 November 1906', unpublished draft from BO 1/30 CWL Heading, 1906–1912, WDA.

up about the whole matter ... I am afraid the Lady of Charity + who attended the meeting as Miss Fletcher's representative rather took the line of saying that the L.O.C Association could be forced to join the Proposed League ...[74]

Worker's rights and fears of socialism caused tensions between the Ladies and Fletcher, perhaps indicating greater class anxieties were at play. Fletcher meant the 'worker' to refer to women who worked outside the home, but here she was misconstrued as purely Leftist.

A liberal attitude towards worker's rights or equity was not in itself problematic for most Catholics. In 1891, Pope Leo XIII had written the encyclical in favour of worker's rights, *Rerum Novarum*, but the Church was now led by the conservative Pius X.[75] Late in 1906, Fletcher capitulated and removed the word 'workers' from the title of the group.[76] The founder wrote in *The Crucible* that the issue was 'wisely weighed in the balance by those whose acceptance or non-acceptance of the scheme will mean much either way.'[77] However, she conveyed the importance that all women should be able to join and the membership fee was kept low enough so that 'everyone above the poverty line' could join.[78] Membership in the CWL was 'open to any Catholic woman possessed of a modicum of social spirit and alive to the duties of citizenship', and further, to utilise 'all the available power and influence of Catholic women in a nation, and opposing them to the de-Christening influences of non-Christian women'.[79] The LofC were unaccustomed to the idea of their social inferiors having such power or agency. Fletcher acknowledged the class issue raised by the LofC and assured the CWL's membership that unlike the Ladies, her group would have 'no enemies, does not know the meaning of the word, has no class distinctions'.[80]

Another issue besides class alienated Fletcher from some of the LofC: women's rights. Some upper-class women found the idea of women's equality too progressive and indicative of radicalism. In *The Crucible*, Fletcher took a clear stance on women's equality and came out in support of Christian feminism. Fletcher incorrectly presumed that all Catholic women would have the same aims. Fletcher wrote of her new group: 'it aims at bringing the influence of Catholic thought on the gradual solution of the position, duties and rights of women, and every public question concerned therewith' and would be concerned with 'work of

---

[74] Lady Edmund Talbot to Archbishop of Westminster, 19 November [1906]. BO 1/30 CWL Heading, 1906–1912, WDA. Capitalisation as in original.
[75] Pope Leo XIII, *Rerum Novarum*.
[76] Fletcher to Bourne, 8 October 1906. Bourne 1/30 1906–1912, WDA.
[77] Fletcher, 'Notes', *The Crucible*, 20 December 1906, pp. 180–4, 180.
[78] Fletcher, 'The Catholic Women's League', *The Crucible*, 25 June 1907, p. 9.
[79] Fletcher to Bourne, 8 October 1906. Bourne 1/30 1906–1912, WDA.
[80] Fletcher, 'The Catholic Women's League', *The Crucible*, 25 June 1907, p. 7.

a semi-public nature'.[81] Clearly, Fletcher always meant for the group to have a feminist bent. This dedication to women's rights in both the secular and sanctified world set the CWL apart from the start.

Top-ranking churchmen like Bernard Vaughan and Bourne supported women's possible contributions to the Church, but women like Talbot were suspicious, and felt matters with a political undertone had no place in church organisations (a stance with which Fletcher agreed). However, what Talbot believed was political, Fletcher believed to be a God-given right, namely, women's equality. Talbot vigorously wrote to Bourne in 1906, emphasising her fears of this proposed classless organisation. She underlined for Bourne the areas she felt were especially sensitive matters: 'I do think that the danger of it's becoming political, women's rights, etc. could be fatal in England, where there is no Catholic party as I understand there is in Germany.'[82] Talbot feared that Fletcher and her group would erode the social order through engaging Catholic women in secular concerns.

The Ladies of Charity finally voted against associating with the new group; three of the board voted for it and four against. The deciding vote was made, tellingly, by the clergyman who acted as the Ladies' spiritual director, Fr Thomas Walsh.[83] Talbot warned Bourne that many of the English upper classes were not prepared to join a mixed organisation, but, over time, many in fact did, coinciding with Fletcher's departure from the day-to-day running of the group.[84] The Victorian mentality of respectability still governed British life in the early Edwardian era, so, despite her ideals, Fletcher required the support of women of status to give consequence to the group:

> Although the main support of the League will at present come from the professional classes, we shall not be altogether without recognition from the class represented by the committee of the Ladies of Charity ... It seems to be generally agreed that ordinary members of the Ladies of Charity would be free to belong to the League.[85]

---

[81] Fletcher, 'Draft suggestions for the Initial Work of organising the Proposed League of Catholic women, to be laid before the Ladies of Charity at their meeting 3 November 1906', unpublished draft from BO 1/30 CWL Heading, 1906–1912, WDA.
[82] Lady Edmund Talbot to Archbishop of Westminster, 19 November [1906]. BO 1/30 CWL Heading, 1906–1912, WDA. The underlining is Talbot's own.
[83] Ibid. If there had been one doctrinal way of thinking on any of these matters then we would not find the breadth of responses to the CWL founding.
[84] Lady Edmund Talbot to Archbishop of Westminster, 19 November [1906]. BO 1/30 CWL Heading, 1906–1912, WDA.; Fletcher, 'Notes', *The Crucible*, 20 December 1906, pp. 180–4, p. 180.; Fletcher, 'The Catholic Women's League', *The Crucible*, 25 March 1907, pp. 189–91, p. 190. She writes, 'a study of the state of things in this country led to the conclusion that there were practically no Catholic associations of women eligible for affiliation'. p. 190.
[85] Fletcher to Archbishop of Westminster, 21 November 1906. BO 1/30 CWL Heading, 1906–1912, WDA.

'Ordinary members' of the LofC did indeed join the CWL, among them Ada Streeter and Miss Wyatt-Papworth. Some aristocratic women, such as Viscountess Enscombe and Dowager Lady Bute, also joined the CWL, demonstrating that Talbot's image of elite women's desire to remain separate was, perhaps, not truly representative of how the majority felt in practice.

Other groups in English Catholic society had mixed opinions about the CWL.[86] Many female religious, who had taken vows of poverty, joined the CWL immediately.[87] Parish priests, long accustomed to being the sole voice of authority over their isolated flocks, felt that their devotional sodalities were sufficient to occupy women of faith, rejecting Fletcher's proposals.[88] Fletcher felt this resistance derived from the priests' status as 'born' Catholics who 'moved in a charmed circle of the other Catholic families', leaving them fearful of a non-devotional women's group as a harbinger of 'irreligion'.[89] Some priests claimed their female parishioners had no interest in *The Crucible* or the CWL because they did not 'read, think, or write'.[90] Fletcher and others in the hierarchy wanted to correct this insular mentality.

In some ways, the Catholic hierarchy enabled Catholic women to independently reinterpret their faith lives and how they expressed their 'Catholicness'. Under the protection of Cardinal Bourne and with the spiritual advice (and liberalism) of the Jesuit Bernard Vaughan, the CWL moved forward.[91] Vaughan, a volunteer, proved to be a sympathetic spiritual advisor and his family connections gave him an air of unquestioned orthodoxy.[92] Fletcher felt he was an ideal candidate to give respect to the new organisation because 'his name will inspire confidence in the minds of the older element'.[93] Vaughan's long-term work in Manchester for disenfranchised Catholics made him empathetic to the class-mixing desired by Fletcher.[94] In Manchester, he was known to have cooked

---

[86] In the end it was left to individual ladies to choose if they would like to be organised under the umbrella of the CWL. Fletcher, 'The Catholic Women's League', *The Crucible*, 25 March 1907 (1905–1913), pp. 189–91.
[87] Those contributing included the Benedictines, Society of the Holy Child Jesus, Sisters of Mercy, and Poor Clares. See Fletcher, 'The Catholic Women's League', p. 10.
[88] Fletcher, *O, Call Back Yesterday*, p. 115.
[89] Ibid.
[90] Ibid., p. 116.
[91] Bernard Vaughan S.J. was the younger brother of the recently deceased Archbishop of Westminster, Cardinal Herbert Vaughan. He was also related to the Archbishop of Sydney, Roger Vaughan, to Francis Vaughan, Bishop of Wales, and John Vaughan, an auxiliary bishop in Salford.
[92] Fletcher to Archbishop of Westminster, 1 December [1905/6/7]. BO 1/30 CWL Heading, 1906–1912, WDA.
[93] Ibid.
[94] 'Father Vaughan, Noted Jesuit, Dies', *New York Times*, 1 November 1922.

dinner for the children of a sick Catholic mother in her home.[95] In 1906 Vaughan gave a number of homilies at Farm Street that took direct aim at upper-class society and its hypocrisy.[96] These actions made Vaughan an ideal match for Fletcher in that he also sought an end to class divisions in Catholic society.[97] He gave Fletcher and the organisation latitude, respecting their autonomy. Fletcher told Vaughan's biographer that he suggested 'that on the secular and practical side we should carve our own way without any criticism and advice from him', which they did.[98]

In its early days, the CWL ran social lectures and debates and even formed an Information Bureau in central London to disseminate information to the national branches and individuals. One debate, held in Mayfair in May 1907, featured Maude Petre arguing in favour of 'personal independence as the highest form of freedom' and Dr Alice Johnson suggesting that 'the monopoly of power by one sex is deteriorating to both'.[99] CWL chapters offered speeches on a variety of topics including cookery and cleaning as trades. The speeches targeted 'working-class girls' who associated with the Catholic settlement movement.[100] The Manchester branch, led by Frances Zanetti, was especially progressive and advocated that lay women were naturally more inclined to help other working-class Catholic women than nuns.[101] These speeches, debates, and the distribution of information enabled Fletcher to connect lay Catholic women with education throughout their lives – and with the workings of the secular world. In the CWL, Catholic women were to engage in social and educational work in larger numbers across the nation.

By 1908, committees had been set up in Manchester, Brighton and Worthing, Bournemouth, Boscombe and Oxford. Branches in the southwest followed at Clifton and Bath. There was no question of the growing popularity of the CWL when over 1,000 women had joined, and headquarters had been organised. As new women joined the organisation, Fletcher stepped back from the fore, and the CWL became more of a social institution. A symptom of this shift away from advocacy was that the CWL distanced itself from *The Crucible* in 1910. The publication remained committed to working-class labour rights and more liberal expressions of Christian feminism, but it folded in 1913. As the CWL gradually became less concerned with women's rights, and more with issues that appealed to conservative middle-class women, Fletcher relinquished a hands-on

---

[95] Ibid.
[96] C. C. Martindale, *Bernard Vaughan S.J.* (London, 1923), pp. 81–3.
[97] Vaughan's mother was also a convert.
[98] Martindale, *Bernard Vaughan*, pp. 113–5.
[99] Fletcher, 'The Catholic Women's League', *The Crucible*, 25 June 1907, pp. 3–11.
[100] Fletcher, 'The Catholic Women's League', *The Crucible*, 25 March 1908, pp. 191–201.
[101] Frances Zanetti, 'Helping Hands', *The Crucible*, 25 September 1907, pp. 157–60.

leadership role. After benefitting from Fletcher's work, women's rights were no longer viewed as a primary concern, and philanthropic interests came to the fore in post-Great War Britain.

Conclusion

Fletcher's status as a middle-class Catholic convert placed her at the crossroads of tensions over and within Roman Catholicism in Britain. Her conversion galvanised her to a life of social work and habilitation of the Catholic woman in Britain. In founding the CWL, Fletcher harnessed the potential in the Catholic Church in Britain to improve the lives of all Catholic lay women. In doing so, she took power out of the hands of the aristocracy and placed it firmly in the hands of the rest of the Church, including the lay community, who valued the trust placed in them. She also organised the influence and support of the hierarchy to create a publication and national group for Catholic lay women. After the CWL, numerous other Catholic organisations for women were founded, such as the Catholic Women's Suffrage Society (1911) and the Union of Catholic Mothers (1913).[102] These groups, open to all Catholic women in Britain, regardless of class, would not have been possible without the work of Margaret Fletcher and the CWL.

This chapter has shown why and how Margaret Fletcher, as the founder of the CWL and *The Crucible*, positioned middle-class women as vital to improving the lives of lay Catholic women in Britain. Fletcher sought to establish an organisation in which Catholic women could connect across classes and educational backgrounds through issues affecting their society. She remained 'convinced that women united in aim and associated in work will accomplish more for the glory of God than they imagine possible while acting in isolation'.[103]

---

[102] Peter Gordon and David Doughan, *Women, Clubs and Associations in Britain* (Abingdon, 2006), pp. 95–143; Caitriona Beaumont, 'Women and Citizenship: A Study of Non-Feminist Women's Societies and the Women's Movement in England, 1928–1950', unpublished doctoral thesis, University of Warwick, April 1996.
[103] Fletcher, 'The Catholic Women's League', *The Crucible*, 25 March 1907, pp. 189–91, 191.

3

'IN THE INTERESTS OF JUSTICE, MORALITY AND RELIGION': ST JOAN'S SOCIAL AND POLITICAL ALLIANCE, 1920s–1930s[1]

Carmen M. Mangion

In 1910, women's suffrage campaigners Gabrielle Jeffery and May Kendall met outside Holloway Prison in London waiting to cheer on released suffragettes. They were allied by their passion for the suffrage cause, but also, as they realised that day, by their Catholic identity. This fortuitous meeting led to the formation of the Catholic Women's Suffrage Society (renamed St Joan's Social and Political Alliance in 1923; then St Joan's International Alliance in 1954).[2] Co-religionists were recruited to the cause of women's suffrage and by 1913, the Catholic Women's Suffrage Society claimed over 1,000 members.[3] Over the next 50 years, the Society expanded to twenty-four countries over five continents.[4] Outlasting most suffrage societies, they successfully moved from their original aim of suffrage for women on the same terms as men, towards broader aims of political, social and economic equalities between men and women.[5] The women of St Joan's Alliance saw their Catholic faith as an integral component of their feminism; they identified their causes for equality between men and women as 'elementary justice' and argued for the 'essential Catholicity of our feminist creed'.[6] In bringing its resolution and aims before Cardinal Archbishop Bourne in 1911, they highlighted

---

[1] Animated discussions with Anne Summers, Naomi Rich and Katharyn Lamontagne have substantially enriched this chapter and focused my thinking. I am also so grateful to the editors for their constructive comments and their support.
[2] Leonora de Alberti, 'History of the Catholic Women's Suffrage Society', *Catholic Citizen* (1928), p. 91. Members often referred to the organisation as St Joan's Alliance or simply the Alliance; this chapter will do the same.
[3] Nancy Stewart Parnell, *A Venture in Faith: A History of St Joan's Social and Political Alliance, Formerly the Catholic Women's Suffrage Society, 1911–1961* (London, 1961).
[4] Anne Marie Pelzer, 'St Joan's International Alliance, a short history, 1911–1977 (1977)', http://www.womencanbepriests.org/interact/pelzer.asp, accessed 7 December 2019. Their international expansion deserves a study of its own but is beyond the remit of this chapter.
[5] 'The Future of St Joan's Alliance', *Catholic Citizen* (1928), p. 97.
[6] Isabel Willis, 'Our Own History', *Catholic Citizen* (1920), p. 39.

'the grave need of admitting women to the parliamentary franchise in the interests of justice, morality and religion'.[7] This chapter identifies how justice, morality and religion were intrinsic to St Joan's Alliance campaigning activities.

Women's movements

The activities of St Joan's Social and Political Alliance were shaped by both the social and gendered politics of the interwar decades and the developing discourse of lay Catholic action. Women had been recruited for jobs vacated by men fighting in the Great War; they worked in munitions factories and as tram conductors, police and civil servants. Yet, as the war ended, women were expected to return to home and hearth to fulfil their gendered supporting roles as wives, mothers and daughters.[8] Some women were given the vote: suffrage was granted to women over thirty who met a property qualification in 1918.[9] The Alliance joined the handful of suffrage organisations remaining active in post-war Britain, to complete the campaign for women's suffrage on equal terms to men. Like many of them, it expanded its aims and acknowledged its widening sphere of activities: 'to establish the political, social, and economic equality between men and women, and to further the work and usefulness of Catholic women as citizens'.[10] It remained a collaborative organisation, joining new and similarly recalibrated suffrage organisations that lobbied for women's equality with men as well as for increased eligibility to social welfare provision. The National Union of Women's Suffrage Societies reinvented itself after 1918 as the National Union of Societies for Equal Citizenship (1918–45) targeting suffrage for all women as their primary aim but also campaigning for legislative changes that promoted the social welfare of women, particularly wives and mothers. They were joined by other organisations espousing a 'new' feminism that highlighted women's gendered differences and contributions to the State, most often linked to motherhood. Organisations such as the Mothers' Union (1885) and the

---

[7] The Women's Library, London School of Economics and Political Science, Records of the St Joan's International Alliance (henceforth 2SJA) 2SJA/A/1/01 'Miss Abadam on the Coverture Qualification', *Universe*, 23 December 1911.

[8] Gail Braybon, *Women Workers in the First World War: The British Experience*, (London, 1981), pp. 85–90. Glew has demonstrated how easily the strictly gendered work of the London County Council was overturned in wartime conditions. Helen Glew, *Gender, Rhetoric and Regulation: Women's Work in the Civil Service and the London County Council, 1900–55* (Manchester, 2016), p. 25.

[9] Representation of the People Act (1918), https://www.legislation.gov.uk/ukpga/1918/64/pdfs/ukpga_19180064_en.pdf, accessed 5 September 2023.

[10] Leonora de Alberti, 'History of the Catholic Women's Suffrage Society', *Catholic Citizen* (1928), p. 105.

National Union of Townswomen's Guilds (1929) dismissed feminism but identified with a domestic ideology that fed their political activism for social welfare benefits for women.[11] They were in ideological opposition to the equal rights feminism espoused by organisations such as the Women's Freedom League (1907–61), the Six Point Group (1921–83) and the Open Door Council (1926–65) which campaigned for equal rights legislation that supported equal employment and pay opportunities for women along with the removal of other legal and economic inequalities between men and women.[12] Non-feminist, 'new' and 'equalitarian' feminist groups were often seen as antagonistic, but despite varied ideologies, they often collaborated on specific political campaigns.[13] The heady activism of the suffrage movement, marked by tactical distinctions, but unified by the objective of women's suffrage changed emphasis by the 1920s, becoming more diverse and ideologically freighted. It did not evaporate as the popular concept of 'first wave' and 'second wave' feminism suggests.[14] Much of the social and political equality and social welfare legislation in place by the 1950s can be credited to the dynamism and exertions of numerous women's lobbying organisations including St Joan's Social and Political Alliance in the interwar years.

Catholic Action

The women of St Joan's Social and Political Alliance were well integrated into the women's social activism of the interwar period – they joined with other groups in their campaigns and their members were also involved with other women's organisations. But, at their core, they identified themselves and their activism as intrinsically Catholic. They saw no contradiction between operating as an 'equalitarian society' directing campaigns for 'true sex equality' and their commitment to their Catholic

---

[11] Caitríona Beaumont, *Housewives and Citizens: Domesticity and the Women's Movement in England, 1928–64* (Manchester, 2013).

[12] The Women's Freedom League, the Six Point Group and the Open Door Council campaigned on equality-based principles that emphasised political, occupational, moral, social, economic and legal equalities between women and men.

[13] Caitríona Beaumont, 'The Women's Movement, Politics and Citizenship, 1918–1950s', *Women in Twentieth-Century Britain*, edited by Ina Zweiniger-Bargielowska (London, 2001), p. 264. Equalitarian was the term often used in the interwar years for equal rights feminism.

[14] The historiography of women's movements suggests a lacuna in women's activism between the 1918 Representation of the People Act and the Women's Liberation Movement of the long 1960s. This chapter follows the lead of numerous scholars who have dispelled this myth of quiescence and inactivity. Adrian Bingham, '"An Era of Domesticity"? Histories of Women and Gender in Interwar Britain', *Cultural and Social History*, 1:2 (2004), pp. 225–33.

faith. Their activism coincided with the emergence of Catholic Action.[15] The Holy See's concerns about its own loss of political power when a liberal, secular state was formed in Italy, and increasing concerns over marginalisation of the Church in an ever more secular society, led to its urging the laity to come to the defence and promotion of Church interests. Catholic Action became the umbrella term for the collaboration of the laity in the apostolic work of the Church and included groups such as the Young Christian Workers, the Catholic Social Guild, and the Catholic Evidence Guild.[16] Pope Pius X's 1905 encyclical, *Il Fermo Proposito*, though directed towards Italy, offered guidelines to all laity involved in organisations addressing issues of public morality and social justice through social action. *Quadragesimo Anno* issued by Pope Pius XI in 1931 encouraged men and women to participate in Catholic social organisations.[17] Defining lay action as an apostolate suggested an official status which reflected lay participation in the 'mission for the glory of God and the salvation of souls'.[18] The groups involved were not simply organisations dedicated to piety. One manual on Catholic Action defined it as:

> the *united action* of clergy and laity, under the direction and guidance of the Hierarchy of each country. It embraces a large variety of Catholic activities, aiming at the promotion of Catholic principles, and of good works of every kind.[19]

Two points were significant to Catholic Action. First, Catholics were meant to work under their bishops or clergy as militant warriors defending their faith. Second, despite this inward-facing philosophy and an emphasis on bishops and clergy as the font of all authority, Catholic Action was socially oriented in outward looking ways that critiqued the socio-political world. It emphasised action, though not denying the significance of prayer. The Young Christian Workers (JOCists) in Belgium and France, with their motto 'See, Judge, Act', exemplified this global movement.[20] Though meant to avoid party politics, Catholics as citizens were not supposed

---

15 'The Future of St Joan's Alliance', *Catholic Citizen* (1928), p. 97.
16 Niall Coll and Alana Harris, 'The Path to Rome: Characteristics and Contours of Theology in Britain and Ireland before the Council', in *Vatican II – Event and Mandate. Intercontinental Commentary on the Council's Documents, their Reception and their Orientation for Church and Theology. Vol. 6. Europe*, edited by Dries Bosschaert and Urszula Pękala (Leuven, 2025).
17 The term Catholic Action was introduced in 1905 by Pius X's encyclical *Il Fermo Proposito*, https://www.vatican.va/content/pius-x/en/encyclicals/documents/hf_p-x_enc_11061905_il-fermo-propos to.html, accessed 5 September 2023.
18 Mgr Luigi Civardi, *A Manual of Catholic Action*, translated by C. C. Martindale S.J. (London, 1935), p. 6.
19 An Irish Priest, *A Manual of Catholic Action* (Dublin, 1933), p. vii.
20 J. Fitzsimons, 'Catholic Action in France', in *Restoring All Things: A Guide to Catholic Action*, edited by John Fitzsimons and Paul McGuire (London, 1939), pp. 165–97, 170.

to be indifferent to politics. Catholic Action was a model for exercising Catholic belief and understanding of social responsibilities.

From its foundation in 1911, St Joan's Alliance participated in political and social Catholicism – both components of Catholic Action. They addressed the 'social questions' of the day with what they believed were Catholic responses of 'elementary justice' rather than through alternative and secular ideologies such as liberalism, socialism and communism. Though not established as part of the Catholic Action movement, the actions of the Alliance were influenced by papal encyclicals. Two features, though, highlighted their divergence from Catholic Action organisations: they did not operate under the direction of the Catholic hierarchy, and they collaborated with non-Catholic organisations. Their decision in 1923 to change their name to the St Joan's Social and Political Union was a response to the Holy See's prohibition of any Catholic society to be represented at a meeting of any 'non-confessional, Protestant, or neutral nature'. From the early days of the Catholic Women's Suffrage Society, organisers were wary of their own independence of action: they did not have a clerical spiritual advisor as was required of Catholic societies. Though they allowed men as 'associate' members, men could not vote or be elected to their governing body. The decision to remove 'Catholic' from their name was painful – but operating as the St Joan's Social and Political Alliance removed any interference from bishops and the Holy See and allowed them the freedom to interact with other feminist organisations.[21] The name change did not hinder their international growth. Involved with and encouraging of co-religionist suffrage campaigns in Europe and beyond from their early days, by 1953 the Alliance was a global institution located on five continents in twenty-four nations.[22]

As chapter one of this volume suggests, there has been minimal scholarship on the lay apostolate in Britain. The historiographical gap is even wider if lay Catholic women's organisations are considered. Groups such as the Catholic Nurses Guild (1897), Dames of St Joan (1926–1999) and the Catholic Mothers' Union (1913) populate the news articles in the Catholic press – but little academic research has examined their activism and how they shaped ordinary Catholic lives. However, a modest historiography exists addressing the Catholic Women's League and the Catholic Women's Suffrage Society. The Catholic Women's League (1906), founded by convert Margaret Fletcher, was a non-feminist organisation concerned

---

[21] 2SJA/A/1/06 Minutes Book No. V 1923–1926, 27 March to 6 June 1923. The painful conversations with Francis Bourne, Cardinal Archbishop of Westminster, are explained in their meeting minutes. Importantly, the Alliance did have some ecclesiastical support despite the name change.
[22] Pelzer, 'St Joan's International Alliance'.

'IN THE INTERESTS OF JUSTICE, MORALITY AND RELIGION' 45

with Catholic women's social education and social welfare issues.[23] A cluster of studies scrutinise the pre-1919 suffrage campaigning of the Catholic Women's Suffrage Society.[24] Extant research acknowledges the significance of faith to the members of St Joan's Alliance as 'a powerful vehicle for their feminism'.[25]

Sources and methods

For its examination of the interwar period this chapter utilises material created and curated by the leadership of St Joan's Alliance. Minute books, pressbooks, their own publication *The Catholic Citizen* (originally the *Catholic Suffragist*, founded in 1915), self-published pamphlets and books and the published work of members of St Joan's Alliance record the campaigns and activism of their members. There is little evidence of what must have been voluminous business correspondence except for the suggestive lists of correspondents found on the pages of meeting minutes. Outside the archive itself, very little material is extant. The organisation has no easily locatable presence in diocesan archives. And unfortunately, the archives of the local branches have yet to be located.[26] Meeting minutes and annual reports document the leadership of a dynamic Executive Committee typically composed of twelve to fourteen dedicated activists.

---

[23] Mary V. Newman, '"To Put into the Field Trained Bands of Women": Margaret Fletcher and the Education of Catholic Lay Women to Engage in the Public Sphere in the Early Twentieth Century', *History of Education Researcher*, 93 (2014), pp. 12–21; Paula M. Kane, '"The Willing Captive of Home?" The English Catholic Women's League, 1906–1920', *Church History*, 60 3 (1991), pp. 331–55; Beaumont, *Housewives and Citizens*. See also Kathryn Lamontagne's contribution in this volume.
[24] Carmen M. Mangion, 'Religious Suffrage Societies', *Routledge Companion to British Women's Suffrage*, edited by Krista Cowman (London, 2024); Jacqueline R. deVries, 'Challenging Traditions: Denominational Feminism in Britain, 1910–1920', in *Borderlines: Genders and Identities in War and Peace, 1870–1930*, edited by Billie Melman (New York, 1998), pp. 265–83; Francis M. Mason, 'The Newer Eve: The Catholic Women's Suffrage Society in England, 1911–1923', *Catholic Historical Review*, 72:4 (1986), 620–38; Elaine Clark, 'Catholics and the Campaign for Women's Suffrage in England', *Church History*, 73 (2004), pp. 635–65; Elaine Clark, 'Catholic Men in Support of the Women's Suffrage Movement in England', *Catholic Historical Review*, 94 (2008), pp. 22–44.
[25] A chapter addressing St Joan's Alliance feminist activism in the 1940s and 1950s can be found in Jessica Bronwyn Thurlow, 'Continuity and Change in British Feminism, c. 1940–1960', unpublished PhD dissertation, University of Michigan, 2006, p. 303.
[26] Leonora de Alberti, 'History of the Catholic Women's Suffrage Society', *Catholic Citizen* (1928), pp. 92–4. Branches included Hastings and East Sussex (1911), Liverpool and District (1912), Brighton and West Sussex (1912), Wimbledon (1913), Plymouth (1913), Edinburgh/Midlothian (1913), Manchester (1913?), Cardiff (1914), Birmingham (1914), Stirling (1914) and Wakefield (1914). Most branch members were transferred to the central London membership during the war as suffrage activities waned and women took part in wartime activities. Only the Liverpool and District Branch remained active.

Volunteers appear plentiful amongst the thousand or so members, though frequent resignations noted in the minutes and the annual reports suggest that women's working lives, both inside and outside the home, often brought a halt to their active exertions.[27] Sadly, membership lists are not extant. Minute books and published obituaries of active members suggest that most members were part of the widening stratum of the Catholic middle classes.[28] As with many such organisations, annual reports suggest financial precarity and gratitude to the more well-off members who paid off the recurring small debts.

The interwar years provide an important period of study coinciding with both the recalibration of the women's movement and the development of Catholic Action organisations.[29] The Catholic Women's Suffrage Society as it developed into St Joan's Social and Political Alliance repositioned its campaigning from political suffrage to legislation that promoted equality between the sexes. In its initial incarnation it understood women's franchise as 'elementary justice' and a stepping-stone to further activism based on the 'moral principle of true sex equality'.[30] St Joan's Alliance espoused an activism based on the politics of equality 'on the same terms as men'. They lobbied on a myriad of issues all reported on in detail on the pages of *The Catholic Citizen*, their annual reports, and both the national and international press. The campaigns, normally ten to twelve each year, were listed in each annual report. Until 1928, the issue that headed the list was for women's enfranchisement. This chapter will explore two categories of campaigns that appeared most frequently in the annual reports and *The Catholic Citizen* during the interwar years. The first, that of women's employment equality, included campaigning for employment opportunities, equal wages and the removal of restrictive employment practices. The second set of campaigns to be examined were those that specifically addressed Catholic moral principles, for example in relation to birth control and divorce. Woven throughout these sections is the question of identity. Paradoxically for modern scholarship which often strictly divides historical actors into the unhelpful categories of conservatives and progressives, St Joan's Social and Political Alliance

---

[27] There was rapid turnover in the executive team, with resignations noted in meeting minutes often mentioning heavy workloads, including family responsibilities. During these two decades those taking such responsibilities more often went by Miss (75%) than Mrs (25%), which suggests St Joan's Alliance was led mainly by unmarried women who were likely to have worked outside the home.
[28] Lists of members who attended the annual meeting and monthly donees and subscribers are recorded in *The Catholic Citizen*.
[29] James Pereiro, 'Who Are the Laity?', in *From Without the Flaminian Gate*, edited by V. Alan McClelland and Michael Hodgetts (London, 1999), pp. 173–8.
[30] Isabel Willis, 'Our Own History', *Catholic Citizen* (1920), p. 38.

proudly declared its Catholic identity as a motivation to its feminism: justice, morality and religion were integral to its equality feminism.

Women's employment and pay equality

It was usual for each campaign to be agreed to by the Executive Committee and discussed at annual meetings. Strategies included holding events and publishing material that educated Catholics on campaign issues; direct protest, often in the form of correspondence with political decision-makers; and collaborative action with other activist organisations. Not unexpectedly, campaign interests overlapped with other feminist and non-feminist organisations and coordinated efforts to lobby the State for new or revised legislation were commonplace. St Joan's Alliance was well connected, in particular, with other equal rights organisations such as the Open Door Council (one of its founder members was Virginia M. Crawford, who was Chair of St Joan's Alliance from 1925 to 1927) and the Six Point Group (Monica Whately was its Honorary Secretary and Chairman and also an active member of St Joan's Alliance). These campaigns, when discussed in the Catholic press, particularly *The Catholic Citizen*, were inflected by the Catholicism of the members of St Joan's Alliance. Rarely theologically explicit, the Alliance's concept of equality was based on the premise of spiritual equality explained in terms of a 'Catholic' morality and justice based on equality.[31]

Outside the parliamentary franchise, St Joan's Alliance's primary campaigning during the interwar years was for equal employment opportunities and wages for women. After the Great War, they acknowledged the wartime circumstances which offered women diverse employment opportunities and expressed their hopes that this was not 'simply a war expedient, but recognised as the application of a principle of justice'.[32] However, women were expected to resume home duties as men returned from the front, and the economic crisis of the 1930s further exacerbated the tensions over women's paid employment. From the 1920s, the marriage bar became the norm in the civil service and government-funded schools and women were regularly forced out of their employment upon marriage.[33] St Joan's Alliance campaigned for the opening up of job opportunities for women, equal pay, and the removal of restrictive employment measures, including the marriage bar.

---

[31] I am indebted to discussions with Naomi Rich and her own unpublished work regarding these points. Gilbert Higgins, 'What the Church has done for Woman', *Catholic Suffragist* (1917), pp. 65–8.
[32] 'February meeting', *Catholic Citizen* (1924), p. 5.
[33] Alison Oram, *Women Teachers and Feminist Politics, 1900–39* (Manchester, 1996), pp. 26–7.

Alliance campaigns often critiqued specific legislation such as the Sex Disqualification (Removal) Act of 1919 which signalled a promising era for women's professional employment. It removed many of the prohibitions to enter professions such as the law or accountancy; it expanded the opportunities for women in the civil service; and it allowed women to be jurors and magistrates.[34] However, women had no right to employment, and restrictive employment practices remained in place despite legal battles.[35] Because it was a piece of permissive legislation, there were no means of enforcing the Act. From 1919 to 1925, St Joan's Social and Political Alliance repeatedly called on the Government to amend the Act so that:

> in practice a person shall not be disqualified by sex or marriage from the exercise of any public function, or from being appointed to any civil or judicial office or post, or from entering or assuming any civil profession or vocation, or from admission to any incorporated society (whether incorporated by Royal Charter or otherwise), and a person shall not be exempted by sex from the liability to serve as a juror.[36]

St Joan's Alliance declared in the *Catholic Citizen* that:

> it should have given women a fair chance in the Civil Service, but it does not. A Clause was inserted reserving to men posts involving service overseas. … all posts in the Diplomatic Service and in the Consular Service are closed to women … It is a strange idea of equality that excludes women from all these posts.[37]

They were also adamant that women should be included in all facets of government, and called on political parties to support women entering the House of Lords on the same terms as men. St Joan's Alliance and other women's groups were outraged when women were not included in the 1931 National Government seeing it as a 'retrograde step' as women had held posts in Government since 1924.[38] They campaigned for 'educational equality', contacting the President of the Board of Education insisting that 'women should be eligible, equally with men, for appointments to the headships of mixed schools elementary, central and secondary, administrative posts, and the inspectorate, and that the best candidate, irrespective of sex, should be appointed'.[39]

---

34   Mari Takayanagi, 'Sacred Year or Broken Reed? The Sex Disqualification (Removal) Act 1919', *Women's History Review*, 29:4 (2020), p. 564.
35   Oram, *Women Teachers and Feminist Politics*, p. 163.
36   'St Joan's Social and Political Alliance, 14th, 1925', *Catholic Citizen* (1925), p. 22.
37   L. de Alberti, 'Victory – After After?', *Catholic Citizen* (1927), p. 72.
38   *The Times*, 25 November 1931, p. 8.
39   2SJA/L/09 1928 pressbook, p. 10, *Universe*, 16 November 1928. Her role was also to challenge or correct press misrepresentation.

The role of the Honourable Press Secretary was to correspond with Catholic, national and local press, making them aware of the organisation's activities and encouraging them to publish items related to Catholic interest.[40] The pages of *The Catholic Citizen* included detailed articles explaining campaign positions and dissecting committee reports and past or potential legislation. It reported scathingly on the findings of the public *Report of the Inter-Departmental Committee on the Admission of Women to the Diplomatic and Consular Services* which concluded: 'that the time has not yet arrived when women could be employed in the Consular Service or in the Diplomatic Service with advantage to the State or with profit to women'.[41] Member Nancy Stewart Parnell, writing in *The Catholic Citizen*, challenged government education bodies to employ female education inspectors and the universities to hire women professors.[42] Her comments in *The Catholic Citizen* were reported in *The Universe* and the *Catholic Herald*.[43] Honourable Secretary Florence Barry's critique that women were not included in the 1931 National Government was taken up in the *Evening Standard*, the *Evening News*, the *Nottingham Evening Post* and at least nineteen other local newspapers.[44]

Collaboration continued to be an important feature of the work of St Joan's Social and Political Alliance. They joined the lobbies and deputations organised by the National Council of Women to make it compulsory that women police officers be appointed to Watch Committees and Standing Joint Committees.[45] The 'Demand for Women Police' was meant to encourage the government and local Watch Committees to train and employ more women as police officers.[46] As part of their direct action, they agreed to join a deputation of sixteen organisations to discuss with the Home Secretary recommendations of the Departmental Committee on the Employment of Policewomen (1924) to create statutory regulations that female police be employed to take statements from women and children where sexual crimes were alleged, and to take custody of women and children in police cells. They advocated for policewomen to be trained by female instructors and that they be appointed to assist HM Inspectors

---

40 'Catholic Women's Suffrage Society Annual Report 1920', *Catholic Citizen* (1921), p. 19.
41 Alberti, 'Victory', p. 72.
42 Nancy Stewart Parnell, 'Inequalities in the Educational Sphere', *Catholic Citizen* (1930), pp. 65–6.
43 2SJA/L/11, 1930 pressbook, pp. 4–5.
44 2SJA/L/12, 1931 pressbook, pp. 6–9, *Evening News*, 11 October 1931. Barry noted: 'we are hearing so much about the need for wise spending and national economy, surely a woman's point of view would have been useful in the Ministry'. This quote can be found in eighteen local newspapers.
45 Watch committees were local government bodies which oversaw policing matters.
46 2SJA/L/09, 1928 pressbook, p. 7, *Catholic Times*, 15 June 1928.

of Constabulary to advise the Home Office and assist local authorities.[47] St Joan's Alliance educated their membership by inviting speakers such as Commandant Allen of the Women's Auxiliary Service who spoke of the delicate cases of interrogations of women and children by qualified policewomen.[48] They worked with local campaigners too. Member Miss Fedden spoke as part of a deputation that met with Rear-Admiral Royds, Assistant Commissioner of the Metropolitan Police, to present a petition for an increase in the number of female police on Hampstead Heath to prevent assaults on children and girls. Other attendees included members of local groups like Hampstead Friends, Hampstead Women's Shelter, Hampstead Temperance Council and Hampstead Hostel for Mothers and Babies.[49] Collaborative relationships were key to suffrage campaigning of the early twentieth century and remained central to the women's organisations' effectiveness in obtaining changes to the political, social and economic position of women in the interwar years.

St Joan's Alliance framed their claims for equality of opportunity for professional work as a matter of justice, not only for women wage-earners but also for Catholics, particularly women and children, in need of their services. Member and journalist, Isabel Willis, wrote in *The Universe*: 'One need hardly point out to Catholics, whose Church is pre-eminently the Church of the poor, what an advantage it would be to many a poor, friendless woman if she could have the help of a lawyer of her own sex in many of the difficulties into which she may have fallen through her ignorance of the law and its intricacies, or through her own fault.'[50] In trying to garner the support of co-religionists, they pointed to the moral value of women's involvement. In advocating for more female police, member Iveigh More Nisbet highlighted: 'The prevention of crime, the prevention of immorality, the protection of the innocent, the salvation of child victims are some of the potential accomplishments which policewoman are striving to obtain.'[51] Such moral arguments utilised an essentialist discourse that pointed to the advantages of women's difference. Scholar Louise Jackson has argued that this was commonplace amongst feminist organisations that endorsed the moral regulation of women and girls as a means of expanding women's place in the police force. This resulted in female police work being defined as separate and distinct from that of policemen. The arguments of St Joan's Alliance and other equality feminists sometimes ran counter to their equalitarian aims that

---

[47] 2SJA/A/1/06 Minutes Book No V 1923–1926, 5 May 1925; 2SJA/L/10, 1929 pressbook, p. 6, *Universe*, 13 December 1929.
[48] 2SJA/L/09, 1928 pressbook, p. 7, *Catholic Times*, 15 June 1928.
[49] 2SJA/L/10, 1929 pressbook, p. 56, *The Vote*, 1929.
[50] 2SJA/L/05, 1918–21 pressbook, p. 34, *Universe*, 17 April 1919.
[51] Iveigh More Nisbet, 'Report of the Royal Commission on Policewomen', *Catholic Citizen*, 1920, p. 79.

woman be employed on the same terms as men. In the case of the police, women were acceptable and employable because of gendered difference, and discourses of both feminised care and control were integral to the policy frameworks in the first half of the twentieth century.[52]

The language of justice was often used to frame their equal pay arguments. In 1925, St Joan's Alliance called upon the Government to establish throughout the Civil Service 'a system of equal pay and opportunities for men and women' hoping this would encourage the private sector to do the same.[53] This became a longstanding resolution, shared by other feminist organisations. In 1929, Press Secretary Helen Douglas Irvine suggested that: 'To pay women at a lower rate than men is not only unjust to the women, who do not receive the fair value of their labour, but also to the men who are exposed to unfair competition, and to the dependents of both women and men.'[54] Campaign tactics included writing and meeting with members of local government bodies and other government departments. In 1928, they forwarded a resolution to the President of the Education Board emphasising the need for equal pay to men and women teachers of equal professional status.[55] In 1930, they cooperated with the Equal Rights Committee to submit evidence to the Royal Commission on the Civil Service regarding equal pay and opportunity.[56] They joined in the campaigns of the London and National Society for Women's Service, which lobbied for equal pay for women in the common classes of the Civil Service only to be defeated in the House of Commons in 1936. Though a loss, the parliamentary vote only came about because of united campaigning by feminist groups.[57] In the 1920s, they joined a mass meeting organised by the National Union for Women Teachers held in Trafalgar Square to protest against the difference in pay scales between male and female teachers.[58] In most of their campaigns, they worked alongside other feminist and non-feminist groups, demanding equal pay and the social rights to work for women as citizens.

The more controversial campaigns of St Joan's Alliance involved restrictive labour practices. The Factories Bill of 1929, like previous factory bills, classed adult women with youth rather than adult males and

---

[52] Louise A. Jackson, *Women Police: Gender, Welfare and Surveillance in the Twentieth Century* (Manchester, 2012), pp. 18–21.
[53] 'St Joan's Social and Political Alliance, 14th Annual Report, 1925', *Catholic Citizen*, (1925), p. 21.
[54] 2SJA/L/10, 1929 pressbook, p.7, *Catholic Times*, 18 January 1929.
[55] 2SJA/L/09, 1928 pressbook, p. 10, *Catholic Herald*, 1928.
[56] 2SJA/L/11, 1930 pressbook, p. 1, *Universe*, 31 January 1930.
[57] Harold L. Smith, 'British Feminism and the Equal Pay Issue in the 1930s', *Women's History Review*, 5:1 (1996), p. 97. The objective of this particular campaign for equal pay was achieved in 1956.
[58] 'Notes and Comments', *Catholic Citizen* (1924), p. 47.

limited female employment, prohibiting nightwork and women's work after childbirth.[59] St Joan's Alliance supported protective legislation that pertained to health, welfare and working hours for all industrial workers, but argued that limiting legislation to women's labour infantilised women, lowered their wages, and narrowed their employment opportunities.[60] Removing protectionist legislation would improve the status of the female industrial worker, as well as allow the employment of women on equal footing with men.[61] To educate its members, St Joan's Alliance invited Mrs Elizabeth Abbott, on her return from the 1928 International Labour Organisation Conference in Geneva, to speak on 'Restrictive Legislation and the Wage Earning Woman'.[62] Monica Whately's presentation at the Catholic Citizen's Parliament, 'Does Restrictive Legislation Really Protect the Woman Worker?', answered the question directly with 'it does not', noting that penalising women drove them to less skilled, overcrowded employment.[63] Whately, along with industrial workers and members of feminist groups including the Women's Freedom League, the Open Door Council and the Six Point Group, met with the Home Secretary urging a change in legislation.[64]

Most controversial of all was St Joan's Alliance's support of the employment of married women. Direct action included lobbying for the amendment of the Sex Disqualification (Removal) Act (1919) so that, in practice, employers including the civil service could not refuse to employ married women.[65] This was controversial, as married women were expected to work in the home, training and educating their children and supporting their husbands. Declining birth rates led to fears of racial decline as 'modern emancipated women' were accused of forgetting their primary function: 'the perpetuation of the race'. Such concerns were commonly mooted in the national press.[66] The Alliance also faced vocal opposition to their stance in the Catholic press. Understandings of Catholic social teaching emphasised women's role as wife and mother, idealising Catholic

---

[59] Harold L. Smith, 'British Feminism in the 1920s', in *British Feminism in the Twentieth Century*, edited by Harold L. Smith (Aldershot, 1990), pp. 59–60. Equality feminists were opposed to the special maternity provisions which prohibited working mothers from working in the first four weeks after giving birth and suggested instead paid maternity benefits.
[60] *The Times*, 5 November 1929, p. 13.
[61] *The Times*, 9 August 1929, p. 8.
[62] 2SJA/L/09, 1928 pressbook, p. 7, *Catholic Herald*, 30 June 1928.
[63] 2SJA/L/09, 1928 pressbook, p. 7, *Universe*, 28 September 1928.
[64] *The Times*, 2 November 1929.
[65] 'St Joan's Social and Political Alliance, 14th Annual Report, 1925', *Catholic Citizen* (1925), p. 22.
[66] As quoted in *Mother and Child*, 3 (1932), pp. 43–4; see Jane Lewis, 'In Search of a Real Equality: Women between the Wars', in *Class, Culture, and Social Change: A New View of the 1930s*, edited by Frank Gloversmith (Sussex, 1980), p. 216.

motherhood as domestic and self-sacrificing but importantly responsible for their own salvation and that of their family.[67] *The Catholic Times* was aghast that St Joan's Alliance would defend 'a mother who refuses to sacrifice her career even at the risk of divesting herself of her primary obligation of training and educating her children'.[68] Father Joseph Dukes S.J., speaking to the Liverpool Catholic Social Guild, opined that the 'ruling of the home was the duty of the mother and it was a whole-time job. ... She had been fashioned by God for the purpose and must not allow anything to interfere with it'.[69] Reverend Joseph Degan of Coalville (Leicestershire) though agreeing with St Joan's Alliance that Catholic married women could 'mould public opinion' and 'render effective social service', insisted the 'private domestic life of the home circle' was more valuable. He saw women's 'withdrawal from our homes of the sacred, spiritualising and educative refinements of motherhood, in the interests of politics or business' as 'surely disastrous'. Degan argued that combining 'the exacting cares of full-time paid employment with the weightier tasks and devotion of motherhood involves, in most cases, a neglect of their husband and their children and a general weakening of family life'. He suggested that St Joan's Alliance redirect its attention to 'inaugurate a movement motherwards for the strengthening of family ties and the restoration of home life'.[70] These attitudes were supported by a great number of Catholics. Londoner E. L. Power suggested that life as a 'sensible wife and mother' was full even for those with children enrolled in boarding schools: mothers were busy caring for husbands and servants; visiting and corresponding with their children at boarding school; attending to their own social life and that was 'sufficient for a sensible wife and mother'.[71] In response, Alliance member C. Madden asked why 'exhort them [women] indiscriminately to bury their talents in the ground?'[72] In 1936, the brief article 'Marriage versus Career' in *The Universe* articulated fears that marriage would become 'not even a secondary career, but a spare-time' occupation.[73] St Joan's Alliance member Christine Spender responded with:

> A normal woman will not neglect her husband and children to their injury, unless she is driven to do so by economic necessity. Married women should

---

67   Martha Kanya-Forstner, 'Defining Womanhood: Irish Women and the Catholic Church in Victorian Liverpool', *Immigrants & Minorities: Historical Studies in Ethnicity, Migration and Diaspora*, 18:2/3 (1999), p. 168.
68   2SJA/L/12, 1931 pressbook, p. 145, *Catholic Times*, 16 October 1931.
69   2SJA/L/19, 1938 pressbook, p. 106, *Catholic Times*, 3 June 1938.
70   2SJA/L/12, 1931 pressbook, p. 145, *Catholic Times*, 23 October 1931.
71   2SJA/L/12, 1931 pressbook, p. 145, *Catholic Times*, 30 October 1931.
72   2SJA/L/12, 1931 pressbook, p. 145, *Catholic Times*, 16 October 1931.
73   2SJA/L/14, 1936 pressbook, *Universe*, 25 September 1936.

be free to decide for themselves whether the family is most benefited by work outside the home or if their duties lie in devoting themselves entirely to the home. That the married woman should be condemned if she decides to follow the former course shows hasty judgement on the part of judges who know none of the circumstances which have led to her decision.[74]

By 1940, St Joan's Alliance was suggesting that women forced to leave their jobs because of a marriage bar could potentially be in even greater moral danger if they turned to cohabitation thus receiving the 'benefits of marriage without entering into a marriage contract'. They argued women not 'domesticated by nature ... would make the home an inferno'. And, of course, the larger community would be deprived of 'the valuable work they do'.[75]

The campaigns for women's equal access to employment opportunities via equal wages and the removal of restrictive practices were a matter of justice for the women of St Joan's Social and Political Alliance. Fully aware of the contentiousness of their actions in a Catholic Church that valorised Catholic motherhood in the home, their arguments rested on the inherent justice of equality and the rights of women to make the decision of working outside the home based on their particular circumstances. They also pointed to the importance of Catholic women's participation in the workforce and public life and their influence on public morality. Much of the heated debate in the press was centred on middle-class married women's employment – though St Joan's Alliance often reminded readers that working-class women's wages were significant to family survival.

Catholic morality

St Joan's Social and Political Alliance sought to 'achieve reforms which must be in no way contrary to Catholic teaching'.[76] While the campaigns discussed above were contentious, two interwar campaigns, those regarding divorce and birth control, were particularly aligned to Catholic teachings on sexual morality.

The Matrimonial Causes Act of 1857 provided the grounds for divorce until 1923: men were required to prove only adultery while women had to prove adultery along with one additional factor (cruelty, incest, bigamy, rape, sodomy, bestiality or desertion). St Joan's Alliance did not seek to overturn civil law to disallow divorce, but, in accordance with its equalitarian position, supported the equalisation of the grounds of divorce as legislated in 1923, when both men and women were allowed to obtain a divorce based on only one criterion: adultery. It was only when additional

---

[74] 2SJA/L/14, 1936 pressbook, *Universe*, 1 October 1936.
[75] 2SJA/L/18, 1940 pressbook, *Huddersfield Daily Examiner*, 30 December 1940.
[76] Parnell, *Venture in Faith*, p. 12.

grounds for divorce were added (desertion, cruelty and unsound mind) with the 1937 Matrimonial Clauses Act, that St Joan's Alliance protested the extension of the grounds for divorce. Their position aligned with Catholic Church teaching on the sacramentality and indissolubility of marriage.[77] They voiced their disappointment with 'the actions of certain Societies', often feminist organisations, 'in pressing for further facilities for divorce'.[78] While equalising divorce legislation was within their remit; extending divorce legislation became an issue aligned with their Catholic identity

Birth control was a contested issue among feminist organisations in the 1920s and 1930s.[79] Some, such as the National Union of Societies for Equal Citizenship, campaigned for the provision of birth control education in government-funded clinics.[80] Equality feminists saw these efforts addressing women's maternal role as a distraction from the equal rights agenda which focused directly on an equal franchise (achieved in 1928) and equal employment and pay. Some feminists believed birth control would 'subject [women] even further to men's carnal desires' and could lead to 'sexual slavery'.[81] St Joan's Alliance played an active role in condemning the 'degrading practice of Birth Prevention'.[82] From 1925, it welcomed the decision of the Ministry of Health to refuse to allow the distribution of birth control information in Infant Welfare Centres maintained by public funds.[83] As this policy changed and 'in certain cases' artificial birth control information was distributed, St Joan's Alliance recorded its disappointment in its annual report and in the press. It urged its members to 'watch the matter in their Local Councils'.[84] Following the Minister of Health's Circular 1408, St Joan's Alliance 'placed on record its opposition to the further widening of conditions under which information on

---

[77] The Catholic Women's League remained silent on the equalisation of divorce law, but similarly became more active once divorce legislation was to be extended. The Church of England, at this time, also insisted on the indissolubility of marriage. Caitríona Beaumont, 'Moral Dilemmas and Women's Rights: The Attitude of the Mothers' Union and Catholic Women's League to Divorce, Birth Control and Abortion in England, 1928–1939', *Women's History Review*, 16:4 (2007), pp 463–85.
[78] 'St Joan's Social and Political Alliance, Twenty-Second Annual Report', *Catholic Citizen* (1933), p. 22.
[79] Marie Stopes's first birth control clinic for married women opened in London in 1921, offering advice about contraception.
[80] Smith, 'British Feminism in the 1920s', pp. 56–8.
[81] Lucy Bland, *Banishing the Beast: Sexuality and the Early Feminists* (New York, 1995), pp. 189–90, 196–7, 213, 221.
[82] 'The Aim of St Joan's Social and Political Alliance', *Catholic Citizen* (1928), p. 39.
[83] 'St Joan's Social and Political Alliance, 14th Annual Report, 1925', *Catholic Citizen* (1928), p. 22.
[84] 'St Joan's Social and Political Alliance, Twenty-Sixth Annual Report', *Catholic Citizen* (1937), p. 26.

artificial birth control' was disseminated.[85] The Alliance often identified two strands to the argument against birth control, one feminist and one Catholic.[86] Member Vera Laughton Mathews at a 1929 meeting of the National Council of Women, a federation of women's groups to which St Joan's Alliance belonged, argued from the feminist point of view that 'artificial' methods of birth control placed all the responsibility for procreation on women when it should be a shared responsibility, would lower 'moral ideals' and would increase immorality among unmarried people. In concluding her talk she argued that birth control was 'contrary to Catholic principles and also to true feminism'.[87] Disappointed when the National Council of Women changed its stance on the dissemination of birth control information, St Joan's Alliance resigned from that organisation though it continued to join them on campaigns with which they were in agreement.[88]

In the interwar years, the values of St Joan's Alliance were strictly aligned to Catholic teachings on sexual morality when it came to issues of divorce and birth control. In both these campaigns, the Alliance continued to work with organisations with which they had differences. As Caitríona Beaumont has pointed out, collaboration remained important to women's organisations despite differences on moral and social questions.[89]

Catholic identities

Members of St Joan's Social and Political Alliance were linked together by their Catholic identity, and despite disagreements with some of their co-religionists, it was Catholic religious values that bound them together. They expressed those values in very traditional ways, noting in their 1914 annual report: 'As Catholics we know that our most effective weapon is prayer'.[90] The Catholic Mass and sacraments were the centre of their feminist community; Mass was offered each month, in London and in branch houses, for the aims of St Joan's Alliance. An annual Mass was

---

[85] 2SJA/L/12, 1934 pressbook, *Catholic Herald*, 21 July 1934.
[86] 'Monthly meetings', *Catholic Citizen* (1929), p. 22.
[87] Vera Laughton Mathews, 'Birth Control: A Policy without Vision', *Catholic Citizen* (1929), p. 87. The primary 'Catholic principles' regarding opposition to contraception rested on the premise that the chief aim of marriage was procreation (1917 Canon Law, 1013 §1), and the 1930 encyclical *Casti Connubii* ('Of chaste wedlock') accordingly asserts that contraception which 'deliberately frustrated [the conjugal act] in its natural power to generate life is an offense against the law of God and of nature' (§56). https://www.vatican.va/content/pius-xi/en/encyclicals/documents/hf_p-xi_enc_19301231_casti-connubii.html, accessed 7 September 2023.
[88] 2SJA/L/10, 1929 pressbook, insert, *Women's Leader*, 22 November 1929.
[89] Beaumont, 'Moral Dilemmas', p. 481.
[90] 'Catholic Women's Suffrage Society, Third Annual Report', *Catholic Citizen* (1914), p. 4.

'IN THE INTERESTS OF JUSTICE, MORALITY AND RELIGION' 57

celebrated for deceased members and associates. The Representation of the People Acts of 1918 and 1928 were celebrated with a High Mass at Westminster Cathedral.[91] From 1918, St Joan's Alliance requested Holy Mass on polling days. In 1924, St Joan's Alliance associate Dom Filbert Higgins C.R.L. offered Holy Mass to 'beg Divine guidance' on male and female electors.[92] In 1914, four hundred members joined in the Mass for the feast of their patron Joan of Arc at Westminster Cathedral where a laurel wreath tied in Alliance colours – blue, white and gold – was laid at her shrine.[93] At the celebration of Joan's canonisation in 1920, several Alliance members attended the open-air Benediction and the procession through the streets of Westminster orchestrated by the Catholic Women's League. In 1939, fifty members of St Joan's Alliance made a pilgrimage to Walsingham to celebrate the twenty-first anniversary of women receiving the vote. Singing hymns and flying the same blue, white and gold banner (designed by Edith Craig) that the Catholic Women's Suffrage Society had first carried in the great suffrage procession of 1912, they prayed their way to the shrine of Our Lady of Walsingham.[94]

Isabel Willis, in recounting the Alliance's history in 1920, acknowledged their struggles with fellow Catholics: 'We still have to try to make clear to many of our co-religionists the essential Catholicity of our feminist creed'.[95] As evidenced by the Catholic response to the more controversial campaigns of married women's work and protectionist legislation, some Catholics questioned feminist equalitarian aims. Members were aware of 'whispering campaigns' and the disapproval of members of the hierarchy and fellow Catholics. It was suggested that their campaigns were 'indelicate' and even 'immoral'.[96] In 1936, Chair Christine Spender found herself justifying their suffrage activism of the 1910s explaining that though suffrage was not always acceptable to all Catholics it did not run contrary to Catholic principles.[97] Perhaps it was these attitudes from co-religionists that caused them to emphasise, repeatedly, papal and episcopal endorsements of their organisation and its aims. Member Annie Christitch, after a private audience with the Pope Pius XI (Ambrogio Damiano Achille Ratti) in 1920, reported the pope approving the aims of the Catholic Women Suffrage Society with the words: 'We should like to

---

[91] Isabel Willis, 'Our Own History', *Catholic Citizen* (1920), p. 39.
[92] 'General Election', *Catholic Citizen* (1924), p. 23.
[93] Alberti, 'History of the Catholic Women's Suffrage Society', pp. 77, 94. Blue was chosen to represent Mary, the mother of Jesus, and gold and white the papal colours.
[94] 2SJA/L/14, 1939 pressbook, p. 137, *The Universe*, 19 May 1939. The Catholic Women's Suffrage Society were suffragists, not suffragettes.
[95] Isabel Willis, 'Our Own History', *Catholic Citizen* (1920), p 39.
[96] Parnell, *A Venture in Faith*, p. 7.
[97] 2SJA/L/14, 1936 pressbook, p. 13, *Catholic Herald*, 17 April 1936.

see women electors everywhere'.[98] The Alliance was keen to publicise the approval of clerics such as the Archbishop of Birmingham, John McIntyre, Archbishop of Liverpool, Frederick Keating, and Auxiliary Bishop of Southwark, William Pella, and their relationship with other Catholic organisations, such as with Father Philip Fletcher of the Our Lady of Ransom Guild.[99] Individual members were certainly held in high esteem. In 1928, the Catholic Citizens' Parliament of Southwark included two St Joan's Alliance members on their council of thirteen: Florence Barry representing St Joan's Alliance and Mrs Mathew representing the Dames of St Joan.[100] Florence Barry also received the Cross *Pro Ecclesia et Pontifice* for her forty years' service as honorary secretary of St Joan's Social and Political Alliance.[101]

Conclusion

Gabrielle Jeffery, one of the founders of what became St Joan's Social and Political Alliance, held two personal guiding principles: 'uncompromising feminism and unswerving loyalty to Holy Mother Church'.[102] These two principals were integral to the campaigns of St Joan's Alliance during the interwar years; they were demonstrated in the campaigns for equal employment, opportunities and wages and the campaigns that addressed divorce and birth control. The Society's imbrication of 'justice, morality and religion' could, however, appear contradictory to both feminists and Catholics. As feminists, the Alliance critiqued socio-political structures and legislation that did not offer women equal opportunities for work and wages joining in with other equality feminists in numerous campaigns. In the eyes of many Catholics, their adherence to the right of married women to employment and their desire to remove protectionist legislation ran contrary to Church teaching that exalted Catholic motherhood. Some questioned their Catholic identity. As Catholics, they remained dedicated to the sexual morality of the Catholic Church opposing further expansion of the grounds for divorce and the proliferation of birth control information. Despite being out of step with some feminist groups, they continued to work alongside them on other matters of equal rights. The aims of the members of St Joan's Alliance were linked to their Catholic faith; they identified with a Catholicism which they connected to the social, political and economic rights of women.

---

98 'London News', *Catholic Citizen* (1920), p. 5.
99 Edith M. Almedinger, 'St Joan's Alliance, English Catholic Women's Suffrage Society, Important Force', *N.C.W.C.* [National Catholic Welfare Conference] *Editorial Sheet* (June 1928), p. 1.
100 2SJA/L/09, 1928 Pressbook, p. 9, *Universe*, 29 June 1928.
101 2SJA/D4, Florence Barry, presentation of Pro Ecclesia et Pontifice by Pope Pius XII.
102 'In Piam Memoriam: Gabrielle Jeffery', *Catholic Citizen* (1940), p. 35.

4

'ITS ACHIEVEMENTS AND ITS HOPES': THE CATHOLIC EVIDENCE GUILD BETWEEN THE TWO WORLD WARS

Richard Finn O.P.

In 1921 the Jesuit Fr Henry Browne published a book entitled *The Catholic Evidence Movement: Its Achievements and its Hopes*. The book set the catechetical and street-preaching work of the Catholic Evidence Guild (C.E.G.), founded in the archdiocese of Westminster three years previously, in the context of earlier and wider public witness to the Catholic faith in Britain. Browne described the many processions and rarer public-speaking engagements undertaken by the Guild of Ransom, membership of which that year had reached some 70,000. He recalled the sale of Catholic Truth Society pamphlets before the Great War by the far smaller 'Book-Barrow Brigade'; and the foundation in 1903 of the Catholic Missionary Society: a group of clerics who held open meetings in rural areas and addressed queries or difficulties about Catholicism posted in a Question Box. He also noted the Christian Evidence lectures aimed since the war at non-Catholics and given by Fr Hugh Pope O.P. and other Dominican friars in town halls and similar venues up and down the country. These had attracted audiences of up to a thousand in Newcastle and Liverpool.[1] The book carried a foreword by the Archbishop of Westminster, Cardinal Bourne, in which the archbishop praised the Catholic Evidence Guild as 'the most recent and in some respects, the most interesting and hopeful of our missionary endeavours in England'.[2] Much was clearly hoped for from the Guild's 'endeavours', which had multiplied since the meeting he had chaired in April 1918 to inaugurate 'a scheme for the instruction of lecturers to speak in the public parks on the fundamentals

---

[1] Henry Browne S.J., *The Catholic Evidence Movement: Its Achievements and its Hopes* (London, 1921), pp. 2, 6–11, 14, 16–18, 20. On the early history of the Catholic Missionary Society, see James Hagerty, 'The Conversion of England: John Heenan and the Catholic Missionary Society 1947–1951', *British Catholic History*, 31:3 (2015), pp. 462–3.
[2] Browne, *Catholic Evidence Movement*, p. vii.

of Christianity'.[3] This chapter examines these hopes and the moves made to fulfil them, to assess how and how far the Guild succeeded in its aims, and so to establish its main achievements in Britain during the first two decades of its existence between the wars.

The central hope occasioned or articulated by the C. E. G. among senior clerics and lay people was that the Catholic faith would publicly and intelligently be set out and widely communicated across the country to non-Catholics, especially to ordinary men and women, many of whom were non-churchgoers. The hope is evident in two handbooks published in 1922. The *Handbook of the Catholic Evidence Guild*, compiled for the Westminster Guild by James Byrne, explicitly stated that it was 'the business of the C.E.G.' to bring the masses untouched by individual Catholics, the 'press and pulpit', within 'the reach of the Church's teaching'.[4] The handbook of the newly formed Birmingham C.E.G. 'or Guild of Diocesan Catechists in Birmingham', opened with a photograph of His Grace Archbishop McIntyre which was followed by a page with three short texts, each taken from a given year: the reader began with 1885 and what was then a 'Vain Hope' for 'mediaeval street preaching'. He or she then read of what was 'Only a Vision' in 1910, when people might 'dream of the day when a friar will stand in the Market Place in Birmingham and Manchester'. Finally, the reader came to 'A vain hope realised! An Empty Dream Materialised!' in 1921, when 'Father Hugh Pope O.P. (in the habit of his Order) preaches every week in the Market Place in Birmingham' along with other priests and 'also laymen'. Out of context the latter phrase might seem at best a grudging acknowledgement of the role lay people might play in meeting the hope for public speaking about the Catholic faith; but in context it served as a bridge to link this hope to the C.E.G. as a predominantly lay organisation which would be the primary vehicle for such nationwide orthodox exposition of Catholic belief and practice. The reader learnt that the 'clarion call' had sounded 'to the laity' and that 'Members of the Catholic Evidence Guild are answering the call'.[5] The Birmingham handbook thus echoed the hopes of Cardinal Gasquet, speaking a few years earlier, who had expressed the 'sure hope and belief that this form of lay apostleship' would 'within a few years, be found in all Christian countries', and of Cardinal Bourne in 1921 that the guild would draw on practice in foreign mission fields and deploy 'the lay catechist to do a work for which a priest cannot find time or, very often, opportunity'.[6] The 1922 Westminster

---

[3] *The Universe*, 26 April 1918.
[4] James Byrne (ed.), *Handbook of the Catholic Evidence Guild* (London, 1922), p. 4.
[5] Birmingham C.E.G. Handbook (Birmingham, 1922?), Birmingham Archdiocesan Archives (BAA), AP/E/8.
[6] Browne, *Catholic Evidence Movement*, pp. 55, vii.

handbook described the Church as 'essentially propagandist' and 'in so far as the laity' possessed 'the spirit of the Church' they, too, would be 'propagandists, and the new institution of the C.E.G.' would 'afford an unlimited outlet for their energies in this direction'.[7] Speaking to the C.E.G. at the London Hippodrome in 1930, Archbishop Williams of Birmingham told the delegates: 'you are the friars of today. I must be careful what I say on this subject because the Provincial of the Friars Preachers is to follow me. But you are the men and women I look to for the work which the friars did in the thirteenth century.'[8] For many, the further hope was that the C.E.G. would in this way make substantial progress towards the reconversion of England, which the Westminster handbook insisted was otherwise merely 'an idle dream'.[9]

To meet these hopes shared by supporters and members, the Westminster C.E.G. had developed a distinctive training programme and institutional structure, both of which would be largely replicated in other dioceses, so that the C.E.G. did not grow into a single institution with a central administration but grew as a movement when new guilds were founded at different times in different dioceses. The guilds collaborated informally by occasionally sharing speakers, and formally by holding two annual events, an Inter-Guild Retreat, normally organised by the Birmingham Guild, and an Inter-Guild Conference hosted by a different guild each year. This structure facilitated episcopal oversight and authority over the movement, not least to establish the credentials of its speakers. This meant that although it was in large part a lay organisation, it was also a highly collaborative institution in which lay members and clerical officers had clearly defined roles. Thus, the Westminster Guild had the Cardinal Archbishop as its President, and the Birmingham Guild was likewise established with Archbishop McIntyre as its President. He appointed a senior cleric, Mgr Cronin, as the Vice-President, and Fr Hugh Pope as the Director of Studies, a post which in the Westminster Guild was long held by Dr John Arendzen, a Dutch Catholic priest and Professor of Scripture at the Ware seminary. The Director chose the lecturers, often clerics, who were to train the lay preachers for their task. The latter individuals would be licensed as catechists in a given subject by the archbishop after examination by a suitable panel, at least one member of which was a priest. The Birmingham Guild was then governed by

---

[7] Byrne, *Handbook*, pp. 3–4.
[8] Archbishop Thomas Leighton Williams, Speech at the Ninth Inter-Guild conference, BAA, AP/E/8.
[9] Byrne, Handbook, p. 5; Hugh Pope O.P., 'What is the Future of the Catholic Evidence Guild?', p. 1, English Dominican Archives (EDA), V, HP 2; *Nottingham and Midland Catholic News* (*NMCN*), 14 August 1926, p. 11.

an eleven-strong executive, of whom only two were clerics.[10] Guilds generally had an elected Lay Master, who served for a year at a time, assisted by a Secretary and other officers. The guilds' memberships of both lay men and women included trained and trainee speakers, but also associate members who supported the speakers by their prayers. Many of those attracted to train as speakers were young adults. When Dr Henshaw, Bishop of Salford, spoke at Burnley in June 1928 he described the C.E.G. as 'comprised of young men and women' whom he praised for addressing those whom ignorance had rendered 'alien to the church'.[11] Members came from a variety of backgrounds: as one leading figure in the movement later wrote, there were 'teachers, typists, bus-conductors, nurses, scientists, housemaids and professors'. Professors though, and university graduates more generally, were few in number.[12] A move to alter the overwhelmingly lay nature of the C.E.G. was floated in 1936. It was suggested at a meeting in Leeds that year 'to make the C.E.G. a body comprising a majority of priests so that it would cease to be a lay organisation'. The motion, however, was defeated: 'Whilst the interest of priests in the work was most essential and desirable it was considered the C.E.G. should maintain its Constitution as a Lay Organisation.'[13]

Within a diocesan guild there might be one or more branches, or centres of activity, each of which normally ran both study classes and one or more 'pitches' or open-air sites at which the qualified (or 'effective') speakers regularly spoke to the crowds. Most followed the practice of the Westminster Guild and had a platform they could erect for the purpose along with a large crucifix. At Reading, and in many other places, the pitch might open for the summer only, and the reopening or other meetings be advertised in the local paper. Sunday evenings were commonly chosen as offering the best opportunity to attract a crowd. The Birmingham branch, for example, ran five meetings on four pitches each week in 1930, three of them on Sundays.[14] Some branches also held series of indoor meetings or lectures, and it became traditional in some guilds to preach the Stations of the Cross at an outdoor meeting on Good Friday.[15] A few

---

[10] Debra Campbell, 'The Catholic Evidence Guild: Towards a History of the Laity', *Heythrop Journal*, 30 (1989), p. 315; Birmingham C.E.G. Handbook, p. 6, BAA, AP/E/8.
[11] *Burnley News*, 20 June 1928.
[12] Maisie Ward, *Unfinished Business* (London and New York, 1964), pp. 82, 89.
[13] Minutes of the Birmingham C.E.G. Quarterly Meeting of the Diocesan Council, May 12, 1936, BAA, CEG 2.
[14] *Reading Standard*, 6 March 1926, p. 8, 11 May 1929, p. 13, and 3 May 1930, p. 11; *Ripley and Heanor News*, 10 June 1932, p. 2; C.E.G., Ninth Inter-Guild Conference Handbook, 1930, p. 28, BAA, AP/E/8.
[15] For lectures at Birmingham, for example, see *NMCN*, September 8, 1928, p. 6. For Good Friday stations, see Francis Leonard, *Fools for Christ's Sake, Being a Short Account of the Catholic Evidence Guilds in England and Wales* (Durham, 2000), pp. 67, 158.

guilds had a library and even a reading room. At Birmingham a C.E.G. centre was initially set up in the Catholic Repository at Dale End with a lending library and reading room in the basement. It opened on 23 January 1922. Three hundred volumes were lent by Bexhill Library, and a further hundred by the Catholic Reading Guild. Three hundred and seventy-five members signed up to use the facility in the first month. A year later the library moved to premises on the second floor of Nelson House 'at the corner of the Bull Ring and Moor St' for a rent of £2/14/0 per week. The site was chosen for its proximity to the guild's major pitch at the Bull Ring.[16] The number of branches reflected the overall size and distribution of the membership within the diocese. In 1933, for example, the Birmingham Guild had branches in Birmingham, Coventry, Wolverhampton, the Potteries and Walsall, though the last of these had no operational pitch that year, when the local guild as a whole ran ten pitches across the archdiocese served by fifty-four effective speakers.[17] Both speakers and associates were urged to devote time to prayer in half-hour blocks before the Blessed Sacrament. The annual report of the Westminster Guild for 1929 recorded four thousand hours spent in speaking and six thousand four hundred half-hours of Adoration.[18] Two years later, the Blackburn branch reported 1,540 half-hours, 149 rosaries, 733 masses, 17 benedictions, 5 stations, 8 novenas and 553 communions.[19]

At the heart of the training programme were evening classes at which trainees listened to lectures, but also practised answering questions. In 1925 Maisie Ward, a major figure in the Westminster Guild, published its *Training Outlines* which gave others a detailed blueprint for how best to run the classes and pitches.[20] For example, Ward described a 'Junior Course' made up of 'subjects which it is reasonable to hope a beginner may learn to handle in a fairly short time'. It could also be called a course on 'The Church founded by Christ'. In each class of the course, a thirty-minute lecture would be followed by fifteen minutes of questions to the class, a further fifteen of questions from the class, and then a half-hour when class members gave short talks on the subject each lasting no more than two to five minutes.[21] The book included fifty-one outlines of lectures on essential topics, including 'technical lectures' on how to develop a theme and handle a crowd, how to deal with hecklers,

---

[16] Birmingham C.E.G. Handbook, p. 17; letter of 2 February 1923, from Haskew as C.E.G. Librarian to Archbishop McIntyre, BAA, AP/E/8.
[17] C.E.G., Twelfth Inter-Guild Conference Handbook, 1933, p. 66, BAA, AP/E/8.
[18] *NMCN*, 2 November 1929, p. 11.
[19] C.E.G. Tenth Inter-Guild conference handbook for 1931, p.47, Archives of the Archdiocese of Westminster (AAW).
[20] Maisie Ward, *Training Outlines* with a Foreword by His Eminence Cardinal Bourne (London, 1925).
[21] Ibid., p. 10.

and how 'chairmen' should run a pitch (when to change speakers, how to give feedback, etc.). A second, 'greatly enlarged' edition was brought out in 1928 with seventy-five lecture outlines, and another in 1939, compiled with Frank Sheed, which contained ninety-five outlines. At Westminster, classes took place on Tuesdays and Fridays and from 1919 were held at the 'Hut' in the cathedral precinct, where a platform was erected similar to that used in Hyde Park.[22] In 1930, the Birmingham Guild held classes on Mondays and Wednesdays; at Leicester the branch held classes for 'juniors' in the Holy Cross School rooms on Wednesdays, and classes for 'seniors' on Fridays in the Upper Room at Holy Cross.[23] As well as licences to speak on individual topics, speakers could obtain after several years' training a chairman's licence, which meant that they could also field questions on any subject, and they could also work towards a general licence after some five or six years, which permitted them to speak on any topic as well as field questions. Even if many speakers did not progress this far, it was expected that they would seek to gain further subject licences each year.[24] A list of Birmingham branch members in 1930 noted that five held general licences, four held chairman's licences, and seven held single-subject licences.[25]

The close collaboration between key clerics and laity is reflected above all in the ministry of Fr Hugh Pope O.P. His extant papers include numerous outlines of talks annotated in ink, such as 'C.E.G. Propaganda' or 'St Paul to the C.E.G.', 'Appeal for C.E.G.', or 'C.E.G. Rally', and stating where the talk was given and how long it lasted.[26] He frequently led the Inter-Guild Retreat, held usually on or around the feast of Pentecost each year. These were held for a number of years in the 1920s at the Cenacle retreat centre at Grayshott in Hampshire, and then for many years at Harborne Hall in Birmingham.[27] One of Pope's notebooks lists ten talks which he gave at the 1929 Retreat and noted '97 present'. He gave eight talks at the 1935 Retreat, ten in 1937, when it seems there were seventy-two attendees. He was also a frequent public speaker on guild platforms. The same notebook among its entries for 1929 had two headed 'Street' detailing when he had spoken at different pitches. For example, he recorded speaking nine times that year at Wimbledon, and thirteen times at Marble Arch.[28] The movement also received considerable report

---

[22] Leonard, *Fools*, p. 36.
[23] C.E.G., Ninth Inter-Guild Conference Handbook, 1930, pp. 28, 18.
[24] Byrne, *Handbook*, p. 22.
[25] List of members at Lent 1930, BAA, AP/E/8.
[26] EDA, V, HP 1.
[27] Campbell, 'The Catholic Evidence Guild', p. 316; *Catholic Times and Catholic Opinion*, 11 or 18 June 1926.
[28] Hugh Pope, Notebook 'Sermons, Lectures, etc. 1926–1938', EDA V, HP 2.

from many of Pope's Dominican brethren, especially the Westminster, Birmingham and Nottingham Guilds, where a Dominican priory existed within the diocese. Thus, Pope gave the first of a set of four lectures to the Birmingham Guild on 1 March 1929, but the other three were also by Dominicans, two of whom were Frs Rupert Hoper-Dixon and Austin Barker.[29] Fr Vincent McNabb O.P. had given a paper on 'Catholic Lay Action' at an early meeting of the Westminster Guild in October 1918, and would occasionally give papers on the work of the C.E.G., as he did at a diocesan rally in the Nottingham Hippodrome in April 1937.[30] He also became one of the movement's most famous street preachers. E. A. Siderman described how 'the appearance of the man immediately attracted attention; a slight figure with bent shoulders wearing his loose, well-worn Dominican habit of coarse black and white material, a haversack slung over his shoulder, thick knitted white stockings, heavy-soled black old-fashioned boots and battered shapeless black hat. His keen lined ascetic face with old-style, steel-rimmed spectacles was known to the thousands that thronged Hyde Park, Sunday after Sunday.'[31] Holy Cross, the Dominican priory in Leicester, provided a space to hold classes and friars to teach them or give retreats, including Frs Hyacinth Koos, Henry St John, Edwin Essex, Mark Brocklehurst and Romuald Horn.[32] It is a mark of the Dominicans' close support for the C.E.G. that Maisie Ward had become a Lay Dominican by October 1921.[33]

Ward was one of two lay members who were particularly important in the successful spread of the C.E.G. movement beyond Westminster, the other being Frank Sheed, who met and later married Maisie in the course of this apostolate. Ward joined the Westminster Guild in 1919 and contributed material to its first handbook in 1922.[34] She served as General Secretary of the Westminster Guild in 1925, and as we have seen published its *Training Outlines* that same year. She married Sheed in 1926, and husband and wife were frequently called upon to advise would-be guild members, and often travelled to support new undertakings. Thus, when the Birmingham Guild was forming, Miss Ward, as she then was, and Dr Arendzen, together with a Mr Jonas from the Westminster Guild, made a four-day visit to the city from 9 May to 12 May 1921. Ward gave

---

[29]   *NMCN*, 2 March 1929, p. 7.
[30]   *NMCN*, 19 April 1937, p. 10.
[31]   *The Universe*, 1 October 1918, p. 6; E. A. Siderman, *With Father McNabb at Marble Arch* (Oxford, 1947), p. 5.
[32]   C.E.G., Ninth Inter-Guild Conference Handbook, 1930, p. 15, C.E.G., Twelfth Inter-Guild Conference Handbook, 1933, pp. 53, 55, BAA, AP/E/8; Leonard, *Fools*, p. 158.
[33]   Dana Greene, *The Living of Maisie Ward* (South Bend, IN, 1997), pp. 56, 215 n. 16.
[34]   Debra Campbell, 'The Gleanings of a Laywoman's Ministry: Maisie Ward as Preacher, Publisher and Social Activist', *Records of the American Catholic Historical Society of Philadelphia*, 98:1/2 (1987), pp. 21–8, 22; Leonard, *Fools*, pp. 34–5.

specimen classes to show how intending speakers could be trained. Before returning to London she addressed a crowd of one thousand in the Bull Ring during heavy rain and, after answering questions, taught the crowd how to say the rosary.[35] Ward was the chief speaker at the inaugural meeting of the Newcastle Guild in June 1925, and returned three months later to open their pitch at the Bigg Market.[36] She once wrote in a letter to Frank Sheed that the C.E.G. was the 'biggest and most glorious thing on earth'.[37] Her enthusiasm inspired a great many others.

The prominent role played by Maisie Ward in the C.E.G. movement, and the guilds' openness to women members raises questions as to what proportion of the members and officers were women, and what roles women played generally within the movement. Much evidence suggests that the proportion of female members, officers, and the roles they played were far from constant in different guilds and at different times. In at least one case, women were the founding members of a branch. When the Jesuit Fr Joseph Howard related the early history of the Preston branch, founded about 1926, he noted the difficulties faced by its few members, 'the chief one being the complete absence of assistance from the male sex'.[38] When the Leeds branch began public speaking on Sunday evenings in the autumn of 1933, their Master was a Mrs Callaghan, and addresses were given by Misses Drywood and Midgley.[39] Similarly, perhaps, when the first five effective speakers of the Hull branch qualified in 1928, a Miss O'Shiel was said to be 'in charge' of the branch.[40] Ward herself highlighted the work and theological acumen of Miss Louisa Cozens, a cleaner, who was appointed a lay examiner in perpetuity by the bishop in the Southwark archdiocese, and who authored *A Handbook of Heresies*, published by Sheed and Ward in 1928.[41] However, the Inter-Guild Conference handbooks from the 1930s suggest that over time men frequently took many of the leadership positions. In four of the years, the handbooks named most of the official delegates in a manner which allows us to ascertain their gender. Thus, the delegates to the 1931 conference comprised twenty-seven men and eighteen women. The 1932 conference delegates comprised thirty-four male and fifteen female delegates; fourteen of the latter were styled 'Miss' and so were presumably unmarried. In 1934, there were thirty-nine male and twenty-five female delegates, the latter all unmarried. In 1938, there were thirty-four male

---

35   Birmingham C.E.G. Handbook, pp. 8–9, BAA, AP/E/8.
36   Leonard, *Fools*, p. 103.
37   Greene, *The Living*, p. 64, citing a letter of 16 April 1925.
38   *NMCN*, 21 December,1929, p. 6.
39   *NMCN*, 7 October 1933, p. 11.
40   *NMCN*, 23 June 1928, p. 6.
41   Ward, *Unfinished Business*, p. 190.

and nineteen female delegates, fifteen of whom were unmarried. The data may well not reflect the proportion of male to female members of the guilds but does suggest that unmarried women in particular were an active minority in the running of the guilds and their branches. The 1930 handbook suggests that these women often assumed secretarial roles. It lists women as General Secretaries in Southwark and Coventry, Honorary Secretaries in Brighton, Wallasey and York, and as Secretary in Derby. By contrast it only listed one woman as Lay Master: Miss Mary Ganderton at Wolverhampton.[42] When the Wimbledon branch elected its officers in 1934, the Chairman, Vice Chairman, Librarian and propaganda secretary were men; but a Miss Roke was the study class organiser, and a Miss Douglas the secretary and treasurer.[43]

With respect to the roles involved in public speaking, the 1930 list of licences held by effective speakers in the Birmingham branch of the C.E.G. can now be revisited to look at the gender of the licensees. All five of the general licences were held by men, and only one of the four chairman's licences was held by a woman. Likewise, while six men held single-subject licences, only one woman did so. Yet this was not typical. At a distribution of catechists' certificates in the Picton Hall, Liverpool, in May 1929, four of the recipients were men, seven women.[44] At an A.G.M. of the Wallasey (Shrewsbury) Guild in 1930, its Master, Mr Cyril Clancy, informed those attending that some twenty speakers had been trained in the previous two and a half years, 'two-thirds of whom were women'.[45] At a rally in Chorley the previous year a Miss Eileen Murphy from the Liverpool branch had spoken on the movement's history and had later given a model lecture on confession from a guild platform erected indoors to demonstrate how the Guild's work was carried out, while other members took the part of hecklers and a Miss Mary McDermott, also from the Liverpool branch, took general questions.[46] Some believed women speakers made a particularly good impression. An Edinburgh Councillor, Mr Andrew Gilzean, who visited the platform at Hyde Park, favourably compared to a 'callow' young man a 'pretty young woman of about 22 years' who 'stated the case for the "Confessional" with a simplicity which must have had a considerable propaganda value'.[47]

The Guilds faced various problems. A practical restriction was the limited amount of funds available to them through subscriptions. Fr Pope lamented 'the ever-recurrent problem of finance. Few or none of

---

[42] C.E.G. Inter-Guild Conference Handbooks, 1930–1938, AAW.
[43] *NMCN*, 10 February 1934, p. 10.
[44] *NMCN*, 18 May 1929, p. 10.
[45] *NMCN*, 15 March 1930, p. 6.
[46] *NMCN*, 5 October 1929, p. 6.
[47] *Edinburgh Evening News*, 5 August 1927.

the speakers are in a position to meet their own expenses in getting out to the scenes of their labours', but neither could these be readily supplied by guild funds, a factor which limited the support speakers in one branch might offer to another.[48] One issue on which Guild members became divided in the period was whether their exposition of Catholic doctrine should include the Church's social teaching, and in particular the teaching of *Rerum Novarum*. Most favoured its exclusion on the grounds that it was hard to tell where the teaching ended and the legitimate diversity of political opinion began, though the two leading Dominicans involved with the movement, Frs Pope and McNabb, both favoured inclusion of the Church's social teaching.[49] Cardinal Bourne ruled against its inclusion in the Westminster Guild, but elsewhere Ward remembered the rule as varying from guild to guild, as their bishops saw fit, though most agreed with Bourne. Fr Pope repeatedly pressed the question at the annual retreats.[50]

There can be no single measure of the C.E.G.'s achievements, or of the extent to which it met the hopes of many. Any adequate assessment, however, should examine, first, the extent of the movement's activities; second, it should study the movement's impact on both its target audience and on its membership. In examining the C.E.G.'s activities, we may begin by considering the number of diocesan guilds and the speed with which they multiplied, together with the small number that failed. The Birmingham Guild was founded in 1921 with initial support from the Westminster Guild, and other early foundations took place in Southwark, Brentwood and Salford.[51] Yet more swiftly followed, though there was often a time-lag between expressions of initial interest and a guild's formal inauguration. On 24 July 1921 a lay Dominican, Leo Edgar, wrote to Hugh Pope about the possible extension of the Catholic Evidence Guild into the Newcastle area by 'members of our Third Order'.[52] Edgar would become a leading figure in the Newcastle Guild, but this was not formally inaugurated until June 1925.[53] Fr Pope, in a paper probably composed in 1927, could state that the movement was 'at present a sort of "snow-ball" ... Guilds are being established everywhere & are flourishing'. He observed that 'for nine years past the work of making English people familiar with what the Catholic Church believes & why she believes it has been carried out winter & summer'.[54] A guild in the Plymouth diocese, active in 1922, had failed by 1930, but by that

---

[48] Pope, 'What is the Future?', p. 8.
[49] Ward, *Unfinished Business*, pp. 189–93.
[50] Ibid., 195.
[51] Leonard, *Fools*, pp. 33–4.
[52] EDA V, HP 1.
[53] Leonard, *Fools*, 103.
[54] Pope, 'What is the Future?', p. 1.

year there were guilds in fourteen dioceses or archdioceses in England and Wales (Westminster, Birmingham, Brentwood, Cardiff, Hexham and Newcastle, Lancaster, Liverpool, Middlesbrough and Leeds, Nottingham, Portsmouth, Salford, Shrewsbury, and Southwark).[55] This was a considerable achievement, given the level of organisation required in training speakers, the high standards expected of them, and the further training and organisation needed to chair and run the pitches. On the other hand, it meant that there were no guilds in south-west England, in East Anglia, or in much of Wales. The same was true in 1938, the last year before the Second World War in which an Inter-Guild Conference was held.[56] This indicates the limited ability of the C.E.G. to reach a non-Catholic audience in rural and other areas remote from major concentrations of the Catholic population.

In Scotland, the C.E.G 's work had been publicised among Catholics by an article in May 1921 in the *Glasgow Observer and Catholic Herald*. Its English author ('J. M.') was eager that the Guild's work 'be known and spread in Scotland' and hoped that this could be done by the members of the Catholic Young Men's Society.[57] The Edinburgh Guild was founded in 1922, but it seems to have had a distinctive and rocky history in which its outdoor work was severely hampered and largely stopped by a sectarian culture.[58] Speakers were attacked at street meetings and attempts made to intimidate them.[59] By 1932 the guild was advertising weekly indoor conferences for 'non-Catholic inquirers' at various venues including the Cathedral Hall, Friary Hall and Lauriston Hall.[60] Guild statistics listed it as having twelve effective speakers, two pitches and two weekly meetings in 1933, dropping to nine speakers and one pitch in 1934 with no numbers given for 1935 and no listing in 1936 and 1937. At Glasgow there had been a clash between supporters of the C.E.G. and the Scottish Protestant League when rival meetings were held in the Cathedral Square in December 1931. In the words of *The Scotsman* 'Sectarian feeling ran high', and the police dispersed the crowd after a minor scuffle.[61] Not long afterwards, a C.E.G. platform near Queen's Park Gate was attacked on a Sunday afternoon in January 1932 during

---

55   Leonard, *Fools* p. 55; C.E.G., Ninth Inter-Guild Conference Handbook, 1930, pp. 51–2, AAW.
56   C.E.G., Seventeenth Inter-Guild Conference Handbook, 1938, pp. 62–3, AAW.
57   *Glasgow Observer and Catholic Herald*, 14 May 1921, pp. 2 and 6.
58   Leonard, *Fools*, 108.
59   *The Scotsman*, 6 July 1934, p. 10.
60   *Edinburgh Evening News*, 16 January 1932, 15 February 1932, 21 March 1932, 6 June 1932.
61   *The Scotsman*, 21 December 1931, p. 10, and 23 December 1931.

which 'Protestant League rowdies' kicked one of the speakers, a fight developed, and several arrests were made.[62]

To assess better the movement's spread and impact, however, we need to examine what was done within the dioceses where it was present, and in particular the history of the many branches. While new branches opened throughout the 1920s and the first half of the 1930s, some soon closed. At Chorley, for example, the branch opened in 1929 closed just four years later.[63] Small branches were vulnerable to the loss of their trained speakers. The difficulties encountered at Oxford, where a branch opened in 1930, can be ascertained from its minute book. It recorded in April 1931 that three members were to leave the district, while a second entry noted that undergraduates could not speak at lunchtimes. A list of which members had passed examinations in which subjects included the names of two 'Cath. Workers', whose entries were annotated as 'Too busy to speak'.[64] The total number of branches across the country in 1933 was forty-two, and the branches ran ninety-seven pitches served by 562 effective speakers.[65] As the 1930s progressed, however, the movement began to lose ground. In 1938, the Birmingham Guild still had five branches, though Wolverhampton had closed and a branch at Stourbridge had opened; but this diocesan guild ran just three pitches served by only twenty-eight effective speakers. The total number of branches for England and Wales that year had dropped to thirty-five; the branches now ran sixty-nine pitches served by 387 effective speakers. Furthermore, a hundred of these speakers (over a quarter of the total), and twenty-three of the pitches (one third of the total), belonged to the original Westminster Guild, which dwarfed the other guilds in numbers of trained speakers (with a hundred in 1938, the next largest being Hexham and Newcastle with fifty-four).[66] Nonetheless, the C.E.G. was active in some of the country's largest cities (Birmingham, Bradford, Cardiff, Leeds, Leicester, Liverpool, London, Manchester, Newcastle and Nottingham), but not most major towns. Some branches had also attempted subsidiary pitches in nearby rural districts. Fr Hugh Pope was an advocate of such village preaching. Among his papers in the English Dominican archives is a notebook for the short-lived Oxford branch of the C.E.G. It included a list of villages with their mileage from Oxford and times when a pitch

---

[62] *Irish Weekly and Ulster Examiner*, 16 January 1932.
[63] *NMCN*, 16 December 1933, p. 7.
[64] Notebook for the Oxford Branch of the Birmingham C.E.G., 1930–1932, pp. 15, 23–4.
[65] C.E.G., Twelfth Inter-Guild Conference Handbook, 1933, pp. 66–7, BAA, AP/E/8.
[66] C.E.G., Seventeenth Inter-Guild Conference Handbook, 1938, pp. 62–3, AAW.

was operated there in the early 1930s, for example, 'Woodstock, 8 m. 1st Tuesday'.[67] Few such attempts, however, met with lasting success. As established at the outset of this chapter, the C.E.G. sought to educate the masses unreachable through church attendance, the Catholic press, or more personal contact between individuals. Having established its limited reach, we must now consider its impact on those who were exposed to it. In many places the C.E.G. found and often held onto an initially attentive audience. The Secretary of the Portsmouth Guild at its annual meeting in 1925 paid a 'pleasing tribute ... to the courtesy of the crowds' at its Sunday meetings in the Town Hall Square.[68] In early October 1926, one Catholic newspaper told its readers that speakers on the beach at Blackpool had 'always received a good reception from the crowd' on most Sunday evenings since meetings had begun in late July.[69] The *Accrington Observer and Times* for 9 June 1928 reported that the Guild had begun a series of open-air meetings on Sunday evenings on the Market Ground. A Mr J. Aspin had spoken on 'The Visible Church' and Mr H. Doyle on confession. The paper told readers that the 'crowd was large, and deep interest was taken in what the speakers had to say'. A week later it related that the second meeting had won 'an even larger crowd than previously'.[70] When the Leeds branch had made their first public appearance in 1933, the meeting had apparently been 'exceptionally well received by a large gathering'.[71] Though we should reckon on some bias in favour of the movement on the part of the Catholic press, it is clear that many C.E.G. platforms were well received by crowds who gave them a place alongside the various other political and religious groups who customarily held open-air meetings in the period.

On the other hand, not every initiative was well received. The Secretary of the Brighton branch recalled in 1928 that the original attitude of the crowds there had been 'decidedly hostile', though it 'was now one of welcome from the majority'.[72] Some pitches were lost when meetings were targeted by organised opponents or hecklers. At Colwyn Bay, where a platform had opened on the promenade in 1926 alongside non-Catholic groups, the Urban District Council in 1927 and 1928 first refused permission for future meetings, and then sought to prevent speakers from taking questions, after representation from what the Catholic press called 'a

---

[67] Notebook for the Oxford Branch of the Birmingham C.E.G., 1930–1932, p. 8, EDA, V, HP 5.
[68] *Portsmouth Evening News*, February 24, 1925, p. 2.
[69] *NMCN*, October 2, 1926, p. 11.
[70] *Accrington Observer and Times*, 9 June and 16 June 1928.
[71] *NMCN*, 7 October 1933.
[72] *NMCN*, 3 November 1928.

very small group of organised hecklers' led by an 'arch-disturber'.[73] In September 1929 Orangemen rushed the platform at New Brighton Sands, Wallasey, damaged the crucifix and ill-treated the speakers, who included a number of young women. As a result, the Wallasey Corporation in 1930 prohibited 'religious propaganda meetings' there.[74] Archbishop Downey of Liverpool claimed that same year to have closed five pitches because of the 'insulting treatment' to which speakers were subjected by 'hooligans who attended for the purpose of breaking up the meetings'.[75] Furthermore, while some pitches remained successful centres of public speaking over many decades, like Marble Arch in London, the Birmingham Bull Ring, and the Bigg Market in Newcastle, others failed at various points to hold a crowd. At the Third Northern C.E.G. Conference, held at Liverpool in 1929, Mr Cyril Lafferty of the St Helens branch delivered a paper on the 'Problem of Languishing Pitches'.[76] Guild libraries could also suffer from declining numbers of readers. At Birmingham, the Librarian stated at a meeting in 1938 that 'there was little to report regarding the Library as this was not used to any great extent'.[77]

This chapter has drawn on newspaper reports that indicate how crowds attended and often responded favourably to C.E.G. speakers. Newspapers were also at times means by which the Guild's meetings were discussed or its teachings more widely broadcast, and sometimes the means by which its work was opposed by the papers' readers. Thus, Mr Frederick Jarvis of Plymouth wrote on several occasions in the *Western Evening Herald* about the Guild meetings held in the city's market place and on the Quay, to describe the 'entertainment' afforded fortnightly 'at the expense of the Guild lecturers'. He thought the Guild secretary had exaggerated the numbers in attendance and assured the readers from his own experience that the majority present had been 'amused at the frantic effort on the part of the Guild lecturers to justify the 'modern novel doctrines of the Church of Rome'.[78] The *Reading Standard* for 7 June 1924 carried an account of what Guild speakers had taught about the Church in relation to the New Testament, and also what they had said about the lectures given on St Thomas Aquinas at Manchester University, which they argued demonstrated the honour now accorded to his teachings by non-Catholics. On 28 June, the paper carried a letter to its editor from a 'Bible Student' who took issue with the speakers' claim that 'the teachings

---

[73] *NMCN*, 1 September 1928.
[74] *NMCN*, 19 March 1930.
[75] *Liverpool Echo*, 14 November 1930.
[76] *NMCN*, 16 February 1929.
[77] Minutes of the Birmingham C.E.G. Committee meeting, 30 September 1938, BAA, CEG 5.
[78] *Western Evening Herald*, 13 February 1922.

of the Church of Rome are in accordance with the New Testament'. The
'Bible Student' row offered 'a few words of friendly criticism'.[79]
The question arises as to whether those who gave the C.E.G. a favourable hearing were swayed by what they heard and, if so, in what way.
Several highly experienced Guild speakers took the view that the crowds'
attitude towards Catholicism and to religion generally changed over the
first decade of the movement's existence. Fr Ronald Knox, speaking at
the Westminster Guild A G.M. in 1925, also claimed there had been a
rise in the number of English converts to Catholicism: whereas these
had numbered some 8,000 a year before the war, they had increased to
12,000 by 1923 and were continuing to climb.[80] He stopped short, though,
of claiming this as the work of the Guild. There were certainly some
conversions due to the Guild: Maisie Ward noted in her autobiography
that 'such conversions as we heard of came more often from lectures on
Confession than on any other subject'.[81] And some, though they did not
become Catholics, reappraised their Christian faith: Frank Sheed once
received a letter which told him that its author, a persistent questioner
at the public meetings, 'was not going to join your Church, but I want
you to know that you have given me back my belief in God and my
belief in Christ'.[32]

Already by 1930, awareness of what the C.E.G. had not done was
reshaping the hopes of its supporters. The Dominican Provincial, Fr
Bede Jarrett O.P., told a C.E.G. Rally in the Leicester Corn Exchange
on Sunday 12 October that year how 'the work of the Guild is not to
convert England, but to convert the temper of mind of the people'.[83]
Frank Sheed had confessed a year earlier that the C.E.G. was 'not in
the least like what an outsider would expect, because ... not in the least
like what its original members did expect'. Enthusiasm in a speaker's
early days, when 'Catholic teaching, never before so well understood'
seemed to 'course through the veins like strong wine' had made one feel
that 'this splendid stuff' had 'only to be shown to the crowd to set them
clamouring for admission to the Church'. He now argued that although
there were converts 'in growing number', they were 'not the object of
the Guild's work' and so 'not the measure of its success'. Rather, the
Guild existed for the 'instruction of the non-Catholic world' and 'results
in that sphere' were 'simply astounding'. Ignorance and prejudice were
being replaced by a better understanding of what Catholics believed.[84]

---

79   *Reading Standard*, 7 June 1924 and 28 June 1924.
80   *Glasgow Observer and Catholic Herald*, 14 November 1925.
81   Ward, *Unfinished Business*, p. 88.
82   Ibid., p. 188.
83   *Leicester Evening Mail*, 13 October 1930.
84   F. J. Sheed, 'Modern Guildsmen', *Commonweal*, 11:5 (December 1929), pp. 139–40.

This claim and the revised hopes which it embodied are of course hard to assess. Just a few years later, Sheed stated in a speech at Walsall in 1932 that ten years previously people had 'definite views on religion', often decidedly Protestant, but now 'it was as though a sponge had been run across their minds' and they held 'no views on religion at all', though they retained a certain suspicion towards Catholicism.[85] On this occasion, however, he did not attribute the change to the Guild's endeavours.

In a joint pastoral letter of 1934, the Catholic bishops of England and Wales announced their intention to establish a National Board of Catholic Action, which by coordinating and overseeing the work of various bodies would form a 'powerful organisation for moulding public opinion and for asserting and defending our Catholic rights'.[86] This was followed by a further joint pastoral in December 1936 on the apostolate of the laity in combatting communism and opposing oppression of the working poor. It was stated that the National Board of this new Catholic Action would consist of the bishops presided over by the Archbishop of Westminster, assisted by a 'small national committee of laymen, with an acting lay president and one of the Bishops as ecclesiastical assistant'. Bishops would then appoint people to their own diocesan boards.[87] The plans reflected the development of the Catholic Action movement in mainland Europe, but they probably also owed something to what the C.E.G. both had and had not achieved in Britain. The C.E.G. held out the promise of something – a power to shape public opinion – beyond its own ability to deliver. It offered a model of clerical and lay collaboration which seems less clerical than the model proposed by the bishops in 1936, and which continued to function effectively on a reduced scale beyond the period considered here, unlike the bishops' model. It seems likely that we should see the C.E.G. as one factor among several, and perhaps the most visible, in effecting greater social acceptance of Catholicism in parts of urban Britain between the World Wars.

Evidence then suggests that the more important achievements of the Catholic Evidence Guilds in the interwar period were internal to the Catholic Church in the British Isles. Dana Greene, biographer of Maisie Ward, has judged that for Maisie and her husband Frank Sheed, the C.E.G. was a 'vocation' that 'gave direction to their lives, deepened their faith, and enhanced their influence on others'.[88] The same was true to a greater or lesser extent for many of the movement's effective speakers and organisers who would often remain such, long after the period considered here. Among the earliest members of the Birmingham Guild were

---

[85] *Rugeley Times*, 8 October 1932.
[86] *NMCN*, 26 May 1934, p. 8.
[87] *Sheffield Independent*, 14 December 1936.
[88] Greene, *The Living*, p. 58.

Messrs Mackey, Ashby and Durk. Minutes of Committee and Council meetings show their commitment as organisers respectively from 1921 to 1948 (the year of Mackey's death), from 1923 to 1953, and from 1924 to 1970.[89] Greene has also noted the movement's innovative nature and success in advancing the study of doctrine by lay men and women.[90] Maisie Ward herself observed another phenomenon: 'fallen-away Catholics brought back to the sacraments'. Previously ill-instructed Catholics 'grew fervent as they learned more about their faith'. In Sheed's view, also, this 'regaining of lapsed Catholics' was 'easily' the Guild's 'most important work'.[91]

Finally, we must also reckon on the symbolic role which the Guild had for the Catholic Church, for which it represented the reasonable nature of the Faith expounded by the Guild, expressed the confidence Catholics had in their Church and its mission, and for some at least modelled the collaborative ministry of clergy and laity, with the latter including women in a variety of roles. In his message of support for the 1938 Inter-Guild Conference at Blackburn, the late Bishop Thomas Henshaw of Salford stated that the Guild was 'as the Hierarchy in their last joint Pastoral declared, "the most important of all forms of Catholic Action" in England. It is essentially the laity's participation in the apostolate of the hierarchy.'[92] As such an ideal or construct, as well as in practice on the platform and in the classroom, the Guild strongly influenced the perception of the laity both by clergy and by the laity themselves.

---

[89] BAA, CEG/2–7.
[90] Greene, *The Living*, p. 59.
[91] Sheed, 'Modern Guildsmen', p. 140.
[92] C.E.G. Seventeenth Inter-Guild Conference Handbook, 1938, p. 5, AAW.

5

CATHOLIC ACTION IN SCOTLAND: THE EARLY YEARS OF THE GUILD OF CATHOLIC TEACHERS

Leonardo Franchi

The Guild of Catholic Teachers was founded in Glasgow in 1934. It was placed under the patronage of St John Bosco and had two principal aims: the social, cultural and religious formation of Catholic teachers and the development of Religious Instruction in schools.[1] Study of the relevant archival material for the early years of the Guild (1934–36) reveals a heightened sense of collegiality and a related determination by lay people to achieve the Guild's ambitious aims.[2] The present chapter will examine the extent to which the aims of the Guild reflected, or were influenced by, the principles of Catholic Action. It will first offer some initial thoughts on Catholic Action in Scotland before focusing on the development of Catholic education in Scotland in the aftermath of the First Word War, in order to understand the varied contexts from which the Guild emerged in 1934. The third section will draw on available archival material to present some of the key moments in the first two years of the Guild. This period offers evidence of the Catholic community's growing self-confidence and a related desire to advance teacher formation in practical ways. The final part will show how 'Religious Knowledge' textbooks,[3] which were underpinned by some new thinking in pedagogy, were one of the early fruits of the Guild.

Catholic Action in Scotland

Catholic Action, as used in the present chapter, is much more than a simple description of the myriad religious, cultural and social interventions

---

[1] 'Religious Instruction' was a common term in Catholic schools in the UK until the 1970s. It would not be used today. It has been replaced by 'Religious Education' or 'Religious Studies'.
[2] The relevant archival material is held in the Scottish Catholic Archives (SCA), Columba House, Edinburgh.
[3] 'Religious Knowledge' textbooks were popular in the UK until the 1970s. Like 'Religious Instruction', the term is not in common use today.

carried out by members of the Catholic Church in early twentieth-century Scotland. In continental Europe, Catholic Action as a *movement* offered the Catholic laity a sense of coherence and shared identity with which to address the significant socio-cultural challenges they faced in the interwar years. In 1928 Pope Pius XI wrote to the German cardinal, Adolf Bertram, with the following definition of Catholic Action:

> The part taken by the Catholic laity in the apostolic mission of the Church with the object of defending the principles of Faith and Morals and of spreading a sane and beneficial social action so as to restore Catholic Life in the home and in Society. This is to be done under the guidance of the hierarchy of the Church, outside and above all party politics.[4]

In seeking to bring Catholic organisations under the authority, some might argue control, of the hierarchy, Pius XI was exploring how to address significant challenges to the Catholic Church from communism and, more immediately, from Mussolini's Fascists in Italy. Pius's letter shows, unsurprisingly, a strictly hierarchical understanding of the Church, and an explicit desire for the bishops to direct lay people in the task of social engagement, including in the ever-fraught field of politics.[5]

Such a top-down understanding of the lay apostolate is, of course, somewhat removed from the vision of Vatican II and subsequent Catholic thinking on the topic. Pope John Paul II's 1988 post-synodal Apostolic Exhortation, *Christifideles Laici*, reminded the Church that the laity's right to form groups 'is a true and proper right that is not derived from any kind of "concession" by authority, but flows from the Sacrament of Baptism, which calls the lay faithful to participate actively in the Church's communion and mission'.[6] This way of thinking does not sit altogether comfortably with the definition of Catholic Action offered by Pope Pius XI.[7]

---

4 Pope Pius XI to Cardinal Segura, 20 July 1928, quoted in Herbert Kildany, 'The Meaning of Catholic Action', *Blackfriars*, 15:174 (September 1934), p. 585.
5 The political dimension of Catholic life in early-twentieth-century Scotland is a mosaic of competing features. The notion of a so-called 'Catholic vote', which implied strong bonds of social, political and cultural solidarity, is only partially correct. The formation of various Guilds could be interpreted as a way to strengthen such bonds. For more on the politics of this era, see John McCaffrey, 'Politics and the Catholic Community since 1878', *Innes Review*, 29:2 (1978), pp. 140–55.
6 Pope John Paul II, *Christifideles laici: On the Vocation and the Mission of the Lay Faithful in the Church and in the World* (1988), §29. https://www.vatican.va/content/john-paul-ii/en/apost_exhortations/documents/hf_jp-ii_exh_30121988_christifideles-laici.html, accessed 11 September 2023.
7 A case could be made that such a response might have been the best way to articulate the Church in Italy's position vis-à-vis the ideological threats from both communism and fascism.

Catholic Action was not unknown in the Scotland of the 1930s. On 8 December 1934, the *Scottish Catholic Herald* carried a report of a talk by Fr Joseph Daniel, Professor of Sacred Scripture, St Peter's College, Bearsden, which was number six in a series of ten talks on Catholic lay societies, entitled: 'Catholic Action – The Obligation from Confirmation – Striving for Souls'.[8] The sub-heading was a quotation attributed to Pope Pius XI: 'Catholic Action is a duty for all. Each one should look on the cause of the Church as his own.' It is not always clear from the article what is being reported and what is direct speech, but it offers a robust defence of the key features of Catholic Action. There is a strong focus on military analogies, such as 'soldier of Christ', 'Christian militia', and 'every apostle becomes necessarily a combatant and every combatant is an apostle'. Such language is similar to the 'soldier of Christ' imagery associated with the sacrament of confirmation. There is no direct mention of education and schooling, and little reference to Scotland, excepting a mention of the Sacred Heart Sodality in the Archdiocese of Glasgow. Nonetheless, it is a window, albeit opaque, into the 'ideals' of Catholic Action as seen by a distinguished member of the Scottish clergy. While this lecture took place after the foundation of the Guild of Catholic Teachers in 1934, it is reasonable to assume that Fr Daniel's audience, who were 'the large number of leaders of Catholic lay societies that attend those meetings', would have contained key figures in Catholic education and thus some form of cross-fertilisation of ideas could have taken place.

Such energy around Catholic Action had the potential to turn Scottish eyes beyond national issues towards wider European Catholic thinking on how best to defend and develop the Christian roots of society.[9] The question of schooling, and the formation of young people more generally, was part of this line of thinking. Pope Pius XI's encyclical *On Christian Education*, published in 1929, was clearly inspired by Catholic Action.[10] As a former diplomat and Prefect of the Vatican Library, Pius had direct knowledge of the political challenges facing the Church from apparently hostile ideologies such as communism and fascism. Furthermore,

---

[8] *Scottish Catholic Herald*, 8 December 1934. N.B. There is no source for the quote from Pope Pius XI which is included at the top of the report. The feature ends with the following: 'The end of Catholic Action is definitely religious, but the means are not necessarily all religious. If the means of attaining the ends of Catholic [sic] are material, they can and must be used, provided, of course, that they are licit and proportionate to the end.'
[9] A Guild of Catholic Teachers was formed in England in 1937, perhaps inspired by the Scottish experience. The Archbishop of Westminster, Arthur Hinsley, communicated the views of the Bishops of England and Wales that the Guild should be 'purely spiritual', with secular matters left in the hands of existing organisations. *The Tablet*, 5 June 1937.
[10] Pope Pius XI, *Divini illius magistri: On Christian Education* (1929), https://www.vatican.va/content/pius-xi/en/encyclicals/documents/hf_p-xi_enc_31121929_divini-illius-magistri.html, accessed 11 September 2023.

he argued that materialist philosophies of education were no less than a denial of the true end of the human person and that the remedy for the attacks on the Christian roots of society lay in a return to authentic Catholic education. To be clear, the promotion and defence of Catholic schools, was, for Pius, an example of 'Catholic Action'.[11] This mission required 'good teachers, teachers who are thoroughly prepared and well-grounded in the matter they have to teach; who possess the intellectual and moral qualities required by their important office'.[12] This template for the ideal Catholic teacher would be the inspiration for the Guild.

Catholic Action and Catholic education in the interwar years

Informed scholarly judgement on the success or otherwise of particular movements in the Church and society requires a level of nuance which recognises the interaction of a host of forces, not all of which can be satisfactorily aligned. With this caveat in mind, a tentative case can be made that Catholic Action as a movement failed to establish itself in Scotland *if* we see the lack of a central organisational structure as evidence of failure as such. For some, this failure stemmed from an attempt 'to establish it, as it were overnight, by higher authority'.[13] This evaluation might be partially true but the failure could also stem from a reluctance of the Scottish hierarchy to be affiliated, albeit loosely, to a movement with robust 'Italianised' political dimensions and which consequently did not fit into the political world in which the Catholics of Scotland moved.[14] The implications of a partnership, even if implicit, between the Scottish Catholic hierarchy and a highly visible Catholic Action movement with very strong Italian connections, could have added to the suspicion and hostility not infrequently directed towards the Catholic community from some extreme Protestant quarters.[15]

The apparent failure of Catholic Action as a template for the Catholic Church's social voice in Scotland did not, of course, mean that the Church in Scotland had little to say on social or educational issues. The period since the restoration of the Catholic hierarchy of Scotland

---

[11] Ibid., §84.
[12] Ibid., §88.
[13] Anthony Ross, 'The Development of the Scottish Catholic Community, 1878–1978', *Innes Review*, 29:1 (1978), p. 22.
[14] We must also bear in mind the apparently strong connection between Glasgow's Italian Club (the *Casa d'Italia*) and the emergence of *fasci di combattimento*, which, in essence, gave a platform to fascism in Glasgow. The *fasci di combattimento* were the shock troops of Italian fascism.
[15] See Terri Colpi, 'The Scottish Italian Community: senza un campanile?', *Innes Review*, 44:2 (1993), pp. 153–67; Tom Gallagher, 'Protestant Extremism in Urban Scotland, 1930–1939: Its Growth and Contraction', *Scottish Historical Review*, 64:2 (1985), pp. 143–67.

in 1878 had been one of burgeoning guilds and other associations which saw the mission to address social inequalities as core to the practice of the faith. Lectures, study circles and public meetings were the common means for the further education of the Catholic community on their social responsibilities: the work of the Catholic Truth Society, the Apostleship of the Sea and the Catholic Young Men's Society are examples of this.[16] The Catholic Social Guild, which was present in Glasgow in the 1930s, was one example of an educational movement for aspirational Catholic workers.[17] Catholics supported an impressive range of initiatives under the auspices of groups such as the Catholic Young Men's Society and the St Vincent de Paul Society.[18] Furthermore, in the interwar years, there was an awakening of Catholic intellectual life in Scotland with the arrival of high-profile converts like Professors John Phillimore (Chair of Greek and Humanity at the University of Glasgow)[19] and Edmund Whittaker (Chair of Mathematics at the University of Edinburgh).[20] This could only add to the sense of dynamism prevalent in Scottish Catholic life at the time.[21]

In matters of schooling, the 1872 Education (Scotland) Act had made education compulsory between the ages of 5 and 11. Its legislative successor, the 1918 Education (Scotland) Act, brought all existing denominational schools into the state system, leading to a new state-funded era in Catholic school education in Scotland.[22] The 1918 Act was not specifically directed at Catholic schools as such but sought equality of opportunity, unconstrained by economic means, in all schools in Scotland.[23] The Act underpinned the increasing professionalisation of the teaching force in Catholic schools. Teachers became part of an ambitious state system, with better working conditions and salaries. Freed from the financial burden of managing schools, the Church's authorities had the space to focus on robust teacher formation and cement the place of teachers in the life of

---

[16] T. Fitzpatrick, 'The Catholic Social Guild: Fr Leo O'Hea S.J. (1881–1976) and the West of Scotland Connection', *Innes Review*, 50:2 (1999), pp. 127–38.
[17] Piotr Potocki, 'The Origins of the Catholic Social Guild in Scotland: "We have not attacked the Socialists professedly"', *Innes Review*, 69:2 (2018), pp. 131–46.
[18] Raymond McCluskey, 'Catholic Education Beyond the School: Sodalities and Public Lectures', in *A History of Catholic Education and Schooling in Scotland: New Perspectives*, edited by Stephen McKinney and Raymond McCluskey (London, 2019), pp. 125–47.
[19] Papers of John Swinnerton Phillimore, https://archiveshub.jisc.ac.uk/search/archives/4fd14455-b730-33d9-affe-bd1bc19929a8.
[20] 'Sir Edmund Taylor Whitaker', Our History wiki, University of Edinburgh, https://ourhistory.is.ed.ac.uk/index.php/Sir_Edmund_Taylor_Whittaker_(1873–1956), accessed 11 September 2023.
[21] Ross, 'Development of the Scottish Catholic Community'.
[22] J. H. Treble, 'The Development of Roman Catholic Education in Scotland, 1878–1978', *Innes Review*, 29:2 (1978), pp. 111–39.
[23] Lindsay Paterson, 'Catholic Schools and the Education (Scotland) Act 1918', *Innes Review*, 71:1 (2020), pp. 85–97.

both Church and society. Indeed, the idealism which had animated the religious orders and teaching congregations in the period between 1872 and 1918 now bore fruit in the formation of corporate bodies for Catholic teachers in the post-war period.[24]

Interestingly, Pope Leo XIII had lauded Scottish Catholic education pre-1918 in *Caritatis Studium: On the Church in Scotland*, issued in 1898.[25] Here, Leo made a point of praising Scotland's schools 'in which the best method of teaching is to be found' and was determined that the Catholic schools should be 'second to none in efficiency'. The work of the religious orders and teaching congregations in developing Catholic education in Scotland before 1918 needs to be rediscovered. It was unfortunate that events commemorating the 2018 centenary of the 1918 Act did not give sufficient emphasis to the contribution that the orders and congregations had made to Catholic education in Scotland before 1918. The 1918 Act did mark 'the beginning of a new era' in the political relationship between Catholic schools and the state but it was not the *beginning* of Catholic schooling in Scotland.[26] After 1918, a more confident Scottish Catholic infrastructure emerged from determined efforts at community-building through explicit educational, cultural and sporting means, albeit manifesting on occasion a somewhat 'defensive and apologetic character'.[27] The 1918 Act was an opportunity for Scotland, living with the aftershocks of the First World War, to unite its people under the banner of Scotland's educational traditions and embed the Catholic community in Scottish society without losing Catholicism's unique theological and cultural traditions. The Guild, therefore, emerged from fertile ground.

---

[24] T. A. Fitzpatrick, Interview with John McKee, 20 February 1978, 'Catholic Secondary Education in South-West Scotland, 1922–72', unpublished PhD thesis (1982), Volume III, Oral Evidence, 3/3. Mr McKee is quoted as follows: 'Remember that one of the reasons for the 1918 Act was that our schools were poorly equipped, our teachers less well qualified than those in the public schools, that education was developing and we couldn't keep pace, in fact, with the development on financial grounds. We did a remarkable job, the Catholics, in the 46 years from 1872 to 1918.' Mr McKee was President of the Glasgow Branch of the Guild after the Second World War had ended.
[25] Pope Leo XIII *Caritatis studium: On the Church in Scotland* (1898), https://www.vatican.va/content/leo-xiii/en/encyclicals/documents/hf_l-xiii_enc_25071898_caritatis-studium.html, accessed 11 September 2023.
[26] Fitzpatrick, p. 35.
[27] Bernard Aspinwall, 'The Formation of the Catholic Community in the West of Scotland: Some Preliminary Outlines', *Innes Review*, 33 (1982), p. 44. See also Tom Gallagher, 'Scottish Catholics and the British Left, 1918–1939', *Innes Review*, 34:1 (1983), p. 35.

The Guild of Catholic Teachers, 1934–36

From the nineteenth century onwards, teachers in Catholic schools in Scotland made various attempts to organise themselves into corporate bodies. In 1872, a gathering of the Association of Certificated Catholic Schoolmasters agreed to draw up a list of resolutions for the development of Catholic schools which would then be submitted to Archbishop Eyre of Glasgow for approval before being sent to Parliament.[28] The report also noted that 'a deputation was also appointed to wait upon His Grace, and explain to him the nature and objects of the Association'. This might challenge any idea that the Catholic laity awaited instructions from the bishops before setting up social movements. Of course, with Archbishop Eyre being fairly new to Scotland it could have been no more than an example of courteous information dissemination.

In 1917, the Catholic Teachers' Union was established as a successor to both the Glasgow and West of Scotland Catholic Teachers' Association, and the Teachers' Branch of the United Irish League.[29] Gradually, the various groups scattered across Scotland merged to form a new national body, the Scottish Catholic Federation, recognised by both the Scottish Catholic Education Council and the Scottish Education Department.

The first Catholic teachers' organisation had been intent on the amelioration of the social and economic conditions of Catholic teachers, focusing on salaries and the fabric of Catholic school buildings. The 1918 Act removed the 'economic grievance' of Catholic teachers on lower salaries than teachers in state schools.[30] The improvement of terms of employment, while an important step forward, did not, however, exhaust the appetite for ongoing socio-cultural and religious formation. The first two years of the Guild, 1934–36, allow us to see a distinct pattern of activity emerging.

It is hard to say precisely when the idea of a new Catholic teachers' guild was first floated. An early indication is a letter sent to all teachers in the Archdiocese of Glasgow on 31 August 1934, signed by Mgr W. M. Daly (the Vicar-General of the Archdiocese of Glasgow) and written on official Archdiocesan notepaper. It invited all schools of the Archdiocese to a meeting in the City Hall in Glasgow on Sunday, 16 September, at 3 p.m.: Donald Mackintosh D.D., Archbishop of Glasgow, would 'meet and address all those engaged in teaching the Catholic children of the Archdiocese'.[31]

---

[28] *The Tablet*, 11 May 1872.
[29] T. A. Fitzpatrick, 'The Catholic Teachers' Union, 1917–1919', *Innes Review*, 41:1 (1990), pp. 132–5.
[30] T. A. Fitzpatrick, *Catholic Secondary Education in South-West Scotland Before 1972* (Aberdeen, 1986), p. 199.
[31] SCA/DE/171/144.

Two things are interesting about this invitation: the first is the expectation that the teachers would use a non-school day (Sunday) to attend a professional gathering at the request of the Archbishop, and the second is the stated aim of the meeting, viz: 'At the same Meeting proposals will be put before the teachers for the formation of a Guild of Catholic teachers to help in the work of instruction in the Catholic Religion.'[32] This seems to be a clear, precise and explicitly professional aim, albeit revealing a merging of the professional and religious identity of the Catholic teaching force. The emphasis on Religious Instruction, as it was called at the time, would eventually lead to a revised syllabus, as will be seen below.

Some preparatory work was, of course, necessary for the first meeting. In an undated, handwritten and unattributed draft version of the Constitution of the Guild, its aim was proposed as follows: 'to unite Catholic teachers in a Guild with a view to the formation of the welfare and effective conduct of Catholic education in accordance with the Encyclical of His Holiness Pope Pius XI. Christian Educ [sic] of Youth.' [33] The reference to Pope Pius XI's 1929 encyclical on education suggests that this particular expression of papal teaching was already familiar to some members of the Church in Scotland and that the encyclical would, in some way, shape the mission of the proposed Guild.

The agenda for the inaugural meeting was set out in some detail. Unsurprisingly, the Archbishop was to address the meeting at the start. The proposal to form the Guild would be advanced by Dr Patrick McGlynn of the University of Glasgow and seconded by Miss Mary Lee, supported by Mr William D. Moore. Dr McGlynn had insisted that, as a teacher in a university setting, he should be part of any organisation for Catholic teachers.[34] Further addresses would be given by four clerics: Right Rev. Mgr Kelly, Rev. Lyden, Rev. McSparran and Rev. Doyle. The meeting would end with a Vote of Thanks, the singing of *Faith of Our Fathers*, and a blessing by the Archbishop. The note also refers to a 'telegram to our Holy Father to be made as desired by His Grace'.[35]

The planned format was designed to strengthen the corporate identity of Catholic teachers. The pre-eminent role afforded to the Archbishop and priests was very much in line with the centralising tendencies of Catholic Action, although it would have been normal practice in Scotland, with or without Catholic Action in the background, to afford a central role to clergy in such meetings. A report in the *Scottish Catholic Herald*, while

---

[32] Mgr Daly's Letter to Catholic Teachers in the Archdiocese of Glasgow, SCA/DE/171/144.
[33] Draft Constitution of the St John Bosco Guild of Catholic Teachers, SCA/DE/171/144. The annual subscription was proposed as two shillings and sixpence.
[34] Fitzpatrick, Interview with John McKee, 20 February 1978, 3/2.
[35] Agenda for Meeting of 16 September 1934, SCA/DE/171/144

rather exaggerated in tone, successfully captured the excitement and hope which surrounded the Guild's early years:

> No more erudite assembly has ever been seen in the city of Glasgow than that which forgathered on Sunday afternoon, in the City Hall, when over two thousand Catholic teachers, men and women, the flower of Catholic educationists, under the chairmanship of his Grace the Archbishop of Glasgow, met for the purpose of forming themselves into a new Guild of Catholic Teachers.[36]

The link with the Holy See is evident via a telegram: 'The most Holy Father, thanking you and the Catholic Teachers who are gathered with you there for homage sent, wishes you everything that is best and sends you his blessing.'[37] It was signed on Pope Pius XI's behalf by the Secretary of State, Cardinal Eugenio Pacelli, the future Pope Pius XII.

Archbishop Mackintosh and Dr McGlynn both addressed the gathering.[38] The Archbishop reminded the audience that, as a bishop, he had the duty to uphold and discharge the Divine Commission of Matthew 28:16–20.[39] He reminded the audience that the work of education was vast and required solid bonds of cooperation between clergy and people.

For Archbishop Mackintosh the mission of Catholic education was urgent, owing to the decline of family, bad housing, and the challenges of 'industrial life in the towns'. Furthermore, it was necessary to find new methods to communicate the abstract truths of theology through high-quality religious instruction in schools. Archbishop Mackintosh was concerned that the children 'pick up ideas which make an impression on them. They give voice to these ideas during religious instruction.' In other words, reform of the Religious Instruction curriculum was pressing if such ideas were to be countered.

Dr McGlynn praised the gathering as 'historical' and made the claim that 'We are at the threshold of a new era in the history of Catholic education in this country.' He then proposed officially the formation of a new Guild under the patronage of St John Bosco.[40] Dr McGlynn noted

---

36 *Scottish Catholic Herald*, 22 September 1934.
37 Ibid.
38 The report in the *Scottish Catholic Herald* contains both indirect and direct speech. The selection above is reproduced as per the original article.
39 In the English Standard Version, this passage reads: 'Now the eleven disciples went to Galilee, to the mountain to which Jesus had directed them. When they saw him, they worshiped him; but some doubted. And Jesus came and said to them, "All authority in heaven and on earth has been given to me. Go therefore and make disciples of all nations, baptising them in the name of the Father and of the Son and of the Holy Spirit, and teaching them to obey everything that I have commanded you. And remember, I am with you always, to the end of the age."'
40 William Dickson notes that Dr McGlynn was instrumental in proposing St John Bosco as patron of the Guild. Dickson also makes a case for the Guild as a form of trade union. See William J. Dickson, 'Don Bosco, Trade Union Patron in Scotland: How the Scottish

that the existing Western Catholic Teachers' Federation already fulfilled many of the objects of the new organisation but that its membership was 'limited', although he did not explain in what way. The Federation supported the proposal for a new Guild which would, as Dr McGlynn noted, 'concentrate on the spiritual aspects of teaching and would provide Catholic teachers with facilities for discussion, elucidation, and helpful guidance on the many special problems associated with Catholic education'.[41] Dr McGlynn's proposal was unanimously adopted. Archbishop Mackintosh accepted the post of Honorary President and appointed Rev. Dr William E. Brown, Catholic Chaplain to the University of Glasgow, as the Guild's Chaplain.

An interim committee was formed to direct the Guild from the initial meeting in Glasgow City Hall in 1934 until the first Annual General Meeting in May or June 1935.[42] The members were: Dr McGlynn (President); Mary Glennan and William Barry (Vice-Presidents); William Moore (Secretary); Louis Dawson (Assistant Secretary); and Mary Roche (Treasurer). The committee also noted: 'It is hoped that the Catholic teachers of the Archdiocese will avail themselves of this opportunity of showing to His Grace, the Archbishop that they yield to no one in their loyalty and devotion to His Office and Person' (underlined in the original).[43] This again suggests a strong but unsurprising commitment to the hierarchy.

The Committee began work quickly. William Moore, in his role as Secretary of the Guild, sent a letter to all head teachers of Catholic schools in the Archdiocese, requesting that they send a representative to a meeting in the Catholic Institute on Friday, 5 October 1934, a few weeks after the inaugural event. The purpose of the meeting was threefold: to investigate difficulties in religious education; suggest how any such investigation be carried out and, crucially, to explore suggestions for the wider activities – religious, cultural and social – which the Guild could undertake in order to strengthen the bonds between its members. He also noted that there were 1,716 members of the Guild at the time of writing, thus showing some indication of its immediate appeal.[44]

By 1935, the Guild was in a position to publish a constitution and a set of by-laws. This is a well-worked document, complete with five full-page

---

Catholic Teachers' Guild Took Don Bosco as Their Patron', in *Percezione della figura di Don Bosco all'esterno dell'Opera salesiana dal 1879 al 1965: Atti del 6° convegno internazionale di Storia dell'Opera salesiana*, edited by Grazia Loparco and Stanisław Zimniak (Rome, 2016), pp. 577–87.
[41] *Scottish Catholic Herald*, 22 September 1934.
[42] Preparatory notes (unattributed and no date) for inaugural meeting of the St John Bosco Guild of Catholic Teachers, SCA /DE/171/144.
[43] Ibid.
[44] Letter to Head Teachers in the Archdiocese of Glasgow, 24 October 1934, SCA / DE/171/144.

adverts from Glasgow businesses. The final page is a membership card. The seven key positions and associated postholders were as follows: President (Patrick McGlynn, who also chaired the Chairman's Committee), Vice-Presidents (William Barry and Mary H. Glennan), Treasurer (Amelia Diamond), Assistant Treasurer (Mary H. McCluskey), Secretary (William Moore) and Assistant Secretary (Louis Dawson). There were five working committees with named coordinators: Religious Activities (Rev. Bro. Germanus), Cultural Activities (Arthur J. Montague), Social Activities (William Melvin), Organisation (William Barry) and Finance (F. E. Davis). Archbishop Mackintosh was Honorary President, and Rev. Dr W. E. Brown was Chaplain.[45] There was also an Executive Council with representatives from seven religious orders (two male, five female) and from primary, advanced, secondary and special schools in Glasgow, Lanarkshire, Renfrewshire, Dumbarton and North Ayrshire. Membership was fairly evenly balanced between male and female, although an exact gender split is impossible to state as some members have only initials before the surname. The constitution had twelve sections. Many of the sections dealt with procedural matters like subscriptions and processes for the election of office-bearers. It did make clear that the aims of the Guild were (a) to provide for the spiritual, cultural and social needs of Catholic teachers and (b) to promote the welfare and conduct of Catholic education in accordance with Pope Pius XI's encyclical on education.[46]

Some detailed and very practical byelaws regarding the administration of the Guild show its ambition to be more than just a low-key support body for teachers. The long-term aim is in line with Dr McGlynn's reference to a 'new era' and it seems that the Guild was planning to energise the profession from the grassroots. While there was a platform for the archbishop and established teaching congregations such as the Sisters of Notre Dame and the Marist Brothers, there was also a concomitant commitment to more collegial, or democratic, ideals in how key personnel were selected.

The early energy around the Guild centred on the Archdiocese of Glasgow, but there was a desire to expand. On 24 October 1934, William Moore, Secretary of the Guild, wrote to Archbishop Andrew MacDonald of St Andrews and Edinburgh to update him on its work. Interestingly, he said that the interim committee had been appointed 'practically by myself in a private capacity – as someone had to initiate proceedings'.[47] Mr Moore also noted that a sub-committee had been formed to study the question of religious education in schools: this seems to be a key theme

---

[45] Guild of Catholic Teachers, Constitution and Bye-Laws, 1935–36, SCA /DE/171/144. The pages are unnumbered.
[46] This is the author's summary of each of the twelve sections.
[47] Letter of William Moore to Archbishop MacDonald, 24 October 1934, SCA /DE/171/144.

and, indeed, desired area of reform. He also noted that meetings of the Guild were now to be held on the first Friday of every month, with groups already formed to study the recent papal encyclical on education. The first event was to be a Guild Mass in St Andrews Cathedral, Glasgow, on 10 November 1934.

By the middle of 1935, the influence of the Guild was more widespread. Its standing was such that the Catholic press published short doctrinal snippets from the Guild on topics such as the Church, the Sacraments, Ritual, Holy Mass, the Missal, the Liturgical Year, Duties of Parents, and Other Educational Works of the Church.[48] Its educational mission now stretched beyond the formation of teachers to the wider catechesis of lay Catholics.

On 23 September 1935, James Campbell, Secretary and Treasurer of the Eastern Branch of the Catholic Teachers' Section of the Educational Institute of Scotland, wrote to the Archbishop of St Andrews and Edinburgh about the possible formation of the Guild of Catholic Teachers in his archdiocese. The branch had agreed that if the archbishop wished the Guild to operate there, they would offer full cooperation and, in the event of the Guild's formation, the existing Eastern Branch of the Catholic Teachers' Federation would cease to exist.[49] On 21 November 1935, James Campbell sent another letter to Archbishop MacDonald about Catholic teacher numbers and an invitation to Dr McGlynn and Mr Moore, both members of the Council in Glasgow, to speak in Edinburgh.[50] Following that, on 6 December 1935, Mr Campbell wrote a third letter to Archbishop MacDonald, this time on the subject of the first meeting of the Guild's Edinburgh Committee which had taken place that same evening. Curiously, he remarked that 'the office-bearers elected will not altogether please Your Grace'.[51] We are not informed of the possible cause of this displeasure although it was noted that Professor Edmund Whittaker had not been elected Chairman, but a Miss Curran was. This suggests that the Archbishop was keen for a high-profile academic to be part of the first leadership team of the Guild in his archdiocese, as had happened in Glasgow with Dr McGlynn and Rev. Dr Brown.

By the end of 1935, the number of Study Circles had grown across Scotland. Their mode of operation favoured an academic approach, unsurprisingly for a Study Circle, yet there was still room to explore the implications for practice of Catholic teaching on education, especially the teaching found in Pope Pius XI's encyclical. Some examples will offer the flavour of the activities on offer: a headteacher in Alloa, A. H.

---

48   *Dundee Catholic Herald*, 14 December 1935. These are the sub-headings of the article.
49   James Campbell to Archbishop MacDonald, 23 September 1935, SCA /DE/171/144.
50   Ibid.
51   Ibid.

Tulloch, is praised for his 'great work in connection with Study Circles in Gregorian Chant'.[52] This is a clear hint to the influence of the Liturgical Movement, which sought greater lay knowledge of and participation in the Church's Gregorian musical heritage. It is not clear who the 'targets' of this initiative were but it is possible, if not probable, that the classes were for teachers who would then share their knowledge with pupils. The Glasgow Study Circle, which met in the Catholic Institute on Monday, 9 December 1935, gave a platform to John Moffat M.A., who addressed the meeting on the topic of Pope Pius XI's encyclical.[53] Key points from the address were as follows: to promote Catholic education in Catholic schools for Catholic youth; classical literature needs Catholic doctrine and a watchful teacher. Mere literacy is not an end in itself; the task of Catholic teachers is, quoting the encyclical, 'the formation of Christian virtue'. This extract shows the tension in Catholic education between secular and religious knowledge – a not uncommon feature in the Church's thinking on education – and underscores the teacher's important role as midwife of knowledge. Movements like the Guild of Catholic Teachers, he argued, are important responses to the Pope's call for teachers to cooperate in the divine mission of the Church. [54] On Monday, 16 December 1935, Canon Patrick Doyle, Chief Inspector of Schools (Archdiocese of Glasgow), spoke to the Glasgow Study Circle on 'The End and Object of Christian Education', again in the Catholic Institute. He referred to Pope Pius XI's emphasis on the divine vocation of the Catholic teacher and the importance of formation. Canon Doyle alluded to 'the anxiety of the Church for preserving the Catholic atmosphere in schools'. There is no hint in the report as to the sources of this anxiety.[55] At the Study Circle in Greenock, James Fitzpatrick BSc. advocated teachers laying strong foundations of faith, especially when parents lacked the 'facilities' so to do. [56] Teachers must show that 'Catholicism is a religion essentially reasonable'. He lamented the amount of time given to religion in schools: half an hour per day was insufficient. The Greenock Circle also enjoyed a talk by James Troy which developed Fitzpatrick's themes.[57] He warned that 'Education of the intellect alone divorced from moral training is futile' and that there

---

[52] *Saturday Catholic Herald*, 28 December 1935.
[53] *Dundee Catholic Herald*, 14 December 1935.
[54] *Saturday Catholic Herald*, 21 December 1935.
[55] *Saturday Catholic Herald*, 28 December, 1935.
[56] Ibid., 6. We do not have the full text of this paper but it seems remarkably contemporary in its lament over parental failure — for whatever reason — to cooperate in education. The observation on the reasonableness of Catholicism could easily be uttered today by advocates of Catholic education, and many would share his concern over the lack of space on the timetable for Religious Education.
[57] Ibid.

were dangers to children's faith and morality from 'immoral literature, the cinema, the stage, the press and false philosophies spread by means of "wireless talks" and street corner oratory, to say nothing of the dangers in workshops.' Troy offered a remedy in suitable after-school care along the lines of Boys Guilds modelled on St John Bosco's oratories.

By the end of 1935, the initial energy and enthusiasm of Guild members had not dissipated. The paid-up membership was 1,711 and the annual Guild Dinner was scheduled for 20 February 1936.[58] Ambitious plans were laid out for a series of four lectures on plain chant by Dom Desroquettes in February and March 1936: the cost was 6*d* per lecture or 2/ for the course. Work on a Children's Drama Festival, the revision of history texts and a list of suitable books for school libraries were going well. A new Study Circle on Salesian education was also planned.[59]

From the available evidence, the corporate life of the Guild made, it seems, a successful start in addressing the religious, cultural and social ambitions it had set out. From 1934–1936, the Guild gave platforms for the exposition of how Catholic education had to engage in serious discussion of wider socio-cultural issues in Scotland.

Religious Knowledge course books

From its early days, one of the stated objects of the Guild was to improve Religious Instruction in schools. This is explicitly outlined in the letter sent to all Catholic teachers in the Archdiocese of Glasgow inviting them to the inaugural Guild event in the City Hall.[60] In a letter of 24 October 1934, William Moore informed Archbishop MacDonald of St Andrews and Edinburgh that a relevant sub-committee had already been formed in the Archdiocese of Glasgow.[61] The general concern around Religious Instruction is explained further in the minutes of a Special Meeting between the Guild and the Archdiocese of Glasgow on 1 June 1939:

> The fact that most children who leave school at fourteen years of age had not had a sufficient grounding in their Religion was stressed. This was a serious position as most of them did not read Religious books nor attend instructions after leaving school.[62]

By the end of 1935, the Marist Brother, Germanus, had reported that a new religious syllabus for Infants was nearly ready and the schemes for junior and secondary pupils were making good progress.[63]

---

58 Ibid.
59 Ibid.
60 Mgr Daly's Letter to Catholic teachers in the Archdiocese of Glasgow, SCA /DE/171/144.
61 William Moore to Archbishop MacDonald, 24 October 1934, SCA /DE/171/144.
62 SCA/DE/126/4.
63 *Saturday Catholic Herald*, 28 December 1935.

A sense of professionalism was in evidence from the outset. The sub-committee sought to listen to the voices of the class teachers. This is not an example of the hierarchy and its lay appointees simply offering instructions to teachers but a much more nuanced and competent, indeed collegial, approach to reform.

Brother Germanus, who coordinated the work of the committee, gave an interim report in the first published *Proceedings* of the Guild, covering the period 1934–35.[64] This would be followed in due course with a full report to the archbishop. He reported that the committee had first met in October and November 1934 to organise a series of consultative meetings ('conferences') at the Catholic Institute for teachers from across the archdiocese.[65] The dates, type of school invited and the number of teachers in attendance at these meetings were as follows:

22 November 1934 Infant Departments 43
28 November 1934 Junior Departments 32
6 December 1934 Senior Departments 42
12 December 1934 Secondary/Central 56
17 December 1934 Special 32

Bro. Germanus' report explained the purpose of the meetings:

> The general purpose of these meetings was to hold a preliminary talk with the teachers concerned, to survey the ground covered by the work of their own department, to learn their difficulties, hear their observations and criticisms, to acquaint them with the leading ideas in our minds and, so far as the limited time allowed, to give a sketch of the work visualized for each section of the Schools.[66]

These words are a call to genuine dialogue. The committee not only wished to hear teachers' views but also to introduce them to new ideas in the field. How much room there was for curricular innovation is unclear, but each category of teacher was invited to respond with some practical suggestions for improvement. The report revealed some degree of independent thinking by the teachers. For example: to use the catechism a bit less and to have a greater variety of activities (Infants); formal use of the catechism should only begin in the Junior stage and scripture should be taught in parallel to catechism and doctrine, not as detached subjects (Junior); the difficulties in learning doctrine by heart are not to be exaggerated and material should be explained first before possible memorisation, as happens in other subjects (Senior); and Religious Instruction should prepare children for modern challenges and not the 'controversies

---

[64] *Guild of Catholic Teachers, Proceedings*, First Annual Issue, 1934–1935, 13–18, SCA/MB/11/9/2.
[65] Ibid., p. 13.
[66] Ibid., p. 14.

of bye-gone days' (Advanced Divisions and Secondary).[67] All of this was infused with the voice of the practitioner wishing to bring about meaningful change in the educational experience offered to the pupils. There were also comments about the unsatisfactory time allocation for Religious Instruction in all types of schools.[68]

Significantly, there was a level of disquiet about what the publication for the general public of the results of the religious examination carried out by the Diocesan Religious Inspector could do to the morale of teachers. The reports proposed 'that the present system of publishing the results of the Religious Examination be superseded by one more acceptable to teachers and not less effective'.[69] This is more evidence of a degree of teacher self-confidence in what is, essentially, a gentle rebuke to those who were responsible for the existing system, whereby the results of the Religious Examination were made public very quickly. Furthermore, there is the controversial suggestion that the Church's processes could learn from practice in other subjects.[70]

The report also had a request for a Manual of Religious Instruction 'giving the Syllabus for the various types of Schools, methods of instruction, helpful notes, lists of useful books, and other illustrative matters'.[71] This again suggests that the material already in use did not meet the teachers' expectations and that more practical support was necessary. The 'General Conclusion' included a revised syllabus and a threefold children's 'Charter of Grace', focusing on (i) 'Sacramental Life', (ii) 'Theory and Practice in Religious Instruction', and (iii) the 'Purpose of the Religious Syllabus'.[72] To address the issues raised by the teachers' responses, the report recommended the production of new Religious Knowledge textbooks. There are two examples of such textbooks available.[73]

The first textbook was written for infants.[74] We read in the foreword that the scheme had been trialled in a number of schools in the archdiocese prior to publication. Feedback from teachers had been sought and there had been some debate over the extent to which the Catechism had been used in the text. The Catechism has to be used judiciously as it would serve as the 'child's manual of Religion for ten years' and the

---

67 Ibid., pp. 14–15.
68 Ibid., p. 16.
69 Ibid., p. 16.
70 Ibid., p. 17.
71 Ibid., p. 17.
72 Ibid., pp. 17–18.
73 SCA/RE 4/5 and 4/6.
74 SCA/RE 4/5. The inside front cover has the following: 'Religious Knowledge A Course for Young Children drawn up by the Guild of Catholic Teacher Glasgow under the Patronage of St John Bosco.'

textbook in question sought only to 'amplify and illustrate it'.[75] Interestingly, the foreword did not claim that the content of the lessons was itself overly radical but rather that it was intended to exemplify a method which 'seeks to ease the task of the teacher, to stimulate the interest of the child and to gather into one the many activities that form a necessary part of religious education'.[76] The volume closed with a section headed 'Our Thanks and Our Hope' signed simply by 'The members of the Committee'.[77] The cautious approach adopted by the writing team recognised the important role of teachers in making the resource work in the classroom. The request for feedback again underlined the importance of collegiality and ongoing dialogue which the writing team had made a key plank of their approach.

In 1943, a new version of the textbook was produced entitled *An Abridged Course of Religious Knowledge for Children in Primary Schools*. This substantial volume of nearly 200 pages had material for all years of the primary school, but owing to the problems caused by the Second World War, including the shortage of paper, it was not as expansive as originally envisaged.[78] In the foreword, Archbishop Mackintosh thanked those who had undertaken this work at a difficult time. He underlined the important educational principle of gradation of knowledge and commended teachers to use the book 'to guide them, not only in the knowledge to be imparted but in the knowledge and method to be followed in their apostolic work'.[79]

Noteworthy in this edition is the chapter headed 'Religious Instruction: A Historical Sketch' which shows a clear understanding of broader international currents in religious pedagogy at that time. It referred to the Munich Method, and the work of individuals such as Rev. Dr Thomas Shields (America), Dr Maria Montessori (Italy) and Canon Francis Drinkwater (England). All three were theorists in Religious Education who had been influenced, to a greater or lesser extent, by new and scientifically more advanced methodological ideas. To what extent the work of Shields, Montessori and Drinkwater had been read as primary sources is a moot point. An article from 1929 in the educationally progressive American journal *Religious Education* had already identified the work of all three theorists and the Munich Method as examples of how up-to-date

---

[75] Ibid., p. 9.
[76] Ibid., p. 7.
[77] Ibid., p. 13.
[78] Archbishop Mackintosh, Foreword, *An Abridged Course of Religious Knowledge for Children in Primary Schools* (Glasgow, 1943), p. 4, SCA/ RE/ 4/6.
[79] Ibid., p. 5.

pedagogy would assist character formation in the Catholic school.[80] It is possible that the journal had acted as the conduit for the new ideas. Nonetheless, perusal of the some of the activities shows the influence of the 'Shields Method' in the style of language used and in the inclusion of prayers, stories and art, as had been requested in the results of the initial consultation with teachers.

In presenting this trio as examples of new thinking in educational methods, the committee showed an openness and intellectual flexibility which is surely not evidence of a subdued laity but, rather, of professionals with wide reading and an international vision In the mind of the authors, the 1943 textbook was an appropriate response to the educational principles sketched out in Pope Pius XI's encyclical. For the contemporary reader, it is convincing evidence of intellectual and practical 'action' by Catholics far from the more defensive mindset of the wider European Catholic Action movement.

Conclusion

The Guild exemplified a Catholicism that was increasingly keen to develop the mission of the lay teacher in the context of openness to new intellectual currents in Religious Education. It is a clear example of how the Catholic community in Scotland in the first half of the twentieth century drew on wider thinking in Catholic cultural life to create a professional association with clearly stipulated intellectual, social and religious aims. It successfully incorporated many layers of 'action' by Catholics but it would be an exaggeration to describe it as a concrete example in Scotland of Catholic Action as understood elsewhere. Its early years in particular show a sense of collegiality and intellectual openness which foreshadow the call in the Second Vatican Council for a renewed lay apostolate.[81]

Looking ahead, there is an urgent need to refresh and give vigour to the study of the history of Catholic education in Scotland since 1872. The formation of the Guild of Catholic Teachers, one of the highlights of Catholic education in Scotland after the First World War, should be central to this story.

---

[80] G. Johnson, 'Character Education in the Catholic Church', *Religious Education*, 24:1 (1929), pp. 54–7. The writer, Rev. Dr George Johnson, was a leading academic on Catholic education at the Catholic University of America. Rev. Dr Thomas Shields had been his doctoral supervisor.
[81] Second Vatican Council, *Lumen gentium: Dogmatic Constitution on the Church* (1964), https://www.vatican.va/archive/hist_councils/ii_vatican_council/documents/vat-ii_const_19641121_lumen-gentium_en.html, accessed 11 September 2023.

6

THE NEWMAN ASSOCIATION AND LAY CATHOLIC SUPPORT FOR EXILED POLISH INTELLECTUALS IN BRITAIN, 1942–1962[1]

Jonathan Bush

> The test of our sincerity in the cause of justice is our concern for the resurrection of Poland, no less, nay, even more, than the liberation of every other persecuted people.[2]

This quotation, taken from a radio broadcast delivered on Sunday 13 September 1941 by Cardinal Arthur Hinsley, Archbishop of Westminster, is a reminder of the important and enduring relationship between the Catholic Church in Britain and the Central European state of Poland. It was spoken in the context of the Second World War and the continuing devastation caused by the German occupation of the country that had begun two years previously, but it remained applicable to the Catholic Church's attitude in the period following that war, when the inhabitants of Central and Eastern Europe fell under the control of Soviet-influenced communist governments. Poles, along with Czechs, Slovaks, Hungarians, Latvians and Lithuanians, fled their homelands to escape from religious persecution, arriving in Britain in their thousands during the late 1940s and 1950s. Many lay Catholic associations, independent from hierarchical control, took it upon themselves to organise initiatives and raise funds for these exiles. This article will examine the role played by one such lay society, the Newman Association, in supporting the tertiary education of Polish exiles in Britain in the Second World War and its aftermath. It will show how the Newman Association worked closely with other Catholic and non-Catholic bodies to create an international centre for the dissemination of information to Polish and other

---

[1] This is a shortened version of an article originally published in the *Downside Review*, 135:4 (2017), pp. 199–222. I am grateful to the Newman Association for supporting me with a generous stipend to research and write this article. I am also grateful to Dr James Kelly, Judith Smeaton and Christine Newman for their comments and suggestions on earlier drafts.

[2] *The Tablet*, 20 September 1941.

Central and East European exiles; to raise money for grants to support Polish students at British and Polish universities; and to arrange cultural exchange programmes between British and Polish intellectuals. Research of this nature provides a case study into how the influx of Polish exiles provided a golden opportunity for an increasingly confident and educated Catholic middle class to assert itself in the Catholic Church in the years immediately prior to the Second Vatican Council.[3]

Despite the vast historiography on the Cold War, Catholic aid to political exiles has generally received little attention. Historians of the Catholic Church have tended to concentrate on the relationship between the Church and Eastern Europe at a political or diplomatic level.[4] Similarly, not one of the many studies by historians of post-war Polish migration to England refers to British Catholic support for Polish exiles.[5] Relatively few published accounts have been written on the work of lay Catholic organisations with persecuted exiles from Central and Eastern European countries, with perhaps the only exception being the work of the Catholic Women's League in Polish displacement camps.[6] The ecumenical work of the Sword of the Spirit and its political involvement in anti-communism has received more attention but this organisation was primarily clerical-led.[7] Recent research on the post-war lay Catholic apostolate also tends to be written from the perspective of the individual spiritual experience which has not included the communal and joint lay politico-theological activism inherent in the work of lay societies.[8] This article will build upon this slim body of work, by highlighting how the Newman Association represented the ambitious vision of Catholic lay societies prior to the Second Vatican Council, thereby transcending the perceived parochial and

---

[3] The increased involvement of lay Catholics in the Church was one of the key achievements of the Second Vatican Council. For its effects, see Alana Harris, *Faith in the Family: A Lived Religious History of English Catholicism, 1945–82* (Manchester, 2013).
[4] See Hansjakob Stehle, *Eastern Politics of the Vatican*, translated by Sandra Smith (Athens, OH, 1981); Jonathan Luxmore and Jolanta Babiuch, *The Vatican and the Red Flag: The Struggle for the Soul of Eastern Europe* (London and New York, 1999).
[5] Sheila Patterson, 'The Polish Exiled Community in Great Britain', *The Polish Review*, 61:3 (1961), pp. 69–97; Jerzy Zubrzycki, *Polish Immigrants in Britain: A Study of Adjustment* (Michigan, 1956); Thomas Lane, *Victims of Stalin and Hitler: The Exodus of Poles and Balts to Britain* (London, 2004); K. Sword, N. Davies and J. Ciechanowski, *The Formation of the Polish Community in Great Britain, 1939–50* (London, 1989); B. J. M. McCook, 'Education in War and Exile: The Polish Experience in Britain, 1940–1954', in *East Central Europe in Exile, Volume 2: Transatlantic Migrations*, edited by Anna Mazurkiewicz (Newcastle, 2013), pp. 291–310.
[6] Catholic Women's League, *History of the Catholic Women's League Relief and Refugee Committee* ([London?], 1981).
[7] James Hagerty, *Cardinal Hinsley: Priest and Patriot* (Oxford, 2008), pp. 303–22; Michael J. Walsh, *From Sword to Ploughshare: Sword of the Spirit to Catholic Institute for International Relations, 1940–1980* (London, 1980).
[8] See Harris, *Faith in the Family*.

inward-looking nature of such societies. The Newman Association was clearly not the only organisation concerned with the plight of post-war exiles but its largely professional and middle-class membership, and the contacts it could and did establish with the higher echelons of British and European institutions, gave it an advantage when dealing with the spiritual and material needs of the educated Polish exile in the post-war world.

The very foundation of the Newman Association in 1942 was an expression of the growing confidence of the lay Catholic middle class during the middle decades of the twentieth century.[9] The organisation was established as a graduate society for both laity and clergy, developing out of a student organisation, the University Catholic Societies Federation. It was heavily influenced by John Henry Newman's concept of an educated laity and its active involvement in the Catholic Church and the wider society.[10] Indeed its main object, as set out in the memorandum of association, was 'to further the mission to the world of the Christian religion with particular reference to the Roman Catholic Church and in the light of the life and work of John Henry Newman, by promoting greater understanding of the Christian faith and the application of its principles to the contemporary world'.[11] From its inception, therefore, the Association wished to foster a deeper understanding of the Catholic faith within the context of the contemporary world, actively encouraging its members to use their skills and knowledge to tackle the theological, social, political and cultural questions of the day from a Catholic perspective. It was the purpose of the Association to utilise lay members of the Catholic Church in this mission and to seek 'to bring greater recognition of the role of lay Catholics both as apostles to the church and as an important voice within the church for greater democracy and accountability'.[12] In 1950, the Newman Association boasted a membership of 1,500 Catholic graduates 'drawn from various professions and walks of life'.[13] As well as a National

---

[9] Hornsby-Smith has noted that Catholics after 1945 were generally 'more upwardly socially mobile than the general population' and were influential at parish level and on various diocesan commissions at the national level. Michael P. Hornsby-Smith, Catholic Education: The Unobtrusive Partner: Sociological Studies of the Catholic School System in England and Wales (London, 1978), p. 87. On the rise of the Catholic middle class, see James Pereiro, 'Who are the laity?', in From Without the Flaminian Gate, edited by V. A. McClelland and M. Hodgetts (London, 1999), pp. 177–8.
[10] John Henry Newman's treatises on this subject were published in The Idea of a University (London, 1852).
[11] Memoranda of Association (1947), Company Registration Papers, D1/A/1, Newman Association Archive, Ushaw College Library.
[12] Clifford Williamson, The History of Catholic Intellectual Life in Scotland, 1918–1965 (London, 2016), pp. 145–6.
[13] H. O. Evennett, 'Catholics and the Universities', in The English Catholics, 1850–1950: Essays to Commemorate the Centenary of the Restoration of the Hierarchy of England and Wales, edited by George A. Beck (London, 1950), p. 320.

Council, it also formed auxiliaries, known as Newman Circles, in most of the major British cities, which were responsible for organising events at the local level. Unlike the Catholic Union, the Newman Association was not under the direct control of the Catholic hierarchy, seeing itself more as 'a partner, if only a junior partner'.[14]

Context

The Newman Association's aid to Polish exiles was affected by a range of social, theological and political factors which influenced Catholic lay activism towards European exiles generally. Firstly, support for migrants was deeply rooted within Catholic social teaching, based around the idea of the common good, in which the social conditions necessary for the 'participation and full development of human beings (including newcomers) need to be provided'.[15] The post-war settlement of 1945, and the advent of the Cold War, brought a fresh set of problems for the Church in dealing with migrants, or more accurately exiles, fleeing to England from religious persecution in the communist-controlled countries of Central and Eastern Europe.[16] Secondly, the Newman Association's lay Catholic and middle-class base would have felt an obvious connection with the largely professional Polish Catholic exile community arriving in Britain. Between 1945 and 1949, a total of 100,875 aliens were admitted for residence as EVWs (European Voluntary Workers), of whom 29,400 were Poles (the next largest group was Latvians, with 13,793).[17] The Polish influx included a substantial number of migrants from the middle and professional classes, such as civil servants, lawyers, teachers, doctors and engineers. Of all the Central and Eastern European nations, Poland had retained the strongest devotion to the Catholic faith. This was not only reflected in the numbers – Poland had the highest percentage of Catholics (95%) – but also in the way in which its national traditions had become inseparable from the Catholic religion.[18] It is little wonder therefore, that the Newman Association, along with other Catholic lay societies with a largely Catholic middle-class and professional base,

---

14   Williamson, *Intellectual Life in Scotland*, p. 146.
15   Donald Kirwin and Jill Marie Gerschutz (eds.), *And You Welcomed Me: Migration and Catholic Social Teaching* (Lanham, MD, 2009), p. x.
16   The word 'exile' will be used throughout this article rather than 'refugee' or 'migrant'. It was felt this more accurately reflects the experience of those exiles who fled religious persecution. The exception are those Hungarians who arrived in Britain following the Hungarian Uprising in November 1956, who are referred to as 'refugees'. This reflects the terms used in the contemporary sources.
17   Zubrzycki, *Polish Immigrants in Britain*, p. 60.
18   Ibid., p. 122.

prioritised the provision of financial, educational, social and spiritual support of the Polish exiles in Britain.

Support for Polish exiles should also be seen within the broader context of the Catholic Church's historic distrust of communism and the rising influence of European federalism on Christian thought. The Vatican had been warning of the dangers of communism since the early nineteenth century[19] but it was the post-war settlement, in which Stalin's Soviet Union swallowed up 10 million Catholics in Eastern Poland alone while new regimes were being installed in Central and Eastern European countries under pressure from the Soviet government, that brought home the reality of the situation to the Catholic Church.[20] Certainly, anti-communism would have been a factor in the willingness of lay societies to assist Central and Eastern European exiles. For the Newman Association in particular, it was only by means of education about the communist system and the Soviet Union, through its lectures and conferences, as well as providing support for their education, that communism could be combatted in the long term. This coincided with the rising influence of European federalism on post-war international relations. A myriad of associations were established in an attempt to achieve the dream of greater European cooperation, including the United Europe Movement in Britain organised by Winston Churchill; the Catholic Nouvelles Équipes Internationales and the Socialist Movement for the United States of Europe in France; and the Europa-Band in Germany.[21] The Newman Association was clearly an active supporter of these developments. It was noted in a history of the International Committee that 'a deep and growing interest in the movements to develop a greater degree of economic and political unity within the Continent' and its contribution towards 'both the universal Church and the world', were of particular interest to many members of the Association.[22] The Christian dimension of European idealism was elaborated further in another Newman Association pamphlet, in which it was argued that Catholic tradition had essentially developed the idea of a 'natural society of nations' that heavily influenced the organisation of international society in the wider world thus making the ideological conditions for European integration possible in the first place.[23]

From the very outset of the formation of the Newman Association, international events were high on the agenda. Indeed, the history of the

---

[19] Luxmoore and Babiuch, *Vatican and the Red Flag*, p. xiii.
[20] Ibid., p. 52.
[21] Derek W. Unwin, *The Community of Europe* (London, 1991), p. 27.
[22] Francis Aylward, *Fifteen Years of International Co-operation: A Survey of the Work of the International Committee of the Newman Association of Great Britain, 1942–1957* (London, 1957), p. 24.
[23] John Eppstein, *Christian Tradition in International Relations* (1944), p. 9.

Newman Association began with a meeting of an 'International Committee' on 5 October 1941, formalised a year later in the drawing up of a constitution for the organisation.[24] In February 1943, the Association responded to a request by the Government to set up 'a body of voluntary organisations interested in material and moral relief in post-war Europe'.[25] It was not until after the war that a more formal policy towards Polish exiles was instigated, however. In November 1945, Frank Aylward, the chairman and secretary of the Association's International Committee, together with the MP for Birmingham Moseley, Sir Patrick Hannon, met with a delegation from the Polish Catholic Graduate Group formed at the recent Pax Romana Congress. At this meeting, it was agreed that the International Committee would provide English-language classes for the benefit of those Poles arriving in England who had recently been liberated from concentration camps in Europe. The International Committee also expressed an interest in establishing an academic assistance committee to provide financial assistance to seminary and university students.[26] Almost from its very inception, therefore, the work of the Newman Association was tied to the fate of the Catholics of Central and Eastern Europe.

The Newman Association was just one of several organisations, lay Catholic and non-Catholic, whose aim was to assist in post-war European reconstruction. Rather than remain isolated working within their own spheres, such organisations soon realised that collaboration was essential to achieve their aims. The Newman Association, with its influential backing and professional contacts, was often in the vanguard of initiatives in this regard, receiving the support of the hierarchy.[27] For example, it worked closely with the Anglo-Polish Catholic Society and the Catholic Council for Polish Welfare in matters affecting Polish relief. It was noted in the published history of the International Committee that 'there has always been a close relationship both with organisations representing the exiles in Britain and with the priests concerned in them'.[28] The Association was also represented on governmental boards. For example, three International Committee members, Dr Helen Chow, Mr Murphy (also a senior official in the Ministry of Labour) and Miss Morath, sat on the Central European Affairs Committee and together they drew up a memorandum on the issue of Polish and other European exile.[29]

---

[24] Newman International Committee Minutes, 6 November 1941, D1/E/1/1, Newman Association Archive. Ushaw College Library; Newman Association, *A Use of Gifts: The Newman Association, 1942–1992* (London, 1992), p. 18.
[25] Newman International Committee Minutes, 2 February 1943.
[26] Ibid., 3 November 1945.
[27] Aylward, *Fifteen Years of International Co-operation*, p. 14.
[28] Ibid., p. 14.
[29] Newman International Committee Minutes, 15 January 1949.

Newman International Centre

It was an undoubtedly lay Catholic initiative, the opening of a 'Newman Centre' by the Newman Association, which provided a focal point of support for exiled Central and Eastern Europeans. Acting as an international hub for overseas Catholic visitors, the Centre at 23 Hereford House, Park Street, London, was given to the Association by a generous benefactor. It was opened on 3 October 1942 by David Mathew, Auxiliary Bishop of Westminster, and the Hon. Anthony J. Drexel Biddle, the United States Ambassador to the Allied Governments in Exile, with an audience of over 200 people from ten different countries.[30] The Centre quickly established itself as the cultural nucleus of the Polish exiled community. Through its hospitality service, it initially played an important role in introducing Catholics from abroad, including allied servicemen during their periods of leave as well as civilians, to British families, aiming 'to provide a place which men and women from Europe and overseas could regard as "home", to meet one another and form enduring friendships'. It is important to point out that events were not only held for Central European countries, but also for groups and individuals from elsewhere, including receptions for parties from France, Germany, the United States and India, with other receptions arranged for delegates of conferences on all sorts of Catholic and non-Catholic topics, such as the Conference of Lawyers and the International Catholic Radio Movement.[31] In this sense, the Newman Centre reached out to Catholics and non-Catholics far beyond its initial remit and helped to establish the Centre's 'place in the intellectual life of London'. During the 1950s, the Association's international events were even included in 'Today's Arrangements' in *The Times*,[32] and by 1957 it could claim that its Centre had 'become known over the past ten years to members of Pax Romana in more than 40 countries, and hundreds of visitors have called each year in search of information, advice and introductions'.[33]

An important cultural activity at the Centre was organising international lecture-discussion meetings, with the main meeting taking place on the first Sunday of each month after Mass. There were also regular weekly meetings to hear a range of respected international speakers lecturing on a variety of topics, as well as monthly 'parliamentary evening' meetings. From these meetings, the audience 'learned of the conditions of life and of Christianity abroad and obtained first-hand accounts of different parts of the British Commonwealth and the Colonial Empire, of the

---

[30] Aylward, *Fifteen Years of International Co-operation*, p. 5.
[31] Ibid., p. 11.
[32] Ibid., p. 11.
[33] Ibid., p. 10.

United States, South America and Asia, as well as of the Continent of Europe'.[34] Central and Eastern Europe began to receive greater attention at many meetings following the Yalta Conference in February 1945, in which 'members were left in no uncertainty ... of the evils to come'.[35] Talks were given on a variety of international topics but lectures on the situation in Central and Eastern Europe remained a popular choice throughout the late 1940s and 1950s. In 1954, for example, a lecture by Dr W. Czerinski of Poland entitled 'Central and Eastern Europe' was delivered in the Newman Centre.[36] There were some notable speakers on the Catholic Church in Poland. Count Balinski Jundzill, who was director of the Polish Institute of Catholic Action in Britain and a Knight of the Holy Sepulchre, 'spoke eloquently' on the subject at Portman Square and was willing to repeat his address to local circles [37]

The Newman Centre also hosted major international conferences on similar themes, many of which proved to be extremely popular. In 1952, a week-long conference was arranged on 'Catholics in Central and Eastern Europe', with speakers from eight different countries. This included lectures by the Polish prelate, Canon Stanislaus Belch, on the persecution of the Church in Eastern Bloc countries (entitled 'The Silent Church'), and on the exiles themselves ('The Exiles in Great Britain'). In the second session, Canon Belch gave a general account of the problems and difficulties faced by the 200,000 Catholic exiles in England, Scotland and Wales, reading reports collected from various exile groups on the work of their organisations. Commenting on this session, the Newman Association *Annual Report* hoped that an account of their situation could be published, 'which is all too little appreciated by many of us'. Two years later, 'The Silent Church' was the title of another conference organised jointly by the Newman Association and the Union of Catholic Students, under the auspices of the University Catholic Federation. It was, as the Association's *Annual Report* described, 'an occasion for the renewal of old friendships and making of news ones among the exiles group in London'. The conference, which was mentioned in the minutes as 'successful and well attended', ended with a 'much enjoyed concert', in which Polish, Hungarian and Byelorussians sang or played music of their own countries.[38]

These conferences at Portman Square were supported by similar themed events at the Newman Association's Summer Schools. The lecture

---

34 Ibid., p. 6.
35 Ibid., p. 6.
36 Newman Association, *Annual Report*, 1954/5, p. 10.
37 *The Newman*, December 1955.
38 Newman Association, *Annual Report*, 1954/5, p. 2; Newman International Committee Minutes, 20 March 1954.

programme of the Festival of Britain Ampleforth Summer School, for example, included 'The Transition from Socialism' by Professor Michael Fogerty, economist, official fellow of Nuffield College, and author of articles and books on industrial organisation and social planning. Similarly, the July 1952 Summer School at Oriel College, Oxford, organised by the Newman Association, featured lectures on 'Modern Europe' and 'International Communism' by Sir Desmond Morton, as well as 'Europe in the Making' by Christopher Dawson. The syllabus for Session 9 included 'The Soviet in Central Europe', with the intention of investigating the 'character of the agricultural communities, their peasant and Catholic character, their political background before today', as well as 'What has happened and is happening to them and what the West is trying to do, and what can be done'.[39]

An essential element of life at the Newman Centre was its social aspect for exiles from different countries. In 1955, the 'At Home' aspect of the Sunday afternoon meetings was expanded 'in order to give Newman members and visitors from abroad the opportunity to meet one another'. This included the hosting of three large receptions during the year for nationals of Central and Eastern European countries, as well as students and graduates from Africa and Asia. At one reception, the Apostolic Delegate was present.[40] As Thomas Lane has argued, such events allowed Poles to feel integrated into the émigré community, thus inhibiting the possibility of developing mental illnesses, such as depression, schizophrenia or hysteria. Polish exiles were far more likely than British nationals to suffer from such illness. For example, the rate of admissions to mental hospitals for all categories of Polish exiles between 1946 and 1950 was 4.42 per thousand males, in stark contrast to the 0.86 of British-born admissions.[41]

Although the Newman Association was aimed at and organised by lay members of the Catholic Church, and thereby free from the direct control of the Catholic hierarchy, patronage was still sought by the Newman Association's International Committee when organising events. As early as 1944, Archbishop (later Cardinal) Griffin visited the Centre within a short time of his appointment and encouraged others to take an interest in its work.[42] The Apostolic Delegate, Archbishop Godfrey, who visited the Centre in 1949, was described as a 'real friend to the Association' and willing to give advice when needed.[43] Following Godfrey's

---

[39] Papers of the Newman Association Summer Schools, D1/H/1, Newman Association Archive, Ushaw College Library.
[40] Newman Association, *Annual Report*, 1954/5, p. 10, p. 16.
[41] Lane, *Victims of Stalin and Hitler*, p. 222.
[42] Aylward, *Fifteen Years of International Co-operation*, p. 6.
[43] Newman Association, *Annual Report*, 1954/5, p. 10.

translation to the archbishopric of Westminster in 1954, members of the Association were delighted to hear of the assurances of his successor, Archbishop G. P O'Hara, at his first visit to the Newman Centre on 18 September. At this visit, the archbishop spoke of his willingness to give the same support as his predecessor towards the international activities of the Newman Association.[44] Indeed, he was instrumental in helping to organise a special reception for exiles from Poland and other Eastern European countries on 14 July 1956. This patronage continued into the late 1950s. On 13 April 1958, for example, a small party was arranged by the International Committee at the Newman Centre, to welcome Mgr Marian Rechowicz, the rector of the Catholic University of Lublin in Poland, with Bishop Craven, Auxiliary Bishop of Westminster, greeting him.[45] For their part, the hierarchy were more than willing to patronise an organisation which accorded with the foreign policy of the Catholic Church generally.

Despite unwavering support from the hierarchy, in its early years the financing of the Centre remained a constant problem for the Newman Association's International Committee. On 8 May 1946, Hereford House was forced to close because the Committee could not afford to keep it open. It was not until December 1948 that a new building, 31 Portman Square in London, was officially opened by Cardinal Griffin.[46] To avoid the financial issues which had beset its previous home, a charitable trust, the Newman International Foundation, was established on 8 April 1946, 'to support the international programme of the Association and to acquire and administer an International Centre'. Subscriptions were sought from members, who were urged to contribute an additional sum of money annually to the International Foundation on top of their Newman membership subscription.[47] This was fully supported by the hierarchy, with the Cardinal promising £1 000 a year for two years for the maintenance of an international office and a further £1,000 a year for several years for the support of the proposed new International Centre.[48] Funds were also sought from a number of charitable trusts including the Carnegie Foundation and the Commonwealth Fund. It was also hoped that Catholics from the staff of working embassies could be persuaded to join to 'strengthen the international atmosphere of the Centre'.[49] Regular collections were taken from churches in support of the International Centre. For example, on European Unity Sunday in January 1950, parish priests were asked

---

44 Ibid., p. 15.
45 *The Newman*, May 1958.
46 Aylward, *Fifteen Years of International Co-operation*, p. 9.
47 Newman International Foundation Minutes, 14 June 1946.
48 Ibid., 14 September 1946.
49 Ibid., 7 December 1947.

to preach on the work of the Newman International Committee and to take a special collection.⁵⁰ This allowed the Newman International Centre the financial stability to establish itself on a firmer footing, with the Newman International Fund trustees recording an annual turnover of £12,000 in 1952.⁵¹

The concentration of the Newman International Committee's activities towards Polish exiles in London reflected the large numbers of Polish exiles residing in the capital (33,000), but there were also significant numbers in other counties, notably Lancashire (14,500), the West Riding of Yorkshire (13,500), and Staffordshire (5,500).⁵² The International Committee did try to assist the local circles in arranging lectures and conferences on international topics by recommending suitable speakers from Britain and abroad.⁵³ When the Newman Association established its Exiles Group on a more formal basis in 1955, it was suggested that the Group should be extended throughout the country and that Veritas – the Polish University Catholic Association – could supply names of the members in local circles who would be willing to assist with this action.⁵⁴ By the late 1950s, however, it was clear that the Association had not been altogether successful in this regard. In the Association's *Annual Report* of 1957/8, it was noted that the high level of its international lecture programme could only be maintained if the local circles in different parts of the UK would share the burden of the work.⁵⁵ Naturally, the London Circle, with its close ties to the national committee and with the largest Polish exile population as a potential audience, benefitted most. Lectures and conferences on Poland, Russia and communism seemed to be a regular fixture of the programme. The records for other circles are patchy for this period and those that do survive barely mention the subject of Central and Eastern Europe as part of their activities, concentrating instead on theological issues. One of the few to record a lecture on the subject was the Swansea Circle. It reported on 5 November 1957 that Fr Eugene Boylan, priest of Caldey, addressed a record audience of 120 people on 'Communism', somewhat controversially advocating the unification of Christianity to save Christendom from the threat of communism.⁵⁶

---

50   Ibid., 19 January 1950.
51   See, for example, ibid., 7 July 1950.
52   Lane, *Victims of Stalin and Hitler*, p. 205.
53   Aylward, *Fifteen Years of International Co-operation*, p. 12.
54   Newman International Committee Minutes, 6 February 1955.
55   Newman Association, *Annual Report*, 1957/8, p. 5.
56   Swansea Circle Minute Book, 5 November 1957, D1/F/2/28/1, Newman Association Archive, Ushaw College Library.

Newman scholarships

As well as providing a cultural hub for the Polish Catholic intellectual community, the Newman Association assisted those students unable to take their degrees in their home country because of the suppression of Polish universities by the communist government. In 1946, the Association decided to set up a programme to help fund scholarships for undergraduate and postgraduate students to undertake a course at a British university, as well as aiding Polish graduates seeking employment in Britain. A grant had already been offered to an unnamed Polish airman to study at Oriel College, Oxford, in 1943 but it was becoming increasingly clear that a more formalised arrangement was required. To fund the venture, an additional charitable fund, the Newman Educational Foundation, was established with Professor A. J. Allmand elected as chairman and Peter Kerr, the Twelfth Marquess of Lothian, as Treasurer.[57] This fund was active until 1949, when its functions were absorbed into the Newman International Foundation.[58] The aim of the Educational Foundation was twofold: firstly, to enable the exiles to preserve the continuity of their Christian culture' and, secondly, 'to enable them to make some useful contribution to their own countries when they returned and to the countries of their adoption while they were in exile'.[59] The Association's stance could thus be viewed as an attempt to bolster the defence of Christianity against the communist persecution of religion in the Soviet satellite states. Through this work of educational assistance, the Association was required to collaborate with Veritas who set up a committee of four Polish professors to deal with the scholarship applications.[60] Lord Lothian agreed to send a letter to the Catholic newspapers, as well as *The Times*, *Telegraph*, *Spectator* and *New Statesman*, and to notify the Catholic hierarchy, publicising the initiative.[61]

The educational assistance programme faced notable difficulties from the outset in post-war Britain. British universities were overcrowded, and Central and Eastern European exiles were required to compete for university places with British servicemen returning from overseas.[62] The first task of the Association was therefore to work with influential figures within the universities to allocate places for Polish exiles. Initial

---

[57] Professor Allmand received a papal knighthood in 1950 for his role in the Newman Educational Foundation. See his obituary in *The Times*, 18 August 1951.
[58] Aylward, *Fifteen Years of International Co-operation*, p. 16.
[59] Newman Educational Foundation, Minutes, 25 March 1946, D1/B/3/3, Newman Association Archive, Ushaw College Library.
[60] Ibid., 25 March 1946.
[61] Ibid., 5 July 1946. For example, notification of the aims of the Newman Educational Foundation was published in *The Times*, 16 August 1946.
[62] Sword et al., *Formation of the Polish Community*, p. 278.

arrangements were made with Irish institutions, perhaps from the belief that they were more likely to be sympathetic towards creating places for Catholic students, but by the late 1940s the Newman Educational Foundation had turned its attention to English universities. In October 1948, two research students were being helped at the University of London with money available for a further student. One of these was a student researching the history of marriage, and the other was the chairman of Veritas, Professor Paul Skwarczyński.[63] Many of the exiles receiving aid to study in England were often in a precarious financial situation, particularly once the Educational Foundation was subsumed into the International Foundation and funds began to dry up. Between 1950 and 1952, the minutes of the Newman International Fund meetings regularly noted the difficulties faced by Polish beneficiaries and extra money was often allocated to relieve their financial difficulties. At one stage, even the Apostolic Delegate was contacted to help fund their fees and expenses.[64] Even following graduation, the difficulties continued. In February 1953, for example, the Association contacted the Catholic Professors of Law in an attempt to find Prof. Skwarczyński an academic post in England 'so that he might be led away from accepting an offer which he has received of a well-paid appointment in Abyssinia', resulting in the loss of his services to Veritas. Recent events in Poland and the death of his mother had upset him and, in his desperation, he was willing to accept a £5 a week job as a clerk which, Dr Aylward argued, could affect his academic job prospects.[65] It was agreed to offer Prof. Skwarczyński £25 immediately from a donation of a Yorkshire friend of the Association.[66]

By the early 1950s, however, these endeavours were beginning to bear fruit. The Newman Association's *Annual Report* confidently proclaimed a number of successes. The trustees noted that, with the exception of the Catholic Council of Polish Welfare, 'no Catholic organisation in Britain has done so much to assist the Poles' with the scholarship programme.[67] Although the work was not continuing at the same rate as in the early years, the report noted that 'many Polish and other students who have received aid in the past have now obtained their first or final degrees at the University of London or elsewhere, one postgraduate student, who was ordained a priest in the United States in June last, is preparing

---

[63] Newman Educational Foundation Minutes, 11 October 1947.
[64] Newman International Foundation Minutes, 25 September 1950, 2 January 1951.
[65] Professor Skwarczyński's difficulties in finding employment were symptomatic of the wider situation for skilled Polish refugees, with only a third having jobs corresponding to their skills between 1947 and 1950. Lane, *Victims of Stalin and Hitler*, p. 200.
[66] Newman International Foundation Minutes, 5 February 1953.
[67] Ibid., 19 January 1950.

for missionary work. The second has just recently been appointed to a professorship of Law.'[68]

Exchange visits

By the late 1950s and early 1960s, the political situation in Eastern Europe was beginning to improve slowly and the Newman Association became more involved with facilitating tours to and from Poland. A three-week study tour of Britain, for example, was arranged by the International Committee for a group of Polish visitors from professional circles. This was organised by Dr F. Sawicki, a Catholic physician from Warsaw, who invited the Klub Intelligencji Katolickiej (Warsaw Club of Catholic Intellectuals) to England. This club was one of a limited number of organisations established to provide a 'discreet outlet for non-Marxist intellectuals in major Polish cities', following the appointment of Wladyslaw Gomulka as the communist leader of Poland in October 1956.[69] These Polish intellectual groups and other media organisations proved vital for providing the Association with information on the religious situation, as the International Committee was keen to recognise:

> It was from Jacek Wozniakowski, Jerzy Turowicz and others connected with the independent Catholic press, re-established after October 1956, that we learned most about the position and needs of Catholics in Poland today. Without the possibility of other organised groups and societies responsibility lies heavily upon them, upon the small group of independent Catholic deputies in the Sejm, and upon the Klubs which now exist in five major cities.

The group arrived on 28 April 1960, meeting various representatives of the Polish community in London, including Mgr Staniazewksi, the Polish Vicar General, and Count Jan Bellinski-Jundzill, secretary of the Catholic Council for Polish Welfare and Chairman of Polish Catholic Action, as well as Canon Stanislaus Belch, the first Veritas chaplain. They were also entertained by Newman members in London, Oxford, Birmingham, Manchester, York, Cambridge and other places.[70] The tour of the provincial areas was particularly appreciated by the Polish visitors who noted the similarities in local customs:

> It was most interesting for us to note that some of these are, in spite of all differences, the same as those we meet in Poland ... Differences between different countries are not as essential as they look, we are all at a more or less advanced stage of the same process of renewal, and the growing awareness of this basic unity and universalism of world Catholicism is surely among the most important and most significant developments of today ...

---

68 Newman Association, *Annual Report*, 1952/3, p. 12.
69 Luxmore and Babioch, *Vatican and the Red Flag*, pp. 79–80.
70 Newman International Committee Minutes, 20 January 1960.

The English Catholic community was far from united in support of this visit. A report in the *Catholic Herald* questioned the Newman Association's part in allowing 'Communist collaborators' into the country. The International Committee's response was to 'damp down any correspondence that may take place in the paper', publishing a supportive article in *The Newman* to allay any fears of the provincial circles.[71] Following the visit, a hope was expressed for a return trip to Poland and this did indeed occur the following year. In an article entitled 'Lublin: so near and yet so far' Dr J. M. Capes described a visit by two Newman delegates to Lublin between 5 and 25 August 1961, as guests of the Klub Intelligencji Katolickiej. The purpose of the visit was 'to attend a seminar organised by the Club, on 'European Tradition and the Future', to see something of Polish life and culture, and to consider some of the problems facing Polish Catholics today'.[72] The Newman Association's *Annual Report* the following year noted how overseas contacts had been maintained by arranging receptions for overseas visitors, including a group of Polish newspaper editors.[73]

The Newman Association also began to develop a strategy to assist students in the Catholic University of Lublin by providing grants to study in England. Mrs Greene,[74] the Honorary Secretary of the Oxford Newman Circle, contacted the International Committee to ask if they could accommodate Professor Mroczkowski, head of the Department of English at the Catholic University of Lublin, who hoped to visit Britain and assist in this matter. Professor Mroczkowski was given a grant by the British Council to visit Britain and attend a meeting with the Chairman of the International Committee. At this meeting, it was agreed that two one-year scholarships could be offered at Oxford University for postgraduate research assistants from Lublin (one man and one woman). A donation of £50 had been offered for this purpose.[75] The two Lublin scholars, Miss Janicka and Mr Swieczkowski, arrived in England in February 1957, with Miss Janicka's fees and expenses being paid jointly by the Catholic Women's League and the Newman International Fund.[76] The following month, it was agreed to contact the Oxford Newman Circle to arrange hospitality for the visiting scholars.[77] Further links were cemented by the Association's agreement with the Rector of Lublin University to provide

---

[71] Ibid., 25 May 1960.
[72] Ibid., 26 April 1961.
[73] Newman Association, *Annual Report*, 1962/3, p. 6.
[74] Wife of the English novelist, Graham Greene. Newman International Committee Minutes, 6 February 1956.
[75] Ibid., 19 November 1956.
[76] Ibid., 4 February 1957.
[77] Ibid., 4 March 1957.

a one-year lectureship in Lublin for a Polish scholar living in England.[78] By the end of 1958, however, the Association seemed to be handing over the financial management of the Polish students to Veritas, who agreed to accept financial responsibility for four students of Lublin University: Dr Ludomir Bienkowski, Mr Euegeniusz Zwolski, Mr Ryszard Bender and Mr Czeslaw Deptula. The Newman Association was only responsible for ensuring that the students were given official letters of introduction to allow them to obtain Polish passports and British visas.[79]

Material support

The Newman Association's support for the education of Polish students was also supplemented by material aid in the purchase of books and other equipment. This had been taking place since the 1940s. In May 1946, the chaplain of Veritas, Fr Belch, required the Newman Association to act as an agent in the forwarding of translated religious books and papal encyclicals to Poland. Veritas had been unable to send the books themselves owing to difficulties with the Polish authorities, but the Newman Association was able to negotiate with the Polish Red Cross for the delivery of regular batches to the Caritas organisation in Gdynia. Polish subscriptions paid for the purchase and transport of the books so the Newman International Committee was not required to make any financial contribution.[80] In November, Miss Gunter was able to report that the plan had been working successfully with a total of £12,000 worth of books being sent from London to Gdynia, with Caritas distributing these books throughout Poland.[81] Aside from books, the Association also agreed to send food parcels to the relations of Polish exiles so that the recipients could send these parcels on to others.[82] Larger gifts were also offered, including a private automatic telephone exchange for the use of Archbishop's House in Warsaw.[83]

Despite the difficulties in raising money for educational assistance towards Lublin scholars, the Newman Association was keen to continue its links with the university through the provision of material gifts. In 1956, money was being collected to provide books for the University but

---

[78] Ibid., 28 April 1958.
[79] Report of the Honorary Secretary of the Newman International Committee, 8 September 1958.
[80] Ibid., 5 May 1946.
[81] Ibid., 2 November 1946.
[82] Ibid., 15 February 1953.
[83] Letter from Cardinal Wyszinski to the Newman Association, quoted in Newman International Committee Minutes, 5 May 1962.

by 1960 the Association was willing to send more substantial gifts.[84] In a letter from Lawrence Roche, trustee for the Newman Association, to Rt Rev. Mgr M. Rechowicz, rector of the Catholic University of Lublin, a decision was made to offer the university machinery for a canteen, including a dishwashing machine, potato peelers, mincing machines, bread-cutting machines, meat-slicing machines, a kitchen thermos, butter-pat machines, and a service counter.[85] In the Soviet satellite states these items would have been impossible to buy domestically and, initially at least, the Association faced great difficulty in even obtaining clearance for this letter to reach its intended recipient. A letter from F. R. McGinnis from the Outward Bag Room, Warsaw, of the Foreign Office, to Mgr Roche, advised Roche that, because of foreign office regulations, he (McGinnis) had been required to destroy his letter to the rector. He had nevertheless been able to pass the information in Roche's letter on to a friend from the university who would attempt to secure clearance from the Polish authorities to allow for the import of the equipment. This was clearly a delicate operation. 'I should perhaps mention', McGinnis's letter concluded, 'that we have to be careful about our contacts with Catholic circles in their interests, and that I am not therefore able to keep in very frequent touch with the university.'[86] Negotiations continued into the following year. A further letter from Roche to the Polish Embassy requested clearance for Mr Joseph Audry of the firm Bernadette Export in London, who were responsible for supplying the equipment, to enter Poland and speak to the university authorities on certain technical issues associated with the equipment.[87] A letter from the rector to Professor Aylward confirmed that the equipment had eventually arrived.[88]

By the early 1960s, the Newman Association began to scale back its aid programme to exiles generally. As early as 1957, the Newman International Committee noted the decreased scale of activity, which it put down to 'declining needs' as well as 'the difficulties in obtaining money for the purpose'.[89] Furthermore, Pax Romana was gradually subsuming the Association's work with Catholic exiles. On the weekend of the 22–3

---

[84] Report of a meeting of the Central and Eastern European Group, quoted in Newman International Committee Minutes, 22 October 1956.
[85] Letter from Mgr Roche to the Rector of Lublin University, undated, International Committee Country Files: Poland, D1/E/2/19, Newman Association Archive, Ushaw College Library.
[86] Letter from F. R. MacGinnis to Lawrence Roche, 7 December 1960, International Committee Country Files: Poland.
[87] Letter from Lawrence Roche to the Polish Embassy, 23 February 1961, International Committee Country Files: Poland.
[88] Letter from the Rector of Lublin University to Francis Aylward, [undated], International Committee Country Files: Poland.
[89] Aylward, *Fifteen Years of International Co-operation*, p. 17.

April 1961, a joint meeting of the Pax Romana Exiles Federations in Britain, the Newman Association, and the Union of Catholic Students was held in which it was decided to form a coordinating committee of Pax Romana Exiles Federations. The objects of this committee included: 'The extension of the work of each national exile federation within the framework of Pax Romana'. Although the Newman Association (and the Union of Catholic Students) was to have representation on this committee, the Association appeared to hand over direct responsibility for aid to Catholic exiles to Pax Romana.[90] Furthermore, in the same year, the Association also agreed to hand over all overseas non-university appointments work to the Catholic Overseas Appointment Bureau.[91]

Conclusion

The Newman Association provides an important case study for the involvement of Catholic lay societies in aiding exiles in the years following the Second World War. This support may have been inspired by a combination of anti-communism, pan-Europeanism, and a genuine altruism informed by Catholic social teaching, but it also emanated from a desire for lay educated Catholics to break out of the confines of their historically subordinate role within the Church, albeit with enthusiastic support and direction by the hierarchy. This encouraged the Newman Association, along with other Catholic lay organisations, to assume greater responsibility for undertaking ambitious initiatives unthinkable earlier in the century. The establishment of the Newman Centre in London, largely staffed by volunteers, was a major achievement, providing a cultural and social hub for Catholics from across the world to meet and take part in educational talks and conferences on subjects of interest. The scholarship programme enabled many Polish students to undertake undergraduate and postgraduate courses in Britain and Ireland which would have been impossible within their own country, and, without the support of the Newman Association in the early years, such opportunities may not have existed at all. The nature of the Newman Association's support to Polish exiles changed over time, reflecting the relative fortunes of the treatment of Catholics in communist countries. In the early post-war years, the priority was to assist Polish exiles in Britain. By the late 1950s, greater links were developed with organisations and individuals within Poland itself. By the early 1960s, however, the Newman Association was relinquishing much of its role in aiding Polish exiles to other organisations, notably

---

90   Pax Romana Papers, 23 April 1961, D1/E/2/1, Newman Association Archive, Ushaw College Library.
91   Newman Association, Annual Report, 1961/2, p. 4.

Pax Romana, who assumed greater control of the Central and Eastern Exile programme for the Catholic Church. Further research needs to be carried out on the work of other lay societies, such as the Catholic Women's League involvement in Polish displacement camps, as well as other Catholic and non-Catholic organisations, to uncover the true extent of the largely hidden involvement of charitable organisations in the post-war world.

7

'BE PROUD TO BE A WORKER GIRL, LIKE CHRIST YOUR WORKER KING': THE TRANSFORMATIVE IMPACT OF THE YOUNG CHRISTIAN WORKERS ON WORKING-CLASS CATHOLIC GIRLS AND YOUNG WOMEN IN THE LONG 1950s

Pat Jones

An early leader in the girls' Young Christian Workers (YCW) in England, Lancastrian Mary Lyons recalled in old age how the Movement had shaped her life, including her choice of husband and how they celebrated their wedding in 1942 She married a fellow YCW, Austin Lyons, and at their wedding, she wrote, 'We sang "Rouse Up" and had the YCW badge as decoration on the wedding cake'.[1] "Rouse Up" was the rallying song of the Movement, shared by both boys and girls, but the girls also had their own songbook. 'Be proud to be a worker girl, like Christ your worker King; for carry on the world could not, save you your labour bring' ran the chorus of one of the songs, set to the tune 'Boys of Wexford'. Another began 'What's that badge, what's that badge, O my brave Jocist girl', and ended with a call to action typical of the YCW spirit:

> So march on, march along,
> Sing our conquering song,
> With shoulder to shoulder, girls advance!
> Till the whole of our land is more Christian, more grand,
> The future is ours, Girls Advance![2]

Whilst sentiments of this kind were not unusual in the defensive and somewhat triumphalist culture of the English Catholic community in the 1940s and 1950s, the specific depiction of the status, dignity and mission of girls, and particularly of worker girls, was distinctive and rare. Working-class

---

[1] Mary Lyons, *Memoir*, unpublished typescript, YCW Archives, hereafter YCWA.
[2] 'Jocist' refers to the French YCW, Jeunesse ouvrière chrétienne (JOC). The girls' version was JOCF.

girls and women had little power, status or attention in the worldview of Catholic teaching or in any other social framework. Their significance lay almost entirely in their destiny as wives and mothers. Women were to occupy what Pius XI in 1930 called 'a truly regal throne' in their homes and he was insistent that it was a 'false liberty and unnatural equality' to claim for women the right to participate in business and public affairs or the right to economic independence.³ In the changed conditions of the post-war world, Pius XII moderated this account of women's vocations, recognising their 'duties in social and political life', but he was still deeply ambivalent: 'Restore woman as soon as possible to her place of honour in the home as housewife and mother!' he pleaded in 1945.⁴ Although he acknowledged that women could also have a mission in the public sphere, particularly those who were unmarried, their task there was primarily to defend and protect the family:

> Therefore every woman without exception is under an obligation – a strict obligation of conscience, mind you! – not to remain aloof; every woman must go into action, each in her own way, and join in stemming the tides which threaten to engulf the home, in fighting the doctrines which undermine its foundations, in preparing, organizing, and completing its restoration.⁵

Pius XII saw nothing but danger in the working life of girls:

> The daughter, who also goes out to work in factory, shop, or office, finds herself deafened by the turmoil in the midst of which she lives; dazzled by the glamour of a tawdry luxury; hungry for equivocal pleasures which distract without giving satisfaction or repose; frequenting the music halls and dancing palaces which, often for purposes of party propaganda, are springing up everywhere to corrupt the morals of the young.⁶

If the Pope's answer to the dangers of working life for Catholic girls was to shore up family life and focus on their domestic destiny, the message and purpose of YCW was the opposite. The Movement was founded on the idea that the milieu of young workers was a vital field of mission where they were to win other young workers – 'the masses' – for Christ, and 'Christianise' their working environment. Their working lives had a theological significance. A 1964 YCW girls' campaign report was very

---

3   Pius XI, *Castii Connubii: Encyclical on Christian Marriage* (1930), §§74–5, https://www.vatican.va/content/pius-xi/en/encyclicals/documents/hf_p-xi_enc_19301231_casti-connubii.html, accessed 11 September 2023.
4   Pius XII, *Questa grande vostra adunata: Women's Duties in Social and Political Life: Address to Members of Various Catholic Women's Associations* (1945), http://www.catholictradition.org/Encyclicals/questa1.htm, accessed 11 September 2023, Chapter I.
5   *Questa grande vostra adunata*, Chapter II.
6   Ibid., Chapter I; see also Pope Pius XI, *Quadragesimo Anno* (1931), §15, https://www.vatican.va/content/pius-xi/en/encyclicals/documents/hf_p-xi_enc_19310515_quadragesimo-anno.html, accessed 11 September 2023.

clear: 'God has a great interest in all our work. He started it off when he created the world, now we are carrying it on. Each day we take part in the continuation of creation.'[7] And each girl mattered: the message that YCW women remembered throughout their lives was that each young worker, including each girl, was more precious than all the gold in the world. The message powerfully conveyed a sense of their value and worth.

This chapter examines the development and impact of YCW on working-class Catholic girls and women in England from the foundation of the girls' Movement until the late 1960s and then discusses its significance for several generations of leaders and members. It draws on oral interviews with six women involved in YCW in the period from 1950 to the 1970s, research in the Salford YCW archive and the author's family history, as well as Church documents and wider secondary literature for contextualisation. By exploring the origins, structure, organisational methods, theology, spirituality and social discourse of YCW for girls in England, it argues that YCW occupied a unique and unexplored place in the formation and life experience of some working-class girls and young women in England, empowering them in the workplace and beyond. A crucial factor was the organisational separation of the female and male branches which meant that the leadership of the girls' Movement was in the hands of the girls themselves.[8] The two branches worked together and joined up for events and other purposes, but the organisational independence of the girls' Movement was crucial in empowering successive generations of Catholic women. In Gerd-Rainer Horn's judgement, this aspect of YCW enabled a process of 'autonomous radicalization' for both working-class boys and girls, which, as he acknowledges, had greater significance for the girls than the boys.[9] The two English branches were merged from 1967 onwards, and whilst strong female participation in YCW leadership structures remained a constant element in later generations, there was no longer a separate space for women as in the founding decades.

The YCW girls' Movement occupied a distinctive space both in relation to ecclesial expectations and narratives regarding girls and young women, and in the wider social context in which working-class women's employment was still largely viewed as either an economic necessity or as a means of occupying girls until they married. Women formed by the YCW became activists, both in the contexts of their working lives and in their local communities. They joined unions, returned to education to

---

[7] *Training for Life; National Campaign Report*, 1964, YCWA.
[8] The female branch was always 'the girls'; the male branch was variously 'the boys' or 'the lads', or less often 'the men'.
[9] Gerd-Rainer Horn, *Western European Liberation Theology 1924–1959: The First Wave* (London, 2009), p. 24.

study for degrees and moved into professional roles in areas such as social work, youth and community work and career guidance, jobs that would have been beyond their reach before their YCW experience. Some, like Peggy McNamara, a YCW organiser in the 1940s and 1950s who became a local councillor and then Mayor of St Helens, Lancashire, later became involved in local politics and held office. After YCW, they were also active in the Church, joining new movements and being likely to hold progressive views in relation to Catholic teaching and liturgy, especially as the Second Vatican Council began the transformation of the Church in the light of modernity. The trajectories of their lives validate Horn's argument for an explicit continuity between YCW/JOC and related movements and the renewal of the Church initiated by Pope John XXIII; 'In that sense, Vatican II can be seen as the ultimate, if unforeseen, product of the energies unleashed by grassroots activists and forward-looking theologians between 1924 and 1959.'[10]

Whilst the primary contours of the YCW girls' experience are clear, there are also areas of paradox, indicating the limits imposed by the social and ecclesial narratives that were dominant in the lives of working-class Catholic girls and women from the 1940s to the 1960s. Although the voices of the girls are spirited, determined and ambitious, they lived within deeply essentialist views of their gender held by those around them, particularly the men in their workplaces and in the Church. The girls themselves were not immune to such views either; articles in 1950s YCW publications, for example, encouraged campaigning against women being expected to do 'unsuitable' or 'defeminising' work. YCW girls took and fully exercised their autonomy while single, but then seemed to accept that this ended when they married and entered the traditional expectations and roles of Catholic wives and mothers, at least in the early decades. YCW was in part implicated in this, as alongside its encouragement of workplace activism, there was a dynamic promoting the Catholic model of marriage and family life with its deep ambivalence about women and employment. Yet YCW may also have been ahead of its time in other ideas about marriage. According to James Chappel, it was a channel for progressive ideas about marriage to reach female working-class awareness and challenge cultural norms.[11]

Despite these contradictions, the YCW Movement was liberative for working-class Catholic girls in the 1950s and beyond, and deserves

---

[10] Ibid., p. 291. For an analysis of the influence on Vatican II of Joseph Cardijn and the priests and bishops he worked with in YCW, see Stefan Gigacz, *The Leaven in the Council: Joseph Cardijn and the Jocist Network at Vatican II* (Melbourne, 2021), https://theleaven.com.au, accessed 11 September 2023.

[11] James Chappel, *Catholic Modern: The Challenge of Totalitarianism and the Remaking of the Church* (London, 2018), pp. 121, 194.

recognition for this. No other Catholic organisation was specifically *for* and *led by* this demographic group, with a focus on their social mission and a powerful message and strategy adapted to their condition and realities. The acute sense of apostolic mission engendered by YCW is still relevant today and the YCW experience can still challenge contemporary concepts and models of personal and social mission.

Origins and growth

The founder of YCW, the Belgian priest Joseph Cardijn, sought a response to the dehumanising and alienating working conditions experienced by the young people of his generation in a rapidly industrialising world. 'My basic concern has always been to bring religion back to the surroundings of real life and the problems these raise', he wrote in *Laymen into Action*.[12] In the early decades of the twentieth century, he studied worker movements and emerging Catholic social teaching and visited leaders such as Ben Tillett in London, looking for answers to the problem of how to reach the working masses. In the aftermath of the First World War, he began to gather his own groups, starting with young seamstresses in Laken and experimenting with a range of structures and affiliations. The world of Catholic associational life was already crowded, and he met resistance from existing organisations, but eventually the form and distinctiveness of YCW emerged, with 1925 as its official date of origin. The Movement (YCW has always asserted that it is a *Movement*, rather than an organisation) spread rapidly in Belgium and France and then internationally, asserting its identity as *specialised* Catholic action in contrast to the larger generic Catholic action structures typical of northern European countries. Its task was both specific and immense: 'The YCW is an organisation which groups, trains, serves and represents the young workers in order that they can: rechristianise the whole of their lives, the whole of their surroundings and the whole mass of their fellow workers'.[13]

In England, the first men's Sections (as local branches were described) began in Wigan in 1937, and within two years, there were twenty-five Sections scattered across Lancashire, London, Yorkshire and Birmingham. It was given an official mandate from the Bishops' Conference of England and Wales in Low Week 1939, and although expansion slowed down in wartime, by 1945 there were eighty-three Sections, and a team of full-time organisers led by Patrick Keegan was established.[14] The development of the girls' Movement, by contrast, was complicated by issues

---

[12] Joseph Cardijn, *Laymen into Action* (London, 1964), p. 32.
[13] Training Section Programme (1947), YCWA, p. 24.
[14] Keegan, from Hindley in Lancashire, left school at 14 and worked as a little piecer in a mill; later he became international president of YCW and an auditor at Vatican II. An

of class identity and paternalistic moves by the bishops. The bottom-up working-class groups initiated by young women around 1939 along the lines of the men's teams became entangled with the Catholic Action Girls Organisation, (CAGO) a top-down attempt by the bishops to organise an English and Welsh version of Catholic Action.[15] CAGO was led by young middle-class Catholic women commissioned by the bishops to set up a range of specialised Catholic action groups. Whilst their approach worked well for the emerging Young Christian Students, also based on Cardijn's vision but drawing membership from Catholic grammar schools, as Dennis Maccagno has shown, it did not work for northern working-class girls.[16] It took some ten years, until 1947, before YCW girls achieved autonomy with their own structures, chaplain, organisers and headquarters. The class adherence and identity tensions embedded in YCW's development are significant: in the early years, there were debates about whether teachers could be members, as they were regarded as a profession, in contrast to the girls who worked in factories and shops. Maccagno concluded that it was only when YCW was released from CAGO that an authentic YCW girls' Movement emerged.[17]

Once the question of class identity had been resolved in favour of working-class self-direction, expansion was rapid. By 1949, there were 297 local YCW Sections, of which 164 were girls' Sections, gathered into eighteen regions, mostly covering industrial cities and towns.[18] There were eighteen national organisers, of whom six were leading the girls' Movement.[19] The peak of YCW growth was in the early 1950s, with around 357 Sections in total in 1952, but numbers held up well through the 1960s and 1970s, although they later declined.[20]

Molly Maddison, a full-time organiser, described the growth of a Section in Hebburn on Tyneside over three years from 1948–51.[21] Analysing the local industries and trades where girls mainly work, the 'centres of influence' that feature in their lives (mainly dance halls and cinemas,

---

unfinished biography of Keegan written by the late Fr John Fitzsimons is now available online at https://patkeegan.josephcardijn.com, accessed 11 September 2023.
[15] Dennis Maccagno, 'The Origins of the YCW Movement', unpublished thesis, University of London, 1971, YCWA, p. 43.
[16] Ibid., p. 44.
[17] Ibid., p. 45.
[18] *Report on the Young Christian Workers Movement in England for the information of the Apostolic Delegate to Great Britain*, January 1949, YCWA, p. 3.
[19] *Minutes of Week at Home*, YCWA, July 1949.
[20] See Sylvia Collins and Michael P. Hornsby-Smith, 'The Rise and Fall of the YCW', *Journal of Contemporary Religion*, 17:1 (2002), pp. 87–100.
[21] *New Life*, 5:4 (1951), pp. 236–52. *New Life* was the YCW journal for chaplains. Maddison was my mother, and I am currently working on a longer study of her life. For further details of her life see pp. 125–6 below.

and a parish youth club), she points to 'the lack of Christian influence and training as to their purpose and role in life'.[22] Their Section began when six girls approached the parish priest to ask for recognition and a chaplain, but the girls were mainly office workers, which 'prevented the growth of the Section by penetrating into the work environment of the masses of factory workers in this district'.[23] The Section grew unevenly for a while until it collapsed. But the chaplain had seen its potential; and 'once a priest has had dealings with the YCW he can't let it go – it is too important'.[24] Consequently he found two keen girls who gathered others into a team of seven leaders and started again, 'full of enthusiasm and zeal and willing to give themselves to be formed as Christian worker leaders for the mass of working girls'.[25] Maddison then describes actions achieved the erection of a danger notice around uncovered pots of boiling solder; action on ventilation; improvement of canteen facilities and first aid capacity; and a YCW leader being elected onto the branch committee of her union. They followed the national YCW campaign on 'The working girl and health', and developed activities related to the four YCW girls' services, concerned with the sick, with marriage training, with publications and with outreach to younger girls, termed Pre-YCW.[26] In Hebburn, they started a library for sanatoria, collecting sweets and sweet coupons (rationing was still in place until the early 1950s) to give to sick girls whom they visited regularly.

The campaigns organised by the girls' Movement in the late 1940s and through the 1950s addressed the girls' lived reality. In 1947, for example, the campaign examined attitudes to work and explored 'the vocational and redemptive nature of work'. In 1948, the campaign theme was 'The Working Girl and Health'.[27] In 1956, the campaign addressed girls' lack of preparation for entry into working life and the choice of a job, themes that crucially led to significant emphasis on school-to-work activities and pre-YCW groups. In 1961, it was still focused on work, asking 'Who is the working girl of today?'

---

[22] Ibid., p. 241.
[23] Ibid., p. 242.
[24] Ibid., p. 243.
[25] Ibid., p. 244.
[26] The *Action Programme* for August 1950 YCWA explains the 'four permanent problems' of each working girl: leaving school and starting work; sickness; the influence of media, cinema, etc.; and the use of leisure time. Hence the four 'services' directed at these.
[27] *Minutes of Organisers' Week at Home*, August 1948, YCWA.

Social and ecclesial attitudes

Young working-class girls were not an easy group to gather and inspire. Most left school at fourteen or fifteen with no qualifications.[28] They moved into local industries, factories and shops, and increasingly into clerical work. Jobs were plentiful, but mostly low status, low paid and classified as low skilled, with few paths to progression open to girls.[29] Little was invested in young women, who were expected to leave work when they married or had their first child. The war had changed their context; domestic service mostly disappeared, and the welfare state was emerging, as was a youth culture based on consumption. In his elegiac description of 1950s working-class culture, Richard Hoggart describes teenage girls in disparaging terms:

> They seem to fill the space between leaving school and marriage with thrice weekly visits to 'musicals' and 'romantic dramas' at the pictures, with fantasy love-stories, and with successive hops at the 'Palais', the 'Mecca', the 'Locarno', or the public baths. Their jobs rarely engage more than a small portion of their personalities, they seem to have little interest as committed individuals in anything, they take no interest in Trade Union activities and little in the home. Surely they are most of them flighty, careless and inane?[30]

Hoggart had clearly never encountered YCW. In a lively article in the Movement's *Young Worker* newspaper, which was sold in large numbers to their peers by YCW members, Rene Tomlin describes her experience of her trade union. Energetically critical about middle-aged men, jargon and rambling speeches, she exhorts other women to get involved, even when the proceedings seem to be conducted in 'double-dutch'.

> It's understandable if you vow never to go to another meeting unless something that directly affects you turns up. THIS WON'T DO! ... Don't wait for something important to turn up, go to your *next* Union meeting. ... Once you have got on the committee, there is no knowing where you will stop.[31]

In Catholic parishes too there was minimal concern for working-class girls once they had left school. At most they might be invited to join the Children of Mary or the Legion of Mary, pious sodalities that did little to address the realities of girls' lives, still less their lives *as workers*. Mary Lyons comments: 'it became apparent that here was something

---

[28] The school-leaving age was raised to 15 in 1947, and to 16 in 1972.
[29] See Stephanie Spencer, *Gender, Work and Education in Britain in the 1950s* (London, 2005), p. 201: in 1950 there were 92,300 boys taking up apprenticeships on entering employment, but only 21,200 girls; by 1955, the number of boys had increased to 96,700, but of girls had fallen to only 15,600; little had changed by 1960. However, three or four times as many girls as boys entered clerical employment across the same decade.
[30] Richard Hoggart, *The Uses of Literacy* (Harmondsworth, 1958), pp. 50–1.
[31] *Young Worker*, undated, YCWA, p. 3.

new, totally different from other parochial organisations – we were in fact to become apostles of our fellow-workers'.[32] The girls joined when they were mostly young teenagers, often before leaving school. YCW statistics from this era are few and fragile, but Hornsby-Smith and Collins note that in the years from 1966 to 1970, 51% of the members were girls, and only 2% were aged twenty-one or over.[33] In the 1950s and 1960s, young women married early, particularly working-class young women. Working-class Catholic girls only featured in the Catholic cultural and vocational horizon once they approached marriage and motherhood, unless they were drawn towards religious life, the only other vocational path for girls promoted by the Church.[34]

Strategy and messages

YCW involvement for most began through social events and simple friendship. The principle of 'sphere of influence' was crucial, and leaders reported each week on whom they had been able to contact. Sheila Wilkinson, who became an organiser aged nineteen, describes 'lots of standing on doorsteps talking about YCW and meeting girls after work'.[35] They were recruited into a structured pattern of formation using the YCW methodology of See-Judge-Act, applied in a series of 'enquiries' which could be either social enquiries or Gospel enquiries.[36] The 'review of life' was another crucial tool. From the beginning, girls were encouraged to bring facts from their daily working life – the 'fact of the week' was an essential element of each meeting and they would send lists of their facts in reports to headquarters – and examine these together, deciding what action was needed to achieve change, and reviewing actions taken when they next met. One former leader described the importance of this step: 'So by knowing you have the group to go back to, to report back to, they were supporting you, how did you get on, what happened, I think that was what actually created the confidence in people to go and do it.' (L., joined in 1967)

---

[32] Lyons, *Memoir* YCWA, p 3.
[33] Hornsby-Smith and Collins, 'Rise and Fall of the YCW', p. 89.
[34] It was not unusual for YCW girls to discover a religious vocation. Lyons mentions the difficulty of replacing her as treasurer as four of the girls working at national level had left to enter religious life. *Memoir*, p. 2. Also see Carmen Mangion, *Catholic Nuns and Sisters in a Secular Age: Britain, 1945–90* (Manchester, 2020), for further discussion of the religious vocation of young women at this time.
[35] 'Flashes on the Infant Girls' Movement', *New Life,* 16:4 (1960) YCWA, p. 115.
[36] The core method of YCW globally; 'see' by examining the facts and realities of a situation; 'judge' in the light of a Catholic theological vision of what God intends for humanity and creation, including what Catholic social teaching described as 'the social order', the structures of society and then determine suitable action to transform the situation.

Although the skills and disciplines of YCW formation were important, there was even greater significance in its core messages to young women. YCW told each girl that she had an inestimable value; that she had her own specific divine vocation and mission.[37] Even thirty to fifty years on, women recalled the impact:

> I think it was about building confidence and having a voice, I think were the messages, you know, it always says, you're worth more than all the gold in the world, well, what does that mean, or you know, they talked about your dignity, well, what does that mean? And things like that really, so you started to value yourself. (L., joined in 1969)[38]
>
> That you're worth more than all the gold in the world. I'll never forget that. Trying to get my head round it and understand it. That's a real Cardijn saying. And I think it was about, the message was that, I can remember, quite naively now when you look back, thinking and feeling that we could do anything we wanted and we *could* change the world. (M., joined in 1979)[39]

The central insight of the YCW worldview was that working life was not a period of drudgery to be endured, nor a place of temptation to be resisted, but a vocation in itself, a cooperation with God's purposes. Cardijn expounded a rich Eucharistic theology of work which spoke directly to the situation of young workers. Their apostolic task was to sanctify the world through their action in their workplaces, making Christ present there just as the Eucharist makes Christ present in the sacrament. If laypeople are faithful to their own apostolate, Cardijn wrote, 'the Mass offered by the priest at the altar will become a Mass prolonged on all those altars of secular life; the worktable, the loom, the lathe, the joiner's bench, the typist's desk'.[40] The first Section training programme in the late 1940s echoed this sacralising of work: 'God intends that they gain their eternal happiness not in spite of their work, their home, their leisure, courtship and marriage, but in and through and because of their work, their home, leisure and marriage'.[41] This theological principle gave dignity and meaning to the smallest acts of workers, whether to do their jobs well or to alter their working conditions. 'The most important of all the services of the Movement are the day to day unglamorous and often unrecorded acts of sacrifice and service of each and every member and leader'.[42] The final verse of 'Be Proud to be a worker girl' encapsulates the theology:

---

37 *Laymen into Action*, p. 33.
38 Anonymised interview.
39 Anonymised interview.
40 *Laymen into Action*, p. 40. Cardijn rarely drew directly from Catholic social teaching texts, working rather from Eucharistic and ecclesiological themes.
41 *Training Section Programme*, YCWA, p. 40.
42 *Report on the Young Christian Workers Movement in England*, January 1949, YCWA, p. 15.

We're heirs of Christ, God's daughters dear
No slaves or beasts are we!
We wish to earn our daily bread
In Christian Dignity.'
So banish hate from out your heart
And face life fearlessly
Your fellow worker, Christ our King
To work gave dignity.

Two other elements were constitutive in the YCW strategy from the beginning. Firstly, the role of chaplains was crucial, particularly at the outset in building a Section. They often found the first leaders, supported their formation, and tied the Movement into the sacramental and spiritual life of the Church. They became friends and colleagues to the leaders and organisers, taking a subsidiary role so that the Movement was truly run by the girls themselves. In the 1950s and 1960s, the chaplains were almost all priests, although the Movement later adopted a broader framework in which other adults, often women religious or laypeople, took on the role of chaplain. For many priests who became chaplains in the early decades however, YCW had a profound impact.

Their role was connected to the second defining principle of YCW; that the only people who can effectively reach and evangelise young workers are other young workers; the principle of like-to-like. This idea was taken up by Pope Pius XI in *Quadragesimo Anno*: 'The first and immediate apostles to the workers ought to be workers; the apostles to those who follow industry and trade ought to be from among them themselves.'[43] The 1947 training programme advised that whilst chaplains will help, and advice will be given, 'none can replace you yourselves in this task'.[44] Mary Gates, a girls' organiser, explained this further, imagining what YCW would say:

> I suddenly thought – I know that the YCW lives in us as individuals, yet if it had *one voice* and was able to speak, what would it say to us?
>
> I helped you to stand back a little and take a look at your life – at the people around you – at the places where you live and work and play. To look well because these things are important to you. Important because among them lies the reason for your life – your mission and vocation.
>
> … As you discovered Christ, I helped you to discover the needs of those around you. To look at your workplace, and think … what would Christ have thought about it? Are those conditions he would have wanted people to work in?
>
> … I brought you out of isolation and gave you the help and support of others so that you became more complete – a better person. I taught you to SEE, to JUDGE and to ACT. But I didn't do it just for you. I did it in order that

---

43 *Quadragesimo Anno*, §141.
44 Training Section Programme, YCWA, p. 5.

with apostolic zeal you would take this to others without considering colour or creed. I tried to make you an apostle.

I asked you to help the girls who were leaving school and had no preparation for the working life you had been talking about – to group them and prepare them. ...

I knew you could do it, because you understood the girls who needed your help.[45]

The insight captured in the principle of like-to-like secures the distinctive character and mission of the early YCW and created an empowering space for young women that they alone can fill.

Leadership

As the preceding exemplifies, the role and nature of leadership at every level from the local Section to the national or international Movement was crucial to the effectiveness of YCW. In his analysis of the Belgian and French JOC Movements, Gerd-Rainer Horn comments that what was truly revolutionary about the YCW/JOC was 'the firm resolve of the founding members to create a youth organisation which could govern its own affairs'.[46] As he points out, this was even more significant for the girls in YCW:

Constantly encouraged to challenge themselves and to take new steps forward, young Christian workers began to discover each other—and themselves! This process of individual and collective personal growth, which was already extraordinary in the way it transformed young male workers' inner selves, was even more astounding when affecting young women workers' lives. ... Young women workers on the road to self-liberation, of course, had at least one more obstacle to overcome than their male cohorts: namely their male cohorts. For this and other reasons, the determined focus on self-government and self-assertion had particularly pronounced effects among young women workers.[47]

The Movement aimed to find and train leaders among ordinary, unskilled teenage girls. The organisers often wrote about finding 'the right sort of girl', those whom they saw as potential leaders – who were then supported to progress through the levels of the Movement to regional and national levels and for some, international meetings. YCW taught its female leaders to speak in public, to organise and run meetings, to write minutes, to look after finances, to plan and lead study weeks for seminarians and rallies for several thousand young people.

---

[45] *New Life*, 15:5 (1959), pp. 154–6.
[46] Horn, *Liberation Theology*, p. 13.
[47] Ibid., pp. 7–8.

The role of organisers deserves particular attention. These were leaders who progressed through the levels and were spotted by those already working at national level and eventually invited to join the full-time team. The process of securing these girls often included speaking to their mothers, who had understandable qualms about their daughters leaving steady jobs to work for no pay and an uncertain future. During the December 1950 organisers' meeting, for example, it is reported that 'Eileen Hanley still has to approach her mother and will bring her to see Molly.'[48] As volunteers, they were provided with accommodation and food either at 'headquarters' in London or in the regions in which they were based. In the early 1950s, full-time organisers were given ten shillings a week for their personal use, but no other wage.[49] They were young when they started – Maddison was twenty-one when she moved from the pit village of Haydock in Lancashire to London to begin work as an organiser, and twenty-four when she became national secretary of the Girls' Movement (in effect, president). They travelled around the country, visiting Sections, contacting priests who might be or were chaplains and speaking at rallies and other events. They organised study weekends, retreats, seminarians' summer schools and YCW holidays. The Movement lived on a shoestring; in March 1949 its bank account had a balance of £5.11.4d, with debts of £1000.[50] Income came from modest member subscriptions, publication sales and a campaign asking members to give a day's pay to finance the Movement.

The transnational nature of YCW had a direct impact on its leaders and organisers. Some attended European and international meetings and maintained links and exchanges with the YCW in other countries. And internationalism was two-way: in the September 1950 campaign newsletter, for example, Maddison's editorial described recent visitors to HQ including:

> Fr Daniel Tawiah from Kumasi, the only African priest of his diocese. He has been released for full-time Catholic action work and is making a short intensive study of the YCW here. Also Florence Triendl, an American girl living in Austria, who is at the moment working in the International secretariat on the preparations for the International study Week.[51]

Such 'matter-of-fact' recording of these encounters indicates how YCW served to broaden its members' worldviews. Maddison grew up in a working-class community where people rarely travelled even to the nearest

---

[48] YCWA.
[49] The average weekly wage in 1950 was £5.60 a week, but women earned less. The average for women in manual work was £4 a week.
[50] *Minutes of Organisers' Week at Home*, YCWA, March 1949.
[51] *Campaign News*, September 1950, YCWA, p. 2.

city or met anyone from outside their tight-knit local world. Another former girls' leader from the late 1960s reflected that in her Durham pit village upbringing, 'There was no such thing as going abroad. I didn't know anyone else who had done that.'[52] The impact on both leaders and members of knowing they belonged to an international Movement was transformative in itself, an impact deepened by visits and international conferences. The same leader described the impact of meeting YCW leaders from South Africa and learning about apartheid: 'I found that absolutely amazing; they were classified according to their colour. And I went home and I told my dad, and he wouldn't believe it; he said that can't be right.'[53]

James Chappel identifies transnationalism as a significant factor in the emergence of what he terms 'Catholic modernity',[54] arguing that it enabled the worldview of Catholic social thought to spread across boundaries and influence diverse political cultures, especially once Catholic teaching began to support democracy as a political project.[55] Chappel's concern is mainly with European political development, and both politics and Catholic action took a different path in England and Wales, but the ground level impact of international exposure matters, opening windows in the often rather narrow world of both Catholic and working-class subcultures.

Spirituality

YCW had a distinct spirituality in which several strands were interwoven. It featured some popular Catholic devotional practices of the time – a dedication to St Therese of Lisieux as patroness of YCW was prominent, while an annual highlight was the rallies organised across the country on the Feast of Christ the King.[56] Prayer was an integral element of every meeting plan, and there were frequent day and weekend retreats. Sacramental practice was encouraged. YCW had its own prayer which asked Christ the Worker to 'Grant me and all my fellow workers the grace to think like You, to work with You, to live in You', so that 'Your

---

[52] Interview with M.
[53] Ibid.
[54] Chappel, *Catholic Modern*, p. 8. See also Susan O'Brien, *Leaving God for God: The Daughters of Charity of St Vincent de Paul in Britain, 1847–2017* (London, 2017), pp. 15–17.
[55] James Chappel, 'Slaying the Leviathan: Catholicism and the Rebirth of European Conservatism, 1920–1950', Unpublished PhD Thesis, Columbia University, 2012.
[56] During the 1950s, annual plans frequently included the 'Teresian campaign'. The Campaign leaflet for September 1952 explains: 'Why do we have a girl and a nun as patroness of young workers? Because the Pope, Christ's representative in earth said so. Because, dying as young as 24, she had become a great saint by her small way of total trust and daily small sacrifices. Because God chooses the weak to confound the strong. Because in her whole being she was an apostle, on fire then and now for the mission of the Church.' YCWA.

kingdom comes in all our factories, workshops, offices, and in all our homes'. Mary Lyons, for one, put this into practice in the Liverpool branch of Maypole Grocers where she was manageress during the war. 'All our staff were Catholics', she recalled, 'We began each day by saying the YCW prayer'.[57]

A more distinctive element was found in the practice of Gospel enquiries, in which the YCW girls from their mid-teenage years on were encouraged to read and interpret the Gospel for themselves. Girls leading the Gospel enquiries might get some help from chaplains at first, but the key element was that they related the Gospel readings to their own lives. In organisers' notes on how to train Sections as they begin, an 'imaginative' approach was recommended: 'Who was there? What were they doing? How did they dress? What did they say? What was Our Lord trying to show people through that? Could we say when we've seen a similar case of this?'[58] In the pre-conciliar era when few Catholics read scripture, and fewer still in working-class homes where books were scarce, bibles even more so, this was a radical practice which gave the girls access to a deeply personal and Christocentric spirituality and empowered them to be agents in their own faith rather than passive recipients.[59]

But YCW spirituality was not simply about devotional practices or reading the scriptures. Cardijn's theological vision was constructed on what he named the 'three truths': the truth of faith, which is the temporal and eternal destiny of every young worker; the truth of experience, which is the contradiction between their real experience and this destiny; and the truth of method, the necessity of an organisation which can help them resolve this contradiction and achieve their destiny. The spirituality of YCW lived in this dialectic, which enabled young workers to see that every detail of their working life was imbued with potential to serve God's purposes and advance God's kingdom.

After YCW: return to the domestic sphere

Once they were married, often to YCW men, girls left the Movement. This meant there was a rapid turnover of leaders, with few staying more than a handful of years. Preparation for a Catholic marriage was part of

---

57   Lyons *Memoir*, p. 3. She had changed jobs 'so that I could influence others'.
58   Minutes of Organisers Week at Home, 16th–23rd February 1954, YCWA.
59   In her analysis of the French YCW girls' Movement, Susan B. Whitney describes an intense version of this spirituality: 'The intimate relationship between Christ and the young female worker depicted in the J.O.C.F. literature could take the form of a mystical union … portraying Christ as a husband, friend, father and lover, and by encouraging young women to forge intimate relationships with him'. *Mobilising Youth: Communists and Catholics in Inter-war France* (London, 2009), p. 125. However, I found no evidence of this intensity in material in the English and Welsh YCW archives.

the formal YCW agenda – many campaign themes covered the practical challenges and moral aspirations associated with a Catholic view of marriage and family life – and also part of the informal reality.[60] Lyons reports that 'The Section ran pre-marriage sessions including practical sessions on how to bath the baby and another on how to bake. We had pre-marriage week-ends at Southport and at the Convent in Leigh.'[61] In this arena, YCW seems to concur with wider society and culture in seeing a woman's place as firmly in the domestic sphere once she married. Even if this consensus was starting to fracture in wider society, it remained almost inviolable in the Catholic world. But although not surprising given the dominant social and ecclesial narratives of the time, it is striking to see the conjunction in YCW narratives of workplace activism and political engagement alongside sessions on baking and bathing babies. Whilst YCW girls questioned and challenged unfair attitudes, practices and structures in their working lives and in wider society, there is no evidence in the archives that indicates any doubt or critique about the future domestic roles designated for them.

The influence of the normative Catholic framework is probably significant here. Historians of 1950s Britain have portrayed this period as transitional, marking a shift to women working in a wider range of jobs. Gender identities became more complex as women experienced greater economic and personal freedom. They became more likely to return to work after children were born, although their maternal responsibilities were not to be compromised.[62] Stephen Brooke argues that 'femininity became less firmly tied to motherhood, while work gradually became accepted as a province of both men and women'.[63] But for young Catholic women, the message imbibed throughout their Catholic lives was that their vocation and destiny was motherhood. For Pope Pius XII, motherhood is:

> a woman's function, a woman's way, a woman's natural bent. ... To this end the Creator has fashioned the whole of woman's nature: not only her organism, but also and still more her spirit and most of all her exquisite sensibility.[64]

Whilst later papal teaching edged towards recognition of women's social, economic and political participation as equally a vocational path, this would not have filtered into working-class Catholic consciousness.

Although the YCW archives are largely silent about the paths taken by the women once they married, oral history interviews and the author's

---

[60] The boys' Movement also often focused on marriage-related issues, taking campaign themes such as 'the choice of a girl' and 'the size of the family' (1948).
[61] Lyons, *Memoir*, p. 4.
[62] Spencer, *Gender, Work and Education*, p. 6.
[63] Stephen Brooke, 'Gender and Working Class Identity in Britain during the 1950s', *Journal of Social History*, 34:4 (2001), p. 774.
[64] *Questa grande vostra adunata*, Chapter I.

personal family history suggest that YCW women still sought outlets for social concern and neighbourhood activism once they married. Many became involved in Family and Social Action (FSA) groups, a movement based on the same principles and using the YCW methodology in a different milieu, but this lost the unique aspect of attention to women *in their working lives*.[65] Some remained single or entered religious life. Whatever the path taken, it is clear both from several memoirs and from oral history interviews that the impact of YCW was lifelong.

Gender and work

The gender essentialism embedded in Catholic teaching – and in prevailing social attitudes of the time – is evident in the way in which YCW publications in the 1950s discussed the work that women might do. An early edition of the *Young Worker* newspaper, for example, ran an article by Jo Jukes, an organiser. In Jukes' view, 'Tradition declines because although woman is now out of the mines she is still on the buses, in the railway stations and hundreds of other jobs that by their very nature are jobs for men'.[66] She continues: 'Work on the whole, does not train girls in exercising their feminine qualities'. Another issue from the same period carried a banner headline 'The Gentle Sex!', and a lead article critical of 'the tendency for women to do defeminising work' such as engineering, trucking and spraying. John Fitzsimons, a YCW national chaplain and rare Catholic priest-sociologist, echoes the same attitude in his book, *Woman Today*, writing that 'there are still many jobs done by women which are of their essence defeminising, unsexing the girls and women who perform them, deforming them in those characteristics that should be the glory of their sex, their grace, their gentleness, their modesty'.[67]

To some extent, these attitudes reflect the post-war concern to encourage women away from the 'transgressive' jobs they had taken up in wartime so that men could return to the jobs they formerly did. It is hard to tell from the available evidence whether and how far such attitudes conditioned or impacted on the girls in YCW. The Section news, the campaign materials and the organisers' meeting records do not replicate the messages found in the *Young Worker* newspaper. The reality was that girls

---

65   FSA flourished in the 1970s and 1980s, but then declined. Some FSA members formed new groups recovering an explicit focus on work issues, and these groups later formed the Movement for Christian Workers, MCW, which still exists and maintains links with adult Cardijn workers movements internationally.
66   *Young Worker*, c. 1949, YCWA. Jukes' brother, John Jukes OFM, became the bishop responsible for the world of work in the Bishops' Conference of England and Wales.
67   John Fitzsimons, *Woman Today* (London, 1952), p. 130.

worked in machine shops, in manufacturing and other 'dirty' jobs, and YCW activists got on with the task of making these better.

It seems possible that YCW women were simply not conscious of how their YCW experience introduced and nourished an expanded horizon of vocation and flourishing which at least partly resisted both Catholic and societal gender essentialism and anticipated feminist aspirations of the 1970s and onwards. Their experience and achievements challenge what Stephanie Spencer terms 'the gendered nature of constructions of citizenship', demonstrating that girls and young women could do more than society and politics, and the Catholic Church, assumed and allowed.[68]

Conclusion

YCW entered the lives of girls living at the lower end of the social scale and showed that they mattered. The Movement enabled working-class girls and young women to discover their potential and expand their horizons, transforming their own lives in a permanent way. Their story deserves to be told because it challenges social and ecclesial assumptions about working-class girls and because they initiated and succeeded in building a new domain of Catholic social mission *for women*. They created a *praxis* of social mission, inspired by Cardijn's vision which mediated theological themes from Catholic sources into accessible messages, rarely citing formal Catholic social teaching. Their praxis was arguably itself a form of Catholic social teaching *from below*, a lived articulation of principles found in later papal texts. Their incremental influence and action as 'leaven in the dough' was mainly local, personal and inserted into workplace systems and structures, and as such, impossible to measure, but nonetheless real, as countless documents in the archives testify.

Paul Misner describes YCW as achieving a breakthrough from 'sheltering paternalism' toward apostolic social mission, a breakthrough he regards as 'unprecedented ... in its daring combination of entrusting the development of youth to the young themselves (with training), of targeting young workers by themselves and firing them with a mission that only they themselves could carry out'.[69] He continues: 'It is no wonder that the influence of the Young Christian Worker Movement was determinative of many of the new developments that would mark social Catholicism for decades to come'.[70] He notes too that what he terms 'social Catholic feminism' is less well documented than the male dimension.[71]

---

[68] Spencer, *Gender, Work and Education*, p. 8.
[69] Misner, *Catholic Labour Movements in Europe*, p. 124.
[70] Ibid., p. 141.
[71] Ibid., p. 143.

It is still not evident in formal social teaching that the Church cares about what young women in exploitative or oppressive work situations experience or what they want to say. Catholic social teaching, although rich in its theology of work, has paid little attention to a gendered analysis or to listening to contemporary voices from young women. YCW enacted for women a counter-narrative to those offered by both society and Church, which although still meshed into traditional expectations of female vocation and roles, created a liberative space in which they could act and lead, and then bring the influence of their YCW formation to bear on the lives of their families and communities.

8

'SOMETHING MORE THAN A MERE CATHOLIC DINING CLUB'? ENGLISH CATHOLIC MASCULINITIES, RELIGIOUS SOCIABILITY AND A CENTURY OF THE CATENIAN ASSOCIATION[1]

ALANA HARRIS

In an after-dinner speech at the 1966 AGM of the Catenian Association, guest of honour and newly appointed Bishop of Arundel and Brighton, David Cashman, light-heartedly urged this nearly sixty-year-old sodality to re-examine its aims and objectives in the post-Vatican II era: 'The image of the Catenians as a section of the People of God dressed for dinner and dancing is not enough.'[2] The Bishop's intentionally provocative questioning of the role of this lay-led association for Catholic men came at a time of profound institutional change within the Catholic church and a reappreciation of the place of the laity as 'active participants' in the liturgy and a 'pilgrim people of God', with their own priestly role.[3] Unsurprisingly, it elicited irritated reactions from the wider membership when reprinted in *Catena*, the Catenians' long-running monthly journal. Letters from members outlined the various philanthropic activities in which they individually participated and rebuked the Catenian leadership for 'improperly briefing the Bishop'.[4] Finally, and most tellingly during a period of wider questioning of tradition and authority, another correspondent was simultaneously *en pointe* in his lack of deference, yet conservative in his insistence on the rules of gentlemanly hospitality,

---

[1] Courtesy of Springer and Palgrave Macmillan, this chapter is reprinted (with amendments) from *Men, Masculinity and Religious Change in Britain since 1900*, edited by Lucy Delap and Sue Morgan (London, 2013), pp. 54–89.
[2] Peter Lane, *The Catenian Association 1908–1983: A Microcosm of the Development of the Catholic Middle Class* (London, 1982), p. 188.
[3] See Second Vatican Council, *Lumen Gentium* (1964), http://www.vatican.va/archive/hist_councils/ii_vatican_council/documents/vat-ii_const_19641121_lumen-gentium_en.html, accessed 30 August 2022.
[4] Lane, *Catenian Association*, p. 188.

when accusing the Bishop of a breach of propriety by 'taking improper advantage of his position as our guest'.[5]

As this opening vignette illustrates, this chapter examines the nature of this association which, throughout its history, has evinced a reluctance to become overly political, but has consistently resisted clerical control and self-reflexively asserted the social *and* spiritual benefits of a forum for male Catholic friendship and class-based sociability. Following a brief outline of the foundation of the association and its function as a form of self-sufficiency in the tradition of 'friendly societies', the chapter sketches the activities of this national (and increasingly transnational) fraternity across the twentieth century and contrasts their 'wining and dining' with other activities more broadly conceived as 'praying and paying'. Through examining a distinctly middle class 'association of Catholic men', a more nuanced picture of English Catholicism beyond ubiquitous working-class and Irish migrant characterisations is delineated,[6] and another type of 'religious sociability' emerges, analogous to but distinct from Callum Brown's interwar 'plebeian male religiosity'.[7] As such, focused attention to this association provides a *longue durée* exploration of transformations in lay identity across the twentieth century and the enduring appeal of a manly yet family-focused spirituality. It thereby offers a contrasting case study to a literature dominated by the increasingly critiqued 'feminisation of religion' thesis from the nineteenth century onwards,[8] or the imprecise concept of 'muscular Christianity',[9] whilst building upon and supplementing emerging studies of modern European Catholic masculinity.[10] It provides yet another example of the complicated relationship and continuing dialogue between concepts of religious manliness and hegemonic masculinities, well into the latter half of the twentieth century.[11]

An exploration of the sodality's operation delineates the dialogue between

---

[5] Ibid.
[6] e.g. James Pereiro, 'Who are the Laity?', in *From Without the Flaminian Gate*, edited by V. Alan McClelland and Michael Hodgetts (London, 1999), pp 167–91.
[7] Callum Brown, *Religion and Society in Twentieth Century Britain* (London, 2006), p. 125.
[8] Tine Van Osselaer and Thomas Buerman, 'Feminization Thesis: A Survey of International Historiography and a Probing of the Belgian Grounds', *Revue d'Histoire Ecclésiastique*, 103:2 (2008), pp. 1–3.
[9] Lucy Delap, '"Be Strong and Play the Man": Anglican Masculinities in the Twentieth Century', in *Men, Masculinities and Religious Change in Twentieth-Century Britain*, edited by Lucy Delap and Sue Morgan (London, 2013), pp. 119–45.
[10] Yvonne Maria Werner (ed.). *Christian Masculinity: Men and Religion in Northern Europe in the 19th and 20th Centuries* (Leuven, 2011); Patrick Pasture, Jan Art and Thomas Buerman (eds), *Gender and Christianity in Modern Europe: Beyond the Feminization Thesis* (Leuven, 2012).
[11] Michael Roper, 'Between Manliness and Masculinity: The "War Generation" and the Psychology of Fear in Britain, 1914–1970', *Journal of British Studies*, 44:2 (2005), pp.

a homosocial, work-based culture – resourced by certain tropes within Catholic tradition[12] – with an emergent cultural valorisation of a conservative male domesticity.[13] As the Bishop of Salford, George Andrew Beck, observed at a banquet to celebrate the golden jubilee of the Association in the late 1950s, as a body of 'laymen ... standing together and living for the principles they professed ... being good Catenians meant being good in the society in which they found themselves and in the professions to which they belonged.'[14] This chapter unpacks the ways in which being 'good men' has changed over the twentieth century, alongside a consistent accent on employment and bread-wining provision,[15] forms of leisure and entertainment, prayer life, familial responsibilities and active citizenship. As the study of this association demonstrates, drawn mostly from the pages of its monthly magazine,[16] for much of the twentieth century a religiously inflected sociability provided an attractive and useful forum for middle-class Catholic men. Such fraternity sustained what the layman editor of *The Tablet*, Douglas Woodruff, described at this same banquet in 1958 as a sociable and 'sound faith', outside and alongside church membership, through which *agape* feasting was an accompaniment to friendship, some theological disputation, and moments of collective prayer.

A friendly society? The origins of the Catenians and middle-class mutuality

Established in May 1908 as the brainchild of the two Mancunian founders of the politically orientated and controversial Salford Catholic Federation (which cut its teeth in opposing the 1906 Education Bill and the perceived threat to voluntary schools),[17] the body initially named the 'Chums Benevolent Association' was conceived for middle-class Catholics

---

343–63; Adrian Bingham, '"An Era of Domesticity"? Histories of Women and Gender in Interwar Britain', *Cultural and Social History*, 1:2 (2004), pp. 225–33.

[12] Alana Harris, '"A Paradise on Earth, a Foretaste of Heaven": English Catholic Understandings of Domesticity and Marriage, 1945–65', in *The Politics of Domestic Authority since 1800*, edited by Lucy Delap, Abigail Wills and Ben Griffin (London, 2009), pp. 155–81.

[13] Martin Francis, 'The Domestication of the Male? Recent Research on Nineteenth- and Twentieth-Century Masculinity', *Historical Journal*, 45:3 (2002), pp. 637–52; Laura King, *Family Men: Fatherhood and Masculinity in Britain, 1914–1960* (Oxford, 2015).

[14] 'In this Jubilee Year', *Catena*, June 1958, p. 159.

[15] Julie-Marie Strange, 'Fatherhood, Providing and Attachment in Late-Victorian and Edwardian Working-Class Families', *Historical Journal*, 55:4 (2012), pp. 1007–27.

[16] Over 100 years of the *Catena* magazine are archived at Head Office, 5 Oak Court, Pilgrims Walk, Prologis Park, Coventry, England, CV6 4QH (hereafter Archives of the Catenian Association, ACA).

[17] Peter Doyle, 'The Catholic Federation, 1906–1929', in *Voluntary Religion*, edited by W. J. Sheils and Diana Wood (Studies in Church History 23; Worcester, 1986), pp. 461–76.

to meet socially, to foster occupational interests and to create a mutual benevolence system. With the blessing of the urbane Bishop Casartelli of Salford,[18] its first meeting was held at Ingham's Hotel, Chorlton Street, under the presidency of John O'Donnell – a mill worker in a velvet factory, who moved into stockbroking. Also present was his friend Thomas Locan (in construction), three men from the textile industry, and John Whittle, who wrote the Constitution and developed the quasi-Masonic rituals of signs, regalia and motto: 'each for all and all for each'.[19] From these humble beginnings, the Manchester membership roll reached 50 in 1908 and would include prominent Catholics such as Alderman Thompson (Mayor of Eccles) and Daniel McCabe (Mayor of Manchester in 1914).[20] A second 'Circle' was opened in London in December 1909 by Edward Hogan of Barnett and he, with four other members, met at the Old Gaiety Club, before enlisting twenty-one more 'Brothers' within a year, including Sir John Knill, Lord Mayor of London.[21] On the insistence of these London members, who tended to be professionals in contrast to the commercial/business orientation of their northern counterparts, there was a desire to 'discard what appeared to be a working-class and socially immature title and adopt one more appropriate to an organisation of aspiring and ambitious Catholic men'.[22] This resulted in a name change in 1910 to 'The Catenian Association' and an annual subscription set at 21 shillings – around a month's pay for a working-class man calibrated against the Old Age Pensions Act 1908.[23] To these subscription costs were added dining charges and outlays for membership regalia, which in a 1917 report from the Bradford Circle were estimated at £7.[24] Unique among Catholic societies in not allowing ordained priests or religious to become members, nor working under a chaplain, from 1910 the Association's influence spread to urban centres in which there were critical concentrations of Catholics. Early Circles were established in Leeds, Liverpool, Newcastle, Blackburn, Hull, Sheffield, Birmingham and Glasgow. By the start of the Great War, there were twenty-seven Circles and 1,593 brothers, and by the war's conclusion, the Catenians could boast within their ranks at least four Conservative MPs (including the highly influential

---

[18] Martin John Broadley, *Louis Charles Casartelli: A Bishop in War and Peace* (Knoxville, TN, 2006).
[19] There are two institutional histories: Lane, *Catenian*, and James Hagerty, *The Catenian Association: A Centenary History 1908–2008* (Evesham, 2007).
[20] Hagerty, *Catenian*, pp. 12, 75.
[21] Ibid., p. 13.
[22] Ibid., p. 1.
[23] Ian Gazeley, *Poverty in Britain, 1900–1945* (Basingstoke, 2003), p. 14.
[24] Hagerty, *Catenian*, p. 46.

Yorkshire grandee and Middle East diplomatic advisor, Sir Mark Sykes).[25] Considering that the middle class were a small proportion of the British population[26] – there were, for example, a mere 168,000 civil servants in 1914[27] – the growth, scale and distribution of the Catenians (in mostly urban, but also rural areas if there was a viable Catholic membership base) was impressive.

Alongside its aim to 'foster brotherly love among the members' through, in the words of Richard Brosch (longstanding Birmingham Circle President and *Catena* editor for nearly three decades) 'consolidating the Catholic laity into a united body for effective action on matters of the moment',[28] other founding members such as W. T. O'Brien thought that the 'sole reason for the existence of our society ... [was] as a purely Catholics [*sic*] *Commercial* undertaking' (italics in original).[29] It is clear that economic and class considerations were an initial impetus to membership, perhaps as a counter to the Masonic business networks from which Catholics were excluded,[30] as West Brook Perceval reflected:

> it is well known that the social and material advantages attaching to membership of some religious denominations are no small factor in their well-being, and bodies such as Freemasons and others make a special feature not only of extending charity to their suffering brethren, but also of exerting influence for the material advantage of their members.[31]

Very early on in the Association's life, a business directory was developed and the first issues of the monthly magazine, *Catena*, included advertisements for the 'favour of your orders', and an exhortation to drink 'Treasure Trove whiskey'.[32] By 1958 *Catena* showcased for its readership advertisements for the unequivocally upper middle-class status symbols of a Ford consul[33] or a foreign holiday organised by Lep Travel.[34]

---

[25] For other MP members, see Hagerty, *Catenian*, p. 75. As a contrast, see another association founded in Manchester in 1909: Joan Keating, 'The Making of the Catholic Labour Activist: The Catholic Social Guild and the Catholic Workers' College, 1909–39', *Labour History Review*, 59:3 (1994), pp. 44–56.
[26] See Joanna Bourke, *Working Class Cultures in Britain, 1890–1960: Gender, Class and Ethnicity* (London, 1994), pp. 2–22, with the working class around 75% of the early twentieth-century population.
[27] Frank Prochaska, *Christianity and Social Service in Modern Britain: The Disinherited Spirit* (Oxford, 2008), p. 66.
[28] Hagerty, *Catenian*, p. 41.
[29] *Catena* 1926, cited in Lane, *Catenian*, p. 19.
[30] Jasper Godwin Ridley, *A Brief History of the Freemasons* (London, 2008), pp. 50, 112, 235.
[31] W. B. Perceval, 'The Catenian Association: Each for All and All for Each', *The Harvest*, 41:491 (1929), p. 289 (Salford Diocesan Archives, Manchester, hereafter SDA).
[32] *Catena*, July 1917, p. 39.
[33] *Catena*, February 1958, p. 44.
[34] *Catena*, October 1962, p. 260.

Despite vast changes to the organisation across the decades, the financial benefits of membership undeniably remained an attraction for some members in changing economic circumstances. In 1963, the *Catena* ran an article on the 'misuse of the Directory' reminding readers that Catenians' personal details were not to be used 'for the compiling of mailing lists, whether for commercial purposes or for sending out [charitable] appeals'.[35] A year later the Bolton Circle investigated 'a brother from Horwich who had the Catenian emblem on his lorries' as a kind of denominational warrant, but concluded that there was no way to prohibit such use.[36] In times of increased occupational hardships and redundancies, Catenian networks were valued as a safety net for redeployment and well into the 1970s many Circles had dedicated 'redundancy officers'.[37]

In many respects, it is tempting to trace the origins of the Catenian Association within the broader history of the proliferation of 'friendly societies' over the long nineteenth century, culminating with the apex of their influence in the Edwardian period.[38] Such an approach would parallel Catenian and friendly societies' lodge structures, promotion of financial interdependency, collective insurance initiatives and convivial settings.[39] Friendly societies of working-class origin were modelled on Freemasonry and developed highly elaborate ritual activities and regalia, prioritising male solidarity and a structured sociability with a strong link to locality. As Daniel Weinbren has explored, such associations offered the opportunity to be part of a 'divinely approved, well-established, financially secure network which provided social support, employment opportunities ... and the prospect of self-improvement'.[40] Comparisons would also foreground the function of these friendly societies as collectivist alternatives to the trade union movement, often taking up the task of benevolent 'social surveillance' in the promotion of health and the regulation of morality (particularly in respect of sexual conduct and temperance).[41]

There are crucial differences however, as unlike the friendly societies (which remained predominantly working class and workplace based), the

---

35   *Catena*, January 1963, p. 17.
36   J. H. Lomax, *The Catenian Association: Bolton Circle No 22, History of the Circle, 1914–1994* (SDA Pamphlet 328), unnumbered page.
37   Ibid.
38   Michael Heller, 'The National Insurance Acts 1911–1947, the Approved Societies and the Prudential Assurance Company', *Twentieth Century British History*, 19:1 (2008), pp. 1–28.
39   Daniel Weinbren, 'Beneath the All-Seeing Eye: Fraternal Order and Friendly Societies' Banners in Nineteenth- and Twentieth Century Britain', *Cultural and Social History*, 3:2 (2006), pp. 167–91.
40   Ibid., p. 169.
41   Ibid., p. 175.

national Catenian Association was resolutely orientated to professionals and businessmen. In his early history of the Association, published in 1929, Perceval triumphantly celebrated the expansion of the Catenians throughout London and the Home Counties, following the extension of the railways, new housing developments and movement into commuter suburbs, concluding that 'only a generation back, the Catholic middle class in this country was almost a negligible quantity, whereas now it is growing very rapidly and in the near future should be a most powerful agency in Catholic life'.[42] As one of the Association's member-historians observed in 1982, the rapid growth of the Catenians and the transformation of its membership across the decades may be viewed as 'a microcosm of the development of the Catholic middle class.'[43] Foundational members, such as Mancunian Brother William O'Dea, seemed to agree. In his *Retrospective and Prospective* (1919), O'Dea glibly concluded – implicitly evoking stereotypes of the Irish Catholic navvy – 'there is nothing in the [Catholic] stock that condemns them to a pick-and-shovel cast or dooms them to serve forever at the tail end of a wheelbarrow'.[44] Alongside these celebrations of a respectable entrepreneurialism, some strains of Catenian rhetoric also revelled in a strategic, separatist recollection of penal suppression, for example celebrating the 'blood of the martyrs in two members' from Accrington.[45] By the middle of the twentieth century, through appeal to the recusant past of former Grand Presidents,[46] and the strategic use of some venues with pre-Reformation histories,[47] some within the Association stressed the native longevity and aristocratic legitimacy of English Catholicism. Across the first half of the twentieth century, the Catenians asserted, simultaneously, their integration into British society as well as a Catholic distinctiveness from the Protestant Establishment.

By the late 1950s there were 171 Circles and over 7,300 members,[48] and while domestic growth slowed in the 1960s and 1970s, this was offset by rapid expansion throughout the Commonwealth and former Empire, most markedly in Australia. At the turn of the twenty-first century, the Association had over 11,000 members and 334 global Circles,[49] outlasting more traditionally constituted friendly societies whose purposes

---

[42] Perceval, 'Catenian Association', p. 290.
[43] Lane, *Catenian*, p. 24.
[44] *A Catholic Retrospective and Prospect*, Manchester Circle, 1919, cited in Hagerty, *Catenian*, p. 60.
[45] A. W. Snape, *The Catenian Association: Accrington Circle (80): A Circle History, 1924–2010* (Preston, 2010), p. 23 (SDA Pamphlet 2069).
[46] See the 'Eminent Catenians' series, *Catena,* August–November 1958.
[47] Snape, *Catenian*, p. 13.
[48] Hagerty, *Catenian*, p. 2.
[49] Hagerty, *Catenian*, p. 2.

were usurped by state-sponsored social welfare and radical changes in working-class culture.[50]

Aside from such class-based differentials, it is also important to recognise the aspirations of the Catenian Association beyond material advancement and a narrow, homosocial conviviality. The second stated aim of the Association was to 'strengthen family life through friendship and faith'.[51] Within the induction ceremony for newly approved members, aspirants pledged their adherence to the exhortation:

> In your domestic relationships we look to find you, if husband, affectionate and trustful; if father, regardful of the moral and material well-being of your children and dependents; if son, dutiful and exemplary; as a friend, steadfast and true. These qualities will dignify our Association and extend its benign influence.[52]

The ideal Catenian was a reliable and respectable breadwinner, but also a good Catholic father, husband, and friend. The role of his faith in supporting and sustaining these social, relational, and spiritual demands should not be underestimated and while a Christian foundation was implicit within many of the Victorian friendly societies, within this association its Catholic framework was foregrounded through its organisational structures and social programmes.

Catholic men: wining, dining, and at leisure

As this brief overview makes clear, one of the enduring attractions of Catenian membership was the opportunity provided for an unabashedly male, collective and respectable sociability. Reviewing the terms of the 1953 'Initiation Ceremony', for example, prospective 'Brothers' were advised: 'We are united not only for the wise purpose of helping each other commercially as far as we possibly can and to assist those who require our aid, but for moderate enjoyment, friendly intercourse and temperate interchange of social feeling.'[53] The stress on 'moderate enjoyment' was a feature from foundation days – Charles Holt identified a disciplined temperance as the chief objective of the Association, with members restricted to two drinks per meeting.[54] This prescription was later reduced to one,[55] in spite of the standard location of most Circle meetings, then as now, in the public house – a space often associated with

---

[50] Heller, 'National Insurance Acts', p. 27.
[51] Hagerty, *Catenian*, p. xii.
[52] Lane, *Catenian*, p. 21.
[53] *The Catenian Compendium*, October 1953, p. 32, ACA.
[54] Lane, *Catenian*, p. 12.
[55] At the suggestion of Charles Holt (the fifth foundational member). Lane, *Catenian*, p. 19.

excessive, working-class and 'feckless' male leisure activities.[56] Monthly Circle meetings early in its history consisted of Association business, light entertainment, and a discussion or lecture to conclude. Reports in *Catena* gave details of whist drives, musical evenings, dinners and picnics, as well as lectures by eminent speakers such as Hilaire Belloc.[57]

Across the decades, forms of entertainment expanded to include charabanc trips (Wigan Circle),[58] wireless evenings (Waterloo and Glasgow Circles),[59] and the creation of sporting societies. Inter-Catenian cricket and golf matches were started after the First World War and the inaugural national cricket tournament began in 1929. Musical theatre also remained a favourite collective outing, with the Bolton Circle patronising St Edmund's Operatic Society performances of *Iolanthe* (1947), *The Mikado* (1949), and *HMS Pinafore* (1950). Local variations in organised leisure also emerged, such as the annual St Helens 'Catenians versus Masons' bowling match from 1930,[60] and the motor-car treasure hunt from 1959,[61] which continued in many Circles well into the 1990s.[62]

Throughout the Association's long history, most of its 'rational recreation' activities were confined to an unabashedly homosocial arena. The founding Manchester Circle held its first 'Ladies Evening' in 1910,[63] but in many branches it was not until the interwar period that Catenian wives were invited to annual dinners or on occasional outings.[64] After the Second World War, as family-orientated activities became more common, a 'Caravanning Fellowship' was established, with a first collective outing to Alton Towers in 1969.[65] These were, however, mostly tangential to the main meetings and social calendar of the Association. In line with the continuance of other longstanding and gender-exclusive religious associations (e.g. the Union of Catholic Mothers),[66] the Association has not yet felt compelled to justify its position that these activities required a single-sex setting. A limited critique of the male-only character of the Catenians was voiced in March 1977, when John O'Callaghan of

---

[56] James Nicholls, *The Politics of Alcohol: A History of the Drink Question in England* (Manchester, 2011).
[57] Hagerty, *Catenian*, p. 12.
[58] Hagerty, *Catenian*, p. 68.
[59] Ibid., p. 67.
[60] Hagerty, *Catenian*, p. 68.
[61] *Catena,* October 1959, p. 218.
[62] Such as Bolton, for example; see Lomax, *Catenian*, unnumbered page.
[63] Lane, *Catenian*, p. 217.
[64] The Swansea Circle, for example, invited wives to the Annual Dinner from 1925, whereas the Edinburgh Circle resisted pressure for wives to attend their Annual Dinner until 1937. Lane, *Catenian*, p. 217.
[65] Ibid., p. 218.
[66] Caitríona Beaumont, *Housewives and Citizens: Domesticity and the Women's Movement in England, 1928–1964* (Manchester, 2015).

the Southport Circle wrote to urge the formation of 'Catenian women's councils'. He continued:

> This would bring together Catenian women with a common bond, where the social and moral affairs of the day, as they affect them and their families, could be discussed at some length. There is here a powerful and untapped Catenian linked source of moral rearmament...[67]

This limited proposal for segregated cooperation was not greeted warmly at the time, and while there have been some local initiatives independent of this call – for example Doncaster Circle wives holding monthly meetings since 1950 and a 'Catenian Ladies Association' founded in Bournemouth in 1965[68] – there has surprisingly been little impetus or external pressure to incorporate women within the organisation itself. Discussions have mostly centred on the question of helping the wives of deceased brothers, with an appeal by the President in 1981 for the establishment of a separate organisation for Catenian widows.[69] At the present time, nearly all Circles have economic and social support mechanisms for posthumous support and continue to invite those bereaved wives to functions intended for Brothers and spouses.[70] Despite these concessions, in a survey of members' views in 2002, there was unabated agreement for continuation of the principle that women should not be allowed to join the Association in their own right, although several Circles suggested a periodic review in future years.[71]

In some respects, single-sex Catenian activities did not vary tremendously from many other Christian associations for laymen or indeed 'secular' working-class leisure groups from the Edwardian period into the post-Second World War years. The Catholic Federation, for example, also offered male members debating opportunities, a rambling club, a library, and organised visits to London, as well as pilgrimages to Lourdes and Oberammergau.[72] Catenian Circles tended to differentiate themselves, however, in the scale and formality of their social occasions, characterised by an annual round of extravagant dinners and black-tie balls. Luncheon clubs in Liverpool and London were established early in the Association's history to cater for weekday sociability and a break from the office.[73] The annual New Year dinner of the Burnley and Accrington Circles in 1957, at which the Bishop of Salford was lavishly entertained, made the

---

67 Lane, *Catenian*, p. 217.
68 Ibid., p. 218.
69 Ibid.
70 Catenian Association Grand Council, *Project 2008: The Report*, 18 May 2002, p. 23 (unpublished ACA miscellaneous).
71 Ibid., 35.
72 Doyle, 'Catholic Federation', p. 467.
73 Hagerty, *Catenian*, p. 68.

pages of the *Accrington Observer and Times* newspaper. The reporter took evident pleasure in describing 'a groaning board surmounted by a boar's head, varieties of fish and meats, sandwiches and a large cake decorated with the emblem of the Organisation'.[74] In a similar vein, the diamond jubilee of the Association was celebrated by all Catenians with finery and much feasting at the Guildhall in London.[75] Reflecting in 1958 on the outlay required in fulfilment 'of his financial and social obligations to his Circle, not forgetting the ladies' [functions]', Brother F. L. Lofthouse from Manchester estimated a price of £100 per annum and linked this 'costly membership' to the loss of good potential members – chiefly young men with family obligations, for whom this considerable outlay prohibited membership.[76] Others were less critical, using humour and self-deprecating parody to reflect on the temperament and generational profile attracted by this emphasis on wining and dining. Brother Bill Wright's illustrated 'Impressions of Personalities at the Weybridge Circle's Annual Dinner and Dance on St Valentine's Night, 1963' featured several middle-aged personalities sporting moustaches and smoking cigars.[77]

In the early years of its foundation, it was taken for granted that an association like the Catenians would adopt a 'uniform', use distinctive titles for office bearers and deploy initiation signs (such as the ritual 'salute' – which was made by placing the index finger under the lapel, with the clenched fist over one's heart – or the crossing of arms to form a 'chain of Brotherhood' as a sign of peace). Details of regalia, on which there was considerable expenditure, are sparse within the literature. By the 1960s, there was a greater openness about the dress code – alongside longstanding use of ribbon sashes and the neck-chains of Office, the Association commissioned 'blue or maroon' Catenian striped bow ties from 'Harrington's Gentleman's Outfitters' and bespoke lapel badges that cost a guinea.[78] In a letter to *Catena* in 1964, Brother Fred Bentley from a Lancashire Circle lamented that such lapel badges were worn only by a minority, exclaiming: 'Rotarians proudly tell the world of their membership of the association, as do the Buffs, the Foresters and the 'Ban the Bomb' supporters – but not us'.[79] Within this eclectic survey of diverse forms of associational culture is an implicit insecurity about the relevance of old-style hierarchies (and the Catenian cause itself) in the socially progressive milieu of 1960s Britain.

---

[74] Snape, *Catenian*, p. 12, citing *The Accrington Observer and Times*, 26 January 1957, p. 8
[75] Ibid., p. 13.
[76] *Catena*, December 1958, p. 291.
[77] *Catena*, April 1963, p. 97.
[78] *Catena*, March 1963, p. 69.
[79] *Catena*, October 1964, p. 275.

From the late 1950s, questions were increasingly being asked about the utility and continuing attractiveness of these ceremonials, particularly to a younger (and more numerous) cohort of Catholic men who might be eligible for admission unlike their more working-class fathers. Extended commentary in *Catena* examined misgivings that the salute was 'childish' but dismissed the critique, voiced in some quarters, that 'to conduct meetings in ceremonial form and to clothe the ceremony in solemn and dignified language' was no longer appropriate.[80] This stimulated a lively correspondence, such as a letter from Brother Leonard Ross in Shrewsbury entitled 'Ritual: Criticism without Disloyalty', which took up an editorial paralleling Catenian ritual with the (pre-conciliar) liturgy of the Church. He concluded: 'We must regard our ritual with respect, yes: but not with awe. Even the liturgy of the Church can be altered by the Church and there have been big changes in recent years.'[81] These 'winds of change', following a 1957 revision of the Catenian Manual's opening prayers for the sick and deceased to strip out 'Edwardian extravagances',[82] were an anticipation of a wholesale critique of Catenian traditions in the early 1960s. Indeed, such self-reflection and renewal paralleled the broader transformations of liturgical form and devotional practice within the Catholic Church associated by many with the Second Vatican Council.[83] Taking up the gauntlet of those who contended that Catenian protocols left them 'ill-at-ease and embarrassed', Bernard Cuming of South London (Circle 10) castigated the rituals as 'vastly overdone ... [with] a faint odour of Freemasonry' and continued:

> Is it really necessary for a number of gentlemen, often middle-aged and frequently (as I am) on the portly side, to link hands across their chests and form a chain with, alas, in so many cases, bulging eyes and indrawn breath? Does it add anything to our dignity that our officers wear beautiful variegated scarfs? In particular, can we not get rid, once and for all, of that sort of Boy Scout salute? ... Please do not let us adhere to our present ritual merely because we dare not break with a tradition which was launched in the formal days of the early twentieth century.[84]

Even correspondents like David J. Bannon from North Manchester, who urged 'let us hold fast to our ritual, but let it be carried out properly and with dignity', acknowledged that the salute should be abolished

---

80   *Catena*, February 1958, p. 25.
81   *Catena*, April 1959, p. 84.
82   *Catena*, October 1964, pp. 297–9.
83   Alana Harris, 'A Fresh Stripping of the Altars? Liturgical Language and the Legacy of the Reformation in England, 1964–1984', in *Catholics in the Vatican II Era: Local Histories of a Global Event*, edited by Kathleen Cummings, Tim Matovina and Robert Orsi (Cambridge, 2017), pp. 245–74.
84   *Catena*, August 1963, pp. 210–11.

as 'meaningless'.[85] Popular sentiment seemed to favour change, with Brother Bernard Daly moving a motion at the Torquay AGM in 1964 for 'a simplification of ritual and regalia, the abolition of the Salute and a possible reduction in the number of Circle officers'.[86] A national questionnaire confirmed these demands, with the abandonment of the salute in 1965 and more informal procedures for Circle meetings incorporated into the 1968 *Manual of Procedure*.[87]

Speaking at the Golden Jubilee Banquet in 1958, the editor of the influential Catholic weekly *The Tablet* drily prodded the Catenians assembled to reflect on their drinking, dining and socialising to ensure the continuing cultivation of a 'high idea of the importance of meeting, conversation and talk' [for] 'there was scriptural authority; "let your conversation be in heaven"'.[88] Reflecting on the abatement of anti-Catholic sentiment which had prompted, in part, the Association's foundation in 1908, Douglas Woodruff exhorted Catenians to guard against:

> another and subtler danger that Catholics would be swamped by secular influences playing upon them by press and books and radio and television ... The Association in its second 50 years would have more to do in counteracting that, keeping Catholics together and keeping public opinion inside the Church.[89]

This prognosis of the challenges facing Catholics in the second half of the twentieth century, and the ways in which the Catenian Association would need to adapt to address the challenges to family life and modern faith, are explored in the next section. It led to much soul searching and experimentation in terms of the Association's *raison d'être*, including a re-examination of the restrictions on 'Catholic Action' or 'political activity' as well as its spiritual function. By the late 1970s, not all Catholic commentators were convinced there was a need for a denominationally exclusive, class-based and invitation-only Association chiefly orientated to 'dressing up' and epicurean enjoyment. As an acerbic and highly critical commentator wrote in the Liverpool-based *Catholic Pictorial* in 1978, which opened with the suggestion that monies spent on regalia should be donated to the Catholic international aid agency, CAFOD:

> It would be cheap and nasty to suggest that old snide – a Catenian was a failed Freemason ... But then I am cheap and nasty. ...The Catenians are outdated. Their society – with cash and social position as a prerequisite – was always one of the Church's less savoury limbs. Today the Society is a total anachronism.

---

[85] Ibid.
[86] *Catena*, September 1964, p. 238.
[87] Hagerty, *Catenian*, p. 126.
[88] *Catena*, June 1958, p. 163.
[89] Ibid.

Let the Catenians take a leaf from the good Knights – the Knights of St Columba. Long ago now, or so it seems, they had the good sense to abandon the frolics of secrecy and enter into the work of the Church ... Perhaps the Catenians could wrest themselves away from solid dinners with solid folk and give something of themselves instead of their cash. It would stop scandal. And think of the warm glow. As costly as any after-dinner Havana taken under the benevolent eye of a chaplain imported to add dignity to a right old binge.[90]

Three decades later in the 'Project 2008' report – an initiative of the Catenian Grand Council to use its centenary as a moment for reflection and evaluation – ordinary members were democratically invited to make submissions on a variety of issues. Over 25% of the total membership responded,[91] with one of the most controversial aspects a grass-roots resistance to the proposed change of the 'crossing of arms' ritual to a simple handshake.[92] While there was a majority consensus that Catenian Circles should have more low-cost functions aimed at young (non-Catenian) men, should programme regular speakers after Circle meetings to enliven proceedings,[93] and should organise a greater number of family-orientated activities, this report also confirmed strong agreement that male-only social functions remained an 'important part of Catenian fellowship'.[94] Well into its second century, the Association retains a sense that a 'religious sociability', centred on breaking bread together and male friendship, lies at the core of its identity and mission as a lay organisation.

Praying and paying: male religiosity and the lay apostolate

It used to be disparagingly said of the pre-conciliar laity that their chief functions were 'praying and paying' (as well as obeying) yet this description, without the associated pejorative overtones, does seem an accurate characterisation of Catenian activity across its history. While there is no express mention of religious activity within the Constitution, implicit within the Association's objectives is an underlying commitment to the strengthening of members' Catholic identities.[95] Men from the London Circle first articulated this awareness when introducing opening prayers to the Holy Ghost before meeting business, and the Southampton Circle innovated further by adding the *De Profundis* (Psalm 130), associated with First World War remembrance.[96] These prayers were nationally mandated in 1923, with controls for subsequent additions to the 'printed

---

90 Cited in Lane, *Catenian*, p. 123.
91 CAGC, *Project 2008*, p. 6.
92 Ibid., p. 8.
93 Ibid., p. 14.
94 Ibid.
95 Lane, *Catenian*, p. 130.
96 Hagerty, *Catenian*, p. 63.

prayer cards' in the years following.[97] From 1921, *Catena* began to report on Rosary Sundays, retreats, and Annual Communion Masses – with large turnouts in Birmingham and Surrey.[98] An unnamed parish priest wrote to the magazine to commend as 'a striking act of faith and devotion', the 'edifying sight' for clergy and congregation of Catenians going 'in a body to the altar rails on Low Sunday'.[99] Services for deceased brothers were held in 1920 in Westminster Cathedral (and continue today)[100] and in 1927 Saints Peter and Paul were adopted as patrons, with an annual Mass during their Octave for Circle Presidents commencing their term of office.[101] It is in the context of this more explicit religious activity that W. B. Perceval's 1929 history provocatively restated that Catenians were 'neither a religious nor a charitable confraternity, and apart from the admission test of being a practising Catholic, no special religious duties are demanded from members'.[102] Concerned to keep membership as wide as possible, Perceval's underplaying of the role of religion within the pages of the diocesan magazine itself was somewhat disingenuous. Increasingly towards the middle of the twentieth century, repeated but glancing references to the faith lives of ordinary members can be gleaned from the official archival record.

This is perhaps best exemplified by Brother Gordon Smith and others from the Norwich Circle, who insisted on reviving the first ever national pilgrimage to Walsingham (against some internal Catenian opposition) in 1934.[103] The pilgrimage became an annual event and in 1958 an illustrated souvenir programme was distributed to the 650 pilgrims who had gifted expensive red vestments to the shrine to celebrate the Jubilee pilgrimage.[104] That same year *Catena* reproduced an image of 'Our Lady of Walsingham' which Brother Dave O'Connell had been commissioned to paint for the Martyrs' church in Eltham.[105] Other Catenians, such as the sculptor Brother Lindsey-Clark, combined a commitment to Catholic sociability with a deep spirituality. As a Carmelite tertiary, he sought to express his faith in material form – sculpting a variety of First World War memorials, commissions for Aylesford Priory and St George's Chapel in Westminster Cathedral and, as a *Catena* photograph featured, a statue of St Bernadette for a church in Scunthorpe when nearly seventy.[106]

---

97 Ibid., p. 90 and a 1945 Prayer Card (unpublished, ACA miscellaneous).
98 Lane, *Catenian*, p. 71.
99 Ibid., p. 68.
100 Hagerty, *Catenian*, p. 67.
101 *Catena*, November 1955, p. 10.
102 Perceval, 'Catenian Association', p. 289.
103 Hagerty, *Catenian*, p. 100.
104 *Catena*, April 1958, p. 84.
105 *Catena*, May 1958, p. 111.
106 *Catena*, August 1958, p. 190.

Devotion to St George as a 'manly', chivalric and 'patriotic' saint was urged upon all *Catena* readers in an editorial which encouraged local Circles to tackle 'religious indifference' and 'national apathy' by doing honour to this military martyr on a scale similar to the way the Irish and Scots 'celebrate their saint's days with unaffected gusto the world over'.[107] More practically in the post-war years, the Shrewsbury circle undertook numerous 'poor parish visits',[108] and Province 11 (encompassing a cluster of Circles in the South of England) introduced collective retreats from 1948,[109] as well as supporting the inaugural 'Catholic People's Week' at which Catenian members, wives and families gathered for prayer, discussion and social activity in Ramsgate.[110] As scholars of pre-conciliar Catholic manliness have observed in other national contexts, male spirituality was often expressed with reference to public Marian devotions and displays of martial prowess and physical strength – such as carrying large crosses or statues in procession. However, from the period after the Second World War these emphases were increasingly displaced by a more family-orientated and domestically located spirituality, emphasising men's traversal of public and private spheres with a new accent on the home and their influence as parental role models.[111]

Alongside this developing post-war religiosity, there was a family-focused charitable ethos built into the work of the Catenian Association from the outset. A benevolent fund for Catenian wives and children was established in 1910, and one of the first grants of £5 from the Manchester general funds was given to the 'widow and family of Brother Callaghan' (London Circle) 'left in very straitened circumstances'.[112] Such a financial safety-net proved invaluable after the Great War and into the hungry thirties, when the Association procured a '"good Catholic home" for the son of a deceased Brother so that he could complete his apprenticeship'[113] or paid £250 in increments to a 'wife and three children without means' to ensure their education.[114] The potential extension of benefits to the wife and children of a Catenian fallen upon hard times or suffering unemployment

---

[107] *Catena*, July 1959, p. 150.
[108] 'Light from Under a Bushel', *Catena,* January 1957, p. 5.
[109] Lane, *Catenian,* p. 176.
[110] Ibid. For more on the Catholic People's Week, see Niall Coll and Alana Harris, 'The Path to Rome: Characteristics and Contours of Theology in Britain and Ireland before the Council', in *Vatican II – Event and Mandate. Intercontinental Commentary on the Council's Documents, their Reception and their Orientation for Church and Theology. Vol. 6. Europe,* edited by Dries Bosschaert and Urszula Pękala (Leuven, 2025).
[111] Harris, 'Paradise on Earth', pp. 167–73, and Richard Hall, Being a Man, Being a Member: Masculinity and Community in Britain's Working Men's Clubs, 1945–1960', *Cultural and Social History,* 14:1 (2016), pp. 73–88.
[112] Lane, *Catenian,* p. 107.
[113] Catenian Association Annual Report 1923, cited in Hagerty, *Catenian,* p. 67.
[114] Lane, *Catenian,* p. 115 (in 1933).

(or grave illness or death), served as a vicarious, fraternal substitution for breadwinner provision, and differentiated the Association from most other friendly societies.[115] These benevolent activities towards its membership and their families have continued unabated across more than a hundred years,[116] yet from the 1950s there was an additional concern to ensure that their considerable financial resources were also utilised beyond Catenian Circles. Catholic education became a key focal point for such initiatives but extensive funds were also made available over the years for pilgrimage to Lourdes, with the Bolton Circle providing £6.16.0 in 1964 to help sick parishioners to go to France,[117] and the combined efforts of Accrington, Burnley, Blackburn, Chorley and Broughton-in-Craven Circles in 1976 sponsoring a new luxury and adapted coach/ambulance, the 'Mark II Jumblance', for pilgrimage purposes.[118]

Nevertheless, increasingly from the late 1950s, it is possible to discern a restless questioning of whether such gentle encouragements of Catholic faith and contributions to selected charitable causes remained sufficient inducements for membership, as 'Catenianism makes few demands on its members except that they should carry out their obligations and practice the Christian virtues'.[119] A letter from G. A. Booth of Maidstone in 1958 articulated this growing sense that something beyond an 'indirect apostolate' was necessary, and under the title 'Catenians in Action' he argued that 'something more than a monthly social gathering is needed, to use to the full the great but dormant potential of the Association to do even more for Catholicism'.[120] This internal critique marked, in many ways, the reanimation of old (and formerly settled) questions about the relationship of the Association to 'Catholic Action' (CA) – defined by Pope Pius XI in 1922 as the participation of the laity in the apostolate of the hierarchy when undertaking work on the direction or mandate of a bishop in fields of dogma, morals, education and charity.[121] In an English Catholic context, organisations such as the Young Christian Workers,[122]

---

[115] Weinbren, 'Beneath', p. 178.
[116] e.g. Francis Boyle (Oldham 140), 'Can more be done for Widows and Children?', *Catena*, October 1964, pp. 274–5.
[117] Lomax, *Catenian*, unnumbered page.
[118] Snape, *Catenian*, p. 14.
[119] Editorial, 'Misplaced Zeal', *Catena*, September 1959, pp. 189–90.
[120] *Catena*, July 1958, p. 151.
[121] See Pius XI, *Ubi Arcano Dei Consilio: Encyclical on the Peace of Christ in the Kingdom of Christ* (1922), https://www.vatican.va/content/pius-xi/en/encyclicals/documents/hf_p-xi_enc_19221223_ubi-arcano-dei-consilio.html, accessed 17 March 2023.
[122] Sylvia Collins and Michael P. Hornsby-Smith, 'The Rise and Fall of the YCW in England', *Journal of Contemporary Religion*, 71:1 (2002), pp. 87–100.

the Catholic Social Guild[123] and the Catholic Evidence Guild[124] explicitly promoted such initiatives and combined Catholicism (often in a male, working-class guise) with forms of social and political action. In its early decades, the stance of the Catenians in relation to 'Catholic Action' was marked by profound ambivalence, considerable anxiety and seeming contradictions. Members were not prohibited from concurrent membership of other societies, or indeed from activity in the wider political arena in an individual capacity, but in 1937 the Association reaffirmed its self-understanding as a 'Catholic fraternity in its fullest sense', which might be a 'force in the nation's middle class life'.[125] Yet as this statement continued: 'in this f[...]tration [members] are carrying the banner of Catholic Action boldly in front of them, not as Catenians but as Catholic laymen' whose 'consciousness of their ability to do so has been clarified and strengthened by their Catenianism'.[126]

Such refined distinctions were often blurred in practice, particularly in the arena of Catholic education initiatives, which were a focus of local Circle activities from their inception. From its Catholic Federation precursors, through to the extensive emphasis on school fees and scholarship provision from 'The Children's Fund',[127] Catenians were at the forefront of championing expanding Catholic secondary provision in the 1920s and 1930s.[128] Symptomatic of changing attitudes to the 'Association in action' was the stance taken by prominent Catenians such as John Finian, W. E. Critchley and C. H. Sheill (of the North-West London Circle and the driving force behind the Catholic Parents' and Teachers' Association), who mobilised every Catenian Circle in 1943 to write in protest to Rab Butler about proposed changes to grant aid and mandated non-denominational acts of worship within all British schools.[129] In the years following the Second World War, increasing educational mobility through the grammar-school system prompted a reoriented focus on tertiary education and, interestingly, some overlap with the Catholic Social Guild (despite its more leftist politics). This took the form of the provision of a scholarship (from 1950 onwards) at the Catholic Workers' College – an adult educational establishment in Oxford modelled on Ruskin College

---

[123] John Martin Cleary, *Catholic Social Action in Britain, 1909–1959: A History of the Catholic Social Guild* (Oxford, 1961).
[124] Debra Campbell, 'The Catholic Evidence Guild: Towards a History of the Laity', *Heythrop Journal*, 30:3 (1989), pp. 306–24.
[125] Hagerty, *Catenian*, p. 77. Also, 'Are Catenians Indifferent to Church Affairs?', *Catena*, June 1937, p. 11.
[126] Hagerty, *Catenian*, p. 77.
[127] Ibid., pp. 112–15.
[128] Ibid., p. 78.
[129] Ibid., p. 155. See Kit Elliott, 'A Very Pushy Kind of Folk: Educational Reform 1944 and the Catholic Laity of England and Wales', *History of Education*, 35:1 (2006), pp. 91–119.

and with an emphasis on Catholic social teaching.[130] By 1962 there were eleven funded male graduates, and continuing impetus for the donation of £2.2s from each Circle to subsidise a bursary annually.[131]

The questions posed with increasingly urgency in *Catena* from 1959 onwards, exemplified by E. Cullen of Leeds' observation that 'we do not make sufficient appeal to individuals to join us in a worthwhile cause [so] as a body let us do something more than eat and drink together',[132] erupted on the magazine's pages in early 1962. This was prompted by an address at a Catenian banquet in Brighton at which the Bishop of Menevia characterised the issue of University Chaplaincies and their funding as 'a national problem [which] would never be satisfactorily settled unless some influential body took it in hand'.[133] Over the next two years, the Association creatively intertwined emerging conciliar thinking on an enhanced role for the laity – beyond liturgical passivity and undue deference for clerical hierarchies, as one writer diagnosed[134] – with the practical question of spiritual provision at Universities in Liverpool, Manchester,[135] Leeds, Sussex and Oxford (where Catenians J. R. R. Tolkien and Frank Pakenham, later Earl of Longford, were prominent members).[136]

Passionate correspondence in *Catena* identified Chaplaincy funding as our 'new cause, a new raison d'être',[137] and an 'ambitious scheme … [tapping] true Catenian spirit' in providing for 'the spiritual needs of the rising undergraduate generation'.[138] More conservatively minded Catenians advocated this unprecedented public activity and expenditure as a way to 'prevent sexual immorality amongst students' and to address the 'dangers of leakage from the church'.[139] An editorial in *Catena* in 1964 celebrated this movement away from a pre-war '"cosy" Catenianism' to a 'rather different brand … with the emphasis on informality and on doing things rather than just sitting back and enjoying fraternal contacts'.[140] A scheme negotiated by the Catenian Association's ruling body and the Bishops of England and Wales emerged in 1964, committing both parties to raising one to two million pounds towards a nationally coordinated

---

[130] *Catena*, September 1962, pp. 194–5; see Keating, 'Making of the Catholic Labour Activist', p. 50.
[131] *Catena*, July 1962, p. 159.
[132] *Catena*, June 1959, p. 138.
[133] Lane, *Catenian*, p. 177.
[134] 'The Role of the Laity', *Catena*, May 1964, pp. 113–15.
[135] *Catena*, July 1962, p. 160.
[136] Hagerty, *Catenian*, p. 133.
[137] Letter from W. B. Whalley (Liverpool 4), *Catena*, May 1962, pp. 116–17.
[138] Editorial, *Catena*, December 1964, pp. 319–20.
[139] See the complaint of R. E. Irvine (Hastings Circle 66), *Catena* March 1965, p. 72, about the 'aide memoire' in *Catena*, January 1965, p. 9.
[140] *Catena*, September 1964, p. 237.

Chaplaincy initiative under Trust deed.[141] The membership body, with some caution,[142] endorsed the scheme in early 1965 in a vote in which only 54 per cent of the total membership participated, but 76 per cent of ballots cast endorsed the scheme.[143]

The last-minute, and unexpected decision of the bishops to pull out of the scheme and revert to differentiated diocesan arrangements in June 1965 was greeted with disbelieving derision, which spoke of members' 'grievous disappointment' but the need to 'swallow any resentments they may feel at the dashing of their hopes'.[144] In a report contemporaneous with the decision, Grand Secretary Laurie Tanner spoke of his 'personal distress' at this 'shattering news', but identified the 'greatest tragedy ... [as] the lost opportunity for the first time in this country of the laity and the Hierarchy tackling a great problem in a true and trustful partnership'.[145] Correspondence in the months following denounced episcopal 'discourtesy' and distrust of 'an active, educated laity'– 'we are deemed to be just a bunch of laymen of no particular importance: our only significance ... is to pay up in the matter prescribed' but we 'get above ourselves when we express ideas on such problems as the spiritual and moral well-being of Catholic undergraduates and graduates'.[146]

In the decades following, the consequences of this episode were an unconscious retreat into more localised charitable initiatives, with falling membership and an insular, Circle-focused sociability. From the late 1970s onwards, a new phase in the Association's history alongside wider changes in British society led to a re-emphasis upon the responsibilities that Catenians articulated in their initiation ceremonies as fathers and family men. In a differentiated rhetoric from that fashionable in the 1950s, but retaining some marked continuities, the Association today re-emphasises family and paternity in recognition of wider societal interrogations of marriage, sexuality, and the place of religion in modern Britain.

Men in the mould of Thomas More: Catenian domesticity and the 'Spiritual Dimension'

The foundational expectation, articulated in the initiation exhortation that Catenians should be 'affectionate and trustful' husbands and mindful of the 'moral and material well-being' of their children and dependents, has

---

[141] Supplement, *Catena*, December 1964.
[142] 'Northern Caut on', *Catena*, January 1965, p. 5, and correspondence from Robert W. Browne (London 2), *Catena*, March 1965, p. 71.
[143] *Catena*, April 1965, pp. 87–8.
[144] As reported a decade later in 'Putting Back the Clock', *Catena*, July 1976, pp. 171–2.
[145] *Catena*, July 1965, p. 177
[146] D. W. C. McCarthy, 'Letter', *Catena*, September 1965, p. 255.

always played a key role in the Association's self-understanding, charitable activities and social initiatives. From the 1950s this pledge to exemplary 'domestic relationships' began to take more explicit and concrete form in the work of Major G. J. Graham-Green (of the Wimbledon Circle),[147] who set up the lay-run Catholic Marriage Advisory Council (CMAC), with financial support from fellow Catenians and offices provided by a Jewish friend. The CMAC augmented, and even influenced other societal initiatives in post-war reconstruction centred on family life and a revivified Christianity,[148] such as the better-known National Marriage Guidance movement under the auspices of churchmen Herbert Gray and David Mace.[149] Catenians were at the heart of the CMAC, evidenced by the observation that all the voluntary male counsellors at the important Birmingham branch were Catenians through its foundational years.[150] Some Catenians working with the CMAC came to prominence nationally – for example Brother Alan Rebello of the Accrington Circle was awarded a papal Bene Merenti for his services to the CMAC, before being made a Knight of the Order of St Gregory the Great in recognition of his efforts over decades as a voluntary medical practitioner on the annual diocesan pilgrimages to Lourdes.[151]

Stable married life, and 'control of fertility' within it, moved to the centre of Catenian preoccupations – as indeed those of most English Catholics – in the mid-1960s with the expectation of a shift in doctrinal teaching on contraceptive methods alongside the modernisation of the Church accompanying the Second Vatican Council. *Catena* included book reviews of influential tomes such as *Handbook for the Catholic Nurse*, Monsignor George Kelly's *Birth Control and Catholics*,[152] and Laurie Tanner's mostly welcomed but provocative opinion piece 'Freedom and Authority – The Wasted Years' which included a forthright condemnation of the church's stance on birth control as vested in an 'inaccurate analysis of the purpose of marriage and even of the sexual act itself':

> Once it is appreciated the primary purpose of marriage is not the biological function but the fostering of mutual love, and when it is seen that the act

---

[147] Graeme J. Graham–Green, 'The CMAC comes of age', *CMAC Bulletin*, 7:4 (1967), pp. 11–15; Alana Harris, 'Love Divine and Love Sublime: The Catholic Marriage Advisory Council, the Marriage Guidance Movement and the State', in *Love and Romance in Britain, 1918–1970*, edited by Alana Harris and Timothy W. Jones (London, 2014), pp. 188–224.

[148] Matthew Grimley, 'The Religion of Englishness: Puritanism, Providentialism and "National Character", 1918–45', *Journal of British Studies*, 46:4 (2007), pp. 884–906.

[149] Sue Morgan, '"Iron Strength and Infinite Tenderness": Herbert Gray and the Making of Christian Masculinities at War and at Home, 1900–40', in *Men, Masculinities and Religious Change*, edited by Delap and Morgan, pp. 168–96.

[150] Lane, *Catenian*, p. 163.

[151] Snape, *Catenian*, p. 23.

[152] *Catena*, December 1964, pp. 323–5.

of intercourse is quite separate and distinct from the act of conception ... a deeper knowledge of sexuality in man will lead in time to a fundamental relaxation in the condemnation of artificial birth control. But in the meantime, in virtue of the rightful magisterium, we must conform with any disciplines they lay on us.[53]

Catenians, like many English Catholics generally, were disturbed by the promulgation of Pope Paul VI's 1968 encyclical *Humanae Vitae*,[154] and a *Catena* editorial headed 'Crisis of Conscience' wrote of the 'agony of mind' for Catholic married couples who: 'Not versed in the finer points of theology ... [confront] problems of an intimate nature, problems they have to grapple with in their daily lives about which the encyclical, though couched in terms of compassion, offers advice which seems to demand the exercise of heroic virtue'.[155] The article concluded that the columns of the magazine would not be opened to correspondence on this issue, implicitly out of deference to the Archbishop of Westminster who called upon Catholic agencies to contain the issue. This decision was also pragmatic, recognising a likely heated diversity of opinions amongst Catenians – compounded by generational differences and subjective assessments of the priority given to conscience. As the editorial concluded, 'Catholics in Britain are divided as never before since the Reformation' and a confusion of voices in these pages 'would inevitably put strain on brotherly love which is the basis of our Association'.[156]

After a brief hiatus, tensions in the arena of a stable married life and its relationship to Catenian membership re-emerged in the late 1980s, undoubtedly related to the rising divorce rates of the previous decade. Acrimonious debates about the 'practising Catholic' criterion for membership and whether such a definition should be determined by an 'objective/legalistic' or 'subjective' test led to the resignation of some divorced Catenians and the denial of membership to others in cases of 'irregular relationships' – explicitly defined as divorced[157] but implicitly including the partnerships of gay Catholics. More recent Catenian publications have continued to stress the degree to which 'Catenianism can help

---

[153] *Catena*, November 1965, pp. 308–9.
[154] Alana Harris, 'A Magna Carta for Marriage: Love, Catholic Masculinities and the *Humanae Vitae* Contraception Crisis in 1968 Britain', *Cultural and Social History*, 17:3 (2020), pp. 407–29.
[155] *Catena*, September 1968, pp. 203–4.
[156] *Ibid*. See also 'Catenian views on Britain's Moral Climate: Statement to the Hierarchy', *Catena*, October 1970, pp. 243–5, which requests an 'honest explanation of the Christian attitude to sexuality and sexual sin', including masturbation, and 'clear guidance' on artificial contraceptives.
[157] Hagerty, *Catenian*, p. 145. See also 'Help for Divorced Catholics', *Catena*, June 1987, p. 128, and more recently CAGC, *Project 2008*, pp. 36–39, 41 where 'loss of good character' could include divorce, adultery, a criminal offence, or tax evasion.

[heteronormative, married] family life, and how families should figure more in our membership',[158] with a correlative in financial provision for Catholic youth. This support frequently takes the form of funding for 'Lourdes youth pilgrimages', World Youth Day, schools and football clubs – spaces 'where fathers are often involved'.[159]

Alongside these tensions within the Association, reflective of changes within wider British society itself and strains on an idealised nuclear family,[160] both the Catenian leadership and broader membership have reanimated long-dormant rhetorics conjuring an isolated, embattled Catholicism needing to insulate itself from corrupting, secularising societal values. In a speech at the AGM in Torquay in 1986 entitled 'The Challenge Ahead', the Grand President John Tominey underlined the importance of male solidarity 'to pursue lives of greater integrity according to the principles of our Catholic faith', to address the contemporary 'social malaise' and to aid the socialisation of children within a Christian framework as 'we must show by our example, particularly within our own homes, that the living care of good Christian parents is essential for young people and their welfare'.[161] As he concluded in this address: 'We must support fervently the sanctity of marriage and the protection of family life in all its aspects. I believe that such witness is a distinguishing mark of a Catenian.'[162] An expressly spiritual strain, annexed to an emphasis on 'Catholic fatherhood' and involved paternity[163] has become more explicit and emphatic within the Association since the late 1970s, and has gently modulated 'Christian mutualism' models to take account of women's changing role in the home and the workplace.[164] Initiatives in this vein have included the addition of prayers to Mary within Circle meetings,[165] prayers for Catenian families (on the model of the Holy Family of Nazareth),[166] and the adoption of Saint Thomas More as the third patron saint of the Association in 1991, given that he was 'the epitome of a Catholic family

---

[158] CAGC, *Project 2008*, p. 25.
[159] Ibid., pp. 32–3.
[160] Claire Langhamer, 'Love, Selfhood and Authenticity in Post-War Britain', *Cultural and Social History*, 9:2 (2012), pp. 277–97; Callum Brown, *The Battle for Christian Britain: Sex, Humanists and Secularisation, 1945–1980* (Cambridge, 2019).
[161] 'The Challenge Ahead', *Catena*, June 1985, p. 126.
[162] Ibid.
[163] Martin Francis, 'A Flight from Commitment? Domesticity, Adventure and the Masculine Imaginary in Britain after the Second World War', *Gender and History* 19:1 (2007), pp. 163–85; Julia Brannen and Ann Nilsen, 'From Fatherhood to Fathering: Transmission and Change among British Fathers in Four-Generation Families', *Sociology*, 40:2 (2006), pp. 335–52.
[164] e.g., Editorial 'Women's Status', *Catena*, March 1968, p. 46.
[165] Prayer Card circa 1964 (unpublished ACA miscellaneous).
[166] See *Catenian Manual of Procedure* 1990 (unpublished ACA miscellaneous).

and professional man'.¹⁶⁷ Catenians were therefore, unsurprisingly, key representatives and organisational volunteers within the National Pastoral Congress in Liverpool in 1980,¹⁶⁸ and provided an impetus to the Catholic Renewal (or Charismatic) Movement in Britain, fostered through *Catena* advertisements for groups in Newport, Basingstoke and Southern England generally.¹⁶⁹

While more explicitly and arguably defensively 'Catholic', the stress on a relaxed 'religious sociability' has remained. In the 1980s and 1990s Catenian and Conservative MP for Hyndburn, Ken Hargreaves, inaugurated annual Masses in the crypt chapel of St Stephen at Westminster through drawing upon a pre-Reformation tradition. Bolton Circle Catenian wives were involved as the lay readers within these liturgies and added incentives to participation were familiar from the dining and fellowship traditions of yesteryear – lunch afterwards provided at the House of Commons, followed by a West End show.¹⁷⁰ This foregrounding of Catholic formation, catechism and prayer has continued until the present. Within the 'Project 2008' Report, reviewing the Association's Centenary and future priorities, a lengthy section based on over 1,300 survey responses was devoted to 'The Spiritual Dimension'. The overarching conclusion of this democratic sounding of members' views was that 'there is strong support for the idea that Catenianism increased our responsibilities towards the faith'.¹⁷¹ Nearly half of those participating advocated for an additional emphasis upon religiously orientated activities (retreats, pilgrimages, daily Mass) and there was near unanimity in refocusing Circle prayers on 'our obligations to the faith, especially in regard to children' and their religious education.¹⁷² In their individual capacities as laymen with parishes, rather than undertaking these tasks as 'known Catenians', virtually all current members were stalwart members of their local church communities, serving as eucharistic 'Special Ministers', lay readers, or volunteers on various parish committees.¹⁷³

Drawing upon the metaphorical and mixed legacy of St Thomas More as the newly elevated patron saint of the Association, and the Catenian soul-searching of the second half of the twentieth century, there are various forms of Catholic masculinity proffered to present-day Catenians. Within More's hagiographical legacy – centred on his monastic-style spirituality

---

167 Proposed by Phil Roberts (Ormskirk Circle); see Hagerty, *Catenian*, p. 147.
168 e.g., Frank Quigley (Droitwich Circle), *Catena*, July 1980, p. 149; Lane, *Catenian*, p. 214.
169 Lane, *Catenian*, p. 213. See John Maiden, *Age of the Spirit: Charismatic Renewal, the Anglo-World, and Global Christianity, 1945–1980* (Oxford, 2022).
170 Snape, *Catenian*, p. 16.
171 CAGC, *Project 2008*, p. 25.
172 Ibid., p. 24.
173 Ibid., p. 23.

and his martyrdom – strains of an English Catholic reformation history and a counter-cultural valorisation of courage and conscience can offer resources from a recusant past to tackle secularisation. In another vein, read through More's embrace of marriage over the religious life and his middle-class respectability as a lawyer, there is confirmation of a longstanding Catenian emphasis on lay spirituality. This is distinct from priesthood and celibacy and centred upon professional respectability and breadwinner capabilities. For yet other members, More's historical representation as an enlightened patriarch (engaged with his children and educating his daughters in humanist teachings) and as a prominent statesman may resonate with desires for more family-orientated activities. Particularly through the 1960s, some members sought an expressly active, publicly visible, and even political Catholicism. Recollecting the abortive University Chaplaincy initiatives of the 1960s, it is interesting that Catenians now part-finance the National Vocations Initiative. In their economic collaboration with the Bishops of England and Wales in a scheme to encourage clerical vocations and the cultivation of candidates for the priesthood within the family, the religious socialisation of Catholic boys is prioritised. The continuing existence of this male-only organisation, despite the erosion of most other homosocial associations and widespread interrogation of traditional, male-only roles within the Church, raises questions about the continuing viability of the Association and its relevance to a younger generation of boys and men seeking support in exploring their identities, relationships and faith.

Conclusion

Existing studies of Catholic organisations and the laypeople and clergymen involved in their establishment and success have tended to focus on politically orientated and working-class 'Catholic Action' initiatives, through the lens of institutional ecclesiastical history or an implicit narrative about Catholic 'lay docility'. Moreover, these are often contrasted to a virile and progressive Continental Catholicism expressed in Christian Democratic parties, and Catholic socialism or syndicalism.[174] In contrast, a focus on the Catenian Association can cast new light on the ways in which an influential group of laymen have negotiated their understandings of Catholic masculinities and their shifting responsibilities as Catholic husbands, fathers, friends and co-religionists across the century. This relatively 'ordinary', grass-roots constituency has, to date, eluded sustained

---

[174] Joan Keating, 'The British Experience: Christian Democracy without a Party, 1910–60', in *Christian Democracy in Europe: A Comparative Perspective*, edited by David Hanley (London, 1994), pp. 168–81.

scholarly analysis – these middle-class men (mostly cradle Catholics, and some from immigrant backgrounds) did not move in the elevated circles of Belloc, Chesterton or other Distributists,[175] nor socialise with the convert intellectuals writing novels or erudite commentaries.[176] A study of this Association, with its religious dimensions increasingly stressed in the later years of the twentieth century but with a predominant emphasis on being 'Catholics at rest', allows for an acknowledgement of an expressive male faith beyond Mass attendance figures and a rigid Weberian/Durkheimian demarcation of the economic and the enchanted, the sacred and profane. In the gender-normative assessment of Richard Brosch in 1935, writing as editor of *Catena*, theirs was a 'practical Catholicism', not of pulpits and platforms but 'in clubs and cafes, in trams and trains, in offices and workshops', tending to 'induce a cultured and well-informed spirit'.[177] Two decades later in 1956, Cardinal Griffin of Westminster would remind Catenians that: 'yours is something more than a mere Catholic dining club ... and the Catenian Association cover[ed] that part of a man's life which was given to recreation; ... not as an end in itself but as a means to strengthening the bond between the members'.[178]

Through the years after the Second World War, and particularly in the period surrounding the Second Vatican Council, English Catholics generally and Catenians specifically felt compelled to look for new solutions to the social, moral and religious problems of the day. The Association took somewhat to heart the jeers of detractors that they were a 'mere body of pleasant drinking companions'.[179] Yet the Catenians survived the rocky post-conciliar period – unlike most other historical lay associations – and the organisation has now stabilised in its mission and membership, helped considerably by its growth beyond English shores (especially now in Goa). Today it is seeking newer forms of expression, with an emphasis on the 'spiritual dimension' and an increasing role for its members as 'Catholic fathers' with enhanced parental responsibilities for children's and grandchildren's inculcation in the faith. At root, these are attempts consistent with, but extending, the Association's original aims – the fostering of 'brotherly love ...[and] develop[ment of] social bonds among the members and their families'.[180] Within this volume's broader examination of lay organisations, this chapter has sought to

---

[175] Adrian Hastings (ed.), *Bishops and Writers: Aspects of the Evolution of Modern English Catholicism* (Wheathamstead, 1977).
[176] James Lothian, *The Making and Unmaking of the English Catholic Intellectual Community, 1910–1950* (South Bend, IN, 2009).
[177] *Catena*, September 1935, p. 4.
[178] *Catena*, November 1956, p. 5.
[179] Hagerty, *Catenian*, p. 135.
[180] *Rules of the Catenian Association* (1961), p. 9 (unpublished ACA miscellaneous).

illustrate the purpose and operation of a sodality speaking to varying British Catholic masculinities, inflected by considerations of class, ethnicity and political orientation. In its nurture and expression of an 'everyday' male, lay Catholicism, the history of this comradely Association presents a case study of the mainstreaming and social mobility of the denomination and its place in wider British society. The Catenian emphasis on a 'practical Catholicism' offering formation and support for laymen, family life and fatherhood – forged through conversation and epicurean conviviality – seems to continue to serve a need today, as it did from its foundation more than a century ago.

9

THE BRITISH CATHOLIC WORKER MOVEMENT AND ITS INFLUENCE ON LAY SOCIAL CATHOLICISM

Anna Blackman

The history of the Catholic Worker movement (CW)[1] within Britain dates from 1935, just two years after the founding of the first community in America. Despite this, relatively little attention has been paid to the movement within the British context, and it is still treated as a distinctly American phenomenon. Whilst swathes of literature abound attesting to the significance of the CW for American lay Catholicism,[2] the way the movement has impacted British Catholicism has been neglected.[3] There is some documentation on the early years of the British movement,[4] but a complete history from its inception until the present day remains lacking. In part, charting a complete history of the CW in Britain is made difficult due to there being very little written documentation;[5] the

---

[1] The Catholic Worker movement does not capitalise the 'm' in movement and this chapter follows that practice.
[2] This is particularly true for the movement's influence on Catholic nonviolence. See, for example, Ira Chernus, *American Nonviolence: The History of an Idea* (Maryknoll, NY, 2004); Nancy Roberts and Anne Klejment (eds), *American Catholic Pacifism: The Influence of Dorothy Day and the Catholic Worker Movement* (Westport, CT, 1996).
[3] For instance, the British Catholic sociologist Michael Hornsby-Smith makes no mention of the movement in *Roman Catholics in England: Studies in Social Structure Since the Second World War* (Cambridge, 1987), nor does he mention the CW in discussions on the development of pacifism and nonviolence. See *An Introduction to Catholic Social Thought* (Cambridge, 2006), especially Chapter 11, pp. 282–318.
[4] See Barbara Wall, 'The English *Catholic Worker*: Early Days', *Chesterton Review*, 10:3 (1984), pp. 275–93; R. P. Walsh, *The Story Behind the 'Catholic Worker'* [Pamphlet] (Manchester, 1949), pp. 1–12. These accounts are written by former CWs.
[5] Most of the literature on the CW focuses on the development of the movement within the US where it was started and where its biggest presence can be felt. A great deal of the literature pertains to the person and influence of Dorothy Day. There has been a tendency, therefore, to treat Day as synonymous with the movement in which her beliefs represent the whole. It is important to note that Day and the CW are correlated, but not identical. There has always been much plurality within the movement, which has continued to evolve since Day's death in 1980, though there are core beliefs and practices that bind the CW family together. For further details see Fred Boehrer, 'Diversity, Plurality and Ambiguity: Anarchism in the Catholic Worker Movement', *Dorothy Day and the Catholic Worker*

years 1959–1993 in particular hold almost no written account.[6] Where the movement has received attention during this period, it is mostly mentioned only in passing during the exploration of other lay societies. Focus on the contemporary movement has also been somewhat atomised, focusing on select activities of the CW, such as their involvement in Ploughshares activism,[7] or Christian anarchism.[8] The present chapter will seek to redress this by offering a holistic history of the movement within Britain, exploring also its impact on lay social Catholicism. Whilst literature on the movement in Britain is limited, archives of the *CW* newspaper have been well preserved;[9] this chapter heavily relies on these primary sources, as well as oral histories taken from those involved with the CW,[10] to provide a coherent narrative.

The birth of a movement

In order to understand the CW within Britain, it is first necessary to understand why and how the movement was founded. The CW movement began in New York in the context of the Great Depression of the 1930s.[11] Unemployment had risen to 30%,[12] resulting in mass poverty and deprivation. Believing that a Catholic response to the Depression was lacking, Peter Maurin, a French Catholic who described himself as a 'peasant-philosopher',[13] together with the American radical journalist

---

Movement: Centenary Essays, edited by William Thorn, Phillip Runkel and Susan Mountin (Milwaukee, WI, 2001), pp. 95–127.
[6] This period was also marked by a decline in CW activities within Britain.
[7] Sharon Erikson Nepstad, *Religion and War Resistance in the Plowshares Movement* (Cambridge, 2008).
[8] Alexandre Christoyannopoulos, *Christian Anarchism: A Political Commentary on the Gospel* (Exeter, 2011).
[9] Copies of the paper are preserved in the British Library. Within the collection are the UK *Catholic Worker* (*CW*) newspaper published in Wigan from 1935 to 1952, before being published in London and changing its name to *Catholic Worker and Family Forum* (*CWFF*).
[10] Special thanks go to Fr Martin Newell, from the London CW, Clive Gillam from the Oxford CW, and Raymond Towey from Catholic Peace Action. Without their generous help this chapter would not have been possible.
[11] For details on the history of the movement in America, see William D. Miller, *A Harsh and Dreadful Love: Dorothy Day and the Catholic Worker Movement* (New York, 1973).
[12] John Cort, 'Dorothy Day, the Catholic Worker, and the Labor Movement', *Centenary Essays*, p. 257.
[13] For further information on Maurin, see Arthur Sheehan, *Peter Maurin: Gay Believer* (Garden City, NY, 1959); Marc Ellis, *Peter Maurin: Prophet in the Twentieth Century* (New York, 1981).

Dorothy Day,[14] established the CW.[15] Day saw the CW as 'filling a need'[16] to reach the marginalised and the poor, which was being met by neither the Church nor wider society. Day and Maurin wanted to reach '*the man in the street with the social teachings of the church*',[17] and sought to provide a viable Catholic form of social action.[18]

Through a particular understanding of Catholic social teaching, one infused by the ideas of personalism, anarchism, nonviolence, communitarianism and voluntary poverty, Day and Maurin sought to challenge social and economic injustice by promoting a 'Christian social order'.[19] Maurin spoke about this in terms of 'blowing the dynamite of the Church', which he argued had failed to be a 'dominant social dynamic force' due to the neglect of the socially and politically radical message of the Gospel.[20] Maurin had come to Day ready with a particular idea of how to make this vision a reality through a programme for action founded on the corporal and spiritual works of mercy.[21] This would work to alleviate the 'immediate needs' within society, through outreach and charity, as well as advocating for structural change.[22]

---

14   For further information on Day, see Jim Forest, *Love Is the Measure: A Biography of Dorothy Day* (New York, 1986). Idem, *All Is Grace: A Biography of Dorothy Day* (New York, 2011); William D. Miller, *Dorothy Day: A Biography* (San Francisco, CA, 1982).
15   Although it was Maurin who initially developed the philosophy behind the CW, as noted, much of the literature focuses on Day. In part, this is because Maurin died in 1949, and Day therefore influenced the movement for much longer. Maurin was also notoriously unwilling to talk about his own life; see Day, 'Introduction', in Maurin, *Catholic Radicalism: Phrased Essays for the Green Revolution* (New York, 1949), p. iii. In contrast, Day wrote numerous autobiographies: *The Eleventh Virgin* (New York, 1924); *From Union Square to Rome* (Silver Spring, MD, 1938); *House of Hospitality* (New York, 1939); *On Pilgrimage* (New York, 1948); *The Long Loneliness: The Autobiography of Dorothy Day* (New York, 1952); *Loaves and Fishes* (New York, 1963); *On Pilgrimage: The Sixties* (New York, 1972).
16   Day, 'To Our Readers', *A Penny a Copy: Readings from the Catholic Worker*, edited by Thomas Cornell, Robert Ellsberg and Jim Forest (Maryknoll, NY, 1995), p. 3.
17   Day, with Francis J. Sicius, *Peter Maurin: Apostle to the World* (Maryknoll, NY, 2004), p. 51. Italicised in the original.
18   Mark and Louise Zwick, 'Introduction: Dorothy Day and the Catholic Worker Movement', in Dorothy Day, *On Pilgrimage* (Grand Rapids, MI, 1999) p. 10.
19   *A Penny a Copy*, p. 43.
20   Maurin, *Catholic Radicalism*, p. 3.
21   Day and Sicius, *Peter Maurin*, p. 51.
22   Maurin also intended to create CW farming communes, which would facilitate a return to the land. These were a much less successful component of the CW model and tended to be short-lived. However, in recent years, CW farms have witnessed something of a revival, in part due to an increased interest in environmentalism, seen, for instance, in the development of the CW Farm based in Hertfordshire which began in 2006 and aimed to grow food to support the community. For further details on Maurin's agronomic ideas, see Francis J. Sicius, 'Peter Maurin's Green Revolution', *U.S. Catholic Historian* 26:3 (2008), pp. 1–14.

Day and Maurin began their programme of action through the publication of *The Catholic Worker (CW)*, in which they intended to raise awareness of structural injustice and the need for renewal. The newspaper's first issue came out on 1 May 1933. As Day wrote in her editorial:

> In an attempt to popularize and make known the encyclicals of the Popes in regard to social justice and the program put forth by the Church for the 'reconstruction of the social order,' this news sheet, *The Catholic Worker*, is started.[23]

There were 2,500 copies of the newspaper printed, to be sold to passersby in Union Square. Bulk subscriptions were also sought from schools and parishes, and within the next three years the newspaper was selling 100,000 copies a year.[24] Shortly after the publication of the first issue, Day and Maurin established the first 'house of hospitality' at Day's flat,[25] to provide accommodation for the homeless.[26]

The *CW* was initially preoccupied with the question of labour, due to the Depression context. Day and Maurin directly aimed to reach out to the working class, presenting Catholic social teaching as a workable solution to their problems, instead of socialism or communism. Day had directly targeted these groups with the naming of the paper. Whilst Maurin had wanted the name *The Catholic Radical*, Day insisted that *The Catholic Worker* would directly counter the communist newspaper, the *Daily Worker*.[27]

The first issue of the newspaper addressed the exploitation of African-American workers in the South of the US, the second focused on farmers' strikes in the Midwest, the third dealt with child labour and textile strikes. Day's voice was dominant on these issues, encouraging nonviolent resistance, such as unionising and striking, as a means of confrontation.[28] However, during the Second World War, the movement saw significant backlash for maintaining its nonviolent and pacifist stance.[29] This only acted to further solidify the CW's nonviolent position, which later extended to include more radical forms of civil disobedience and direct action. Alongside the newspaper, this radical nonviolence became a dominant

---

[23] Day, 'To Our Readers', *A Penny a Copy*, p. 3.
[24] Zwick and Zwick, 'Introduction', *On Pilgrimage*, p. 11.
[25] Ibid. See also Day and Sicius, *Peter Maurin*, p. 51.
[26] Zwick and Zwick, 'Introduction', *On Pilgrimage*, p. 11.
[27] Ibid.
[28] Day, *From Union Square to Rome* (New York, 1978 edition), p. 145.
[29] Sandra Yocum Mize, '"We are Still Pacifists": Dorothy Day's Pacifism During World War II', *Centenary Essays*, p. 465.

mode of action for the CW in aiming to give witness to an alternative societal reality.³⁰

The Catholic Worker in Britain: the early years

The British inception of the CW began in a similar way to its American counterpart, through the publication of a newspaper, the first issue of which was published in 1935. During the preceding decade, there had been a marked general decline in social Catholicism within Britain,³¹ as the Catholic hierarchy became more concerned with internal problems, such as the status of Catholics within Britain, and the Education Acts,³² and less interested in the social question.³³ Church leaders, following the example of Cardinal Manning,³⁴ encouraged the laity to work through existing political avenues, such as political parties, rather than forming their own modes of Catholic social and political activity.³⁵ However, elements of social Catholicism, such as the Distributist League and Catholic Land Association, were still active, even if their impact on the episcopate was limited.³⁶ However, after 1935, when Cardinal Hinsley,³⁷ an ardent supporter of Catholic Action, was appointed as Archbishop of Westminster, social Catholicism underwent something of a revival. The CW was at the forefront of this resurgence.³⁸

The British CW came out of the meeting of Bernard Wall and Edmund Howard,³⁹ who had met as undergraduates at Oxford. They had been

---

30   Charles Curran, *American Catholic Social Ethics: Twentieth Century Approaches* (South Bend, IN, 1982), p. 132.
31   Aspden, Fortress Church, p 153.
32   Between 1929 and 1930 three education bills were proposed which included clauses that would allow local authorities the right to appoint teachers if they had funded school repairs. There were worries that Catholic concerns would be ignored in regions that showed anti-Catholic hostility, such as Liverpool. See Aspden, *Fortress Church*, pp. 178–9.
33   Ibid. pp. 179–80.
34   Henry Edward Manning (born Totteridge, 15 July 1808; died London, 14 January 1892), Cardinal from 15 March 1875.
35   Aspden, *Fortress Church*, p. 156.
36   Ibid. pp. 182–4.
37   Arthur Hinsley (born Carlton, Yorkshire, 25 August 1865; died Hare Street House, Hertfordshire, 17 March 1943), Cardinal from 13 December 1937.
38   Aspden, *Fortress Church*, pp. 204–5.
39   Bernard Wall (1908–1974) was a British Catholic writer, journalist and translator who specialised in Italian and Spanish culture and history, as well as translating several works by Teilhard de Chardin. In 1973 he won the Society of Author's John Florio Prize for his translation of Luigi Santucci's *Wrestling with Christ* (London, 1972). The writings of Bernard Wall and his wife Barbara can be accessed at Georgetown University Library. See *The Catholic Herald*, 10 May 1974. Edmund Bernard Carlo Howard (1909–95) was a writer, soldier and diplomat. After studying Law at Oxford, he went on to practice as a barrister before working at the Stock Exchange. During the Second World War he served

inspired by copies of the American newspaper, which Howard had acquired in America.[40] Wall stated in his autobiography that:

> When I saw it, it made a deep impression on me. Peter and Dorothy ... seemed to me to be putting into practice the Christian revolution. Whereas many of us were theorising, they had set out to put the Sermon on the Mount into operation in their daily lives.[41]

As with the American newspaper, Wall and Howard aimed to produce a publication that would reach working-class Catholics. Wall had previously founded and edited *Colosseum*,[42] a Catholic quarterly periodical that focused on reviews of literature and discussion of current political and intellectual thought.[43] However, after reading the work of Maurin, Wall concluded that '*Colosseum* was all very well, but it appealed to an elite or privileged class. It said nothing to the masses in England who had never heard of Maritain or Berdyaev'.[44]

The newspaper began as a two-page, double-sided broadsheet. Like its American counterpart it was sold for 'one penny a copy' and contained similar material such as woodcuts, quotations from the Bible, the Mass and papal encyclicals, as well as Catholic teachings on contemporary issues. Articles focused on issues such as anti-rearmament, in light of the rise in Nazism and fascism, support for the League of Nations, championing of labour rights, book reviews, correspondence and readers' questions.[45] Theological topics were also covered, as were political matters such as bills being debated in parliament and local and national elections.[46] Published monthly, the newspaper aimed to spread Catholic teaching on the social questions, and 'show all workers that the Catholic Church is their Church'.[47]

However, the newspaper faced problems in garnering interest. The group, formed of Howard with Wall and his wife Barbara,[48] aimed to

---

in the King's Royal Rifle Corps and in intelligence for the invasion of Italy. Subsequently he worked for the Foreign Office in Italy. See the *Daily Telegraph*, 11 June 2005.

[40] Wall, 'The English *CW*', p. 275. Howard's father was British ambassador to America, as a result of which Howard spent time in the US.
[41] Bernard Wall, *Headlong into Change* (London, 1989), pp. 96–7.
[42] See Barbara Wall, 'Bernard Wall and the *Colosseum* (1934–1939)', *Chesterton Review*, 7/3 (1981), pp. 198–224.
[43] Wall, 'The English *CW*', p. 276.
[44] Wall, *Headlong into Change*, p. 96.
[45] The authorship of many of these articles was unattributed. See Wall, 'The English *CW*', p. 281.
[46] Ibid., pp. 281–2.
[47] *CW Bulletin*, January 1940, p. 3.
[48] Barbara Wall née Lucas (1911–2009) was a Catholic author who was highly involved in the Catholic peace movement throughout her life. In 1972 she was awarded the Bene Merenti medal for her work for peace. As detailed below, she was fundamental in the

increase awareness by selling the papers on the streets and at Speaker's Corner.[49] As a small newspaper, they could not afford to advertise in other publications, but they were able to exchange adverts with papers with similar interests, such as the *Catholic Herald*.[50] By January 1936 the sales of the newspaper had reach 64,000 and it was being distributed in the streets and through parishes, as well as through the Catholic Social Guild and Catholic Workers' College.[51] Like the US newspaper, the British *CW* addressed Catholics who would otherwise be drawn to other political affiliations, and thus the newspaper was also distributed at communist and fascist meetings.[52]

Despite this, like its American model, the British *CW* also faced accusations of communism.[53] As Barbara Wall noted, this meant that the CW, 'on the whole', 'had great difficulties with bishops and priests', due to anti-communist sentiments amongst the British clergy in light of the increasing support for the Communist Party due to increasing economic depression.[54] Even the title of the paper, 'Worker', attracted instant suspicion due to its closeness to the communist newspaper the *Daily Worker*. She stated the group found this strange as they saw themselves as following in the footsteps of the papal social encyclicals *Rerum Novarum* (20; 54) and *Quadragesimo Anno* (46) in advocating for worker's rights and a just wage.[55]

However, whilst there was suspicion within the Church, the newspaper also received modest clerical support, including from Hinsley.[56] The group aimed to build relationships with parish priests so that they would place bulk orders for the newspaper which they would display in their churches after Mass, which many did. For instance, Fr Rochford, parish priest of Poplar, ordered one hundred copies each month which helped to solidify a working-class group of supporters in London. Soon similar groups appeared all over England, including Leeds, Middlesbrough, Nottingham, Northampton, Birmingham and Newcastle.[57]

Whilst Bernard Wall initially edited the newspaper, it sought a permanent editor who would be representative of its readership, and therefore

---

formation of both the Young Christian Workers movement and PAX within Britain. See Valerie Flessati, 'Champion of Faith and Justice', *Chesterton Review*, 35:3/4 (2009), p. 709.
49   Wall, 'The English *CW*', pp. 284–5.
50   Ibid., p. 285.
51   Ibid., pp. 279, 277.
52   Walsh, *The Story Behind the 'CW'*, p. 7.
53   *CW Bulletin*, January 1940, p. 2; *CW Bulletin*, Summer 1936, p. 3.
54   Wall, 'The English *CW*', pp. 278–9.
55   Ibid., p. 279.
56   Wall, 'The English *CW*', p. 280.
57   Ibid., pp. 279–80.

drawn from the Catholic working class.[58] In April 1936, Bob Walsh, who had worked for the *Catholic Herald*, took over as editor.[59] Although the founders had no ambitions beyond starting a paper,[60] Walsh more closely followed the American model instituting the first British house of hospitality in Wigan in December 1936.[61]

The Wigan community sought to meet both the physical and spiritual needs of those seeking help, who were regarded not as 'applicants or cases' but as 'human beings ... Ambassadors of God'. Working to 'combat the spirit of materialism', the community condemned the class and wealth divide, arguing against both 'patronising pity' for the poor who were forced 'to accept "charity"' and indifference to their plight by those 'secure in the knowledge that the State will look after them'. Rather, the community aimed to 'shock the rich into realising their brotherhood with the poor, and the essential Christian duty of helping the poor out of their surplus'. Echoing both the personalism and anarchism of the movement's founders, the community stated that 'we endeavour to correct, in a little way, the impersonalism and ruthless efficiency of the State organisations by the personal care and love of Christianity'.[62]

The community assisted in various acts of charity, such as providing clothes and food, but also provided advice in legal affairs, for example on the 1935 Housing Acts, the 1934 Unemployment Insurance Act and the 1934 Unemployment Assistance Board regulations, as well as providing representation in the Court of Appeal.[63] Within the first year, the community estimated that they had distributed 1,500 items of clothing, supplied 525 meals, provided shelter for 160 nights and dealt with over 2,000 legal inquiries. Donations were sought through appeals placed in the *CW* as well as other Catholic papers, such as *Blackfriars*.[64]

Growth and decline

Soon after the founding of the British *CW* newspaper, discussion groups began to appear throughout Britain. These were started in Manchester, London and Leeds,[65] and as Walsh notes, many of the members of these

---

[58] Ibid., p. 277.
[59] Ibid., pp. 287–8, 275, 277, 292. Walsh served as the editor of the paper until its cessation in 1959, after nearly twenty-five years of publication.
[60] Ibid., p. 275.
[61] Ibid., p. 290.
[62] Wigan CW, 'House of Hospitality', *Blackfriars*, 19:23 (1937), pp. 936–7.
[63] Walsh, *The Story Behind the 'CW'*, pp. 7–8.
[64] 'House of Hospitality', p. 937.
[65] Walsh, *The Story Behind the 'CW'*, p. 7.

groups were former students of the Catholic Workers' College.[66] By 1936, CW shops that sold the newspaper and related Catholic literature, had opened in Manchester and Liverpool.[67] These aimed to counteract 'the influence of the mass distribution of Communist literature',[68] and were supported by the clerical hierarchy. The Bishop of Salford blessed the Manchester shop at its opening in 1936,[69] and letters of support for the movement were received from Cardinal Hinsley. Richard Downey, Archbishop of Liverpool, Fr Gosling, former editor of *The Sower*, and Donald Mackintosh, Archbishop of Glasgow.[70]

The *CW* continued efforts to expand its readership, planning for circulation in Liverpool and Westminster, by holding a press exhibition and campaign in the dioceses. Similar plans were proposed for Middlesbrough, Manchester and Birmingham.[71] By 1936, 700 sellers for the newspaper had been recruited,[72] and the CW rapidly began to expand. Between 1937 and 1939, houses opened in Wigan, East, South-east and North London, and Airdrie.[73] By 1939, further bookshops had been opened in Wigan, Bolton, Blackburn, Stamford Hill, Croydon, London, and an additional shop in Liverpool.[74] Offices were located in Liverpool, London and Manchester, with the head office in Wigan.[75] Further CW groups were located in Newcastle, Glasgow and Clydebank.[76]

The Second World War, however, had a devastating impact on the movement,[77] on both sides of the Atlantic. In the United States, the newspaper continued to advocate for a complete pacifist stance, which proved unpopular. However, unlike the American *CW*, the British newspaper argued that whilst 'Peace at any price' could not be supported, defensive wars were permissible.[78] Although the British newspaper continued to

---

66   Ibid. The Catholic Worker's College, Oxford, was founded to train Catholics for trade union movements or for the Labour Party. See Villis, *British Catholics and Fascism*, p. 202.
67   *Bulletin*, Summer 1936, no 1, p. 6.
68   'Worker Shops', *CW*, March 1938, p. 7.
69   *Bulletin*, Summer 1936, p. 1
70   *Bulletin*, January 1940, pp. 2–3. Richard Downey (born Kilkenny, Ireland, 5 May 1881; died Liverpool, 16 June 1953), was Archbishop from 3 August 1928. Donald Mackintosh (born Inverness, Scotland, 10 October 1876; died Bearsden, Scotland, 8 December 1943), was Archbishop from 24 February 1922.
71   *Bulletin*, Summer 1936, p. 5.
72   Ibid., p. 1.
73   'Another house of hospitality', *CW*, March 1938, p. 5; 'London's House of Hospitality', *CW*, April 1939, p. 2
74   Walsh, *The Story Behind the 'CW'*, p. 7. See also *CW*, January 1939, p. 2.
75   *Bulletin*, Summer 1936, p. 8.
76   *CW*, May 1938, p. 2; *CW*, January 1939, p. 2.
77   *Bulletin*, January 1940, p. 6.
78   'War.. War.. War.. War.. There is a Christian Attitude', *Catholic Life and Family Forum (CLFF)*, 13 (1956), p 1.

be published, and some meetings were held by groups in Highbury and Islington, many of the pre-war volunteer groups broke down.[79] Sellers were lost as they were recruited for military service, and many Catholic societies suspended activities until the end of the war.[80] By January 1940, the newspaper was only circulating 21,000 copies, leaving the *CW* in ever-increasing debt.[81] Sales continued to drop to 17,000 and the newspaper lost almost all its sellers.[82] The Wigan house was forced to close in 1945,[83] and by the end of the war the only meeting groups that remained were those in Wigan, London, Manchester and Glasgow.[84]

In the aftermath of the war, the newspaper was forced both to limit its output due to paper rationing and to increase its price from $1d$ to $2d$.[85] In 1947 the decision was made to start running adverts in the newspaper to further help cover the costs of publication.[86] By 1948 circulation had increased to 30,000. However, Walsh estimated that the newspaper needed to sell 50,000 copies in order to be sustainable. Due to newsprint rationing, this was unattainable and the newspaper had to rely on donations.[87] Numerous appeals were launched for 'propagandists' who would distribute throughout their networks to widen the readership,[88] and by 1949 circulation had risen to 37,380.[89] Due to this increase in demand, Walsh announced that the newspaper would be reduced to four pages, rather than eight, to allow the publication of the same amount of copies for circulation, rather than decreasing the numbers of newspapers produced to meet with paper ration restrictions.[90]

However, the newspaper never recovered its pre-war sales, and the remaining elements of the movement looked somewhat different to before the war. After the closure of the Wigan house, the CW moved on to suggest the development of 'propaganda groups' which would consist of 'groups of Catholics working out ways and means of influencing their own neighbourhood', each centred in their own 'action house' within the local parish.[91] Though St Joseph's house of hospitality in London

---

79 Walsh, *The Story Behind the 'CW'*, p. 11.
80 *Bulletin*, January 1940, p. 6.
81 Ibid., pp. 6–7.
82 R. P. Walsh, 'A New Year's Letter to You', *CW*, January 1948, p. 2.
83 'News from other CW Houses' *CW* [America], January–February 1997, p. 4.
84 *CW*, January 1944, p. 2.
85 *CW*, February 1951, p. 4.
86 'The "Catholic Worker" and Advertising', *CW,* February 1947, p. 2.
87 Walsh, 'A New Year's Letter to You', p. 2.
88 See, e.g., the pamphlet *The Catholic Worker Looks Forward* (Manchester, 1946).
89 R. P. Walsh, 'We Report to Our Readers', *CW*, December 1949, p. 4.
90 'Explaining Four Pages', *CW*, May 1948, p. 4.
91 The CW pamphlet *Two Problems of Propaganda for Your Attention* (Manchester, 1948).

survived the war.[92] this wider vision never came to fruition. Throughout the 1950s, the newspaper struggled to maintain circulation, and was faced with increased costs from both printers and postage rates. Walsh continuously urged readers to send donations and help increase circulation.[93] In 1951 a further increase in price was made to 3*d*.[94] By 1952, the CW only held bases in Wigan, Surrey and Glasgow.[95]

By January 1955, sales had dropped to around 20,000,[96] and by the end of 1955 Walsh was reporting that the newspaper was considering ceasing publication due to financial difficulties.[97] Instead, however, Walsh took the decision to try to widen its appeal, both through increasing the topics covered, and reaching a global audience. In 1955 the CW began to release *Catholic Life*, an 'overseas edition' of the newspaper circulating 'throughout the English-speaking world'.[98] Readers of the British newspaper were encouraged to fund deliveries of the overseas edition to missions abroad.[99] Walsh also began to doubt the appeal of the British version of the newspaper. He argued that the country was not facing the same poverty as before the war, and due to the impact of the Welfare State, there was not the same need for it. As he saw it, the main activity of the newspaper was now supporting the Association of Catholic Trade Unionists.[100]

In August 1951, Bob Walsh's wife, Molly, began a family section of the newspaper, and the *CW* increasingly focused on issues that threatened traditional family life such as increased divorce rates.[101] In 1955 the title 'Family Forum' was interwoven into the paper's name, to represent its support for the Christian Family Movement.[102] Walsh further argued that the name 'Catholic Worker' acted as a 'barrier' in certain areas of Britain,[103] and that he was told repeatedly by readers and sellers that 'our name is a handicap'. He argued that '[t]hey think it is political; they think it is for men only; they think it sounds communistic; they are not

---

92 'St Joseph's House', *CW*, September 1945, p. 4.
93 R. P. Walsh, 'The Latest on Our Position', *CLFF* (1956), p. 8.
94 *CW*, February 1951, p. 4.
95 *CW*, April 1952 p. 4.
96 R. P. Walsh, 'Progress Report', *CWFF*, January 1956, p. 7.
97 Ibid.
98 *Catholic Life (CL)*, December 1955–January 1956, p. 1.
99 *CL*, March–April 1956, p. 6.
100 R. P. Walsh, 'The Story Behind this Paper', *CWFF*, January 1959, p. 8.
101 *CWFF*, April 1956, p. 1.
102 Walsh, 'Catholic Worker: Catholic Life: 21 Years Old', p. 7. The Christian Family Movement began in the early 1940s in America and aimed to help married couples and their families to strengthen their faith commitment and live out their Christian vocation in their community through meetings with other couples and by using Cardinal Cardijn's See-Judge-Act method.
103 Ibid., p. 7.

interested in the social apostolate, for economics and sociology sound too much like school'.[104] It was proposed that 'Catholic Life', the title of the overseas edition, would be deemed more acceptable,[105] extending interest to the whole of the lay apostolate, not just the social.[106]

However, in the October 1955 edition, Walsh stated that he had received great resistance to this from readers who argued that the title took away from the special focus of the newspaper.[107] Whilst it aimed to be bipartisan and present a range of views, this was met with criticism by some readers who saw it as being insufficiently radical.[108] Whilst it did retain a core group of supporters and committed sellers,[109] with readers arguing that it was one of the only ways the Church could reach working-class Catholics,[110] the newspaper ultimately failed to retain and gain enough sales to make it sustainable. In July 1958 a decision was made to stop the publishing of a special issue for the overseas paper.[111] In September 1959, after nearly twenty-five years of publication, the last edition of the British newspaper was issued.

Impact and influence

Despite the struggles faced by the CW, it had a notable impact on lay Catholicism within Britain. In particular, the newspaper acted as a vehicle to give expression to more marginal Catholic voices. The most unique contribution came from the newspaper's anti-fascist position.[112] This was unusual within Britain, at a time when most Catholics tended to favour fascist regimes that supported the institutional Church against the anti-clericalism of Republicans.[113] Pro-fascist sympathies were common within the Catholic press,[114] leaving most Catholic anti-fascist voices in Britain either isolated or absorbed into the secular mainstream.[115] This

---

[104] Walsh, 'A Letter to Every Reader', p. 2.
[105] Walsh, 'Catholic Worker: Catholic Life: 21 Years Old', p. 7.
[106] Walsh, 'A Letter to Every Reader', p. 2.
[107] *CWFF*, October 1955, p. 1.
[108] Brendan P. Murphy, 'I am an Academic Worker: Make the Paper Revolutionary and Political', *CWFF*, June 1959, p. 6; 'Readers Have Views', *CWFF*, July–August 1959, p. 6.
[109] R. P. Walsh, 'Our Future', *CWFF,* March 1959, p. 1.
[110] 'What Readers Say About Our Crisis', *CWFF,* March 1959, p. 6.
[111] R. P. Walsh, 'End of an Era', *CWFF*, July 1958, p. 3.
[112] However, this was not uncontroversial amongst the readers of the paper and regular letters were received that criticised the CW's stance. See Tom Villis, *British Catholics and Fascism: Religious Identity and Political Extremism Between the Wars* (London, 2013), pp. 199–200. Indeed, Bob Walsh spoke of how he felt his anti-Franco stance 'ostracised him from other British Catholics', ibid., p. 203.
[113] Ibid., p. 6.
[114] Ibid., p. 8.
[115] Ibid., p. 198.

meant that Catholic anti-fascist voices, such as PAX, had to rely on 'niche publications', such as the *CW*, to promote their voices.[116]

The newspaper also gave voice to those within the peace movement, especially, again, to PAX, even if it did not share their commitment to total pacifism. However, as Barbara Wall described, there was much 'cross-fertilization' between the CW and PAX due to their shared vision of spiritual renewal, the pursuit of peace, and a new resultant social order.[117] Indeed, Bernard and Barbara Wall were among the first members of the organisation.[118] The newspaper included articles on issues of peace, and on Catholic attitudes towards war, and advertised and promoted the work of peace activists, such as the activities of Spode House.[119] The newspaper also condemned other forms of violence, decrying antisemitism[120] and the racism of the Ku Klux Klan.[121]

The CW was also instrumental in enabling the birth of several other Catholic social movements including the Young Christian Workers (YCW) and Association of Catholic Trade Unionists in Britain (ACTU).[122] The newspaper published the first pamphlet of the YCW, allowed them to use their office space from which to initially base their work, and also published updates on the activities of the YCW, encouraging wider support and participation.[123] The newspaper supported the ACTU in much the same way.[124]

The CW also supported existing Catholic social bodies such as the Catholic Social Guild (CSG)[125] and the Catholic Worker's College in Oxford. The CW was concerned with spreading Catholic teaching on 'the social questions', by raising awareness of similar organisations such as the CSG, seeking to move beyond itself to create a wider network of

---

[116] Ibid., p. 199. PAX was a British Catholic peace society that challenged Church teaching on just war. It ran from 1936 to 1971, when it merged with Pax Christi. See Valerie Flessati, 'PAX: The History of a Catholic Peace Society in Britain, 1936–1971', unpublished doctoral thesis, University of Bradford, 1991, p. 8. Certain other periodicals did provide a Catholic anti-fascist stance, such as *Blackfriars* and *The Sower*. See Villis, *British Catholics and Fascism*, p. 198.
[117] Wall, 'The English *CW*', p 291.
[118] Villis, *British Catholics and Fascism*, p. 199.
[119] See for instance 'If Nuclear Race is Madness What Ought We Do?' *CLFF*, 9 (1956), pp. 4–5; 'Your Guide to Nuclear War', *CWFF*, August 1957, p. 6.
[120] 'Anti-Semitism Attacked'. *CW*, May 1943, p. 2.
[121] 'Ku Klux Klan Active Again', *CLFF*, 9, 1956, p. 5.
[122] Walsh, 'The Story Behind this Paper', p. 8.
[123] 'YCW Leads the Way', *CLFF*, 9, 1956, p. 8.
[124] *CLFF*, 11, 1956, p. 3.
[125] Founded in 1909, it professed similar views to the CW, interpreting *Rerum Novarum* as anti-capitalist, yet not supporting the corporatism of fascism. See Villis, *British Catholics and Fascism*, p. 202.

likeminded Catholics, though there was no formal connection.[126] Arguably, the largest and most lasting impact from the CW came not from the growth of the movement itself, but from the way in which it influenced, promoted and supported the development of other like-minded groups. As Walsh stated, 'I have always thought that the great thing about this paper was not the paper itself but the activities that grew up around it'.[127]

Cross-fertilisation

Despite the demise of the newspaper, and lack of a formal community, the CW still permeated British lay Catholicism after 1959 and segments of a loose CW network remained. However, this network became much more closely linked with the American CW. In lieu of a British counterpart, the American newspaper received letters from Britain that demonstrated continued interest. In 1959 Betsey Hines asked to be sent copies of the US newspaper and stated that the 'Catholic Worker is very well known over here'.[128] The December 1963 American *CW* featured updates from the Scottish poet and activist Eddie Sean Linden, about English interfaith and nonviolent efforts, writing on behalf of both PAX and the Catholic Committee for Nuclear Disarmament.[129]

Whilst Britain lacked any 'official' CW houses, the work of the American forebear exerted considerable influence of the formation of the Simon Community.[130] Begun by Anton Walloch-Clifford in 1963, the community drew significantly on the CW model of hospitality. Indeed, the first house used had been a former CW house during the Second World War.[131] As Day herself stated, the Simon House 'was very much like a Catholic Worker'.[132] Linden, also involved in the formation of the Simon Community, provided updates to the American paper, and the American CW included these as part of their wider CW network.[133]

It was also during this period that the American CW came to exert more influence over how the movement would develop in Britain. Whilst American CWs, such as English and Bondy, had visited Britain, it was not until 1963 that Day herself made the journey. This visit was particularly influential in bringing British CW interests into more close alignment with

---

[126] *Bulletin*, January 1944, p. 1.
[127] Walsh, 'The Story Behind this Paper', p. 8.
[128] Betsey Hines, 'London Peace Walk', *CW* [America], August 1959, p. 3.
[129] Eddie Sean Linden, 'Letter', *CW* [America], December 1963, p. 4.
[130] The Simon Community, founded in 1963, aims to provide community hospitality for homeless people, especially those to whom others forms of care are inaccessible. It is still active today in London and Ireland.
[131] Day, 'On Pilgrimage', *The Catholic Worker* [America], December 1967, p. 2.
[132] Ibid.
[133] Eddie Sean Linden, 'Non–Citizens', *CW* [America], December 1964, p. 4.

the wider peace movement. In October 1963 Day journeyed to England where she gave the keynote speech at Spode Conference, at Spode House, Staffordshire, sponsored by PAX.[134] Her talk focused on draft resistance, civil rights, direct action and pacifism.[135] Wicker argues that after this visit, the connection between American and British Catholic peace groups 'became more or less regular', through figures such as Eileen Egan, who had organised Day's visit, Gordon Zahn, and the Berrigan brothers.[136]

During the late 1960s and early 1970s, a small resurgence occurred when Peter Lumsden founded a CW-inspired house of hospitality in Notting Hill. Having travelled to America to engage in farming near the CW farm in New York, Lumsden founded the house upon his return to London in 1958.[137] Day saw Lumsden as following the example of Ammon Hennacy, a CW who was heavily committed to nonviolence and anarchism. She wrote of how Lumsden earned little and lived poorly, 'in order to get out of paying taxes for armaments'.[138] According to Lumsden, the house eventually closed down when it was taken over by a heavy metal band.[139]

However, CW-inspired radical activism continued to spread within Britain. In January 1973 a four-day meeting was held in Huddersfield sponsored by the Student Christian Movement and attended by 350 people. As Adrian Mitchell stated, the meeting was held 'in response to a widespread feeling among radical Christians, that a re-examination of our faith – in the context of our more usually articulated political radicalism – was long overdue'.[140] The meeting featured lectures from American CW Jim Forest, and Fr Daniel Berrigan who was highly influential in Catholic anti-war activism and had deep connections to the American CW.

Daniel Berrigan, alongside his brother Phillip, was one of the founders of the Plowshares Movement which was heavily inspired by the CW.[141] This form of activism went beyond protest and focused on resistance actions that directly aimed to undermine government action, such as entering military bases and disabling weaponry, whether symbolically or

---

134 W. D. Miller, *Dorothy Day. A Biography* (San Francisco, CA, 1982), p. 473.
135 Miller, *Dorothy Day*, p. 472.
136 Brian Wicker, 'Making Peace at Spode', *New Blackfriars*, 102:1101 (2021), pp. 763–71.
137 John Sullivan, 'Peter Lumsden, 1935–2007', *CW* [America], August–September 2007, p. 5.
138 Day, 'On Pilgrimage', *CW* December 1967, p. 2.
139 Martin Newell 'Obituary: Peter Lumsdaine: An Unusual Disciple', *London CW*, Christmas 2007, pp. 4–5.
140 Viv Broughton, *Seeds of Liberation: Spiritual Dimensions to Political Struggles*, edited by Alistair Kee (London, 1973), p. viii.
141 Nepstad, *Religion and War Resistance*, p. 53.

actually. This formed a new mode of action amongst radical Catholics,[142] and in America it became synonymous with the CW.

In 1982, inspired by the direct action of the American CW and the Berrigan brothers, Catholic Peace Action (CPA) was founded.[143] Founding members, Dan and Carmel Martin had worked at the Sacramento CW. Joined by other activists, such as Pat Gaffney, Sarah Hipperson,[144] and Raymond Towey,[145] the group emulated the spirit of the CW through outreach to homeless peoples and campaigned for nonviolence and nuclear disarmament. The CPA also continued to promote cross-fertilisation. Dan, then working for Justice and Peace Southwark Diocese, organised another three-day retreat in 1985 at which Daniel Berrigan and other American CWs shared their experiences. The form of action that the Berrigans and American CWs emulated was to be incredibly influential in the renewal of the CW in Britain, as was CPA.

Renewal and revival

In 1993 the Oxford CW opened. Founding members, husband and wife Clive Gillam and Mena Remedios,[146] were both inspired by the American CW and CPA. Whilst working in New York in the 1980s, Clive had been active in Catholic social outreach which brought him into contact with the New York CWs, and their form of resistance. Upon returning to England, inspired by what he had witnessed, he became involved in the CPA. During this time, Clive met Mena, who had attended the 1985 CPA retreat. Together, they visited American CWs in New York and California, and subsequently founded the house in Oxford. After initially providing hospitality to local homeless, the purpose of the house shifted to provide accommodation to asylum seekers in response to increasing restrictions in immigration law, such as the Immigration and Asylum Acts of 1993, 1996, and 1999, which limited social security benefits, the right to work, and local authority responsibility to support and house asylum seekers,

---

[142] Ibid., p. 46.
[143] See 'Welcome', Catholic Peace Action website, https://catholicpeaceaction.org/
[144] Hipperson spent 17 years living at Greenham Common and protesting against nuclear weapons. For more information on her life see her oral history, stored at the Imperial War Museums: 'Sarah Hipperson' [Recording] *Imperial War Museums*, https://www.iwm.org.uk/collections/item/object/80019678, accessed 11 September 2023. Hipperson also wrote about her experiences in *Greenham: Nonviolent Women v the Crown Prerogative*, edited by Beth Junor (London, 2005).
[145] Towey writes about the example of Day and Daniel Berrigan in his *Homily for Franz Jagerstatter Memorial Service*, organised by Pax Christi, London, Westminster Cathedral, 9 August 2018, https://catholicpeaceaction.org/2018/, accessed 11 September 2023.
[146] The January 1994 American paper reported on the opening of the Oxford house. See 'Correspondence on Cult, Culture, and Cultivation', *CW* [America], January 1994, p. 4.

leaving many destitute. Alongside this, the community also engaged in acts of resistance against militarism, organising weekly vigils, and published their own paper, *Strangers and Pilgrims*.[147]

Shortly afterwards, the Liverpool CW emerged from a Ploughshares action, the title given to the forms of activism that were inspired by their American counterparts. In January 1996, a group of three women, from a larger group of ten who had planned the action, entered a British Aerospace factory in Lancashire to disarm aircraft intended to be sold to Indonesia for the invasion of East Timor. This action, known as the Seeds of Hope Ploughshares, resulted in the arrest of four members of the group, who were charged with criminal damage and conspiracy to cause damage. They were refused bail and kept in prison for six months,[148] but were later fully acquitted, the first time this happened in the history of the Plowshares movement.[149]

A key difference between the American Plowshares and the British movement was that the US activists were often part of CW communities which provided them with a strong infrastructure and support network, for both planning and engaging in the activities, and providing support after arrest.[150] However, Ciaron O'Reilly, an Australian CW, with experience in both Australian and American CW activism, had come to Britain to support the Seeds of Hope activists,[151] knowing members Andrea Needham, who also had involvement in the American CW and Plowshares movement as well as Oxford CW, [152] and Angie Zelter, who was fundamental in forming the Trident Ploughshares in Scotland.[153] In 1997 the Liverpool CW was formed from the support offered to the Ploughshares activists.[154] It focused on hospitality for families and friends

---

[147] See Ashley Beck, *Dorothy Day: Devoted Daughter of the Church* (London, 2008), p. 66.
[148] This action is documented in Andrea Needham, *The Hammer Blow: How 10 Women Disarmed a War Plane* (London, 2016).
[149] Nepstad, *Religion and War Resistance*, pp. 182–7. For further information, see Ciaron O'Reilly, 'For Swords into Plowshares, the Hammer Has to Fall!', *Mutual Aid: Newsletter of the West End Catholic Worker* (1996). O'Reilly also detailed the Seeds of Hope Ploughshares in a letter to the American *Catholic Worker*. See O'Reilly 'The right place at the right time', *CW* [America], August–September 1996, p. 5.
[150] Harry Browne, *Hammered by the Irish: How the Pitstop Ploughshares Disabled a U.S. Warplane with Ireland's Blessing* (Edinburgh, 2008), p. 17.
[151] Ciaron O'Reilly, 'Ploughshares and the Catholic Worker Movement' Presentation for the Nonviolent Action Research Project, July 1996. Summary available online at https://civilresistance.info/challenge/9-ploughshares, accessed 11 September 2023.
[152] Nepstad, *Religion and War Resistance*, pp. 182–7.
[153] Browne, *Hammered by the Irish*, p. 16.
[154] 'News from other CW Houses', *CW* [America], 1997, p. 4.

visiting inmates at Liverpool jail, refugees from East Timor,[155] and support for further resistance actions.

The community's commitment to resistance was reflected in its newspaper which closely documented updates in the Ploughshares movement. Their June/July 1999 issue, for example, relayed the details of the Preston Ploughshares trial, where charges were brought against Swedish Ploughshares activists accused of having sought to disarm the Trident submarine HMS *Vengeance* in VSEL shipyards at Barrow-in-Furness.[156] The newspaper also covered news of other CWs involved in activism internationally, such as the arrest of CWs at NATO HQ in Brussels whilst protesting the Balkan war in May 1999.[157]

The community also engaged in direct action by offering solidarity to other activists, such as those involved in the Preston Ploughshares and the Bread not Bombs Ploughshares,[158] as well as involvement in resistance actions themselves. For instance, on 19 May 1999, the Liverpool CWs gathered alongside other peace activists to make a statement on the NATO attacks on Kosovo and Serbia. O'Reilly blockaded the doors to the office at Preston Air Force and Navy Recruitment Centre, which closed the office for the rest of the day. O'Reilly was arrested for breaching the peace and was held for two hours before having the charges dropped.[159] The community also engaged in the wider Catholic peace movement. For example, alongside Pax Christi, the Liverpool and Oxford CW organised a vigil outside the Indonesian Embassy, from June to August 1999, to protest what was seen as the Indonesian military's meddling in the upcoming ballot on autonomy for East Timor.[160]

In 1998 another community emerged in Glasgow in reaction to the increasing number of refugees and asylum seekers entering Britain, and what they saw as the inadequate response from the government. With help from the St Vincent de Paul Society, the community founded their own house of hospitality in Maryhill. They also undertook their own resistance action, focusing heavily on Trident and related nuclear weapons issues,[161] as well as collaborating in resistance actions with the wider CW community.[162]

---

[155] Ibid.
[156] Ciaron O'Reilly, *Liverpool CW*, June/July 1999, pp. 2–3.
[157] Ibid., pp. 2–3.
[158] Ibid., p. 3.
[159] Ibid., pp. 2–3.
[160] Ibid.
[161] This is something that the community still takes part in today. See Frances Gallagher, 'Scotland's Christian Peace Groups Campaign at Faslane', *Independent Catholic News*, 24 January 2022, https://www.indcatholicnews.com/news/43924.
[162] Glasgow CW, 'Catholic Worker Glasgow – a previous incarnation', Glasgow CW website, http://Catholicworker.org.uk/UploadIS/CatholicWorkerGlasgowHistory.pdf, accessed 11

In 1999, hostility towards CW's resistance actions surfaced as the Liverpool community was infiltrated by a corporate spy from British Aerospace, helping to force its closure.[163] However, they persisted in their resistance efforts, which would go on to form the London CW. This too was born out of Ploughshares activism. On 3 November 2000, Fr Martin Newell, a British Passionist priest who had been involved in the Liverpool CW,[164] and Susan van der Hijden, a Dutch CW, entered the air station RAF Wittering in Cambridgeshire to disable the Trident nuclear weapons convoy vehicle.[165] The action, known as 'Jubilee Ploughshares 2000', resulted in the arrest of both and drew together a network of supporters who shared a 'long sensed … need for a Catholic Worker community of hospitality and resistance in the world's second imperial city'.[166] These supporters included O'Reilly and Lumsden, both of whom supported Newell and van der Hijden until their release from prison in May 2001.[167]

Conclusion

By 2001, the London *CW* newspaper was reporting CW supporters in Glasgow, Liverpool, Manchester, Norwich, Oxford and Portsmouth.[168] In October 2005, the London community began running the Urban Table soup kitchen; in June 2006 it opened the community's first house of hospitality, Dorothy Day House; and in June 2007 the community opened Peter's Community Café named after Lumsden. In 2010, the community moved to Giuseppe Conlon House in Haringey, where it still resides.[169] Fr Newell went on to found a Passionist House of Hospitality in Birmingham, which has since closed. In 2006, Scott and Maria Albrecht established the CW Farm in West Hyde, Hertfordshire, to provide hospitality for female

---

September 2023. For newsletters of the Glasgow CW from 2013 onwards, see the Glasgow CW website, http://Catholicworker.org.uk/Articles/InfoSheet.aspx, accessed 11 September 2023. In 2009 the house of hospitality in Maryhill closed due to a lack of support. However, the community was reborn as a network of individuals who take part in resistance actions, community outreach and roundtable discussions.
163   Browne, *Hammered by the Irish*, p. 16.
164   Newell had also been involved with the Simon Community for over twenty years, from 1989 to 1990 living in the house at Malden Road that the community had inherited from the first London CWs. It was here that Newell learned about the CW and met Judith Dawes, another founding member of the Oxford CW, who also had previous experience of the CW in America.
165   See London CW, 'Jubilee Ploughshares', London CW website, http://www.londonc-Catholicworker.org/jubilee_ploughshares.htm, accessed 11 September 2023.
166   London CW, 'Who We Are', London CW website, http://londoncCatholicworker.org/wwa.html, accessed 11 September 2023.
167   London CW, 'Jubilee Ploughshares'.
168   'Other Catholic Worker Contacts', *London CW*, November 2001, p. 4.
169   Beck, *Dorothy Day*, p. 67.

asylum seekers and refugees and their children.[170] Former members of the London community founded a Quaker offshoot, Martha House, in Tottenham in 2014.[171] London CW, Br. Johannes Maertens, helped to open a house offering ministry to the refugee camps in Calais in 2016.[172] In 2017 a CW group emerged in Kent, holding vigils at Dover docks, and providing outreach to the homeless.[173]

Whilst the present incarnation of the British movement looks very different to that of the early CW, continuity is still apparent. The movement still functions on the basis of disseminating a newspaper and offering hospitality, though it is much more heavily involved in resistance action and a commitment to nonviolence, reflecting the direction the CW has taken in America. Direct links between the first iteration and that of today can also be witnessed through the continued involvement of individuals, such as Lumsden who provided a pivotal crossing-point.[174] Both manifestations have also been influential in opening up alternative methods of political and social engagement for lay Catholics, from involvement in strikes and trade unions, to nonviolent resistance and Ploughshares activism. Both have also offered a theological critique of societal structures, producing a Catholic analysis of pressing issues of the day. Again, the two embodiments have continuously advocated for a more widespread engagement by lay Catholics in an active commitment to Catholic social teaching.

In 1938 H. A. Reinhold wrote, comparing the CW to other contemporary Catholic movements of the time, that it differed in its reluctance 'to become anything like an Organisation and its firm determination to remain a movement, a leaven in the minds of Catholics'.[175] Today the movement continues to engage with other like-minded Catholic organisations, such as Pax Christi, Caritas, and the National Justice and Peace Network.[176] The movement has received attention in prominent Catholic

---

[170] *The Catholic Worker Farm*, available at https://www.thecatholicworkerfarm.org/, accessed 11 October 2023.
[171] 'About', *Martha House Wordpress*, https://marthahouse.wordpress.com/about/, accessed 11 September 2023.
[172] 'Maria Skobtsova House', European CW website, http://www.eurocatholicworker.org/index.php?id=33, accessed 11 September 2023.
[173] @KCatholicWorker, 'Kent CW', Twitter, https://twitter.com/KCatholicWorker; 'Kent CW', CW website, https://catholicworker.org/directory/int-uk-kent-cw-html/, accessed 11 September 2023.
[174] Newell, 'Obituary: Peter Lumsdaine'.
[175] H. A. Reinhold, 'The Catholic Worker Movement in America', *Blackfriars*, 19:222 (1938), pp. 640–1.
[176] See 'Directory', National Justice and Peace Network website, https://www.justice-and-peace.org.uk/external-contacts/name/london-catholic-worker/, accessed 11 September 2023; 'London CW', Caritas website, https://www.caritasvs.org.uk/london-catholic-worker-539.php, accessed 11 September 2023; 'Pax Christi at Faslane', Pax Christi Scotland website, https://www.paxchristiscotland.org/news/, accessed 11 September 2023.

newspapers, such as *The Tablet*,[177] and in 2014 Cardinal Vincent Nichols, Archbishop of Westminster, and Justin Welby, Archbishop of Canterbury, visited Giuseppe Conlon House.[178] More recently, the Bishop of Westminster, Paul MacAleenan, joined the London CW in a vigil for refugees outside the Home Office.[179] The London CW has also been highly influential in the growth of Christian Climate Action, of which Newell was a founding member.[180] Whilst the CW model of action still remains far from mainstream, it has left a lasting impression on the British Catholic socio-political imagination. Today, Reinhold's definition remains fitting.

---

[177] *The Tablet*, 9 May 2020 and 20 November 2016.
[178] Henrietta Cullinan, 'Cardinal and Archbishop of Canterbury Visit Giuseppe Conlon House', *London CW* Easter 2014, pp. 1, 2, 9.
[179] *The Tablet*, 20 June 2023.
[180] Christian Climate Action, the Christian branch of Extinction Rebellion, engages in direct action in favour of policy changes to address the climate crisis. See the Christian Climate Action website, https://christianclimateaction.org/, accessed 11 September. Newell has also spoken about his involvement; see *Lacuna Magazine*, 10 February 2016.

10

'TODAY IT IS NOT THE GREAT SAINT WHO IS THUNDERING FORTH': THE LAITY AND CATHOLIC CHARISMATIC RENEWAL IN ENGLAND[1]

John Maiden

'The exciting thing about the renewal in the 20th century is that it is being achieved through the people'. So argued a lay writer in a mid-1970s issue of *Goodnews*, the English Catholic charismatic magazine. He asserted:

> The Lord takes each one of us as he finds us – then uses it. Perhaps he is also taking our generation as he finds it, with its higher degree of education, its thirst for the spiritual, its greater facility in movement and communication, and is using these elements for his greater purpose.
>
> However it may be, today it is not the great saint who is thundering forth for the Lord. It is the ordinary person – the bank clerk, the housewife, the religious, the secular priest – who is being called by the Lord, not merely to personal holiness in life, but to be his instrument of salvation to others.[2]

The *Goodnews* article echoed various Second Vatican Council utterances about the diversity and oneness of ministry in the Church, including *Apostolicam Actuositatem*, the 'Decree of the Apostolate of the Laity' (1965), with its description of the laity's 'apostolate of evangelization and sanctification'.[3] Identifying antecedents in the Liturgical Movement and Cursillo, the writer in *Goodnews* claimed such movements represented a profound shift in the recognition and empowerment of the laity in the Church. It is necessary to juxtapose the optimism of the author with recent analysis of the Catholic laity in the post-1945 period,

---

[1] I am grateful to Kristina Cooper, the former editor of *Goodnews*, for sharing various research notes: 'Notes of a conversation with Lady Bronwyn Astor' and Bob Balkam, 'Charism and Institution, 1968–1978'.
[2] Anthony Pyle, *Goodnews*, 7 (December 1976/January 1977), pp. 3–4.
[3] Paul VI, *Apostolicam Actuositatem*, 18 November 1965, https://www.vatican.va/archive/hist_councils/ii_vatican_council/documents/vat-ii_decree_19651118_apostolicam-actuositatem_en.html, accessed 15 January 2024.

which has sought to describe and explain an erosion in lay participation. Stephen Bullivant describes a 'Mass exodus', citing evidence of a decline in attendance at Sunday Mass in England and Wales from 2,114,000 in 1965 to 1,644,000 in 1980.[4] He attributes this in part to social and cultural turbulences, but also suggests that the sheer scope of the reforms of Vatican II was such that the Council's work must surely have contributed to a trend of decline. The contribution of charismatic renewal to the laity post-Vatican II must be considered in this context of secularisation in the English Church.

Catholic charismatic renewal, or 'Catholic pentecostalism' as it was often known in the United States in the early 1970s, has been understood primarily as a lay movement.[5] The American priest Fr Kilian McDonnell O.S.B. of the Collegeville Institute who, along with Cardinal Suenens was the leading theologian of Catholic charismatic renewal in the 1970s, claimed, 'the movement is dominantly lay in character. The theology and rhetoric are essentially lay.'[6] As we shall see, English Catholic charismatic renewal, in its origins, organisation, leadership and characteristics, had important lay dimensions. Bullivant argues that in the environment of post-Vatican II Catholicism, the more physical and material expressions of devotion, such as rosary beads, were increasingly replaced by the 'verbal and cerebral' – patterns of ministry requiring 'a certain amount of literate self-confidence'.[7] He includes as an example, but only in passing, the extemporising prayers of charismatic worship. At the same time, as Alana Harris's work on Lourdes has shown, mid-century cultural trends had increasingly shifted towards the therapeutic. Just as Lourdes was, after the Second World War, increasingly reimagined 'within a cultural framework that embraced a widely popularised psychological awareness and the desire for an experiential spirituality', so charismatic renewal operated within a context of increased emphasis on self-actualization.[8] This chapter offers a new perspective on post-Vatican II lay devotion in the light of wider cultural developments, looking for the first time at the historical development of English Catholic charismatic renewal.

The global influence of American Catholics on charismatic renewal means that what follows in this chapter also includes a transnational

---

[4] Stephen Bullivant, *Mass Exodus: Catholic Disaffiliation in Britain and American since Vatican II* (Oxford, 2019), pp. 267–8.
[5] On 'Catholic pentecostals' see Kevin and Dorothy Ranaghan, *Catholic Pentecostals* (New York, 1969).
[6] Quoted in Joseph Fichter, *The Catholic Cult of the Paraclete* (New York, 1975), p. 12.
[7] Bullivant, *Mass Exodus*, p 193.
[8] See Alana Harris, 'Lourdes and Holistic Spirituality: Contemporary Catholicism, the Therapeutic, and Religious Thermalism', *Culture and Religion*, 14:1 (2013), p. 27.

component. As argued by the author elsewhere, the upper Midwest university cities of South Bend and Ann Arbor were the 'cockpit' for Catholic charismatic renewal in the United States and beyond.[9] The ecumenical 'covenant' communities of True House and People of Praise (South Bend) and The Word of God (Ann Arbor) were the centres for a multi-million-dollar charismatic media operation – producing the magazine *New Covenant*, the widely used *Life in the Spirit* course (an introduction to charismatic discipleship) and key texts by authors such as Kevin and Dorothy Ranaghan, Steve Clark and Ralph Martin – and largely oversaw the annual international Catholic charismatic conference held at the Notre Dame University football stadium. The patterns of charismatic renewal endorsed by these communities – and by extension the Catholic Charismatic Renewal Service Committee (CCRSC) in the United States – was of a particular type, tending to emphasise lay leadership, but in a 'complementarian', or male-dominated, mould. In this chapter we shall see that English charismatics, middle class and cosmopolitan, often drew on influence from the United States. However, the English scene was marked by some important differences in relation to the dominant model in America, for example regarding gender and various emphases around issues of authority, discipleship and healing. By paying attention to the transnational context of lay involvement, therefore, what follows also sheds light on the 'glocal' dynamics of the movement and the distinctiveness of the English Catholic charismatic scene.

Laity and the emergence of English Catholic charismatic renewal

The conventional narrative of Catholic charismatic renewal has been that it began with an 'outpouring' of the Spirit amongst the students and Faculty of Duquesne University in 1967. An implication of this storyline, of course, is that renewal was an American export. Like many such origin myths of modern Christian movements, this is misleading. Nevertheless, this historical narrative was widely accepted by English participants in the renewal.[10] A 1978 *Goodnews* article, for example, charted the emergence of the renewal from small American beginnings to global international conferences: '1967, a handful at Duquesne, Pittsburgh; 1975, the Rome Conference; and now, 1978, the astonishing experience of over 20,000

---

[9] John Maiden, *Age of the Spirit: Charismatic Renewal, the Anglo-World, and Global Christianity, 1945–1980* (Oxford, 2023), pp. 113–17. Valentina Ciciliot has examined this power base in greater detail in 'The Origins of the Catholic Charismatic Renewal in the United States: The Experience at the University of Notre Dame and South Bend (Indiana), 1967–1975', in *Transatlantic Charismatic Renewal, c. 1950–2000*, edited by Andrew Atherstone, Mark Hutchinson and John Maiden (Leiden, 2021), pp. 144–64.
[10] On origins 'myths', see also Maiden, *Age of the Spirit*, pp. 50–64.

people at the International Conference in Dublin.'[11] Linear narratives, of course, have their attractions; nevertheless, in reality the beginnings of Catholic charismatic renewal in England were organic, involving transatlantic exchange but also indigenous emergences.

Individual charismatic prayer groups were being established in England at the turn of the decade. One was organised in London by a laywoman, Gill Davies, who had been influenced by American literature, specifically a copy of the South Bend charismatics Kevin and Dorothy Ranaghan's *Catholic Pentecostals*, published the previous year.[12] Another was established in Wimbledon by Tim and Mimi Turner, which met on Tuesday nights and included a minority of Protestants.[13] The Turners' approach to renewal had been informed by American influences: indeed from 1973 they were running a European distribution centre for the Ann Arbor magazine *New Covenant*.[14] The circulation and popularity of American literature was a prominent factor in the rise of renewal in England. When in 1977, the charismatic priest Fr Ian Petit O.S.B. recalled the early stages of renewal in the country, he described how it had often spread 'by word of mouth and by books', listing various titles associated with South Bend and Ann Arbor.[15]

In contrast, various other prayer groups which emerged were the product of interactions with English pentecostalism and had no obvious connection at all with American mediation in their inception.[16] Esmond Gwatkin was 'baptised' through the ministry of pentecostals at a congregation in Portsmouth, and he soon established a prayer group in the tiny village of West Meon, meeting in the presbytery of St Laurence Church.[17] Hockley Pentecostal Church in Birmingham was particularly successful in persuading individual Catholics they had been missing a dimension of spiritual life. One visitor was a Catholic schoolteacher, Gabrielle Twomey, who then established a small, ecumenical (75% Roman Catholic) prayer meeting in Edgbaston.[18] Fr Peter Hocken, who was to become a historian

---

[11] 'You shall be my witnesses', *Goodnews*, August/September 1978, p. 4.
[12] Gill Davies, 'One of the organisers of the first London Days of Renewal shares her memories', *Goodnews*, 146 (2000), pp. 22–3.
[13] *List of Catholic Sponsored Prayer Groups, 1975–76* (National Service Committee, 1975), 7. 'England', *Goodnews*, April/May 1992, pp. 68–9.
[14] *Day of Renewal* newsletter December–January 1973. Mary Ann Jahr, 'Regional distribution centres', *New Covenant*, 3:3 (September 1973), pp. 21–2.
[15] Ian Petit, 'Where are we?' *Goodnews*, 9 (April/May 1977), pp. 2–4, 2.
[16] Various authors have described this dynamic, including Peter Hocken in 'Baptism in the Holy Spirit: A Spiritual and Theological Journey', in *Children of the Calling: Essays in the Honour of Stanley M. Burgess and Ruth V. Burgess*, edited by Eric Nelson Newberg and Lois E. Olena (Eugene, OR, 2014), pp. 299–300.
[17] Balkam, 'Charism and Institution'; *List of Catholic Sponsored Prayer Groups*.
[18] *List of Catholic Sponsored Prayer Groups*, 4; 'England', *Goodnews*, April/May 1992, pp. 68–9.

of charismatic renewal, was amongst those who visited Hockley around this time.[19] In Oxford, Fr Simon Tugwell and various other Dominicans encountered pentecostals at a nearby prayer group and soon began to run meetings at Blackfriars Hall.[20] These 'indigenous' beginnings of renewal, as Catholic laity, religious and clergy encountered local forms of pentecostalism, help account for something of the distinctiveness of the movement in England. According to Hocken, Tugwell, one of the dominant figures in the early phase of renewal in England, was 'uninterested in the new movement arriving from the United States, which we saw as pre-packaged and highly organized'.[21]

The laity also played a role in the appearance of another important early node for renewal which was the product of transatlantic ecumenical networks. A key actor was Bob Balkam, an American lay Catholic convert from Congregationalism, who since 1966 had been Chair of the Gustave Weigel Society, an organisation named after the Maryland liberal Jesuit theologian who had been an advisor to the Secretariat for the Promotion of Christian Unity, which organised ecumenical retreats.[22] In 1967, when visiting Freiburg, Germany, for a meeting of the International Ecumenical Fellowship, Balkam met Lady Bronwen Astor. She was something of a celebrity figure, whose late husband, Viscount Astor of Cliveden, had been caught up in the media frenzy around the Profumo spy affair. At this stage, Lady Astor, an Anglican, was interested in mysticism, notably the work of Russian P. D. Ouspensky and the French Jesuit Teilhard de Chardin.[23] The year after the conference, Balkam experienced baptism in the Spirit; and meanwhile Astor had begun to understand a 'Damascus' experience she had in 1959 as having received the Holy Spirit.[24] Balkam was persuaded by Lady Astor – who converted to Catholicism – and Mary Tanner, another ecumenist, to move with his wife and six children to England. Around 1971, they inaugurated the charismatic lay Community of Christ the King next to Astor's Tuesley Manor home, near Godalming.[25] The American layman was to become a leading figure in the English charismatic scene, working closely with the Fountain

---

[19] Hocken, 'Baptism in the Holy Spirit', pp. 299–300.
[20] 'England', *Goodnews*, April/May 1992, pp. 68–9.
[21] Hocken, 'Baptism in the Holy Spirit', pp. 299–300.
[22] 'Miscellany', *Christianity Today*, 19 January 1968, p. 42; 'Weigel Society Meets', *The Living Church*, 8 May 1966, pp. 6–7.
[23] On Astor's spirituality, see Peter Stanford, *Bronwen Astor: Her Life and Times* (London, 2000). On the history of the IEF, see Kate Davson and Nagypál Szabolcs (eds), *Living Today the Church of Tomorrow: Forty Years of the International Ecumenical Fellowship* (Brussels, 2009).
[24] Cooper, 'Notes'.
[25] 'England', *Goodnews*, April/May 1992, pp. 68–9; Bob Balkam, 'The Spirit blows where it pleases', *Goodnews*, 146 (2000), pp. 8–9.

Trust, an interdenominational Protestant charismatic service agency, and organising with the support of the Astor Foundation several ecumenical conferences in the early 1970s.[26]

By mid-decade there were an estimated 135 'Catholic-sponsored' prayer groups in England, with significant clusters of these meetings in London, Surrey, Essex, West Yorkshire, Cheshire and Greater Manchester.[27] Of these groups, a total of sixty-four were lay led, with a further three jointly led by lay and religious and one group led a lay person and parish priest. There were opportunities also for married couples to lead prayer meetings together: a total of fifteen groups were organised on this basis. Alongside these, thirty-three groups were led by religious and another thirty-one by parish priests. Lay-led groups included large meetings such as the Turners' Wimbledon gathering, which attracted forty or more, and a group in Soho, with attendances between thirty and fifty. However, most were smaller, with many groups reporting twenty or fewer usually in attendance. Only 31 groups had more, and of these, 27 reported usual attendances of 40 or less. The larger groups were sometimes held in convents such as Holy Cross in Gerrards Cross, and Notre Dame, at Mount Pleasant, Liverpool, or priories, such as a Monday night meeting at the Olivetan priory in Cockfosters, London, which could attract 100. Larger meetings also took place in schools, such as La Retraite, Bristol, which was attended by between 40 and 50, and Ratcliffe College in Leicestershire, where 60 were drawn to a Wednesday night term-time group. Although a total of 37 prayer groups were entirely Catholic in membership, the majority were to some degree ecumenical, albeit usually with a Catholic majority (53 groups were in the 80–99% Catholic range). Some groups, however, were Protestant majority, with twelve groups less than 40% Catholic. The lay and ecumenical dynamics of renewal could result in some unique situations: with, for example, one lay woman, Christine Donaldson, leading a group at a convent in Erdington, Birmingham, which was 75% Protestant.

By the mid-1970s, the number of Catholic charismatic prayer groups was modest, the products of word-of-mouth witness, American media, and encounters with English pentecostals. The laity made an important contribution to the overall picture, leading approximately half of all prayer groups. Around fifty of the total of 135 prayer groups listed appear to have met in private homes. Like renewal in Protestant denominations, the movement amongst Catholics often occupied domestic spaces.

---

[26] Cooper, 'Notes'; Balkam, 'Charism and Institution'.
[27] All information in this paragraph is taken from *List of Catholic Sponsored Prayer Groups*.

Leadership of Catholic-sponsored prayer groups in England by category

lay	lay couple	lay and religious	lay and priest	priest	religious	Anglican or unknown	total
49	15	3	1	31	33	3	135

Proportion of Catholics in attendance at Catholic-sponsored prayer groups in England

100%	80-99%	60-79%	40-59%	under 40%	unknown	total
37	53	14	9	12	10	135

Attendances at Catholic-sponsored prayer groups in England

1-20	21-40	41-60	61-80	81-100	unknown	total
100	27	1	2	1	4	135

[Source: 'List of Catholic Sponsored Prayer Groups, 1975–1976'. For 'Attendances', where a range was given, the analysis uses the mean figure.]

National leadership, teaching and gender

In the United States in the early 1970s, Catholic charismatic renewal was spreading across the country, through prayer groups, 'days of renewal' events, and later *Life in the Spirit* seminars. The leaders of Catholic charismatic groups in South Bend and Ann Arbor, along with a few others, began to feel called to put in place services and structures to support and guide a movement which had for several years been growing organically. A Catholic Charismatic Renewal Services Committee (CCRSC) – later known as the National Service Committee – was incorporated in 1971. The group of seven, which was entirely male, consisted of a mix of laity and clergy, and soon appointed Joseph McKinney, Auxiliary Bishop of Grand Rapids, as an episcopal advisor, in order to liaise with the Church hierarchy. The group had oversight over a vast media operation, Charismatic Renewal Services, which produced teaching materials and a pastoral newsletter which became the glossy and widely read *New Covenant* magazine. Later, alongside national conferences, regional leadership structures and events were also established. The CCRSC had no formal power. However, the group of men felt a great sense of responsibility for the emerging national movement.[28] In particular, they saw a need to foster sound teaching and pastoral work. They recognised that their influence, supported by the media organisation, gave their committee an 'intrinsic authority'.[29] The CCRSC would later be criticised as wielding too much power, with the Notre Dame theologian Josephine Massyngberde Ford describing it as an 'oligarchy'.[30]

The basics of the model of CCRSC were soon duplicated in England, as well as in various other national contexts. In December 1973, a National Service Committee (NSC) met for the first time. There was a sense that God was doing something new, and that the committee should seek and expect guidance. A Bible reading from Isaiah 48:7, given during the opening time of prayer, runs: 'Now I am revealing new things to you, things hidden and unknown to you, created just now, this very moment, of these things you have heard nothing until now, so that you cannot say, "Oh yes, I knew all this"'. Like their American counterparts, the group saw itself as having a unifying function, trying to bring some sense of coherence to diverse local movements. The aim, the NSC felt, was to 'facilitate communication between all the areas in the country and be a bond of unity to all'. The purposes of the committee would be to 'serve and to offer advice', mediate and pray. In keeping with the democratising impulse of the renewal, the committee specifically thought it should be 'a means of giving fullest opportunity to everyone to discover and develop the gifts in their particular ministry'.[31] The NSC supervised the production of a newsletter, which printed teaching from 'Days of Renewal' events (the name was borrowed from the United States) organised around the country. From 1975, this was known as *Goodnews*, with 1,300 copies printed of the first issue.[32] A first, landmark national NSC conference – involving laity, religious and clergy – was organised at Hopwood Hall, Greater Manchester, in 1974.[33] In 1976, in an indication of the growing interest of the Catholic hierarchy, Langton Fox, Bishop

---

[28] Maiden, *Age of the Spirit*, pp. 113–15.
[29] Sword of the Spirit archive (online), Catholic Charismatic Renewal Service Committee minutes, 21 June 1971, https://swordofthespirit.app.box.com/s/5vhqezztl37z3zfl77wzm18yy8g500jx, accessed 3 March 2023.
[30] See Ciciliot, 'The Origins of the Catholic Charismatic Renewal in the United States: Early Developments', p. 256; J. Massyngberde Ford. *Which Way for Catholic Pentecostals* (New York, 1976), p. viii.
[31] National Service Committee papers (hereafter NSC papers), NSC minutes, 17 December 1973, private collection.
[32] Editorial, *Goodnews*, 2 (January 1976), p. 1.
[33] *Newsletter of the National Service Committee for the Catholic Charismatic Renewal*, July 1974, p. 1.

of Menevia, was appointed as a liaison between the charismatic renewal and the episcopal conference.[34]

The laity had a key role in the emerging leadership of renewal. Alongside Fr Ian Petit O.S.B., of St Alban's Church, Warrington, and Sr Bernade of Holy Cross Convent at Chalfont St Peter, the early NSC consisted of a lay majority: Bob Balkam, now settled in England, Jilyan Bray, who ran a prayer group in the Midlands, Alan Guile, a lecturer in electrical engineering at Leeds University (a scientist who also had a particular interest in the healing ministry) who led a group in the city's Notre Dame School, and Lisa Reynolds, a school teacher based in Wimbledon. In 1976, after diocesan teams were set up by the NSC to coordinate renewal locally, the laity similarly took on leadership. In that year, for example, the Liverpool Diocesan Team consisted of six laity, two priests and three nuns; while in Lancaster, there were no priests, and the team was led by 'four relatively inexperienced members'.[35] The 'Days of Renewal' events – gatherings for worship, teaching and ministry which by 1976 were taking place in eleven locations in England – were nearly all organised by laity.[36] Importantly, lay leadership was not only practical. While most teaching at these events came from priests and religious, laity, such as Bob Balkam and Lisa Reynolds, also spoke.[37] At a second national conference at Hopwood Hall in 1975, teaching workshops saw clergy, religious and laity sharing platforms; with, for example, Fr Mike Gwinnell of South London, Tim Turner of the Wimbledon group, and a couple, David and Rosemary Billaux, speaking on how to lead the Ann Arbor community's *Life in the Spirit* seminars. These seminars, developed by The Word of God community in Ann Arbor, explained salvation, the Spirit-filled life and discipleship in the context of Church and community, and had an important role in introducing not only Catholics but also Anglicans and (other) Protestants to charismatic renewal.[38] They were popular with prayer groups – an important tool for recruitment – and were often coordinated by lay leaders.

In assessing the role of the English laity, the gender dimension is highly significant. In the United States, the teaching and practice of the influential communities in South Bend and Ann Arbor were complementarian, believing men and women to be equal in dignity but expected to fill distinct roles. The CCRSC was also male-only. Although its Advisory

---

[34] Editorial, *Goodnews*, 4 (June 1976), p. 1.
[35] NSC papers, Reports of Diocesan Teams, 1 November 1976.
[36] *Newsletter of the National Service Committee for the Catholic Charismatic Renewal*, July 1974, p. 13.
[37] Lisa Reynolds, 'The Spirit and Mary', *Newsletter of the National Service Committee for the Catholic Charismatic Renewal*, July 1974; *Goodnews*, January 1976, pp. 2, 10.
[38] *The Life in the Spirit Seminars: Team Manual* (South Bend, IN, 1973).

Group included a diversity of views on gender, in 1974 only two of its twenty-seven members were women.[39] The teaching in *New Covenant* magazine was almost entirely male, and speakers at the conferences within this milieu were usually male. Sometimes teaching on this national platform in the United States explicitly recommended submission to male authority.[40] This attitude towards gender roles was a considerable frustration to Josephine Massyngberde Ford, an eminent scholar of the New Testament and Rabbinic teaching, and the first woman at Notre Dame to receive tenure in the Faculty.[41] As Ford became increasingly public in her criticism of the leadership – in 1970, according to one report, she tried to 'seize a microphone' at a meeting and then 'refused to take a seat after she was subdued'[42] – there were attempts to keep her, and her books, away from charismatic gatherings.[43] The situation in England offered a sharp contrast, with both women religious and female laity heavily involved. It was possible even for lay women to teach jointly with priests. At one Day of Renewal in 1972, for example, Lisa Reynolds spoke with Fr Mike Gwinnell on 'relationships and chastity', with Reynolds asserting 'We all need each other; we cannot live a one-sex existence.'[44]

This more liberal approach to women's leadership is one indication that English charismatic renewal was of a different character to the dominant American model. There were other contrasts, too. Compared to the teaching evident in the American *New Covenant* magazine, the Days of Renewal and *Goodnews* rarely addressed issues such as authority and submission, or controversial matters such as supernatural deliverance. An indication of the emphases of the English scene is found in an article by Fr Joe Laishley, of Heythrop College, from 1974:

> Vatican II summarised much reflection when it described the people of God as a <u>prophetic,</u> priestly and royal people. This means that all Christians share knowledge of the mind of God to be communicated to others. And people are beginning to take seriously the idea that they have as Christians their own charisms – gifts of the Lord for the building up of the Body of Christ (cf. 1 Cor. 12), gifts which are often rooted in natural and acquired abilities, as teachers, as healers, gifted nurses, doctors and counsellors of all sorts who

---

[39] 'The Service Committee: An Updated Report', *New Covenant*, 3:7 (February 1974), pp. 17–18.
[40] Bert Ghezzi, 'Love and Order: Ways to bring Peace to our Relationships', *New Covenant*, 3:5 (December 1973), pp. 12–16, 15.
[41] See Ciciliot, 'The Origins of the Catholic Charismatic Renewal in the United States: The Experience', pp 161–2; also John Maiden, 'Charisma, Gender and "Glocality": Catholic Charismatic Women in the 1970s', *Journal of Modern and Contemporary Christianity*, 2:1 (2023), pp. 91–114.
[42] 'Pentecostalism should not be Confused with Drug Experiences, Meeting Told', *NC News Service*, 23 June 1971.
[43] Maiden, 'Charisma, Gender'.
[44] *Day of Renewal* newsletter (November 1972), pp. 1–3.

help to heal people's psychic hurts, and so on and even as good organizers (cf. 'administrators' in 1 Cor. 12:28).⁴⁵

The primary emphasis of teaching in English renewal was on healing. This was often concerned with psychological aspects – and therefore issues such as inner healing, personality and interpersonal relationships. In the Westminster Diocese, according to Gill Davies, groups would discuss themes like 'loving oneself, finding oneself (like trees which grow upwards, downwards and sideways – their branches touching the trees next to them) and knowing oneself, expressing oneself, being oneself and accepting oneself'.⁴⁶ Speakers at events included the psychologist Dr Bernard Gilsenan, who in July 1973 spoke to the Marylebone Day of Renewal on the subject of 'Psychology of Religion', discussing the supernatural dimension of Jung; and Frank Lake, the Anglican founder of the Clinical Theology Association who, in 1977, spoke to a conference for priests on 'Dark Nights, Depth Healing and Personality Change'.⁴⁷ This interest in healing of the mind could lead to invitations for American speakers, but these visitors tended to come from outside the dominant South Bend/Ann Arbor milieux. The main speaker for the 1974 Hopwood conference, for example, was Dr Carole Bandini, a psychotherapist from Fordham University.⁴⁸ The next year's conference saw a visit from Fr Francis MacNutt, the well-known Franciscan healer, and the recommended reading ahead of the event was mostly not from the conservative side of the American charismatic spectrum, and included the likes of the Jungian therapist and Episcopalian priest Morton Kelsey, the Anglican healer Agnes Sanford, and the Jesuit theologian Donald Gelphi.⁴⁹

This is not to say that linkages with South Bend and Ann Arbor were absent. Visitors to England included Kevin Ranaghan, of the People of Praise community. There were reports in *Goodnews* of English visits to the upper Midwest communities. When layman Mark White described a trip to Ann Arbor's The Word of God community in 1975, he clearly felt that the Americans had put into practice what the English had hoped for: 'This is how it was always meant to be. This is nothing new here. It's what we have been preaching all the time.'⁵⁰ The profile of those upper Midwest

---

45   Fr F. J. Laishley, 'Baptism of the Holy Spirit', *Newsletter of the National Service Committee for the Catholic Charismatic Renewal*, July 1974, pp. 2–4.
46   NSC papers, Conferences of Diocesan Service Committee's Representatives, 2–4 February 1979.
47   Dr Bernard Gilsenan, 'Psychology and religion', *Day of Renewal*, July 1973, pp. 4–5; Goodnews (February–March 1977), p. 10.
48   'Report on the Fruit of the Spirit Conference', *Day of Renewal*, November 1974, pp. 3–4; Goodnews (August–September 1976), p. 11.
49   Seek Ye First, conference programme, 1975.
50   Mark White, 'Reflections on a visit to Ann Arbor's "Word of God" community', *Goodnews* (December 1975), p. 8.

charismatic communities was growing in the early and mid-1970s due to their relationship with Cardinal Suenens, who advocated a 'policy of presence' – that the Church should seriously engage with the charismatic renewal, as Suenens himself did, attending a Notre Dame conference in 1973.[51] Overall, however, the English scene had more in common with what Josephine Massyngberde Ford described as the 'Type 2' American Catholic charismatic renewal. In contrast to the 'Type 1' approach of South Bend/Ann Arbor, this did not place emphasis on women's submission to men. Instead, women were 'accepted as equals and not kept separate, and they minister similarly to men except for sacerdotal powers'. Type 2 placed little emphasis either on 'discipleship' or 'shepherding'. Ford also said of 'Type 2' Catholic charismatics, that while they encouraged the role of the laity, they were 'clerically and sacramentally orientated'.[52] In the early 1970s, as Valentia Ciciliot has described, there was some criticism of South Bend and Ann Arbor as having too much authority, with fears that they were in practice setting up structures parallel to the Church. In 1973, when Fr Francis O'Connor, a prominent Notre Dame theologian, resigned from the American CCRSC, he described how 'In the eyes of many, the Service Committee seems to have become a kind of private magisterium or pastorate for the Renewal.'[53] If this *was* the case, in contrast, Fr Peter Hocken urged at a 'Day of Renewal' gathering at Marylebone, London, in 1973, 'We should have no distinct doctrine (that is the mark of a sect)'.[54] From the very early stages of the renewal in England, there was a commitment to integrating new patterns of ministry with the life of the Church.

Lived renewal: the Catholic laity and the prayer group

There were two main everyday contexts for Catholic charismatic renewal. Some charismatics became involved in communities, where a group of people intentionally lived according to a common set of principles and practices, sometimes – as with the most prominent American communities – in 'covenant' agreement to one another. The Community of Christ the King, in Godalming, was one early community. Others, such as The House of the Open Door community, a residential 'extended family'

---

51 Valentina Ciciliot, 'The Origins of the Catholic Charismatic Renewal in the United States: Early Developments in Indiana and Michigan and the Reactions of the Ecclesiastical Authorities', *Studies in World Christianity*, 25:3 (2019), pp. 250–73.
52 Ford, *Which Way*, p. 67.
53 Ciciliot, 'The Origins of the Catholic Charismatic Renewal in the United States: Early Developments'.
54 Peter Hocken, 'Prayer Groups, Christian Community and World Transformation', *Day of Renewal*, March 1973, pp. 1–3.

established in Slough in 1975, were focussed on individuals with particular troubles and addictions.[55] Such communities were an important part of the overall Catholic charismatic ecosystem in England; however, as only a minority of charismatics were involved in them, they are not discussed in this chapter. Rather, the focus here is the prayer group as an everyday context for charismatic renewal. These gatherings varied in their size and strength. The Diocesan Team for Portsmouth in 1976, for example, estimated that there were five 'strong' prayer groups, eight 'middling' and a majority of ten which were 'weak'.[56] Furthermore, as we shall see, by no means were all groups recognisable as 'Catholic pentecostal'; indeed, such was the variety of devotionalism in these groups that the term is less valid in the English context. Another Diocesan Team report for this period described small groups springing up but admitted that 'not all of these would profess to be extensions of the Charismatic renewal'.[57]

There was, as we have seen, a preponderance of lay leadership. Prayer groups could open up significant new opportunities for laity. One lay woman, Joan Williams, described getting an impression from God that she should pray for the gift of preaching and put this to use in prayer groups. The example underlines how the notion of gifting for the body of the Christ could empower laity and allow them to move beyond their comfort zone. Williams initially responded to God by thinking, 'You must be joking Lord, a middle-aged, Catholic, nearly elderly lady of a nervous disposition and not a bit intellectual, to pray for preaching?' But she then had a dream of 'preaching to a congregation about the power of the Spirit in men's lives'.[58] For lay women and men, however, a prayer meeting could bring with it a complex set of issues, relational, theological and ecclesiological, which could mean significant pastoral challenges. As one priest, Fr Tony Moran S.J., said in an article on 'Discernment of Spirits' in 1973, potential pitfalls such as emotionalism, or too much emphasis on tongues, required sound, measured pastoral authority. It was common, he suggested, to hear the claim 'The prayer meeting does not need a priest'. He was not opposed to this view but was adamant that every prayer group leader 'does need access to someone with experience more objective than our own'.[59] A Diocesan Team report said of Leeds in 1976 that 'most groups felt the lack of leadership and had great need of sound teaching'.[60] This was a problem common to charismatic renewal

---

[55] 'The House of the Open Door', *Goodnews*, April/May 1992, pp. 22–3, https://www.houseoftheopendoor.org/community/history/, accessed 11 March 2023.
[56] NSC Papers, 'Reports of Diocesan Teams', 1 November 1976.
[57] NSC papers, Diocesan Report, n.d.
[58] Joan Williams, 'Are you joking Lord?' *Goodnews*, 3 (April 1976), p. 9.
[59] Fr Tony Horan S.J., 'Discernment of Spirits', *Day of Renewal*, February 1973.
[60] NSC papers, Diocesan Report, n.d.

more broadly – Protestant-led groups often reported the same issue. For this reason, 'tape ministry', the use of teaching cassettes in prayer groups, was common. A 1976 new year edition of *Goodnews* explained, 'we need to use our resource and energies this year in developing leaders, not so as to neglect the flock, but so the flock will be better served'.[61] The democratisation of authority which prayer groups afforded also opened up pastoral gaps which, so far as the NSC was concerned, were a particular challenge to the direction of renewal.

Some groups were marked by a new commitment to prayer, or greater use of the Bible, but not by experimentation with the supernatural gifts.[62] Alan Guile, a lay member of the NSC based in the Leeds area, asserted in 1976: 'I can honestly say that among Catholic groups ... I have not seen undue attention on such gifts as prophecy, healing or tongues.' Like various other Catholic charismatic leaders, while Guile was relaxed with the intended theology of 'baptism in the Holy Spirit', he was uncomfortable with the terminology, because of the Catholic teaching on the reception of the Spirit at baptism. He preferred the notion, taken from St Thomas, of the 'new sending' of the Spirit, and the experience of an increase in grace.[63] Prayer meetings moved at different paces into experimentation with the supernatural in ministry. One prayer group in Surrey, largely made up of parishioners (not 'fanatically traditionalist' but 'conservative in their attitudes') and students, did not rush into the charismatic gifts. The parishioners instead treated the group 'as a journey towards God'. This involved discussion of the Catholic hierarchy's idea of a 'New Pentecost' and consideration of the Scriptural arguments for 'indwelling of the Holy Spirit, and that there are gifts'. It would not be helpful, a group leader argued, to try to replicate the free-flowing charismatic practices which people imagined occurring in the United States (or 'to talk of fifty thousand people praying together in Kansas City, remarkable as that may be'). This responsible caution was well received by the local priest.[64] By no means were all Catholic charismatic prayer meetings spectacles of supernaturalism.

Very often, when there was a more supernatural dimension to prayer group ministry, inner healing was the central theme. The prayer group in Huttlecote, for example, found that a series of crises felt by individuals

---

61 Ian Petit, 'Putting you in the Picture', *Goodnews*, 2 (January 1976), pp. 2–4, 4.
62 NSC papers, 'Meeting of NAC and NSC', n.d. (c. 1979).
63 NSC papers, Alan Guile, 'Comments arising from the message of the Canadian Bishops of April 1975 on the Charismatic renewal', 13 March 1976.
64 'A New Prayer Group in Surrey', *Goodnews*, 13 (December 1977/January 1978), pp. 8–9.

led them to seek after 'deep healing'.[65] Alan Guile offered the following description of the dynamics of prayer groups:

> It is wonderful to see how the love of God flows between people when they become able, within the security of a small praying community, to drop their masks and barriers built up over the years for defence against further hurt, and ask others to pray that God will help them. We have seen people, some of whom were almost out of action as Christians, receive deep inner healing and then in time God has used them to help others. We try by our fellowship and our prayer to help God to build others up to realise that He loves them deeply and that He wants to breathe new life into the gifts which He has given them, so that they can play their allotted part in the working of the Body of Christ, and that the whole community needs each one of them.[66]

Prayer groups were spaces for self-actualisation in the context of community.

Activism, evangelisation, and secularisation

Many English Catholic charismatics had perceived a crisis of the Church in the 1970s. Looking back at the end of the decade, one Redemptorist priest recalled, 'The years of the Council and those directly after were years of profound crisis of: the priesthood; the religious life; the parishioners – the devotional life of Catholics declined; the prayer life of the parish – also declined; the prayer life of the family – ditto.'[67] For some involved in the renewal, there was a real sense that its reanimated Christianity and new patterns of ministry and community were desperately needed by the Church. It is therefore salient to ask what difference the renewal made on the ground.

Many examples indicate that charismatic renewal could foster new activism in the lives of laity. Alan Guile found 'It is remarkable how many people one meets in prayer groups who are active for such causes as Justice and Peace, anti-abortion work, and concern for the elderly or for young people.'[68] While a frequent criticism of Catholic charismatics in the United States was that they retreated from the world, in England this disparagement of the renewal was less commonly found. Prayer group members often seem to display a strong commitment to the life of a parish. A prayer group in Basingstoke, for example, claimed that its members were involved in 'parish schools, hospitals, parish magazine, pilgrimage, overseas aid fund, liturgy and worship, lectors, instructors for

---

[65] 'Things that have happened', *Goodnews*, 3 (April 1976), pp. 2–6, 3–4.
[66] Guile, 'Comments arising'.
[67] NSC papers, Conference of Diocesan Service Committees' Representatives (England), 2–4 February 1979.
[68] Guile, 'Comments arising'.

confirmation, eucharist and folk choir'.[69] From the mid-1970s the NSC placed a particular emphasis on engaging the wider church – to the extent that they hoped their impact could be such that the label of 'charismatic renewal' would no longer be necessary. The Basingstoke group concurred with this view: 'the time has come for the thrust to be made towards the renewal of the parish and not just to part of it'. Involvement in renewal, too, could result in engagement with the wider world. A 'census' of visitors to the Basingstoke group one evening found that their number included a French priest, missionaries from the Philippines, Assam and Nigeria, and visiting women religious from India and Ecuador.[70] The global flows of Catholic charismatic renewal contributed to a religious cosmopolitanism amongst middle-class laity.

Drawing on figures from a *Catholic Herald* survey, the NSC estimated in 1977 that 83% of the newspaper's readers had heard of the 'renewal'.[71] However, in terms of numbers, growth in England was small. The distribution of *Goodnews* increased from its first edition in 1975, but only to 3,500 copies by 1980.[72] When faced with news of significant expansion and large conferences elsewhere, it was easy for English Catholics to feel disappointed. An editorial in *Day of Renewal* in 1975 asked:

> Are you just a little tired of hearing, repeatedly if not constantly, of the 'amazing' growth of the Charismatic Renewal in the US, in Australia and New Zealand, and more recently in Ireland? Do you wonder sometimes if the Spirit has chosen not to blow quite so strongly around here, or do you simply dismiss slower growth as the result of British reserve?

The editorial expressed the hope that despite frustration at 'more rapid growth' being held back by 'what seemed to be the "stiff upper lip"', a more mature growth was occurring at a deeper level in the English renewal.[73] However, despite occasional optimism with the news of prayer group expansion, renewal did not achieve the kind of scale many hoped for. There were frustrations about seepage, too Leaders of prayer groups acknowledged a 'revolving door syndrome' – a similar dynamic was noticed by charismatics in other Anglo-world countries – whereby Catholics would attend for a short time, and then move to another group or leave the renewal entirely.[74] In 1977, the NSC discussed Cardinal Suenens's recent suggestion that there was a need for 'bold and public re-affirmation' of renewal in the Church. The minutes noted:

---

69 'Things that have happened , *Goodnews*, 3 (April 1976), pp. 2–4, 2.
70 Ibid.
71 NSC papers, NSC minutes 23–24 March 1977.
72 'Bad News about Goodnews', *Goodnews*, February–March 1980, p. 6.
73 Editorial, 'The Spirit blows where it will', *Day of Renewal*, January 1975.
74 NSC papers, 'Meeting of NAC and NSC', n.d. (c. 1979).

As Catholics, at every level, we all need <u>encouragement</u>, a great upsurge of hope. The potential of grace within each of us needs energising. Awareness of this need is becoming more and more apparent as so much we have taken for granted is disintegrating around us. Do these considerations lead us to see that the time has come to offer people the opportunity of re-affirming and declaring openly their belief in and sub-mission to the Lordship of Jesus Christ in a joyous celebration at National level?[75]

Plans were mooted for a such an event at Wembley Stadium. However, perhaps tellingly, the idea does not seem to have gone ahead.

The ecumenism of charismatic renewal could also bring ecclesiological challenges. A report by the Commission for Ecumenism for England and Wales in 1975 described the renewal as a 'tremendous blessing in itself and for the Church' but was conscious of the ways in which pentecostals and Protestant mainline charismatics, who might appear 'experts in the charismatic field', could have significant influence on teachings in Catholic meetings. There was also the danger that Catholics could be drawn into a charismatic world which operated in parallel to the structures of the Church – with slogans like 'we believe in Christianity not Churchianity'.[76] A dynamic of the ecumenism of the charismatic scene was that Catholics were drawn towards independent charismatic congregations and house churches, which appeared to some to operate more along New Testament lines than the parish church did. While the charismatic prayer group could bring new energies to the Catholic laity, it could also provide a kind of 'gateway drug' towards expressions of Spirit-filled worship and ministry which ultimately led away from the Church.

Conclusion: presenting a 'middle-class Jesus?'

By the end of the 1970s, the NSC had supported the expansion of a movement in the Church which reenergised many Catholic laity. It had helped foster patterns of leadership and ministry which had empowered some laity to take a greater role. It had, too, mediated a form of spirituality which was well suited to a cultural environment now pervaded by expressive individualism. Not surprisingly, as Stephen Bullivant has said of various post-Second Vatican Council innovations more generally, this tended to attract middle-class Catholics.[77] Alan Guile admitted 'We are sometimes criticised because at the moment in England there are many [more] professional people, particularly teachers, than 'working-class' people in the groups. This is not of our choosing, and we shall

---

75 NSC papers, NSC minutes 23–24 March 1977.
76 NSC Papers, 'The Commission for Ecumenism for England and Wales', n.d. (c. 1975).
77 Bullivant, *Mass Exodus*, p. 193.

be glad when there is a proper balance.'[78] A meeting of the NSC and its advisory committee around the same time was wary of 'the danger of presenting a middle-class Jesus'.[79] While the renewal proved highly attractive to some middle-class Catholics, there were plenty of secular activities and opportunities competing for the attention of this group. The demographic of renewal, too, meant it struggled overall to make a larger contribution to resisting secularising trends. Some had hoped it would. On attending the national conference of the NSC in 1974, one priest had told a member of the committee that 'If all Masses were like that ... there would be no lapsing from the Church.'[80] Ultimately, while the renewal revitalised some groups and parishes, it did not bring the resurgence the priest hoped for. As a *Goodnews* piece admitted in 1977, 'So far the renewal is only scratching the surface in this country'.[81] The data record of decline remains stark for the late decades of the twentieth century – even though it is reasonable to wonder if without the renewal, the situation could have been worse. At the end of the decade, Bob Balkam of the NSC argued its mission was now 'spiritual renewal'. The term is significant, for it was deliberately chosen to appeal in the broadest possible terms to the Catholic Church. Indeed, he looked forward to the 'dissolution of Catholic Charismatic Renewal as an identifiable movement or organisation'.[82] The renewal was increasingly being recognised as part of the life of the wider Church: in Easter Week of 1978, Basil Hume, the newly enthroned Archbishop of Westminster, was the main celebrant for a conference at Hopwood Hall for priests 'geared for the renewing of their priesthood'.[83] Where the laity were concerned, if the charismatic 'New Pentecost' did not prevent Catholic decline in the late twentieth century, it did establish itself as one strand of devotional expression in the English post-Second Vatican Council environment.

---

[78] NSC papers, Guile, 'Comments arising'.
[79] NSC papers, 'Meeting of NAC and NSC', n.d. (c. 1979).
[80] NSC papers, Guile, 'Comments arising'.
[81] Fr Ian Petit, 'Where are we?', *Goodnews*, 9 (April/May 1977), p. 3.
[82] Bob Balkam, 'The way ahead', *Goodnews*, 23 (August/September 1979), p. 7.
[83] 'Stop Press', *Goodnews*, April–May 1978, no. 11, 15.

11

HIV AND AIDS IN ENGLAND AND WALES: HOW LAY PEOPLE LED THE CATHOLIC RESPONSE

Vincent Manning

Sex makes HIV problematic for the institutional Church. That was true when AIDS first emerged in the early 1980s and it remains true today. The Catholic Church is the largest private provider of healthcare for people living with HIV globally today,[1] but tensions have always been evident between effective HIV prevention, education and treatment strategies, and the teaching of the Church on matters of sex and sexuality. When it comes to any discussion about the Catholic Church and HIV, this apparent conflict between Church doctrine and widely accepted approaches to public health has dominated public debate for more than forty years now, overshadowing the important contribution the Church has made and continues to make today.

This chapter will argue that the inability of the Catholic Bishops of England and Wales to reconcile this tension explains, in part, why the institutional Church was slow to respond to the reality of AIDS in England and Wales. Without any coordinated response from the Bishops Conference to what eventually became an international health emergency, it fell to lay people to take responsibility for the moral leadership, HIV education and pastoral care required, on behalf of the Catholic Church.

The first national Catholic conference on AIDS was held in 1986. Sponsored by the Dominicans, the contribution of lay people was important for the learning. This chapter will describe some of the ways in which lay people took action after this conference, providing the effective Catholic leadership that was needed at a time of national crisis. Drawing from newsletters from the charity Catholic AIDS Link (CAL) issued

---

[1] UNAIDS 2012. *UNAIDS requests Pope Benedict XVI for support in efforts to stop new HIV infections in children*. News article. UNAIDS website, accessed January 2024. Anthony Egan, 'Global Health, AIDS, and the Catholic Church in Africa', in *HIV & AIDS in Africa: Christian Reflection, Public Health, Social Transformation*, edited by Jacquineau Azetsop (Maryknoll, NY, 2016), p. 240.

from 1989–1998.[2] previous research and the author's own experience and recollections, it will describe the creation of a national network of concerned people and clergy. Selected examples will illustrate how CAL activists led the way in educating and supporting members of the church to respond to the reality of AIDS in our society and the Church.[3] The role that lay people living with HIV had in assisting the church to understand, reflect upon and bear witness to the Gospel during the time of AIDS, in England and Wales, will be emphasised throughout. Following a discussion and summary of issues raised, the chapter will conclude with a postscript exploring the reasons for the closure of CAL in 1999 and describing the legacy of CAL today.

To begin with, however, it is important to situate AIDS in historical context and be reminded how responses to AIDS have been defined from the very start by fear and stigma. An understanding of HIV-related stigma is essential if we intend to reflect theologically on HIV and AIDS as a sign of the times to which Christians are called to respond.

A minority disease and threat to the nation?

It is difficult to convey now just how frightening the AIDS pandemic was. The story starts in the United States where a number of cases of what was later called AIDS were identified in 1981. Commentary, in the early years especially, always referenced the increasingly gruesome story of AIDS as it unfolded first in the North American context. Historians agree that governments were slow to respond to the emergence of this deadly new disease. Some argue that the medical and scientific community was caught off-guard. The last pandemic to impact the Western world had been the Spanish flu of 1918–20, and a virus that attacked the immune system had not been known before.[4] The fact that the first recorded deaths were of young gay men and that AIDS emerged within the gay community was without doubt a significant contributory factor in the failure to act with greater urgency in the face of AIDS.[5] If only

---

[2] A selection of CAL newsletters from 1989 to 1998 are held at The Wellcome Collection, Euston Road, London.
[3] 'The Church' refers to the Roman Catholic Church including clergy, bishops, and laity. Varying emphasis between different aspects of the life of the Church will hopefully be clear. When referring to 'the church' we mean to include Christians from other traditions.
[4] V. A. Harden and D. Rodrigues, 'Context for a New Disease: Aspects of Biomedical Research Policy in the United States before AIDS', in *AIDS and Contemporary History*, edited by Virginia Berridge and Philip Strong (Cambridge, 2002), pp. 182–202.
[5] The first diagnosed cases of what would come to be called AIDS were identified in the United States Centers for Disease Control *Morbidity & Mortality Weekly Report* (MMWR) in June and July 1981. Cases amongst men with haemophilia, women and children, were also identified in MMWR reports from 1982.

by comparison with how governments have responded to the Covid-19 pandemic internationally, it is clear that AIDS was unanticipated and that institutions were remarkably slow to act within the first five years.

By the mid 1980s the majority of Western governments understood that if left unchecked, AIDS could result in the deaths of hundreds of millions of people. Such was the concern, that a nationwide Public Health Campaign was launched in the UK.[6] From 1986–87, the government coordinated a massive media response previously unknown in peacetime.[7] Every household received the information leaflet 'Don't Die of Ignorance' in 1987.[8] By today's standards, what was broadcast in the 1980s was very conservative. Across all television and radio channels 'AIDS Week' smashed through previously taboo subjects. Nineteen hours of AIDS-related television made it practically impossible to avoid condom-use demonstrations and explicit discussion about safer sex. The screening of the (in)famously alarming 'Tombstone' and 'Iceberg' adverts in cinemas and on television made it clear that this new killer disease should concern everyone. Ignorance could mean death. AIDS was extremely frightening.

To some extent, public ignorance was understandable. Prior to 1987, TV news bulletins and documentaries had observed the emergence of AIDS within the gay community,[9] and the myth of a 'gay plague' had been

---

[6] Department of Health Minister Norman Fowler played a major role in galvanising the political will and resources needed, but he encountered significant resistance. Not everyone was convinced. Some accused him of an obsessive overreaction. Defending his actions, he responded 'We were all driven by the urgency of the issue. Delay would cost lives.' Fowler was convinced that knowledge about AIDS must be made widely available so that the general population became aware of the risks of infection. Fear of an exponential rise of HIV within the heterosexual population compelled the government to act. Virginia Berridge, *AIDS in the UK: The Making of Policy, 1981–1994*, (New York, 1996), pp. 131–2.

[7] Virginia Berridge refers to the period 1986–7 as 'The War Years': 'AIDS was officially established as a high-level national emergency, as a national crisis on a par with the Falklands or the Second World War.' Berridge, *AIDS in the UK*, p. 7. As with actual war, the perceived threat of impending disaster justified government action. Measures that might otherwise be unthinkable were needed. Objections that the public health education campaign was an overreaction, too shocking, or too explicit in bringing into ordinary homes topics such as homosexuality, condom use, anal sex and intravenous drug use, were set aside. In 1986 the government ran the first nationwide campaign with full-page newspaper adverts that had the title 'Don't aid AIDS'. The dramatic nature of the nationwide campaigns across television, radio and cinema and in the printed press reflects the sense of urgency and panic that existed at the time.

[8] The leaflet is reproduced in full in N. Fowler, *AIDS: Don't Die of Prejudice* (London, 2014), pp. 277–82.

[9] The BBC Horizon programme *Killer in the Village* was first broadcast in 1983. It charted the spread of AIDS in the USA amongst the gay community and concludes by asking 'Do we already have the hidden seeds of an epidemic here?' Available at: https://www.bbc.co.uk/iplayer/episode/p01z2lbp/horizon-19821983-killer-in-the-village, accessed February 2024.

fuelled by sensationalist stories in the press. Tabloid coverage especially promoted the idea that AIDS only affected a small and despised group of gay men. Cases of HIV infection amongst intravenous drug users, sex workers, haemophiliacs or Africans, only reinforced the notion of AIDS as a minority disease. The newspapers consistently described AIDS as a consequence of the immoral behaviour of people on the margins of society, with whom ordinary 'decent' people had little in common. However, this myth of AIDS as remote was a dangerous idea. Creating a false but emotionally reassuring distance in the minds of many, those who thought themselves 'safe' need not change their behaviour. At the same time, paradoxically, ignorance about the transmission of HIV led to exaggerated fears of contagion. All too easily fear of infection translated into fear of the infected.[10] By 1986 the government understood that to prevent the onward transmission of HIV, individual behaviour change on a national scale was required. The awareness campaigns emphasised that heterosexual people living ordinary 'normal' lives could also be infected with the virus that led to AIDS.

Naturally, the lack of any cure, the painful ugliness of a death from AIDS and the ostracisation or 'social death' that people with AIDS were subjected to, combined powerfully as good reasons to fear infection. The government's AIDS Week campaign heightened public anxiety.[11] In this regard it worked. People took notice. Unfortunately, widespread public fear often also results in the tendency to attribute blame, or scapegoat those groups or individuals whom we consider to be bearers of that which threatens us. Moral panic reinforced by sensationalist tabloid coverage compounded pre-existing prejudices held about gay men, black people, intravenous drug users or sex workers, in the minds of many. Those thought to be infected or at risk often suffered discrimination and prejudice.[12]

An appreciation of the extraordinarily powerful stigma attached to AIDS is essential for any understanding of the impact and meaning of the pandemic. HIV was first identified within already stigmatised communities and the genesis of HIV stigma existed long before the actual emergence of AIDS. It has deep roots in multiple historical prejudices,

---

[10] There are numerous stories of patients not being served food except at a great distance from worried nurses in hospitals; of parents being told that it would be better if their child did not return to school; of funeral directors refusing to collect corpses; priests refusing to conduct funerals and congregations being concerned about 'catching' AIDS from the chalice during the Eucharist. See also notes 12 and 56.
[11] The National AIDS Helpline was set up to respond to public inquiries. Berridge, *AIDS in the UK*, p. 128.
[12] Public attitudes to the acceptability of same-sex relationships hardened through the 1980s. Nearly two-thirds of people thought that sexual relations between same-sex adults were always wrong in 1987, up from half of people surveyed in 1983. A. Park et al. (eds), *British Social Attitudes: The 30th Report* (London, 2013). See also notes 10, 56.

traditions and practices of fear and ignorance. The long Christian tradition of associating sex and disease with sin is an example of one source and contributory factor for the religiously generated aspects of HIV stigma.[13] With the very first naming of this strange new disease as 'the Gay Plague', HIV- and AIDS-related stigma manifested itself like a malignant tumor in the body of society. Almost no one could be safe. AIDS was to be feared and some people were dangerous. The significance of stigma cannot be overstated.

The silence of the institutional Church and stigma

Even in a secular society the views of religious leaders still command public attention, especially during a crisis or in response to controversial issues. AIDS represented both controversy and crisis, but the Catholic bishops made very few public statements. Behind the scenes the then Archbishop of Westminster, Cardinal Basil Hume, and the Archbishop of Canterbury, Robert Runcie, had been engaged in extensive discussion with officials and ministers about the government's strategy to combat AIDS. Their public silence on the issues cannot be interpreted as complacency or ignorance.[14]

---

[13] Whenever sex and sexuality have been associated with danger, disease and sin, the moral judgments made create a powerful societal impact. It is important to note this recurring feature in history, in order to be alert to this more or less persistent tendency to attribute blame in response to fears. The dynamics of guilt and innocence, blame and scapegoating, are evidenced in response to the threat which HIV represents. The inherited myth linking sex, disease, sin and punishment, and the affective response this creates, remain an actual and operative factor that generates and maintains HIV stigma in different societies today. On the historical association of sex and moral danger, see e.g. P. L. Allen, *The Wages of Sin: Sex and Disease, Past and Present* (London, 2000); F. Mort, *Dangerous Sexualities: Medico-Moral Politics in England since 1850*, Second Edition (London, 2000).

[14] The UK government consulted mainstream religious leaders knowing that their intended public health approach, including AIDS Week and education within schools, would be controversial. They undoubtedly wished to minimise the potential for a major backlash or objections from mainstream religious leaders that might undermine the effectiveness of the campaigns. The cooperative stance taken by Cardinal Hume and Archbishop Runcie may be appreciated when contrasted with others advocating more extreme measures. For example, in written submissions to the Social Services Committee on Problems associated with AIDS, which convened in 1986–7 in the House of Commons, the Conservative Family Campaign (CFC) amongst other recommendations called for: AIDS to be a notifiable disease; mandatory testing of all visitors to the UK from Africa; repeal of the 1967 Sexual Offences Act and the re-criminalisation of homosexuality; the value of marriage to be taught in schools along with the risk to public health of homosexuality; and contraceptives (condoms) to be made available for married couples only. They argued that government funding should be withdrawn from the Terrence Higgins Trust and the Family Planning Association, because the former promoted homosexuality and the latter encouraged promiscuity, and that funding should be diverted to Christian counselling services to help homosexuals refrain from their practices. They denounced the 1987 media campaign as distasteful, offensive and counter-productive. They asserted that the key to an effective

However, the silence of mainstream religious leaders in the UK allowed ample space for the supposed Christian view of AIDS to be mediated publicly in three main ways.[15] The headline 'AIDS is the Wrath of God, says Vicar'[16] typifies how religious opinion was repeatedly presented in the popular press. Secondly, public figures who claimed to be Christian grabbed headlines with judgmental and condemnatory statements, the most notorious of these coming from the then Chief Constable of Greater Manchester, James Anderton, who in 1986 described people with AIDS as 'swirling around in a cesspool of their own making'. Interviewed later on BBC Radio Four he claimed that God was speaking through him.[17] Thirdly, dogmatic and fundamentalist views of church leaders in the USA were heard loudly across the world. Often quoted are Rev. Jerry Falwell, who said on national television that 'a god who hates sin has stopped [homosexuality] dead in its tracks by saying "Do it and die. Do it and die"', and Cardinal John O'Connor, Catholic Archbishop of New York, who defended his stance on the prohibition of condoms in Catholic hospitals by saying: 'Don't blame the Church if people get a disease because they violate Church teaching.'[18]

Simplistic and theologically dubious statements reinforced the distinction between those considered 'innocent' and those whose 'lifestyles' made them blameworthy. Many concluded that the Church was unsympathetic to those directly affected by or suffering with AIDS, and hostile towards HIV prevention efforts which represented a threat to public morality.[19]

---

response to AIDS was 'whether the Government is prepared to make a moral stand on what is essentially a disease spread by immoral behaviour'. The CFC Memorandum submitted to Parliament is reproduced in L. K. Clarke and M. Potts (eds), *The AIDS Reader: Documentary History of a Modern Epidemic* (Boston, MA, 1988), pp. 270–4. In contrast, Hume and Runcie gave qualified support to the government's liberal approach to public health, including on matters of sexual health education. Publicly, however, they neither endorsed nor denounced the government's policies and they failed to respond to the government's invitation to collaborate strategically at a national level. Virginia Berridge concludes that whilst less extreme than some representations of Christian views, the official Anglican and Roman Catholic position in the UK amounted to 'loving the sinner whilst hating the sin'. Berridge, AIDS in the UK, pp. 135–7.

15   I am not arguing that individual bishops or leading religious figures were wholly unsympathetic or unconcerned but that more thoughtful or pastorally sensitive responses, when they were made, went mostly unnoticed or unheard in the public domain. See also note 37.

16   *The Sun*, 7 February 1985.

17   Berridge, *AIDS in the UK*, pp. 109, 137; Simon Garfield, *The End of Innocence: Britain in the Time of AIDS* (London, 1995), pp. 113, 123–4.

18   T. F. Murphy, 'Is AIDS a Just Punishment?' *Journal of Medical Ethics*, 14 (1988), pp. 154–60; A. R. Jonsen and J. Stryker (eds), *The Social Impact of AIDS in the United States* (Washington, DC, 1993), p. 131; Allen, *Wages of Sin*, pp. 121, 143

19   Vicky Cosstick (ed.), *AIDS: Meeting the Community Challenge* (Slough, 1987), p. 48; S. Pattison, 'To the Churches with Love from the Lighthouse', in *Embracing the Chaos: Theological Responses to AIDS* edited by J. Woodward (London, 1991), pp. 8–19; Jonsen

The first and loudest voices heard in the public space, claiming to speak in the name of the church, were condemnatory and judgmental. The message that individuals were to blame for AIDS as a result of their own sinful behaviour was loud and clear.[20]

The importance of lived experience and lay expertise for theological inquiry

Cardinal Hume issued a public letter about AIDS in early 1987,[21] but unlike their American counterparts, no collective statement from the Catholic bishops in the UK was ever issued. A collective official statement might have been controversial or have done more harm than good. Perhaps the bishops were unsure as to how to respond.[22] As Diane Winston observes: 'AIDS represented a minefield for a Church that taught homosexual acts were immoral and condoms were forbidden.'[23] Writing in 1990, Martin Pendergast noted that 'If society ... shows discomfort in dealing with ... the ... major issues ... AIDS raises ... then it is hardly surprising that the Churches have been faltering in their first steps to respond.'[24] As

---

and Stryker, *Social Impact*, p. 119; Patrick Dixon, *The Truth about AIDS and a Practical Christian Response,* Fourth Edition (London, 2004), pp. 151–2.

[20] 'In the near absence of constructive leadership by churches on these issues, the public has been left with the judgmental theological attitudes voiced by some conservative church spokespersons and TV evangelists that AIDS is God's punishment of homosexuals and IV drug users. With the churches largely remaining silent, society can hardly be faulted for assuming that this perspective is representative of the total Christian community.' David G. Hallman (ed.), *AIDS Issues: Confronting the Challenge* (New York, 1989), p. xvii.

[21] Basil Hume, 'AIDS: Time for a Moral Renaissance', *The Times*, 7 January 1987.

[22] Public controversy had followed the publication of 'The Many Faces of AIDS: A Gospel Response' by the Administrative Board of the Catholic Bishops Conference in the USA in 1987, which was later amended by 'Called to Compassion: A Response to the HIV/AIDS Crisis', issued by the bishops in 1989. See: United States Catholic Conference Administrative Board, *The Many Faces of AIDS: A Gospel Response* (1987), and National Conference of Catholic Bishops, *Called to Compassion and Responsibility: A Response to the HIV/AIDS Crisis* (Washington, DC, 1989). Cardinal O'Connor was a leading critic of the earlier document as was Cardinal Ratzinger, then head of the Congregation for the Doctrine of the Faith (CDF), who in a letter to the US Bishops appeared to criticise them for having issued their earlier statement without consulting Rome and warned against the appearance of condoning immoral practices. See for example P. Steinfels, 'Catholic Bishops Vote to Retain Controversial Statement on AIDS', *New York Times*, 28 June 1989, and R. Chandler and J. Dart, 'Bishops' Panel Rejects Condoms in AIDS Battle', *Los Angeles Times*, 13 October 1989. See also note 35 below.

[23] D. Winston, 'Shame, Fear and Compassion: Media Coverage of Catholicism during the First Decade of the AIDS Crisis', in *In the Logos of Love: Promise and Predicament in Catholic Intellectual Life*, edited by J. L. Heft and U. M. Cadegan (New York, 2016), pp. 171–95.

[24] Martin Pendergast, 'HIV in Britain 1982–1990: The Christian Reaction', *New Blackfriars*, 71:840 (1990), Special Issue: *Christians and AIDS: An Anglo-French Assessment*, pp. 347–53.

the number of cases rose and public anxiety heightened, some Christians began to understand HIV and AIDS as a sign of the times to which they must respond. Many Catholic gay men were directly affected. Catholic lay people working in the health and social services sectors were confronted by the suffering. Increasingly, AIDS touched the lives of individuals and families in parishes across the country. Many ordinary Christians and some clergy began by volunteering in one or other of the newly emerging voluntary sector AIDS agencies.

The first major national Christian conference on AIDS, entitled 'The Catholic Church and AIDS', was hosted by the Dominican Order. The weekend gathering took place at the Dominican House at Spode, Staffordshire, in early November 1986, with the collaboration of the Terrence Higgins Trust (THT).[25] It was attended by more than one hundred Catholics.[26] With backing from a major religious order and the approval of the Catholic bishops, the conference qualifies as a response from the institutional Church. More importantly, it relied upon the expertise of lay people, doctors and others with frontline experience of the struggle with AIDS. This active participation of both lay people and clergy makes this conference significant as the first organised attempt to reflect theologically on the meaning of AIDS in a manner that was inclusive of the whole Catholic community.

The organisers realised that to understand the phenomenon of AIDS in society, the facts, as they were known at the time, mattered. The nationwide public health campaign had not yet begun and there was widespread ignorance of the basic facts, for example about how the virus was transmitted. Organisers also recognised that they too were subject to the negative mythologising of AIDS and the anxieties and fears that this induces. During the conference, experts shared their knowledge of the latest scientific and medical facts as the starting point to counter ignorance. Clinicians and pastoral workers helped the participants to explore the social and interpersonal aspects of this frightening disease. Unsurprisingly several trained theologians made important contributions

---

[25] The leading voluntary sector HIV agency formed by a small group of the friends of Terry Higgins in 1982, one of the first gay men to have died from AIDS in the UK. The involvement of THT recognised the need to work with secular agencies and draw from their expertise and experience. It also reflects an awareness within the mainly secular HIV sector of how they needed to work with allies within faith communities to address matters at the intersection of AIDS and religious faith. Earlier in 1986 the 'AIDS Faith Alliance' produced a pamphlet for distribution through THT entitled 'Is AIDS God's Wrath?' to combat often-expressed fundamentalist views, and the THT AIDS and Faith working group issued a leaflet giving guidance on receiving holy communion in response to fears amongst churchgoers that AIDS might be passed on through the communal sharing of the chalice. Berridge, *AIDS in the UK*, p. 135; Pendergast, 'HIV in Britain', p. 349; Bill Kirkpatrick, *AIDS: Sharing the Pain: Pastoral Guidelines* (London, 1988), p. 121.

[26] Pendergast, 'HIV in Britain'.

as part of the programme and Fr Michael Lopes O.P. who coordinated the AIDS Ministry of the Archdiocese of San Francisco shared his insights and experience of pastoral ministry. A shared-learning approach was apparent. During this conference the presentations of experts, the workshops and dialogue between all who attended, contributed in important ways to the process of inquiry and mutual learning.

Above all, the inclusion of lay people living with HIV and AIDS was of utmost importance.[27] The voices of people living with HIV and AIDS were heard. Amongst others there was Benedict, whose body bore the purple lesions of Kaposi's Sarcoma[28] and who 'made of his suffering a preaching'.[29] He told his story and answered questions from participants. At the close of the Conference, this 'church at Spode' gathered around Benedict, and they prayed with him and for each other as he was anointed with oil. Benedict died a few months later from AIDS.

The full participation of people living with HIV demythologised AIDS. Their presence ensured that an abstract reduction of pastorally complex and theologically challenging issues was avoided. Through them, AIDS was embodied in that place at that time and HIV was given a human face. The learning that took place, any transformation of attitude, any diminishment of fear or anxiety, any prejudice challenged, any pain revealed, any deeper theological understanding gained, happened because Benedict and other lay men and women touched by AIDS had a central role during the weekend. The Conference became a place where the embodied encounter with AIDS was allowed and actualised, and that could only happen because Benedict, people living with HIV, and those directly affected by AIDS were invited to share their experience and had the courage to be present and do so.

This approach stands in stark contrast to that taken at the first Vatican Conference on AIDS some three years later in 1989. Vatican officials ignored approaches from both the National Catholic AIDS Network (NCAN) in the USA and the lay-led Catholic AIDS Link (CAL) in the UK, who had argued that people living with HIV willing to speak openly about their experience should be invited to address the conference as part of the formal programme. At the Vatican Conference people living with HIV or AIDS were talked about but excluded from meaningful participation. Anyone present living with HIV was to remain silent. When, increasingly frustrated, CAL delegates Peter Larkin and Fr John White, both living with AIDS, protested that people living with HIV had no

---

[27] Timothy Radcliffe writes that Benedict, who was living with AIDS, contributed most to the conference. Radcliffe, 'The Church and AIDS', *The Tablet*, 8 November 1986, p. 26.
[28] Kaposi's Sarcoma is a type of cancer, previously thought very rare, often producing purple lesions on the skin and is an AIDS defining illness.
[29] Timothy Radcliffe, 'The invitation to meet Christ', in *AIDS*, ed. Cosstick, pp. 115–21.

voice at the Conference, they attracted international press coverage.[30] The voices of lived experience were absent, except as protest from the margins. Larkin and White made themselves heard around the world. They made a noise but were not listened to. They were noticed but not encountered in the sense that we mean it. To truly encounter someone requires a willingness to be vulnerable. An openness to the possibility that we might be changed by the person before us. As a consequence of this approach, presentations at the Conference lacked the reflections of those with lived experience of AIDS. Instead, mostly abstract arguments, with just a veneer of reflection, restated the fixed official positions of the magisterium on public health education, human sexuality and the prohibition of condoms.[31]

It is the priority given to those with lived experience of AIDS at Spode, replicated at public events in the ministry of CAL in the following years, that is especially noticeable. The involvement of lay men and women, especially those diagnosed with HIV, is instructive. Meaningful theological reflection starts by paying attention to the experience of those who have lived with HIV at sites of suffering. At Spode, discernment of a response faithful to the Gospel began with a deep and attentive listening, and the vulnerable encounter with people living with AIDS was central.

The invitation to meet Christ

The title of Timothy Radcliffe's account of the conference 'The Invitation to meet Christ' summarises this approach to learning in theological language.[32] Namely, the Christian belief that through those who suffer, there is the opportunity to encounter Christ in a particular way. Recognising our own fears and anxieties and overcoming them sufficiently so that those who are marginalised may be seen and heard, allows the Holy Spirit some room to move among us, between us and in us. When we

---

[30] Peter Larkin had publicly challenged the conference organiser, Archbishop Fiorenzo Angelini, about this lack of representation; Fr John White held up a sign at the conference which read 'The Church has AIDS' whilst announcing: 'I am living with AIDS, and people with AIDS have no voice at this conference.' The Vatican security men quickly bundled him out and he was detained by the Vatican police. 'The Church has AIDS' was the headline relaying the story in the next day's press, adding to the already controversial worldwide coverage of this conference. Vincent Manning, *Encountering Christ through the Passion of HIV: An inquiry into the theological meaning of HIV in the Church*, doctoral thesis, St Mary's University, London, 2019, pp. 29–30; Garfield, *The End of Innocence*, pp. 169–71.
[31] I refer only to presentations that included matters of theology, not the presentations of scientists who attended. See: Pontifical Council for Pastoral Assistance to Health Care Workers, *Proceedings of the Fourth International Conference. To Live: Why? AIDS* (Vatican City, 1990).
[32] Radcliffe, 'Invitation'. Timothy Radcliffe O.P. was Prior of the Dominican Priory at Oxford at the time and was one of the main organisers of the Spode Conference.

meet this Christ in need, through others, we may be changed in ways that are never forgotten.

Encounters of this kind are repeated frequently in Christian accounts of this time, described often as types of conversion experience. The pastoral worker or priest who discovers that it is they who are ministered to by the ones they intended to serve. The one in need of help becomes the teacher. Numerous testimonies recount how gay men living and dying with AIDS cared for each other, exemplifying the very love-in-action that Christians profess.[33] Theological phrases like 'the Church has AIDS' may remain little more than shallow theological abstractions, but for encounters such as these, when the Love of Christ is enacted and embodied. Benedict was physically placed at the centre of the church gathered in prayer at Spode, and through him, with him and in him, the body of Christ living with HIV became real and present.

At the end of the Spode conference, a statement, agreed unanimously, summarised the shared learning. Participants acknowledged the urgency of the situation and the need to provide accurate information to minimise further new infections. Restating the Christian duty to care for the sick they recognised the reality of prejudice and stigma: '… when their need for love and support is greatest …' people with HIV or AIDS often experience rejection from family or friends, becoming for our society the outcasts with whom Jesus had associated. The statement called for all Catholic people to act and asked the '… bishops to give their active support to this work of Christ; for it is His Body which has AIDS.'[34]

A post-conference working group concluded that an effective Catholic response needed coordination. An inter-diocesan consultation also identified the need to appoint a national Catholic coordinator. The group submitted a report to the bishops outlining a number of steps that should be taken to facilitate a national pastoral response to HIV and AIDS. It was a call to action but nothing more came of it from the Bishops Conference.[35]

---

[33] 'A new command I give you: Love one another. As I have loved you, so you must love one another. By this everyone will know that you are my disciples, if you love one another.' John 13:34–5 (New International Version).

[34] Radcliffe, 'Invitation'.

[35] The failure of the bishops to answer the request from the Spode Conference that they coordinate a national Catholic pastoral response in the UK can be contrasted with the example of the Irish bishops who set up a national task force on AIDS in 1987 and appointed Fr Paul Lavelle as the Pastoral Care Coordinator. It may also provide some clues as to why the English and Welsh bishops did not take a similar initiative. The Irish bishops, perhaps under pressure from Rome, withdrew funding and ended their association with the task force just two years later, following controversial comments made by Fr Lavelle about the acceptable use of condoms. See Ann Nolan and Shane Butler, 'AIDS, Sexual Health, and the Catholic Church in 1980s Ireland: A Public Health Paradox', *American Journal of Public Health*, 108:7 (2018), pp. 908–13; also Gerald M. Oppenheimer, 'The Catholic

The urgent need for a Catholic response

By late 1987 the pastoral needs of those affected and infected were impossible to ignore. Matters of policy and practice in different settings needed to be decided upon.[36] AIDS had become a matter of wider public concern and heightened anxiety. Increasingly those directly affected were subjected to public vilification, hostility, prejudice and exclusion. The failure of the bishops to take a lead role in coordinating a national response caused increasing frustration for Catholics actively engaged in HIV and AIDS ministry.[37] The need for adequate pastoral care was urgent.[38] Misrepresentations of the Christian view as hostile and condemnatory dominated public and private discourse, adding religious weight

---

Church, AIDS, and Sexuality in Ireland: Uncovering Part of the Story', *American Journal of Public Health*, 108:7 (2018), pp. 850–1. See also note 22 above.

36 After the national public education campaign more people came forward for testing. Rates of diagnosis were rising amongst gay men and drug users. Women were learning that they had been infected. Children were being born with HIV. Adults receiving treatment for haemophilia were being diagnosed with AIDS and parents were being taken aside discreetly, to be told by a doctor that their child had been infected. Hospital chaplains and parish priests were being approached secretively by worried families seeking guidance. The negative mythology and fears of contamination in the public imagination meant that teachers in Catholic schools, for example, were having to decide on what their policy should be in regard to the inclusion or exclusion of any pupil with AIDS. Directors of priestly formation were considering whether candidates for seminary should be tested for HIV or not.

37 It is important to distinguish between the lack of a nationally coordinated response from the Bishops Conference and more positive responses from individual bishops. In this essay, each of the bishops named provides an example of a concerned pastor who was supportive of CAL and sought to fulfil their role as bishop thoughtfully and responsibly. For example, Cardinal Hume was known to be understanding of issues affecting and pastorally supportive of LGBT Catholics (see also note 48). Hume was influenced by his encounters with Peter Larkin, mentioned above. Larkin was also a Director of the AIDS self-help support group 'Frontliners' for whom Cardinal Hume made office space available at the Church of Notre Dame de France, Leicester Square, London. CAL News, no. 4, March 1990. Similarly, the Archdioceses of Westminster and Southwark appointed clergy or religious sisters as HIV chaplains or coordinators, and in 1989 Southwark became the first diocese to formulate a pastoral policy on HIV and AIDS. CAL News, no. 1, February 1989.

38 An HIV or AIDS diagnosis was always shocking news. At that time, subjectively, diagnosis meant that a person was likely to face the onset of an ugly and painful disease. They could spend weeks or months in hospital. Losing any independence, their body, perhaps their mind too, would weaken, until they appeared thinly skeletal. In time, helpless and incapacitated, surrounded by loved ones or isolated and alone, death from AIDS was considered inevitable by almost everyone. From HIV infection to death, the most optimistic prognosis generally believed at the time was ten years. Those diagnosed with AIDS might expect to live for just a matter of months. The personal and family crises that an HIV diagnosis provoked should not be underestimated. A diagnosis was and still is both subjectively and communally experienced. HIV impacts an individual, whether affected or infected, always within the context of their relationships with others.

to the stigma attached to AIDS. For Catholics volunteering or working in the HIV sector this association was more than embarrassing.[39] More importantly, as the Spode declaration had realised, religiously generated stigma created a barrier to practical and spiritual support at precisely the time when individuals and affected families were most in need of well informed and sensitive pastoral care.[40] Religiously generated stigma and the lack of any coordinated response added to the isolation of people living with or directly affected by AIDS. For those Catholics closest to the unfolding phenomenon of AIDS in society, it was not stories in the press about priests with AIDS or disputes amongst bishops about condom use that scandalised as much as the silence and inaction of the Church.[41]

The stigma attached to HIV and AIDS, the lack of organised pastoral support for increasing numbers of affected and infected people, the apparent indifference of the institutional Church, the need for guidance and accurate information, and the general perception of Christian hostility towards people living with and affected by HIV, demanded a more coordinated national Catholic response.

Catholic AIDS Link (CAL) established

In 1988, CAL was formed, coordinated jointly by volunteers Krystyna Fuchs, Martin Pendergast and Peter Harris, to offer 'non-judgemental, spiritual, emotional and practical support' to anyone affected by HIV and

---

[39] Within the HIV and AIDS sector, there was a reasonable suspicion of anyone who claimed allegiance to a religion that was apparently so ready to condemn gay men, even in sickness. That leaders or Christian spokespersons contributed to the stigma surrounding AIDS understandably created antagonism. The voluntary sector charities that had been set up to provide support, were places where gay men or any woman or man living with HIV or AIDS expected to feel welcome and safe. Catholic priests and religious sisters who volunteered in HIV sector agencies often avoided wearing clerical clothing lest their visible presence and association with institutional religion cause offence or upset. Lay Catholics working in the NHS or Social Services reported hiding their Catholic identity for the same reason. For any Catholic person working or volunteering in AIDS ministry, there was also a need for them to be provided with pastoral support and training.

[40] The impact of stigma cannot be overstated. Many people with HIV or AIDS kept their diagnosis secret. Because of the stigma and shame attached to homosexuality and to AIDS, families often maintained the strictest privacy possible. The inevitability of public shame and the affective power of internalised stigma can be illustrated by the many stories of funerals where no mention of the person's death from AIDS was allowed by the family. In many cases it went unmentioned or was denied that the young man being mourned and buried was gay. The exclusion from the funeral rites of people living with HIV or gay friends, perhaps including a lover, was not uncommon. Official death certificates avoided naming AIDS as the cause of death to lessen the distress caused to family members, or simply to keep the reality secret and avoid the gossip, judgment and vilification of others.

[41] For examples of Press coverage, see Sandra G. Boodman, 'Priests and AIDS: Will Church Minister to its Own?' *The Washington Post*, 7 February 1987; Miles Corwin, 'Priest With AIDS — "It's Important That People Know"', *Los Angeles Times*, 16 February 1987.

AIDS.[42] Initially, CAL operated out of a small room in an East London community building, moving later to a more spacious office in Camden. Volunteers managed the office, compiled resources and took phone calls from people seeking help. Collaborating with other HIV-sector groups and agencies, CAL represented the Catholic contribution to the infrastructure of newly created HIV support organisations, clinics and self-help groups developing rapidly across the country. The coordinators were supported by a wider CAL Board, which included lay people living with HIV or AIDS from the start.[43]

CAL soon became a central point of reference, communication and support for Catholics and other Christians engaged in HIV ministry. For Catholic organisations and diocesan bodies, CAL was a trusted source for training and education, consistent with Catholic teaching and practice. Over the following decade, CAL organised liturgies and conferences, published resources and cooperated with governmental, NHS and voluntary sector agencies within the HIV sector. Regular CAL newsletters were circulated to thousands of people, and included news items and updates about the ministry, practical guidance, theological reflections, letters and poems from readers and accounts of ministry from the UK and around the world.[44] CAL created a network of concerned lay people and clergy, so that informed and sensitive pastoral care became more available throughout the country. A monthly 'Positively Catholic' peer support group was established in London. Retreat weekends for Catholic and other Christian people diagnosed with HIV, led by people living with HIV, took place around the country. CAL equipped lay people and clergy for HIV ministry and created spaces within which serious theological reflection upon HIV and AIDS could happen. By establishing links with NCAN in the USA,[45] the International Christian AIDS Network (ICAN)

---

[42] Martin Pendergast had been a social worker at St Thomas Hospital and later became the HIV coordinator for an East London local authority. Krystyna Fuchs was a volunteer at THT. Peter Harris was a secondary school teacher at this time. In 1994 he was ordained as a priest in the Diocese of Westminster.
[43] Amongst others, Peter Larkin and Rev. John White, mentioned above, were both actively involved with CAL from the outset. I was formally appointed to the CAL Board in 1991.
[44] By 1993, 216 organisations subscribed to CAL Newsletters; by 1995, CAL News had 1,100 individual subscribers. CAL News 15 and 17.
[45] The first national gathering of Catholics working in HIV/AIDS ministry in the USA took place at Notre Dame University in 1988. Following the conference, the National Catholic AIDS Network (NCAN) was founded in 1989 by a diverse group of leaders in the Catholic Church, including clergy and lay people, as the only organisation devoted exclusively to helping the Catholic Church respond with compassion and understanding to the HIV/AIDS crisis. Loyola University Chicago. Archives & Special Collections. National Catholic AIDS Network Records, 1986–2007.

and CARITAS Internationalis,[46] CAL extended its influence beyond national borders.[47]

From its founding in 1988 until its closure in 1999, CAL was the authoritative Catholic body representing the voices of lay Catholics, ordinary clergy and people living with HIV. Whilst maintaining independence as an organisation, and often critical of statements issued in the name of the Church,[48] CAL always sought to operate fully within the structure of the Church. An important aspect of CAL's mission was to inform, assist and influence the bishops in their various roles as leaders. With the active support of several individual bishops including Cardinal Hume and the tacit support of the Bishops Conference, this lay-led Catholic charity became not only a resource for, but also the effective voice of the Catholic Church in the UK in regard to HIV and AIDS.[49]

Liturgy: helping the Church to pray

CAL's inaugural 'Mass for World AIDS Day' on 1 December 1988, with Bishop John Crowley presiding, at the French Church in Leicester Square,

---

[46] CARITAS Internationalis (CI) is the coordinating umbrella body for Catholic relief, development and social services organisations globally. It has headquarters in Vatican City and representatives at the United Nations.

[47] Cafod, the official aid agency of the Catholic Church in England and Wales and a CI member agency, became the lead agency for the CI Working Group on AIDS. In 1994 Martin Pendergast and Vincent Manning attended the first CI Theological Weekend Symposium on AIDS in Dublin. By this time the reality of HIV and AIDS as an enduring global pandemic was clear. Theologians and practitioners from Continental Europe, Great Britain, Ireland and the USA gathered for theological reflection upon HIV in the light of faith, in the hopes of establishing theologically sound Christian responses. A series of regional theological consultations held by CI in Africa, Asia, North America, Latin America and Europe followed in subsequent years.

[48] For example, CAL representatives were highly critical of the 'Letter to the bishops of the Catholic Church on the Pastoral Care of Homosexual Persons' insensitively issued by the CDF in 1986 at the height of the AIDS crisis. This letter is still remembered for its description of same-sex desire as 'a more or less strong tendency ordered toward an intrinsic moral evil' and 'an objective disorder' (para. 3). Whilst it makes no direct mention of AIDS, it implies an inevitable link between gay sexuality, sickness and death (para. 9). It is relevant to note that the 1986 CDF letter appears to contradict the earlier *Declaration on Certain Questions Concerning Sexual Ethics* (Humana Persona), published by the CDF in 1975, which, whilst viewing homosexual genital behaviour as wrong, regards homosexual orientation as morally neutral. Aware of the distress caused by the 1986 letter and, advised in part by CAL members, Cardinal Hume issued letters in 1993 (*Some Observations on the Teaching of the Catholic Church Concerning Homosexual People*) and 1997 (*Note on the Teaching of the Catholic Church Concerning Homosexual People*) to both ameliorate and clarify the teaching of the Church in regard to homosexuality.

[49] For example, whilst Cardinal Hume corresponded with government ministers, CAL was also consulted by ministers and Members of Parliament when, in 1992, Christian conservative groups and MPs sought to remove HIV from the national education curriculum. (CAL News 10).

London,[50] coincided with the World Health Organization's first ever international day for global health.[51] A few months later, in April 1989, a 'Mass of Anointing' was held at St Aloysius Church in East London, attended by over 200 people from the city and surrounding counties. The great majority of those present were anointed with oil, along with Bishop Victor Guazzelli[52] and the assisting priests. CAL volunteers organised religious services and published various liturgical resources each year, in support of a more adequate ritual and sacramental response to the AIDS crisis. As awareness of the pandemic spread within society over the following decade, CAL prayer resources might be used, for example around World AIDS Day, in many parishes. As well as public liturgy for particular occasions, the Eucharist or other forms of communal prayer were an important element in most CAL training events or conferences. There was usually an ecumenical dimension to any Mass, healing or memorial service organised by CAL. People living with HIV/AIDS, their partners, family members and friends, staff from hospitals, activists from the HIV voluntary sector, and people from other churches were regularly in attendance.

A service entitled 'A Celebration of Life' provides one example of this awareness of the need to ensure that liturgy was as inclusive and welcoming as possible.[53] I led the planning group which brought together Catholics, Anglicans and Buddhists to organise a service which would enable people of all faiths and none to pray, grieve and remember loved ones in their own way. At each of three entrance doors to the church, a person of faith and someone from one of the HIV sector agencies, together, greeted every person as they arrived.[54] Designated counsellors were on hand to speak with anyone who needed individual support. After

---

50 CAL News, 1 February 1989.
51 Today there are numerous designated global public health day campaigns intended to raise awareness and mobilise support for action, from the local community to the international stage. It was the global threat posed by AIDS and the need to exert pressure on governments to act quickly that led to the very first such international day. AIDS campaigners first devised this now widely applied model for public health promotion.
52 Victor Guazzelli (1920–2004), then auxiliary bishop in the Diocese of Westminster, concelebrated and preached the sermon.
53 Held to mark World AIDS Day at the Cathedral Church of Saints Peter and Paul in Clifton Diocese, to the best of my recollection in 1993.
54 For example, welcomers included Fr Dominic Mansi, a monk from Downside Abbey near Bath, accompanied by the lead nurse from the Bristol Royal Infirmary HIV clinic, both of whom dressed in ordinary attire. As a Catholic charity, we had arranged for the event to take place at Clifton Cathedral, because of the centrality of the venue and because the internal beauty and physical space of the Cathedral allowed for workshops to take place. However, we were aware that for some people, the prospect of just entering a Catholic church to attend an AIDS-related service, might cause anxiety. This was true, not only because of the general stigma and fear attached to AIDS, but also because of a suspicion within the HIV sector and those communities most directly impacted, not least gay men,

an initial introduction and welcome, eighty people took part in facilitated workshops, contributing their stories, music, symbols, mementos and favourite readings, to co-create the liturgy that followed.[55] About one quarter of the people who came said that it was the first time they had been in any church in many years.

Most CAL liturgy was more traditionally sacramental in style and format than this example. This chapter has included it to emphasise how organisers were aware that any liturgy inevitably attracted people of all faiths and none, some who had an uneasy relationship with religion and many who felt let down or hurt by the Church. At a time of great suffering, whether celebrating Mass or a less formalised time of prayer and worship, CAL liturgy always aimed to be pastorally relevant for those who may not be Sunday Mass-attending Catholics. Attention was given to the language used, so that those alienated from faith, or excluded by the Church, felt included and welcome. At a time when so much hostility and fear was directed at people living with or affected by AIDS, a CAL liturgy became an act of solidarity with those who had been marginalised. Through prayer and fellowship, it provided a public witness and call to repentance on behalf of the whole church.

Liturgy: helping the priest to preach and pray

Dedicated liturgical events were very often initiated and organised by concerned lay people. Not every priest felt comfortable presiding at a liturgy that explicitly addressed the AIDS pandemic.

Clergy may have been concerned about negative reactions from local people. Some parishioners had argued that children with HIV should be excluded from church schools to avoid any risk to other children. Some Christians advocated that testing for HIV should be compulsory for some groups of people or that homosexuality be made, once again, illegal. Parishioners might have felt upset or threatened by the visible presence of people with AIDS in their sacred space.[56]

---

that the Catholic Church was an unhelpful or hostile agent, rather than an ally or friend to people living with HIV and AIDS.

55   In the publicity for the service, people had been alerted to the workshops and invited to bring anything that they wished which might be included as part of the liturgy. We invited participants to join one of four workshops on 'the word', music, symbols, or 'preparing our shared space and decoration'. Some came with favourite music and others were involved in decorating the area around the baptismal font, where the liturgy took place. In 'the word' group one woman had brought a poem that she had written about her friend who had died. A mixture of story, grief, lament and anger, she read it aloud as part of the service. The workshops were intended as a time of sharing and reflective preparation for the liturgy that followed.

56   Despite the government adopting a liberal approach to the AIDS pandemic, opinion amongst the general public, including many churchgoers, was at the time decidedly hard-line

Individual clergy also knew that their words and actions might be scrutinised. The exercise of clerical discipline by an increasingly centralised and conservative magisterium created an atmosphere of anxiety that extended to the level of parish practice. Reflecting wider society, debates about the acceptability or not of gay relationships and contraception, and sexual morality more generally, had intensified since the close of Vatican II. Positions became more polarised during the AIDS crisis, with attitudes to homosexuality and condoms becoming the touchstones for a rigid type of Catholic orthodoxy. From this viewpoint, any impression given that the Church was accepting of gay relationships or contraception, for example, would be an intolerable compromise with the truth of Catholic doctrine. As described below, for any priest or bishop engaging in HIV ministry, even presiding at liturgy, posed a potential risk to his reputation, and invited criticism from parishioners and possible censure from his superiors.[57] As a public action in the wider community, bringing

---

and illiberal. For example, a survey of 12,000 people undertaken for *The News of the World* and published in March 1987 had clear majorities in favour of making homosexuality illegal; the sterilisation of people with AIDS; compulsory testing for unfaithful sexual partners; the compulsory isolation of people with AIDS; the right not to work alongside someone with AIDS; and compulsory testing and exclusion of immigrants with HIV. Even funeral directors had complained that they and those attending funerals were at risk of 'catching AIDS' because of the government's refusal to make HIV or AIDS a notifiable disease. There were reports of attacks on people thought to have AIDS in some parts of the country and of homes being burnt. Berridge, *AIDS in the UK*, p. 134. See also notes 10 and 12.

[57] For example, regarding ministry with homosexual people, magisterial teaching insisted that 'All support should be withdrawn from any organisations which seek to undermine the teaching of the Church, which are ambiguous about it, or which neglect it entirely. Such support, or even the semblance of such support, can be gravely misinterpreted. Special attention should be given to the practice of scheduling religious services and to the use of Church buildings by these groups ... such permission to use Church property may seem only just and charitable; but in reality it is contradictory to the purpose for which these institutions were founded, it is misleading and often scandalous.' CDF, *Letter to the Bishops of the Catholic Church on the Pastoral Care of Homosexual Persons* (1986). This more pastorally rigid approach was enforced by the Vatican and led to the expulsion of numerous local chapters of the American Catholic LGBT organisation 'Dignity' from Catholic Church premises. Enforcement of this approach in the UK created conflict between Cardinal Hume and the LGBT Catholic support group 'Quest'. Under pressure from the Vatican, Cardinal Hume instructed that Quest's listing in the official Catholic Directory be suspended because of their refusal to endorse official Church teaching on homosexuality. See Basil Hume, 'Why Quest was excluded', *The Tablet*, 13 March 1999. Attempts to enforce this type of rigid orthodoxy can also be seen in the case of attacks on CAL and a later campaign against Cafod. In the Catholic press a columnist asserted that the 'non-judgmental approach to people living with HIV or AIDS' stated as a CAL aim was incompatible with any claim to Catholic identity (Editorial, CAL News, 8 July 1991). In 2004 a vigorous campaign was launched to defund Cafod, attacking the Bishops Conference and urging parishioners to cease donations, in protest against Cafod's HIV prevention strategy which made some allowance for the use of condoms as a health protection measure. See Ann Smith, 'Where Cafod Stands', *The Tablet*, 25 September 2004; P. Donovan, 'Cafod faces criticism over HIV policy', *The Tablet*, 23 October 2004.

HIV or AIDS into the Church, in any way, was potentially controversial and not without some degree of risk for those involved.

More positively, sensitive clergy were also concerned, when presiding at Mass or conducting the funeral of someone taken by AIDS, for example, that their actions and words be pastorally helpful. A competent priest was aware of his responsibility to find the right words to say in the face of such suffering. As Bishop Crowley acknowledged in his sermon at that first CAL Mass, an insensitive use of language might 'offend carelessly', which mattered because 'language does influence attitudes'.[58] CAL resources and the advice of CAL activists were often sought by a priest or bishop wishing to fulfil their role in a pastorally sensitive manner and in a way that did not contribute further to stigma, prejudice or the negative stereotyping of those most directly affected.

A liturgy is also an opportunity for health education. At a basic level, an informed priest avoided adding to public ignorance by conflating HIV and AIDS or speaking about AIDS as though it might be 'caught', like a common cold, from ordinary social interaction. A properly informed priest would have noted how AIDS affected family members, men, women and children, taking care not to speak of HIV as confined within gay communities. Those with an awareness of how stigma is reproduced avoided language that depersonalised or 'othered' people. A sensitive pastor would not add to the stigma by speaking in the language of innocence and guilt or labelling those diagnosed with HIV as 'AIDS Victims' rather than people living with HIV.

At a time of heightened moral panic, how might a priest avoid reinforcing any sense that AIDS was divine retribution? How to speak about the dignity of love expressed between gay men within the context of AIDS? At that first CAL Mass, as he began his homily, Bishop Crowley's honest admission was indicative of some anxiety: 'Let me first begin with a confession. When I was asked to celebrate this Mass and preach on the occasion of World AIDS Day, though I was happy to be asked and glad to say "yes", I soon became aware of all sorts of pressures, mainly from within.' Describing most of the concerns already mentioned above, he concluded his opening remarks: 'Those then were some of my initial rather anxious thoughts, and I mention them if only to share the tensions which others too might experience in different ways.'[59]

Whenever a priest was asked to lead or preside, it is perhaps too obvious to say that CAL activists would think carefully about who to approach and ask those who they felt would be both open to the invitation and sufficiently aware of the need for care. The invitation alone was a kind of

---

[58] Text of Bishop Crowley's sermon in CAL News 1.
[59] CAL News 1.

permission for the priest or bishop to undertake a liturgical duty that he might otherwise avoid, for whatever reason. CAL activists were sensitive to the anxious thoughts that any priest might have because these were shared concerns. The wisest priests knew that they must prepare to lead the people in prayer and in this time of crisis, they had a responsibility do so in an informed and pastorally sensitive manner. Countless priests and bishops drew upon the expertise of lay people involved with CAL to educate and advise them, informally and formally

Training and education in the language of faith

As the reality of AIDS within families and communities across the country became more difficult to ignore, CAL provided training and education for Christian lay societies, in parishes and schools, at conferences and for clergy. In the main participants were motivated to attend because they had been touched personally by HIV in some way. Very often attendance represented the first tentative steps to confront a painful personal reality which could no longer be denied.

Despite the government's public health campaign, ignorance and myths about people affected or infected persisted. CAL training included a presentation of the latest scientific and epidemiological information, allowing time for questions to be addressed. We insisted there were never any 'stupid' questions. Ignorance of scientific fact is always an obstacle to learning and within the Church, the misrepresentation of scientific evidence contributed to confusion.[60] Along with prejudice, shame and exclusionary practices, ignorance is one of the pillars of stigma. Still today, an aim of any education workshop is to challenge HIV stigma. Any confusion about the basic epidemiological data or transmission routes, for example, must be clarified before more meaningful reflection can begin.

Our approach to learning was dialogical and workshops always began with an agreement that Chatham House Rules and principles of confidentiality would apply. Participants agreed to listen to one another as far as possible in a spirit of openness without judgment. No one was immune from the prejudice and moral panic that AIDS provoked. Fear and shame had created a culture of secrecy and discrimination, meaning that any association with HIV, once known, could have devastating consequences in the community, at work or in the family. Sharing personal information was a decision for the individual concerned, not something to be revealed in casual conversation or idle gossip. For anyone diagnosed with HIV

---

[60] For example, arguments made prohibiting condoms have sometimes been supported with misleading statements regarding the efficacy of condoms as preventative of HIV transmission.

or directly affected, careful thought about who to share any information with and the effect that might have on wider relationships was needed. The explicit agreement that anything said would not be repeated elsewhere in a way that identified individuals was necessary. Paradoxically, confidentiality created the conditions of trust within which the silence of secrecy might be broached, and honest sharing became possible.

Equally, for anyone who had already suffered prejudice and discrimination this agreement provided some reassurance that they would not be subjected to the judgmentalism of others. Whether a mother anxious for her gay son, the father unsure how to explain hospital visits to his family, a friend, teacher or pastor wanting to be supportive, the young woman struggling to come to terms with her diagnosis and that of her newborn baby, or someone worried about coping when they became sick, people came from diverse situations and backgrounds. Each person came with their own particular relationships, wanting to make sense of intensely personal and often complex dilemmas. The intention was to enable each person some space and time to process their own thoughts and feelings in response to a disease which was inevitably disruptive and disturbing. Confidentiality was essential to create as safe a learning environment as possible, so that all participants might be able to reflect upon and learn from their own experience and that of others.

Creating spaces for vulnerable sharing

One example that illustrates CAL's approach to training is a workshop for clergy delivered in 1996 in the Birmingham Archdiocese. Around a dozen priests participated in a one-day workshop, facilitated by Martin Pendergast and myself.[61] Unsurprisingly, because of the stigma attached to HIV, a culture of secrecy also existed amongst the clergy. Reflective of the tensions that Bishop Crowley alluded to, the honest sharing of personal experience, or raising questions about Church teaching or the challenges of HIV ministry, could be risky for a priest's career prospects, reputation or standing.

The youngest priest in attendance identified himself as a heterosexual man whose gay brother had received an AIDS diagnosis. Even though it had been widely promoted by the archbishop, he had not told the parish priest with whom he lived that he was attending the training day. Instead, he had lied, requesting permission to change his usual day off in order to attend a family occasion. He had heard his superior make judgmental comments about people living with AIDS. He shared his anxiety that his

---

[61] This account is taken from an audio recording of this training workshop, is anonymised, and is used with the permission of the participants. Original recording held by the author.

brother priest would question him and not allow him to attend. After all there were other priorities in the busy parish and what had AIDS to do with them? The young priest worried that intrusive questions might be asked about his motivation for attending or that assumptions might be made about his sexuality.

During the day he shared some of his concerns for his brother and their family. He spoke about his love for his brother and how their lives were very different. He wondered how he might be most supportive and acknowledged how his brother's choices and relationships contrasted with his own. He admired the love that was evident amongst his brother's friends and how they cared for each other. At the same time there were aspects of his brother's life, of gay life, that he found difficult to understand or accept. Confronting the reality of this debilitating disease and the prospect of his brother's death from AIDS challenged him to love authentically and caused him to question the teaching of the Church and his role as a priest.

The testimony of a lay person living with or directly affected by HIV was usually central for CAL training. As at Spode, the personal story of someone diagnosed with HIV, and what that meant for their relationships with God and family and the Church, served to demythologise AIDS. Usually coming during the first part of any training day, through this personal testimony, the participants had an opportunity to encounter someone living with HIV and learn from them. The willingness to share deeply personal and painful experience served as an example for others. For anyone wanting to come to terms with or make faith-sense of their own situation, the sharing of a mother or father, someone living with HIV or a lover grieving the loss of their partner, provided a model of sharing to follow. Their courage to be vulnerable was often the encouragement that others needed to speak.

On this occasion, a Catholic gay man in his early thirties (we shall call him John) shared how his diagnosis in 1987 had been profoundly shocking. 'I couldn't believe it. It was too much to bear, too difficult to accept.' John's initial coping strategy of total secrecy lasted for two years but eventually denial had to give way to facing the truth. He needed to plan for the prospect that he would become very sick and die from AIDS. Fearing rejection, he spoke about how painful it had been to tell his partner about his diagnosis. Holding back tears John said that his failure to share the news sooner with someone he loved intimately had been his 'biggest sin'. He described how, as a young adult, he had been sincerely determined to live in accordance with God's will for him and how this led him to explore the possibility of a priestly vocation. The practice of faith had always been precious and central for his life. At the same time his Catholic upbringing created an irreconcilable conflict within, between his sexuality and the teaching of the Church, which he kept secret. He spoke about how shocked his parents would be if they knew he was gay. Growing up, John felt totally unprepared to navigate his feelings of same-sex attraction which, he had been taught, were disordered. Confusion and the attendant feelings of shame had consequences for his relationships. He had come to understand that self-loathing and fear of his deepest desires had predisposed him to HIV infection. John explained how, after diagnosis, his own internalised homophobia, now compounded by the natural fear of death and the stigma attached to HIV, brought these conflicts into painfully sharp focus: 'I can no longer live in denial ... To deny myself and the way God has made me became too much to bear and the truth will out one way or another ... I plunged headlong into confronting my fears.' John arranged to take the needed time off work. He travelled for several hours each week to attend peer support groups in London. He did not want to risk being seen locally. In the long process of coming to a greater degree of acceptance of himself as a Catholic gay man living with HIV, his faith remained his touchstone:

> I reminded myself that God has made me and God loves me, that I am saved and I am good ... even though I am separated from God, I am not disordered. The virus has in a very real sense compelled me to journey more quickly and with greater vigour towards God ... I must learn to love myself, rather than deny myself ... learn to be myself ... I've had to learn to see my sexuality as a gift from God ... it is in all of me, part of my being ... so I better learn how to express it positively.

John concluded with his belief in the God who, in the words of the psalmist, loves each of us as we are wonderfully made. The God who knows us better than we know ourselves, from whose presence we can never hide, who guides us always.[62] The God revealed in Christ, from whose love, in the words of St Paul, nothing can separate us.[63] At the same time, John's statement of faith also served as an indictment upon the Church to which he still belonged:

> God has called me first to be who I am, to be who God has made me ... And anyone or anything that prevents me or obstructs me from being truly myself, is not from God. Anyone who encourages me to hide, to be fearful, to deny myself, to wear masks, to pretend to be somebody else is not from God, because God has created me to be me ... [this is] God's will for me.[64]

Towards the end of the day, the oldest priest there, in his late sixties or seventies, shared a personal experience. I sensed his nervousness, as though he had been weighing up whether or not he could tell the story.

---

[62] An allusion to Psalm 139.
[63] Romans 8:31–9.
[64] John did not die from AIDS. At time of writing John is alive and well and is a person for whom Catholic faith and identity remains central to his life.

His voice nearly cracked as he spoke quietly. The preamble in what he said was just that, as though hesitating on his way to the main point. It was when he spoke about having presided at Mass for Quest, a support network for Gay Catholic men and women, regularly, he said, over several years, that I heard him revealing something that took courage to share.[65] Before then, he had not told any other priests that he was involved in this ministry to gay people, he said. I remember him still and the compassion I felt for him in that moment. This old man who had kept what was clearly a painful secret and carried it alone for years, did something important that day. He showed something of himself to his brother priests trusting that they would understand. And we listened. Perhaps John's sharing gave him the courage to be vulnerable. It felt like a moment of grace to me. A gift for others and a liberating act for him.

Whilst this example draws from the experience of training for clergy, workshops were more often delivered for mixed groups of lay people and clergy. This is just one example that illustrates how trust and a non-judgmental approach enabled participants to share very personal stories and receive encouragement. Although important, the passing on of scientific or medical facts was not the main aim. Rather, CAL workshops helped participants to face often painful situations, and speak with others honestly in the language of faith. Whether the mother feeling that God was punishing her and her gay son; the father who felt abandoned, even by God; the young woman who could not forgive her partner; or someone afraid of death and judgment; these and many other religious and spiritual questions, not adequately addressed in more secular HIV environments, could be named. For any Christian, too anxious or afraid to speak about HIV in the presbytery or church, a CAL workshop invited them to share their joys and hopes, griefs and anxieties, with others who were willing to listen and could understand. CAL workshops helped lay people and clergy to make faith-sense of HIV as sisters and brothers in Christ.

There is no comprehensive account of the ministry of CAL. A fuller story of how members of the Church, lay and ordained, responded to the emergence of AIDS in the UK is yet to be written. This essay has identified just some of the ways in which lay people led the Catholic response to AIDS in the UK, and described how the identification of HIV with the gay community, and perceptions of AIDS as a minority disease, resulted in complacency. The initially slow response gave way to urgent action only when the predicted, potentially devastating impact of HIV within the general population was accepted and understood.

---

[65] Being open about any association with Quest was a potentially risky thing to reveal, given that Quest was viewed as a controversial organisation by many lay Catholics, clergy and bishops, and given the CDF 1986 instruction that support should not be provided for LGBT groups who dissented from magisterial teaching on homosexuality. See note 57.

Stigma is too wide a subject to be explored adequately here, but this chapter has outlined how ignorance, fear and moral panic contributed to the stigma which remains a defining feature of HIV to this day. People living with HIV and dying from AIDS were viewed as a threat. Subjected to prejudice and discrimination, they acquired a status comparable to the outcasts of Jesus' time. In His life, Jesus risked the condemnation of religious authorities and caused scandal by associating with those considered public sinners. His solidarity with people on the margins of society, at least in part, brought Jesus to the site of disgrace, outside the walls, where the greatest sign of God's love for us was revealed through the utter humiliation and public shame of crucifixion. The crucified Christ embodies the stigma of every age and time and challenges us to consider, what do we risk? In this sense, the story told here raises questions about how willing or able Christians have been to follow the example of Jesus. What have we still to understand about the willingness of Jesus to accept and take upon Himself the stigma of the Cross?[66]

This chapter has described how individual bishops and many clergy were willing to respond but in many cases were inhibited by religiously generated stigma, as well as a rigid type of Catholic orthodoxy and the enforcement of clerical discipline. The Bishops' Conference could not provide the leadership asked of them. For many priests, the tension between respectful and sensitive pastoral practice and their obligation to uphold the official teaching of the Church on matters of gay sexuality created situations within which they felt conflicted and morally compromised. The clerical-hierarchical structure of the Church, and magisterial teaching about sexuality, problematised what would otherwise be a clear Christian obligation to care for the sick.

More coordinated Christian leadership, in this account provided by Catholic lay people, also took more than five years to begin. The proximity of AIDS and encounters with people who were suffering compelled some Christians to act. Throughout, the meaningful involvement of people living with HIV as essential for any attempt to make faith-sense of the pandemic, has been emphasised. The Vatican Conference revealed the impoverishment of a Church which seeks first to control the voices of those who suffer rather than listen to them. The selected examples above illustrate how important engaging with lived experience has been, collectively and individually, for theological reflection, discernment and action. We have seen how lay people assisted the clergy in presiding at liturgy and preaching. CAL workshops provided safe spaces for priests and other Christians to reflect on their faith in a time of AIDS. The courage and willingness of Christians living with or directly affected by HIV to share

---

[66] See Galatians 3:13; Hebrews 12:2; 1 Corinthians 1:18–25.

their faith with others, provided a prophetic witness to wider society and the church, at a time when any association with AIDS invited suspicion, judgment, fear and hostility. The CAL network provided occasions for mutual support and education. Christians were afforded opportunities to more honestly reflect upon their own experience and the ways in which HIV both disturbed and deepened their faith.

Postscript: the closure and legacy of CAL

A CAL General Meeting in 1999 made the controversial decision to disband the charity. Whilst minutes from this meeting are not available, there is sufficient evidence to argue that this decision was influenced by the following societal and ecclesial factors.[67] From 1997, the introduction of anti-retroviral drugs (ARVs) radically changed the prognosis for anyone diagnosed. The treatment became known as the Lazarus effect' as people nearing death from AIDS were visibly restored to life. I recall discussions at CAL board meetings in 1998 where it was proposed that given these remarkable medical advances, CAL's work could shift away from engagement with HIV as an issue for the gay community. Instead, CAL should focus on issues affecting women and children and the devastation of AIDS in Africa. Some argued that there was plentiful support for gay men within the secular HIV sector, whilst the needs of women were neglected and the vast numbers of people with AIDS globally now demanded attention. Others, myself included, argued that HIV could not be reduced to a medical issue. Pastoral care and support for people *living* with and affected by HIV was every bit as important as caring for gay men dying from AIDS. CAL had consistently raised awareness of AIDS as a global issue, and pro-actively supported ministry for women.[68] Retreats for people living with HIV always included women and heterosexual men and these efforts should continue. However, amongst the theologically disruptive and challenging truths revealed by the AIDS crisis was that the Church had neglected and marginalised gay people. That the

---

[67] My research has not located minutes or notes from this meeting. As I was living and working in Scotland at the time I did not attend this meeting. Conversations that I have had with some people who attended confirm my analysis but others report being confused or not remembering why the motion to close CAL was passed.

[68] For example, an active CAL member, Sr Elaine Kelly, of the Helpers of the Holy Souls Congregation, started 'Centrepeace' in 1991 on the ground floor of a Convent in Camden, providing care and support for mostly African women and their families. This and other initiatives for women, children and young people were actively supported by CAL members. To raise awareness, CAL produced a poster showing women of different ethnic groups, entitled 'AIDS it's a women's issue too', with links to support from CAL. Concern for women was not new. The issue was highlighted by the 1990 theme for World AIDS Day, 'Women and AIDS'.

prognosis had changed did not mean that we could now abandon gay men and women or their families. Medical advances, even the vast impact of AIDS on millions of lives globally, should not be an excuse for CAL to neglect people affected by HIV in our midst, including gay men, who at that time remained the largest directly impacted community in the UK. This discussion brings us back once again to the wider ecclesial context and tensions between orthodoxy or right-doctrine and orthopraxy or right-practice, identified throughout this essay. As noted above, debates within the Church about human sexuality, and gay sexuality in particular, intensified during the AIDS crisis. The exercise of clerical discipline had resulted in several well-publicised cases of theologians and priests being censured by the Vatican. The strategy to enforce conformity in both doctrine and pastoral practice, under the lengthy pontificate of John Paul II, had an impact, not just upon the bishops, theologians or parish clergy, but upon lay people as well.[69]

There is no evidence that pressure from the Vatican was directly applied to close CAL, although that may yet come to light.[70] However, a decade of pastoral ministry with gay men living with HIV in particular, and solidarity with what was then coming to be called the LGBT community in general, had undoubtedly resulted in a weariness, or at least discomfort, for some clergy and lay people attending the 1999 General Meeting. In my opinion, the potential for disagreement over Church teaching and the possibility of dispute between lay people and the bishops tasked with enforcing it, influenced the vote.

The advances in treatment in Western society, the devastating impact of AIDS globally, and the fact that AIDS ministry took a heavy emotional toll on so many who had been actively involved, were factors that combined to justify the closure of CAL. In my view, the disjuncture between the official stance of the Church, whether in regard to condoms or homosexuality for example, and the reality of HIV pastoral ministry, also influenced the decision. Disengaging from HIV ministry within the gay community meant that thorny theological and pastoral issues around sexuality could be ignored, and tensions between lay people, clergy and the magisterium more easily avoided.

However, the ministry of CAL continued when a successor charity, Catholics for AIDS Prevention and Support (CAPS), was founded in 2003. At a CAPS Conference to consider afresh how the Church should respond to the continuing reality of HIV in our midst, Christian people living with HIV attending a workshop clearly restated their need for pastoral care.[71]

---

[69] See note 57 above.
[70] See note 57 above.
[71] Many of the people most closely associated with CAL were also involved with establishing CAPS, including Martin Pendergast and myself. The first trustees of CAPS were:

In response to the question 'why are you here?' an Evangelical Christian expressed the desperation that she and her friends felt: 'We saw the words HIV and Christian and even though this is a Catholic conference, we just had to come.' Christians living with HIV spoke about how, within the HIV sector, religious belief was rarely understood. Sometimes, they were treated with suspicion or outright hostility because of their faith. At the same time, stigma within churches meant that they could not be open with their fellow Christians, including family members. They spoke of the ignorance of their priests or pastors. How sermons or judgmental comments reinforced notions about HIV as indicative of personal moral failure, God's disfavour, or punishment for sin. And how this silenced them. As one African woman later put it: 'I could not possibly speak about my diagnosis with anyone in my church. They would think I have been a bad wife.'[72] In short, Christians living with HIV still experienced judgment, shaming and rejection within both the HIV sector and their faith community. Participants welcomed the opportunity to speak honestly about the impact of HIV on their lives and relationships with fellow Christians. To share how shocking their diagnosis had been, so often leaving them confused and frightened. About the ways HIV had challenged their understanding of God and the meaning of suffering. How isolated they had become, often feeling abandoned even by God. How diagnosis had been undergone as a type of Gethsemane experience. They reported how relieved they felt to finally explore these and many other faith-related questions with others who could understand.

To this day, HIV disproportionately impacts already poor, disadvantaged or marginalised groups in the UK. The principle in Catholic Social Teaching of the preferential option for the poor challenges the Church to support ministry with and for people living with HIV. Research also shows that compared to the general population, where religious identity is in decline, faith matters more to people living with HIV in the UK.[73] Christian faith and spirituality have been shown to contribute to the health and wellbeing of people living with HIV.[74] For these reasons, ministry

---

Robert Loftus, Rev. Dr Bernard Lynch, Anne Gayer, Roy Parr, and Rev. Stephen Portlock. The first CAPS Conference took place at Vaughan House, Westminster.

72 Comment made during a Positive Faith retreat weekend, Douai Abbey.
73 Among people living with HIV, 51.6% identify as Christian. Of those identifying as belonging to any religion, 65.7% report their religious beliefs as very or fairly important; A. Aghaizu et al., *Positive Voices: The National Survey of People Living with HIV. Findings from 2022. Report summarising data from 2022 and measuring change since 2017.* Demographic Data Tables (London, 2023). In the general population just 38% identify as Christian and 52% state that they have no religion; J. Curtice, E. Clery, J. Perry, M. Phillips and N. Rahim (eds), *British Social Attitudes: The 36th Report* (London, 2019).
74 B. R. Doolittle, A. C. Justice, and D. A. Fiellin, 'Religion, Spirituality, and HIV Clinical Outcomes: A Systematic Review of the Literature', *AIDS and Behavior*, 22:6 (2018), pp. 1792–1801.

for people living with HIV ought to be a priority for the Church.[75] However, as these short accounts demonstrate, in 2004 the pastoral and spiritual needs of Christians living with HIV were not being met within their churches.

Following this workshop, the HIV peer support ministry 'Positive Faith' began.[76] From the first meeting in London in 2004 when seven Christians, heterosexual and gay, met to pray together, Positive Faith has grown. Since then, Christians living with HIV have met regularly in London, Essex, Manchester and Cambridge. Led by lay women and men living with HIV, the members meet for a time of prayer, reflection on Scripture, sharing experience and a meal together. Retreat weekends held throughout the year allow members the time to deepen friendships.

This chapter has illustrated how CAL made the resources of Catholic faith more accessible and relevant during the AIDS crisis. The many challenging theological issues raised by AIDS have not gone away. More importantly, people living with HIV in the UK continue to have need of the pastoral care and spiritual support of their faith communities. The guidance and encouragement in faith so often desired by people with HIV is not the responsibility of secular HIV agencies or clinicians. When the institutions of the Church struggled to respond to AIDS, lay people took a lead. Through CAPS and Positive Faith lay people living with and affected by HIV continue to provide a prophetic witness to the Gospel. With the service of sensitive priests, Christians living with HIV, heterosexual and gay, black and white, rich and poor, welcome each other into a community of acceptance and understanding and minister to each other. As each person makes sense of their experience in the shared language of faith, hope is restored. As Christ is encountered in loving community the wounds of stigma may be healed. As sisters and brothers, the members of Positive Faith are strengthened in faith, hope and love to live ever more positively as disciples of Jesus, our teacher, brother and Saviour.

---

[75] 'to whom should (we) go first? When we read the Gospel we find a clear indication: not so much our friends and wealthy neighbours, but above all the poor and the sick, those who are usually despised and overlooked, "those who cannot repay you" (Lk 14:14) ... Today and always, "the poor are the privileged recipients of the Gospel", and the fact that it is freely preached to them is a sign of the kingdom that Jesus came to establish. We have to state, without mincing words, that there is an inseparable bond between our faith and the poor. May we never abandon them.' Pope Francis, *Evangelii Gaudium: The Joy of the Gospel.* (London, 2013), §48.

[76] When the peer support ministry began it was called 'Positive Catholics' but later renamed 'Positive Faith' to better reflect the diverse ecumenical membership and remove any perceived barrier to inclusion amongst Christians from denominations other than Roman Catholic. Positive Faith has a membership of several hundred Catholics and Christians from other denominations, living with and affected by HIV in the United Kingdom.

BIBLIOGRAPHY

Ecclesiastical documents referenced

PAPAL PRONOUNCEMENTS

Leo XIII, *Arcanum Divinae: On Christian Marriage*, 10 February 1880.
Leo XIII, *Rerum Novarum: On Capital and Labour*, 15 May 1891.
Leo XIII, *Caritatis stadium: On the Church in Scotland*, 25 July 1898.
Pius X, *Tra Le Sollecitudini: On Sacred Music*, 22 November 1903.
Pius X, *Il Fermo Proposito: On Catholic Action in Italy*, 11 June 1905.
Pius XI, *Ubi Arcano Dei Consilio: On the Peace of Christ in the Kingdom of Christ*, 23 December 1922.
Pius XI, *Divini Illius Magistri: On Christian Education*, 31 December 1929.
Pius XI, *Casti Connubii: On Christian Marriage*, 31 December 1930.
Pius XI, *Quadragesimo Anno: On the Reconstruction of Society*, 15 May 1931.
Paul VI, *Apostolicam Actuositatem: On the Apostolate of the Laity*, 18 November 1965.
John Paul II, *Christifideles Laici: On the Vocation and the Mission of the Lay Faithful in the Church and in the World*, 30 December 1988.
Francis, *Evangelii Gaudium: On the Proclamation of the Gospel in Today's World*, 24 November 2013.

COUNCIL DOCUMENTS

Second Vatican Council, *Lumen Gentium: Dogmatic Constitution on the Church*, 21 November 1964.

EPISCOPAL COMMUNICATIONS

United States Catholic Conference Administrative Board, *The Many Faces of AIDS: A Gospel Response* (1987).
National Conference of Catholic Bishops, *Called to Compassion and Responsibility: A Response to the HIV/AIDS Crisis* (1989).
Basil Hume, *Some Observations on the Teaching of the Catholic Church Concerning Homosexual People* (1993).
———, *Note on the Teaching of the Catholic Church Concerning Homosexual People* (1997).

CURIAL COMMUNICATIONS

Congregation for the Doctrine of the Faith, *Persona Humana: Declaration on Certain Questions Concerning Sexual Ethics*, 29 December 1975.
———, *Letter to the Bishops of the Catholic Church on the Pastoral Care of Homosexual Persons*, 1 October 1986.
Pontifical Council for Pastoral Assistance to Health Care Workers, *Proceedings of the Fourth International Conference. To Live: Why? AIDS*; special issue of *Dolentium Hominum*, 13:1 (1990).

CATHOLIC NEWSPAPERS, NEWSLETTERS AND REVIEWS

Blackfriars
Catena
The Catholic Citizen
The Catholic Herald
The Catholic Suffragist
The Catholic Times
The Catholic Worker
The Commonweal
The Crucible
Day of Renewal
Dundee Catholic Herald
Goodnews
Mutual Aid: Newsletter of the West End Catholic Worker
New Covenant
New Life
The Newman
Newsletter of the National Service Committee for the Catholic Charismatic Renewal
Saturday Catholic Herald
Scottish Catholic Herald
The Tablet
The Universe

Books and journal articles cited

Pauline Adams, *English Catholic Converts and the Oxford Movement in Mid 19th Century Britain: The Cost of Conversion* (Bethesda, 2010).
A. Aghaizu, V. Martin, C. Kelly, H. Kitt, A. Farah, V. Latham, A. E. Brown, and C. Humphreys, *Positive Voices: The National Survey of People Living with HIV. Findings from 2022. Report summarising data from 2022 and measuring change since 2017* (London, 2023).
Peter Lewis Allen, *The Wages of Sin: Sex and Disease, Past and Present* (London, 2000).

BIBLIOGRAPHY

Patrick Allitt, *Catholic Converts: British and American Intellectuals Turn to Rome* (Ithaca, NY, 2000).

Kester Aspden, *Fortress Church: The English Roman Catholic Bishops and Politics, 1903–1963* (Leominster, 2002).

Bernard Aspinwall, 'The Formation of the Catholic Community in the West of Scotland: Some Preliminary Outlines', *The Innes Review*, 33 (1982), pp. 44–57.

Francis Aylward *Fifteen Years of International Co-operation: A Survey of the Work of the International Committee of the Newman Association of Great Britain, 1942–1957* (London, 1957).

Caitríona Beaumont, 'Women and Citizenship: A Study of Non-Feminist Women's Societies and the Women's Movement in England, 1928–1950', unpublished doctoral thesis, University of Warwick, 1996.

———, 'The Women's Movement, Politics and Citizenship, 1918–1950s', *Women in Twentieth-Century Britain*, edited by Ina Zweiniger-Bargielowska (London, 2001), pp. 262–77.

———, 'Moral Dilemmas and Women's Rights: The Attitude of the Mothers' Union and Catholic Women's League to Divorce, Birth Control and Abortion in England, 1928–1939', *Women's History Review*, 16:4 (2007), pp. 463–85.

———, *Housewives and Citizens: Domesticity and the Women's Movement in England, 1928–64* (Manchester, 2013).

Ashley Beck, *Dorothy Day: Devoted Daughter of the Church* (London, 2008).

Virginia Berridge, *AIDS in the UK: The Making of Policy, 1981–1994* (New York, 1996).

Adrian Bingham, '"An Era of Domesticity"? Histories of Women and Gender in Interwar Britain', *Cultural and Social History*, 1:2 (2004), pp. 225–33.

Lucy Bland, *Banishing the Beast: Sexuality and the Early Feminists* (New York, 1995).

Fred Boehrer, 'Diversity, Plurality and Ambiguity: Anarchism in the Catholic Worker Movement', in *Dorothy Day and the Catholic Worker Movement: Centenary Essays*, edited by William Thorn, Phillip Runkel, Susan Mountin (Milwaukee, WI, 2001), pp. 95–127.

Joanna Bourke, *Working Class Cultures in Britain, 1890–1960: Gender, Class and Ethnicity* (London, 1994).

Julia Brannen and Ann Nilsen, 'From Fatherhood to Fathering: Transmission and Change among British Fathers in Four-Generation Families', *Sociology*, 40:2 (2006), pp. 335–52.

Gail Braybon, *Women Workers in the First World War: The British Experience* (London, 1981).

Martin John Broadley, *Louis Charles Casartelli: A Bishop in War and Peace* (Knoxville, TN, 2006).

Stephen Brooke, 'Gender and Working Class Identity in Britain during the 1950s', *Journal of Social History*, 34:4 (2001), pp. 773–95.

Viv Broughton, Preface to *Seeds of Liberation: Spiritual Dimensions to Political Struggles*, edited by Alistair Kee (London, 1973) pp. vii–viii.

Callum Brown, *Religion and Society in Twentieth Century Britain* (London, 2006).

———, *The Battle for Christian Britain: Sex, Humanists and Secularisation, 1945–1980* (Cambridge, 2019).

Harry Browne, *Hammered by the Irish: How the Pitstop Ploughshares Disabled a U.S. Warplane with Ireland's Blessing* (Edinburgh, 2008).

Henry Browne S.J., *The Catholic Evidence Movement: Its Achievements and its Hopes* (London, 1921).

Tom Buchanan, 'Great Britain', in *Political Catholicism in Europe, 1918–1965*, edited by Tom Buchanan and Martin Conway (Oxford, 1996), pp. 249–74.

Stephen Bullivant, *Mass Exodus: Catholic Disaffiliation in Britain and American since Vatican II* (Oxford, 2019).

James Byrne (ed.), *Handbook of the Catholic Evidence Guild* (London, 1922).

Debra Campbell, 'The Gleanings of a Laywoman's Ministry, Maisie Ward as Preacher, Publisher and Social Activist', *Records of the American Catholic Historical Society of Philadelphia*, 98:1/4 (1987), pp. 21–8.

———, 'The Catholic Evidence Guild: Towards a History of the Laity', *Heythrop Journal*, 30:3 (1989), pp. 306–24.

Joseph Cardijn, *Laymen into Action*, translated by Anne Heggie (London, 1964).

Hilary M. Carey, *Truly Feminine, Truly Catholic: A History of the Catholic Women's League in the Archdiocese of Sydney, 1913–87* (Kensington, 1987).

Catholic Women's League, *History of the Catholic Women's League Relief and Refugee Committee* ([London?], 1981).

James Chappel, 'Slaying the Leviathan: Catholicism and the Rebirth of European Conservatism, 1920–1950', unpublished doctoral thesis, Columbia University, 2012.

———, *Catholic Modern: The Challenge of Totalitarianism and the Remaking of the Church* (London, 2018).

Ira Chernus, *American Nonviolence: The History of an Idea* (Maryknoll, NY, 2004).

Alexandre Christoyannopoulus, *Christian Anarchism: A Political Commentary on the Gospel* (Exeter, 2011).

Valentina Ciciliot, 'The Origins of the Catholic Charismatic Renewal in the United States: Early Developments in Indiana and Michigan and the Reactions of the Ecclesiastical Authorities', *Studies in World Christianity*, 25:3 (2019), pp. 250–73.

———, 'The Origins of the Catholic Charismatic Renewal in the United

States: The Experience at the University of Notre Dame and South Bend (Indiana), 1967–1975', in *Transatlantic Charismatic Renewal, c. 1950–2000*, edited by Andrew Atherstone, Mark Hutchinson and John Maiden (Leiden, 2021), pp. 144–64.

Luigi Civardi, *A Manual of Catholic Action*, translated by C. C. Martindale S.J. (London, 1935).

Elaine Clark, 'Catholics and the Campaign for Women's Suffrage in England', *Church History*, 73:3 (2004), pp. 635–65.

———, 'Catholic Men in Support of the Women's Suffrage Movement in England', *Catholic Historical Review*, 94:1 (2008), pp. 22–44.

Loren K. Clarke and Malcolm Potts (eds), *The AIDS Reader: Documentary History of a Modern Epidemic* (Boston, 1988).

John Martin Cleary, *Catholic Social Action in Britain, 1909–1959: A History of the Catholic Social Guild* (Oxford, 1961).

Niall Coll and Alana Harris, 'The Path to Rome: Characteristics and Contours of Theology in Britain and Ireland before the Council', in *Vatican II – Event and Mandate. Intercontinental Commentary on the Council's Documents, their Reception and their Orientation for Church and Theology. Vol. 6. Europe,* edited by Dries Bosschaert and Urszula Pękala (Leuven, 2025).

Sylvia Collins and Michael P. Hornsby-Smith, 'The Rise and Fall of the YCW in England', *Journal of Contemporary Religion*, 71:1 (2002), pp. 87–100.

Terri Colpi, 'The Scottish Italian Community: Senza un campanile?', *The Innes Review*, 44:2 (1993), pp. 153–67.

Yves Congar, *Lay People in the Church* (London, 1965).

Thomas Cornell, Robert Ellsberg, and Jim Forest (eds), *A Penny a Copy: Readings from the Catholic Worker* (Maryknoll, NY, 1995).

Jay P. Corrin, *Catholic Intellectuals and the Challenge of Democracy* (South Bend, IN, 2002).

———, *Catholic Progressives in England after Vatican II* (South Bend, IN, 2013).

Vicky Cosstick (ed.), *AIDS: Meeting the Community Challenge* (Slough, 1987).

Virginia M. Crawford, 'The Coming of Age of the CSG (Catholic Social Guild)', *Studies: An Irish Quarterly Review*, 19:75 (1930), pp. 456–66.

Charles Curran, *American Catholic Social Ethics: Twentieth Century Approaches* (South Bend, IN, 1982).

J. Curtice, E. Clery, J. Perry, M. Phillips and N. Rahim (eds), *British Social Attitudes: The 36th Report* (London, 2019).

Kate Davson and Nagypal Szabolcs (eds), *Living Today the Church of Tomorrow: Forty Years of the International Ecumenical Fellowship* (Brussels, 2009).

Helena Dawes, *Catholic Women's Movements in Liberal and Fascist Italy* (Houndmills, 2014).

Dorothy Day, *The Eleventh Virgin* (New York, 1924).
———, *From Union Square to Rome* (Silver Spring, MD, 1938).
———, *House of Hospitality* (New York, 1939).
———, *On Pilgrimage* (New York, 1948).
———, *The Long Loneliness: The Autobiography of Dorothy Day* (New York, 1952).
———, *Loaves and Fishes* (New York, 1963).
———, *On Pilgrimage: The Sixties* (New York, 1972).
Lucy Delap, '"Be Strong and Play the Man": Anglican Masculinities in the Twentieth Century', in *Men, Masculinities and Religious Change in Twentieth-Century Britain*, edited by Lucy Delap and Sue Morgan (London, 2013), pp. 119–45.
Jacqueline R. deVries, 'Challenging Traditions: Denominational Feminism in Britain, 1910–1920', in *Borderlines: Genders and Identities in War and Peace, 1870–1930*, edited by Billie Melman (New York, 1998), pp. 265–83.
William J. Dickson, 'Don Bosco, Trade Union Patron in Scotland: How the Scottish Catholic Teachers' Guild Took Don Bosco as Their Patron', in *Percezione della figura di Don Bosco all'esterno dell'Opera salesiana dal 1879 al 1965: Atti del 6° convegno internazionale di Storia dell'Opera salesiana*, edited by Grazia Loparco and Stanisław Zimniak (Rome, 2016), pp. 577–87.
Patrick Dixon, *The Truth about AIDS and a Practical Christian Response*, Fourth Edition, (London, 2004).
B. R. Doolittle, A. C. Justice, and D. A. Fiellin, 'Religion, Spirituality, and HIV Clinical Outcomes: A Systematic Review of the Literature', *AIDS and Behavior*, 22:6 (2018), pp. 1792–801.
Peter Doyle, 'The Catholic Federation, 1906–1929', in *Voluntary Religion: Papers Read at the 1985 Summer Meeting and Winter Meeting of the Ecclesiastical History Society*, edited by William J. Sheils and Diana Wood (Oxford, 1986), pp. 461–76.
———, 'Episcopal Leaders and Leadership', in *The Oxford History of British and Irish Catholicism, Volume IV: Building Identity 1830–1913*, edited by Carmen M. Mangion and Susan O'Brien (Oxford, 2023), pp. 36–55.
Anthony Egan, 'Global Health, AIDS, and the Catholic Church in Africa' in *HIV & AIDS in Africa: Christian Reflection, Public Health, Social Transformation*, edited by Jacquineau Azetsop (Maryknoll, NY, 2016), ch. 20.
Kit Elliott, 'A Very Pushy Kind of Folk: Educational Reform 1944 and the Catholic Laity of England and Wales', *History of Education*, 35:1 (2006), pp. 91–119.
Marc Ellis, *Peter Maurin: Prophet in the Twentieth Century* (New York, 1981).
H. O. Evennett, 'Catholics and the Universities', in *The English Catholics,*

1850–1950: Essays to Commemorate the Centenary of the Restoration of the Hierarchy of England and Wales, edited by George Andrew Beck (London, 1950), pp. 291–321.
Joseph Fichter, *The Catholic Cult of the Paraclete* (New York, 1975).
T. A. Fitzpatrick, 'Catholic Secondary Education in South-West Scotland, 1922–1972: Its Contribution to the Educational, Religious, Cultural and Social Aspects of the Change in Status of the Catholic Community of the Area', unpublished doctoral thesis, University of Glasgow, 1982.
———, *Catholic Secondary Education in South-West Scotland Before 1972* (Aberdeen, 1986).
———, 'The Catholic Teachers' Union, 1917–1919', *The Innes Review*, 41:1 (1990), pp. 132–5.
———, 'The Catholic Social Guild: Fr Leo O'Hea S.J. (1881–1976) and the West of Scotland Connection', *The Innes Review*, 50:2 (1999), pp. 127–38.
John Fitzsimons, *Woman Today* (London, 1952).
John Fitzsimons and Paul McGuire (eds), *Restoring All Things: A Guide to Catholic Action* (London, 1939).
Valerie Flessati, 'PAX: The History of a Catholic Peace Society in Britain, 1936–1971', unpublished doctoral thesis, University of Bradford, 1991.
———, 'Champion of Faith and Justice', *The Chesterton Review*, 35:3/4 (2009), p. 709.
Margaret Fletcher, *Light for New Times* (New York, 1905).
———, *O, Call Back Yesterday* (Oxford, 1939).
J. Massyngberde Ford, *Which Way for Catholic Pentecostals?* (New York, 1976).
Jim Forest, *Love Is the Measure: A Biography of Dorothy Day* (New York, 1986).
———, *All Is Grace: A Biography of Dorothy Day* (New York, 2011).
Norman Fowler, *AIDS: Don't Die of Prejudice* (London, 2014).
Martin Francis, 'The Domestication of the Male? Recent Research on Nineteenth- and Twentieth-Century Masculinity', *Historical Journal*, 45:3 (2002), pp. 637–52.
———, 'A Flight from Commitment? Domesticity, Adventure and the Masculine Imaginary in Britain after the Second World War', *Gender and History*, 19:1 (2007), pp. 163–85.
Tom Gallagher, 'Scottish Catholics and the British Left, 1918–1939', *The Innes Review*, 34:1 (1983), pp. 17–42.
———, 'Protestant Extremism in Urban Scotland, 1930–1939: Its Growth and Contraction', *Scottish Historical Review*, 64:2 (1985), pp. 143–67.
Simon Garfield, *The End of Innocence: Britain in the Time of AIDS* (London, 1995).
Ian Gazeley, *Poverty in Britain, 1900–1945* (Basingstoke, 2003).
Stefan Gigacz, *The Leaven in the Council: Joseph Cardijn and the Jocist Network at Vatican II* (Melbourne, 2021), https://theleaven.com.au.

Helen Glew, *Gender, Rhetoric and Regulation: Women's Work in the Civil Service and the London County Council, 1900–55* (Manchester, 2016).
Peter Gordon and David Doughan, *Women, Clubs and Associations in Britain* (Abingdon, 2006).
Dana Greene, *The Living of Maisie Ward* (South Bend, IN, 1997).
Matthew Grimley, 'The Religion of Englishness: Puritanism, Providentialism and "National Character", 1918–45', *Journal of British Studies*, 46:4 (2007), pp. 884–906.
Gerry C. Gunnin, *John Wheatley, Catholic Socialism, and Irish Labour in the West of Scotland, 1906-1924* (Abingdon, 1987).
James Hagerty, *The Catenian Association: A Centenary History, 1908–2008* (Evesham, 2007).
———, *Cardinal Hinsley: Priest and Patriot* (Oxford, 2008).
———, 'The Conversion of England: John Heenan and the Catholic Missionary Society, 1947–1951', *British Catholic History*, 31:3 (2015), pp. 461–81.
Richard Hall, 'Being a Man, Being a Member: Masculinity and Community in Britain's Working Men's Clubs, 1945-1960', *Cultural and Social History*, 14:1 (2016), pp. 73–88.
David G. Hallman (ed.), *AIDS Issues: Confronting the Challenge* (New York, 1989).
V. A. Harden and D. Rodrigues, 'Context for a New Disease: Aspects of Biomedical Research Policy in the United States before AIDS', in *AIDS and Contemporary History*, edited by Virginia Berridge and Philip Strong (Cambridge, 2002), pp. 182–202.
Alana Harris, '"A Paradise on Earth, a Foretaste of Heaven": English Catholic Understandings of Domesticity and Marriage, 1945–65', in *The Politics of Domestic Authority since 1800*, edited by Lucy Delap, Abigail Wills and Ben Griffin (London, 2009), pp. 155–81.
———, *Faith in the Family: A Lived Religious History of English Catholicism, 1945–1982* (Manchester, 2013).
———, 'Lourdes and Holistic Spirituality: Contemporary Catholicism, the Therapeutic, and Religious Thermalism', *Culture and Religion*, 14:1 (2013), pp. 23–43.
———, 'Love Divine and Love Sublime: The Catholic Marriage Advisory Council, the Marriage Guidance Movement and the State', in *Love and Romance in Britain, 1918–1970*, edited by Alana Harris and Timothy W. Jones (London, 2014), pp. 188–224.
———, 'A Fresh Stripping of the Altars? Liturgical Language and the Legacy of the Reformation in England, 1964–1984', in *Catholics in the Vatican II Era: Local Histories of a Global Event*, edited by Kathleen Cummings, Tim Matovina and Robert Orsi (Cambridge, 2017), pp. 245–74.
——— (ed.), *The Schism of 68: Catholics, Contraception and Humanae Vitae in Europe, 1945–1975* (Basingstoke, 2018).

———, 'A Magna Carta for Marriage: Love, Catholic Masculinities and the *Humanae Vitae* Contraception Crisis in 1968 Britain', *Cultural and Social History*, 17:3 (2020), pp. 407–29.

——— (ed.), *The Oxford History of British and Irish Catholicism, Volume V: Recapturing the Apostolate of the Laity, 1914–2021* (Oxford, 2023).

Adrian Hastings (ed.), *Bishops and Writers: Aspects of the Evolution of Modern English Catholicism* (Wheathamstead, 1977).

———, *A History of English Christianity, 1920–1990* (London, 1991).

Michael Heller, 'The National Insurance Acts 1911–1947, the Approved Societies and the Prudential Assurance Company', *Twentieth Century British History*, 19:1 (2008), pp. 1–28.

Peter Hocken, 'Baptism in the Holy Spirit: A Spiritual and Theological Journey' in *Children of the Calling: Essays in the Honour of Stanley M. Burgess and Ruth V. Burgess*, edited by Eric Nelson Newberg and Lois E. Olena (Eugene, OR, 2014), pp. 298–310.

Richard Hoggart, *The Uses of Literacy* (Harmondsworth, 1958).

David Holmes, 'Catholic Spirit of Association: Catholic Popular Culture, Confraternities, Guilds and a Restored Community in the Industrial Diocese of Late Victorian–Early Edwardian West Riding of Yorkshire', *Northern History*, 57/2 (2020), pp. 229–49.

Gerd-Rainer Horn, *Western European Liberation Theology, 1924–1959: The First Wave* (London, 2009).

Michael P. Hornsby-Smith, *Catholic Education: The Unobtrusive Partner: Sociological Studies of the Catholic School System in England and Wales* (London, 1978).

———, *Roman Catholics in England: Studies in Social Structure Since the Second World War* (Cambridge, 1987).

———, *Roman Catholic Beliefs in England: Customary Catholicism and Transformation of Religious Authority,* (Cambridge, 1991).

———, 'A Transformed Church', in *Catholics in England, 1950–2000: Historical and Sociological Perspectives*, edited by Michael Hornsby-Smith (London, 1999), pp. 3–25.

———, *An Introduction to Catholic Social Thought* (Cambridge, 2006).

Kathryn Hurlock, 'The Guild of Our Lady of Ransom and Pilgrimage in England and Wales, c. 1890–1914', *British Catholic History*, 35.3 (2021), pp. 316–37.

———, 'Army Style, We Marched: War and Peace in the Cross-Carrying Pilgrimages to Vézelay and Walsingham, 1946–1948', *British Catholic History*, 36:4 (2023), pp. 410–30.

An Irish Priest, *A Manual of Catholic Action: Its Nature and Requirements* (Dublin, 1933).

Louise A. Jackson, *Women Police: Gender, Welfare and Surveillance in the Twentieth Century* (Manchester, 2012).

G. Johnson, 'Character Education in the Catholic Church', *Religious Education*, 24:1 (1929), pp. 54–7.

A. R. Jonsen and J. Stryker (eds), *The Social Impact of AIDS in the United States* (Washington, DC, 1993).

Beth Junor (ed.), *Greenham: Non-Violent Women v the Crown Prerogative* (London, 2005).

Paula M. Kane, '"The Willing Captive of Home?" The English Catholic Women's League, 1906–1920', *Church History,* 60:3 (1991), pp. 331–55.

Martha Kanya-Forstner, 'Defining Womanhood: Irish Women and the Catholic Church in Victorian Liverpool', *Immigrants & Minorities: Historical Studies in Ethnicity, Migration and Diaspora*, 18:2/3 (1999), pp. 168–88.

Joan Keating, 'Roman Catholics, Christian Democracy, and the British Labour Movement, 1910–1960', unpublished doctoral thesis, University of Manchester, 1992.

———, 'The British Experience: Christian Democracy without a Party, 1910–60', in *Christian Democracy in Europe: A Comparative Perspective*, edited by David Hanley (London, 1994), pp. 168–81.

———, 'The Making of the Catholic Labour Activist: The Catholic Social Guild and Catholic Workers' College, 1909–1939', *Labour History Review,* 59:3 (1994), pp. 44–56.

———, 'Faith and Community Threatened? Roman Catholic Responses to the Welfare State, Materialism and Social Mobility, 1945–62', *Twentieth Century British History,* 9:1 (1998), pp. 86–108.

James E. Kelly and John McCafferty, 'Series Introduction' in *The Oxford History of British and Irish Catholicism, Volume V,* pp. xvii–xxv.

Herbert Kildany, 'The Meaning of Catholic Action', *Blackfriars*, 15:174 (September 1934), pp. 583–8.

Laura King, *Family Men: Fatherhood and Masculinity in Britain, 1914–1960* (Oxford, 2015).

Timothy Kinnear, 'Statistical Appendices', in *The Oxford History of British and Irish Catholicism, Volume V,* pp. 357–77.

Bill Kirkpatrick, *AIDS. Sharing the Pain: Pastoral Guidelines* (London, 1988).

Donald Kirwin and Jill Marie Gerschutz (eds), *And You Welcomed Me: Migration and Catholic Social Teaching* (Lanham, MD, 2009).

Kathryn G. Lamontagne, *Reconsidering Catholic Lay Womanhood: Pious Transgressors in Late Nineteenth and Early Twentieth Century England* (Abingdon, 2024).

Peter Lane, *The Catenian Association, 1908–1983: A Microcosm of the Development of the Catholic Middle Class* (London, 1982).

Thomas Lane, *Victims of Stalin and Hitler: The Exodus of Poles and Balts to Britain* (London, 2004).

Claire Langhamer, 'Love, Selfhood and Authenticity in Post-War Britain', *Cultural and Social History*, 9:2 (2012), pp. 277–97.

Francis Leonard, *Fools for Christ's Sake, Being a Short Account of the Catholic Evidence Guilds in England and Wales* (Durham, 2000).

Jane Lewis, 'In Search of a Real Equality: Women between the Wars', in *Class, Culture, and Social Change: A New View of the 1930s*, edited by Frank Gloversmith (Sussex, 1980), pp. 208–39.

J. L. Lilly and Edmund Talbot, *Manual of the Ladies of Charity* (London, 1926).

James R. Lothian, *The Making and Unmaking of the English Catholic Intellectual Community, 1910–1950* (South Bend, IN, 2009).

Jonathan Luxmore and Jolanta Babiuch, *The Vatican and the Red Flag: The Struggle for the Soul of Eastern Europe* (London and New York, 1999).

Dennis Maccagno, 'The Origins of the YCW Movement', unpublished thesis, University of London, 1971.

Mary M. Macken, 'The German Catholic Women's League', *Studies: An Irish Quarterly Review*, 20:80 (1931), pp. 555–69.

John Maiden, *Age of the Spirit: Charismatic Renewal, the Anglo-World, and Global Christianity, 1945–1980* (Oxford, 2023).

———, 'Charisma, Gender and "Glocality": Catholic Charismatic Women in the 1970s', *Journal of Modern and Contemporary Christianity*, 2:1 (2023), pp. 91–114.

Carmen M. Mangion, *Catholic Nuns and Sisters in a Secular Age: Britain, 1945–90* (Manchester, 2020).

———, 'Religious Suffrage Societies', in *Routledge Companion to British Women's Suffrage*, edited by Krista Cowman (London, 2024).

Vincent Manning, 'Encountering Christ through the Passion of HIV: An Inquiry into the Theological Meaning of HIV in the Church', unpublished doctoral thesis, St Mary's University, London, 2019.

Francis M. Mason, 'The Newer Eve: The Catholic Women's Suffrage Society in England, 1911–1923', *Catholic Historical Review*, 72:4 (1986), pp. 620–38.

Peter Maurin, *Catholic Radicalism: Phrased Essays for the Green Revolution* (New York, 1949).

John McCaffrey, 'Politics and the Catholic Community since 1878', *The Innes Review*, 29:2 (1978), pp. 140–55.

Raymond McCluskey, 'Catholic Education Beyond the School: Sodalities and Public Lectures', in *A History of Catholic Education and Schooling in Scotland: New Perspectives*, edited by Stephen McKinney and Raymond McCluskey (London, 2019), pp. 125–47.

B. J. M. McCook, 'Education in War and Exile: The Polish Experience in Britain, 1940–1954', in *East Central Europe in Exile, Volume 1, Transatlantic Migrations*, edited by Anna Mazurkiewicz (Newcastle, 2013), pp. 291–310.

L. McKenna, 'An Irish Catholic Women's League', *The Irish Monthly*, 45:528 (1917), pp. 53–568.

Hugh McLeod, 'Building the Catholic "Ghetto": Catholic Organisations, 1870–1914', in *Voluntary Religion: Papers Read at the 1985 Summer*

Meeting and Winter Meeting of the Ecclesiastical History Society: Studies of Church History, edited by William J. Sheils and Diana Wood (Oxford, 1986), pp. 411–44.

Stuart Mews, 'The Sword of the Spirit: A Catholic Cultural Crusade of 1940', Studies in Church History: The Church and War, 20 (1983), pp. 409–30.

William D. Miller, A Harsh and Dreadful Love: Dorothy Day and the Catholic Worker Movement (New York, 1973).

——, Dorothy Day: A Biography (San Francisco, CA, 1982).

Sandra Yocum Mize, '"We are Still Pacifists": Dorothy Day's Pacifism During World War II', in Dorothy Day and the Catholic Worker Movement: Centenary Essays, edited by William Thorn, Phillip Runkel, Susan Mountin (Milwaukee, WI, 2001), pp. 465–73.

Sue Morgan, '"Iron Strength and Infinite Tenderness": Herbert Gray and the Making of Christian Masculinities at War and at Home, 1900–40', in Men, Masculinities and Religious Change in Twentieth-Century Britain, edited by Lucy Delap and Sue Morgan (London, 2013), pp. 168–96.

Frank Mort, Dangerous Sexualities: Medico-Moral Politics in England since 1850, Second Edition (London, 2000).

T. F. Murphy, 'Is AIDS a Just Punishment?' Journal of Medical Ethics, 14 (1988), pp. 54–160.

Andrea Needham, The Hammer Blow: How 10 Women Disarmed a War Plane (London, 2016).

Sharon Erikson Nepstad, Religion and War Resistance in the Plowshares Movement (Cambridge, 2008).

Mildred Neville, 'The Changing Nature of Catholic Organisations', in Catholics in England, 1950–2000: Historical and Sociological Perspectives, edited by Michael Hornsby-Smith (London, 1999), pp. 99–121.

Newman Association, A Use of Gifts: The Newman Association, 1942–1992 (London, 1992).

John Henry Newman, The Idea of a University (London, 1852).

Mary V. Newman, 'The Educational Work of the Catholic Women's League in England, 1906–1923', unpublished doctoral thesis, Institute of Education, University of London, 2010.

——, '"To Put into the Field Trained Bands of Women": Margaret Fletcher and the Education of Catholic Lay Women to Engage in the Public Sphere in the Early Twentieth Century', History of Education Researcher, 93 (2014), pp. 12–21.

James Nicholls, The Politics of Alcohol: A History of the Drink Question in England (Manchester, 2011).

Ann Nolan and Shane Butler, 'AIDS, Sexual Health, and the Catholic Church in 1980s Ireland: A Public Health Paradox', American Journal of Public Health, 108:7 (2018), pp. 908–13.

Susan O'Brien, *Leaving God for God: The Daughters of St Vincent de Paul in Britain, 1847–2017* (London, 2017).
Gerald M. Oppenheimer, 'The Catholic Church, AIDS, and Sexuality in Ireland: Uncovering Part of the Story', *American Journal of Public Health*, 108:7 (2018), pp. 850–1.
Alison Oram, *Women Teachers and Feminist Politics, 1900–39* (Manchester, 1996).
Alison Park, Caroline Bryson, Elizabeth Clery, John Curtice and Miranda Phillips (eds), *British Social Attitudes: The 30th Report* (London, 2013).
Nancy Stewart Parnell, *A Venture in Faith: A History of St Joan's Social and Political Alliance, Formerly the Catholic Women's Suffrage Society, 1911–1961* (London, 1961).
Patrick Pasture, Jan Art and Thomas Buerman (eds), *Gender and Christianity in Modern Europe: Beyond the Feminization Thesis* (Leuven, 2012).
Lindsay Paterson, 'Catholic Schools and the Education (Scotland) Act 1918', *The Innes Review*, 71:1 (2020), pp. 85–97.
Sheila Patterson, 'The Polish Exiled Community in Great Britain', *The Polish Review*, 61:3 (1961), pp. 69–97.
Stephen Pattison, 'To the Churches with Love from the Lighthouse', in *Embracing the Chaos: Theological Responses to AIDS*, edited by James Woodward (London, 1991), pp. 8–19.
Martin Pendergast, 'HIV in Britain, 1982–1990: The Christian Reaction', *New Blackfriars*, 71: 840, special issue, *Christians and AIDS: An Anglo-French Assessment* (1990), pp. 347–54.
James Pereiro, 'Who Are the Laity?', in *From Without the Flaminian Gate: 150 Years of Roman Catholicism in England and Wales, 1850–2000*, edited by V. Alan McClelland and Michael Hodgets (London, 1999), pp. 167–91.
Piotr Potocki, 'The Origins of the Catholic Social Guild in Scotland: "We have not attacked the Socialists professedly"', *Innes Review*, 69:2 (2018), pp. 131–46.
Maria Power, 'The Catholic Church and Human Rights: A Case Study of 1980s South Africa', *Catholic Archives*, 41 (2021), pp. 65–77.
——, 'Ecumenism and Interfaith Relations', in *The Oxford History of British and Irish Catholicism, Volume V*, pp. 229–48.
Frank Prochaska, *Christianity and Social Service in Modern Britain: The Disinherited Spirit* (Oxford, 2008).
Kevin and Dorothy Ranaghan, *Catholic Pentecostals* (New York, 1969).
H. A. Reinhold, 'The Catholic Worker Movement in America', *Blackfriars*, 19:222 (1938), pp. 640–1.
Jasper Godwin Ridley, *A Brief History of the Freemasons* (London, 2008).
Nancy Roberts and Anne Klejment (eds), *American Catholic Pacifism: The Influence of Dorothy Day and the Catholic Worker Movement* (Westport, CT, 1996).

Frederick S. Roden, 'Michael Field, John Gray, and Marc-Andre Raffalovich: Reinventing Romantic Friendship in Modernity', in *Catholic Figures, Queer Narratives*, edited by Lowell Gallagher, Frederick S. Roden and Patricia Juliana Smith (Basingstoke, 2007), pp. 57–68.

Michael Roper, 'Between Manliness and Masculinity: The "War Generation" and the Psychology of Fear in Britain, 1914–1970', *Journal of British Studies*, 44:2 (2005), pp. 343–63.

Anthony Ross, 'The Development of the Scottish Catholic Community, 1878–1978', *The Innes Review*, 29:1 (1978), pp. 30–55.

Olivier Rota, 'Margaret Fletcher and the Roman Catholic Thinking on Women before the First World War: An Idea of Woman and Woman's Higher Education', *Women's History Magazine*, 58 (2008), pp. 34–7.

H. E. Salter and Mary D. Lobel (eds), *A History of the County of Oxford: Volume 3, The University of Oxford* (London, 1954).

Adam Schwartz, *The Third Spring: G. K. Chesterton, Graham Greene, Christopher Dawson, and David Jones* (Washington, DC, 2005).

Mary G. Segar, *Margaret Fletcher, 1862–1943* (London, 1945).

Arthur Sheehan, *Peter Maurin: Gay Believer* (Garden City, NY, 1959).

Francis J. Sicius, *Peter Maurin: Apostle to the World* (Maryknoll, NY, 2004).

——, 'Peter Maurin's Green Revolution', *U.S. Catholic Historian*, 26:3 (2008), pp. 1–14.

E. A. Siderman, *With Father McNabb at Marble Arch* (Oxford, 1947).

Bonnie G. Smith, *Ladies of The Leisure Class: The Bourgeoises of Northern France in the Nineteenth Century* (Princeton, NJ, 1981).

Harold L. Smith, 'British Feminism in the 1920s', in *British Feminism in the Twentieth Century*, edited by Harold L. Smith (Aldershot, 1990), pp. 47–65.

——, 'British Feminism and the Equal Pay Issue in the 1930s', *Women's History Review*, 5:1 (1996), pp. 97–110.

A. W. Snape, *The Catenian Association: Accrington Circle (80): A Circle History, 1924–2010* (Preston: 2010).

Stephanie Spencer, *Gender, Work and Education in Britain in the 1950s* (London, 2005).

Peter Stanford, *Bronwen Astor: Her Life and Times* (London, 2000).

Hansjakob Stehle, *Eastern Politics of the Vatican*, translated by Sandra Smith (Athens, OH, 1981).

Julie-Marie Strange, 'Fatherhood, Providing and Attachment in late Victorian and Edwardian working-class Families', *Historical Journal*, 55:4 (2012), pp. 1007–27.

Morgan V. Sweeney, 'Diocesan Organisation and Administration', in *The English Catholics, 1850–1950: Essays to Commemorate the Centenary of the Restoration of the Hierarchy of England and Wales*, edited by George Andrew Beck (London, 1950), pp. 116–50.

K. Sword, N. Davies and J. Ciechanowski, *The Formation of the Polish Community in Great Britain, 1939–50* (London, 1989).

Mari Takayanagi 'Sacred Year or Broken Reed? The Sex Disqualification (Removal) Act 1919', *Women's History Review*, 29:4 (2020), pp. 563–82.

Susan L. Tanabaum, 'Rescue Work: Catholic Care in Britain from the 1880s to 1920s', *Journal of the History of Childhood and Youth*, 12:1 (2019), pp. 45–67.

Jessica Bronwyn Thurlow, 'Continuity and Change in British Feminism, c. 1940–1960', unpublished doctoral thesis, University of Michigan, 2006.

J. H. Treble, 'The Development of Roman Catholic Education in Scotland, 1878–1978', *The Innes Review*, 29:2 (1978), pp. 111–39.

Tine Van Osselaer and Thomas Buerman, 'Feminization Thesis: A Survey of International Historiography and a Probing of the Belgian Grounds', *Revue d'Histoire Ecclésiastique*, 103:2 (2008), pp. 1–31.

Derek W. Unwin, *The Community of Europe* (London, 1991).

Tom Villis, *British Catholics and Fascism: Religious Identity and Political Extremism Between the Wars* (London, 2013).

Barbara Wall, 'Bernard Wall and the *Colosseum* (1934–1939)', *Chesterton Review*, 7:3 (1981), pp. 198–224.

———, 'The English "Catholic Worker": Early Days', *Chesterton Review*, 10:3 (1984), pp. 275–93.

Bernard Wall, *Headlong into Change: An Autobiography and a Memoir of Ideas since the Thirties* (London, 1989).

Michael J. Walsh, *From Sword to Ploughshare: Sword of the Spirit to Catholic Institute for International Relations, 1940–1980* (London, 1980).

———, 'Ecumenism in War-Time Britain: The Sword of the Spirit and Religion and Life, 1940–1945', *Heythrop Journal*, 23:3 (1982), pp. 243–58; 23:4 (1982), pp. 365–76.

R. P. Walsh, *The Story Behind the 'Catholic Worker'* (Manchester, 1949).

Maisie Ward, *Training Outlines* (London, 1925).

———, *Unfinished Business* (London and New York, 1964).

Daniel Weinbren, 'Beneath the All-Seeing Eye: Fraternal Order and Friendly Societies' Banners in Nineteenth- and Twentieth-Century Britain', *Cultural and Social History*, 3:2 (2006), pp. 167–91.

Yvonne Maria Werner (ed.), *Christian Masculinity: Men and Religion in Northern Europe in the 19th and 20th Centuries* (Leuven, 2011).

Susan B. Whitney, *Mobilising Youth: Communists and Catholics in Inter-War France* (London, 2009).

Brian Wicker, 'Making Peace at Spode', *New Blackfriars*, 102:1101 (2021), pp. 763–71.

Clifford Williamson, *The History of Catholic Intellectual Life in Scotland, 1918–1965* (London, 2016).

Diane Winston, 'Shame, Fear and Compassion: Media Coverage of Catholicism During the First Decade of the AIDS Crisis', in *In the Logos of*

Love: Promise and Predicament in Catholic Intellectual Life, edited by James L. Heft and Una M. Cadegan (New York, 2016), pp. 171–95.

John Wolffe, 'Anti-Catholicism', in *The Oxford History of British and Irish Catholicism, Volume IV,* pp. 191–208.

Jerzy Zubrzycki, *Polish Immigrants in Britain: A Study of Adjustment*, (Michigan, 1956).

Mark and Louise Zwick, 'Introduction: Dorothy Day and the Catholic Worker Movement', in Dorothy Day, *On Pilgrimage* (Grand Rapids, MI, 1999), pp. 1–64.

INDEX

Abadam, Alice   28, 41
activism   1–2, 7, 42–47, 95, 97,
   115–116, 128–129, 130, 171–179,
   194–195, 199, 213, 216–217
Africa, Africans   31, 102, 125–126,
   201, 202n, 222n, 223, 225
AIDS   198–226 *passim*
AIDS Faith Alliance   205n
AIDS Week public health campaign   200–201, 202n
Allmand, Arthur John   105
Anderton, James   203
Anglo-Polish Catholic Society   99
anti-Catholicism   6, 14, 69–72, 79,
   144, 163n
anti-communism   2, 104, 111, 165
Apostleship of the Sea   80
Apostolicam Actuositatem
   (1965)   180
Arcanum Divinae (1880)   29
archdiocese, *see* Birmingham;
   Glasgow; San Francisco;
   Southwark; Westminster
Arendzen, John   61
Association of Catholic Trade
   Unionists   169, 171
Association of the Ladies of
   Charity of St Vincent de Paul,
   see Ladies of Charity
Astor, Bronwen   184–185
asylum seekers   174–175, 176,
   177–178
Australia   27, 138, 175, 195
autonomous radicalisation   115
Aylesford Priory   146
Aylward, Frank   99, 106, 110

Balkam, Bob   184, 188, 197
Baptism in the Spirit   183–184, 193
Barry, Florence   49, 58
Belch, Stanislaus   101, 107, 109
Belloc, Hilaire   8, 140, 157

Bender, Ryszard   109
Bernadette Soubirous, Saint   146
Berridge, Virginia   200n, 203n
Berrigan, Daniel   173–174
Berrigan, Philip   173–174
Bienkowski, Ludomir   109
Birmingham   63–65, 67, 68, 70,
   72, 74, 99, 107, 117, 135, 136,
   146, 152, 165, 167, 177, 183, 185
Birmingham, Archdiocese of   69,
   218; *see also* McIntyre, John
birth control   16, 46, 54, 55–56, 58,
   152–153
Bishops' Conference of England
   and Wales   117, 129n, 198,
   208, 209n, 212, 215n, 222
Black, Clementina   32
Blackburn   63, 75, 135, 148, 167
Blackfriars Hall, Oxford   184
Bolton   137, 140, 148, 155, 167
Bourne, Francis   15, 26–27, 33, 34,
   36, 37, 40, 44n, 59, 60, 68
Bournemouth   38, 141
Boylan, Eugene   104
Bray, Jilyan   188
Brown, William E.   85, 86, 87
Browne, Henry   59

CAFOD   144, 212n, 215n
Cardijn, Joseph   116n, 117, 118,
   122, 127, 130, 169n
Caritas   109, 128
CARITAS Internationalis (CI)   212
Caritatis studium (1898)   81
Casartelli, Louis Charles   135
catechism   90, 91, 155
catechists   60, 61, 67
Catena   132, 134n, 136–137, 140,
   142, 143, 145–147, 150, 152,
   153, 155, 157
Catenian Association   132–158
   passim

Catholic Action 13, 41, 42–45, 65, 74, 75, 76–79, 83, 93, 101, 107, 117, 118, 125, 126, 144, 148–149, 156, 161, 163
Catholic Action Girls' Organisation (CAGO) 118
Specialised Catholic Action 117, 118
Catholic Agency For Overseas Development, *see* CAFOD
Catholic AIDS Link (CAL) 198–199, 206, 210–224 *passim*
Catholic Bishops' Conference, USA 204n
Catholic Bishops of Ireland 208n
Catholic Charismatic Renewal Service Committee (CCRSC) 182, 186–187, 188, 191
Catholic Citizen 45–49 *passim*
Catholic Council for Polish Welfare 99, 106, 107
Catholic Evidence Guild 43, 59–75 *passim*, 149
Catholic Federation 7, 134, 141, 149
Catholic Herald 49, 108, 165, 166, 195
Catholics for AIDS Prevention and Support (CAPS) 224, 226
Catholic Land Association 163
Catholic Marriage Advisory Council 152
Catholic Missionary Society 59
Catholic Mothers' Union 44
Catholic Needlework Guild 34
Catholic Nurses Guild 44
Catholic Overseas Appointment Bureau 111
Catholic Parents' and Teachers' Association 149
Catholic Peace Action 160n, 174
Catholic People's Week 147
Catholic Renewal Movement 155
Catholic Social Guild 9–10, 24n, 32, 43, 53, 80, 149, 165, 171
Catholic social teaching 2, 4, 9, 13, 16, 52–53, 68, 97, 111, 117, 121n, 122n, 126, 128, 130–131, 149–150, 161, 162, 164, 171, 178, 225
Catholic Teachers' Union 25
Catholic Truth Society (CTS) 59
Catholic Union 5, 97
Catholic University of Lublin, Poland 103, 108–110
Catholic Women's League 14–16, 20–39 *passim*, 44, 57, 108, 112
Catholic Women's Suffrage Society 14, 15, 39, 40, 44–45, 57; *see also* Saint Joan's Social and Political Alliance
Catholic Worker movement 159–179 *passim*
Catholic Worker (newspaper) 162, 165–170 *passim*
Catholic Workers' College 14, 23, 149, 165, 167, 171
Catholic Young Men's Society 69, 80
Celebration of Life, Clifton Cathedral (1993) 213–214
celibacy 156
Central Europe 94–104 *passim*
Centrepeace 223n
chaplaincy
  hospitals 209n
  universities 85, 150, 156
  Young Christian Workers 118, 119, 123, 125, 127, 129
Chappel, James 116, 126
charismatic renewal 18, 155, 180–197 *passim*
  communities 182, 188, 190–192, 194
  gender 186–189
  healing 182, 188, 190, 193–194
  literature 183
  origins in England 182–184
  prayer groups 183–186, 188, 191–196
  United States 181–182, 186, 187, 188–189, 193, 194
charitable works; charity 3, 21n, 103, 105, 136, 137, 147, 148, 151, 152, 161, 166, 198, 210n

children 29, 38, 49–50, 52–53, 84,
    89–92, 120, 128, 139, 147, 149,
    151, 154, 155, 156, 162, 178,
    199n, 209n, 214, 223
Children of Mary 120
Christ the King 113, 123, 126–127,
    184, 226n
Christian Anarchism 160, 161,
    166, 173
Christian Climate Action 179
Christian Evidence Lectures 59–75 *passim*
Christian Family Movement 169
Christian feminism 14, 16, 25n,
    28, 35–36, 38, 40, 45
Christifideles laici (1988) 77
Clark, Steve 182
class (social) 2, 3, 7–9, 10, 14–16,
    33–35, 38, 123, 139–142, 144
  working class 11, 29, 32,
    113–131 *passim*, 135, 137, 149,
    162, 164, 165–166, 170
  middle class 7, 20–21, 23–25,
    30, 39, 46, 54, 95–96, 97,
    134, 136, 138, 149, 156–157,
    181, 182, 195, 196–197
  upper class 34–35, 36, 39, 138
clergy 6–7, 15, 17, 24, 43, 75, 83,
    84, 96, 146, 165, 167, 184, 186,
    187, 188, 199, 205, 211, 212,
    214–215, 221, 224
Clifton 38
  Cathedral 213–214
Clinical Theology Association 190
Cold War 95, 97
Collins, Sylvia 121
Colosseum 164
Communion, *see* Eucharist
communism, communists 9, 11,
    44, 77, 78, 94, 97–98, 104–105,
    107, 162, 165, 167
Community of Christ the
    King 184, 191
condom (prophylaxis) 202,
    202–204, 207, 208n, 210, 215,
    217n
confidentiality 218

Congregation for the Doctrine of
    the Faith (CDF) 204n, 212n,
    215n, 221n
Congregationalism 184
conscience 153, 156
Conservative Family Campaign
    (CFC) 202n–203n
contraception 55n, 56n, 152, 153n,
    215
converts 3, 6, 7n, 8, 20–39
    passim, 44, 73, 80, 157, 184
Covid-19 200
Crawford, Virginia 31, 47
Craven, George Laurence 103
Crowley, John 212, 216, 218
Crucible 20–39 *passim*
crucified, crucifixion 222
Cursillo 180
Czechoslovakia, Czechs 23, 94

Daly, William 82
Dames of St Joan 44, 58
Day, Dorothy 159n, 161–162,
    172–173
Days of Renewal 186–189 *passim*
Deptula, Czeslaw 109
diagnosis, *see* HIV diagnosis
Dignity (organisation) 215n
diocese, *see* Birmingham; Clifton;
    Glasgow; Nottingham;
    San Francisco; Southwark;
    Westminster
direct action 162, 173–174, 176
discrimination 201, 217, 218, 222
Distributist League 163
Divini illius magistri
    (1929) 78–88 *passim*
divorce 16, 46, 54–55, 56, 58, 153,
    169
Dominicans (Order of
    Preachers) 28n, 59–61,
    64–65, 68, 70, 73, 184, 198,
    205, 206, 207n
Dorothy Day House 177
Douai Abbey 225n
Downey, Richard 72, 167
Downside Abbey 213n
Drinkwater, Francis 92

Eastern Europe 94–95, 97–101, 104, 105, 107, 112
ecumenical, ecumenism 12–13, 18–19, 95, 182–185, 196, 213, 226n
Edinburgh 45n, 67, 69, 80, 86, 87, 89, 140n
education 3, 5, 11, 14, 23–26, 28, 30–32, 38, 48–49, 51, 76–93 *passim*, 98, 105–106, 109, 115–116, 118, 134, 147–148, 149, 155, 163, 180, 202n, 203n, 212n, 217–218
  public health education 198, 200n, 209n, 216
Education (Scotland) Act, 1872 80
Education (Scotland) Act, 1918 80–81, 82
employment equality 42, 46–52, 54, 55, 58, 114
Encounter 206–208, 222, 226
equalitarian feminism 42, 50–51, 57
Eucharist 17, 122, 155, 195, 201n, 213; *see also* Mass
Eucharistic Ministers 17, 155
European Voluntary Workers 97
Evangelisation 2, 3, 123, 180, 194
Eyre, Charles 82

Falwell, Jerry 203
family 29, 31, 53–54, 84, 100, 114, 116, 133–134, 139–158 *passim*, 169, 175, 194, 205, 208, 209n, 210, 217, 219, 224, 225
Family and Social Action (FSA) 129
Family Planning Association 202n
fatherhood 139, 143, 154, 156–158
Farm Street, Mayfair 22, 31, 38
Fascism 77, 78, 79n
feminisation thesis 133
feminism 14, 16, 20–58 *passim*, 130
First World War 4, 10, 41, 47, 81, 93, 117, 135, 140, 145, 146
Fitzsimons, John 118n, 129

Fletcher, Margaret 14, 20–39 *passim*, 44
Fletcher, Philip 58
Ford, Josephine Massyngberde 187, 189, 191
Fowler, Norman 200n
Fox, Langton 187–188
Francis, Pope 226n
Frauenbund 25
Freemasons 136–137, 143, 144
French Church of Our Lady of Notre Dame, London 212–213
friendship 23, 100, 101, 110, 121, 123, 133–134, 139, 145, 156, 205n, 208, 210n, 213, 219, 226
Fuchs, Krystyna 210

Gaffney, Pat 174
Gates, Mary 123
gay 153, 198–226 *passim*
Gay Plague 200–202
Gayer, Anne 225n
Gdynia, Poland 109
gender 14, 23–29, 30–31, 33, 37, 41–42, 44–45, 51, 61–62, 66–67, 75, 86, 128–129, 131, 133, 140–141, 155–158, 182, 188–189
  gender and women's work 32, 51, 47–54, 129–130
  gender essentialism 29, 116, 130
George, Saint 146–147
Germanus, Brother 86, 89–90
Glasgow 69–70, 76, 79n, 84–89 *passim*, 135, 140, 167, 168, 169, 176, 177
  Archdiocese 78, 82, 86; *see also* Eyre, Charles; Mackintosh, Donald
Glasgow and West of Scotland Catholic Teachers' Association 82
Goa 157
Godfrey, William 102–103
Gomulka, Wladyslaw 107

Goodnews 180, 182, 187–190, 193, 195, 197
Great War, *see* First World War
Greene, Dana 74–75
Greene, Vivian 108
Griffin, Bernard William 102, 157
Guazzelli, Victor 213
Guild of Catholic Teachers 76–93 *passim*
Guild of Ransom 58, 59
Guile, Alan 188, 193, 194, 196
Guiney, Louise Imogen 26, 27
Gustave Weigel Society 184
Gwinnel, Mike 188, 189

Harris, Alana 3, 181
Harris, Peter 210, 211n
healing 182, 188, 190, 193–194, 213
Helpers of the Holy Souls Congregation 223n
Hexham and Newcastle, Diocese of 69, 70
Higgins, Terry 202n
Hinsley, Arthur 78n, 94, 163, 165, 167
Hipperson, Sarah 174
HIV 198–226 *passim*
　diagnosis 199n, 207, 209n, 210n, 217–218, 219–220, 225
　stigma 199, 201–202, 208, 210, 213n, 216, 217, 218, 220, 222, 226
Hocken, Peter 183–184, 191
Hoggart, Richard 120
holiness 180
Holy Child Convent, London 26
Holy Cross School, Leicester 64
Holy Family 154
Holy See 43–44, 84
Holy Spirit 145, 184, 193, 207
homosexual, *see* gay
Horn, Gerd-Rainer 115–116, 124
Horn, Romuald 65
Hornsby-Smith, Michael 4, 6, 8, 17, 96n, 121, 159n
House of the Open Door Community 191–192

Howard, Edmund 163–164
Howard, Joseph 66
Howard, Mary 34
Hull 66, 135
Humanae Vitae (1968) 17, 153
Hume, Basil 197, 202–204, 209n, 212, 215n
Hungary 9

Il Fermo Proposito (1905) 43
immigrants, immigration 5, 95, 97, 133, 157, 174, 215n
International Catholic Radio Movement 100
International Christian AIDS Network (ICAN) 211–212
Ireland, Irish 3, 5, 6, 8, 11, 22, 34, 82, 106, 111, 172n, 195, 208n, 212n

Jarrett, Bede 73
Jeffery, Gabrielle 40, 58
Jesuits 4, 22, 31, 37, 59, 66, 184, 190
Jeunesse ouvrière chrétienne (JOC, JOCF) 43, 113, 116, 124
Joan of Arc, Saint 28, 57
John Bosco, Saint 76, 84, 89
John XXIII, Pope 16, 116
John Paul II, Pope 77, 224
Johnson, Alice 38
Johnson, George 93n
Jukes, Jo 129
Jundzill, Balinski 101
Justice and Peace (movement) 18, 174, 178, 194

Keating, Frederick William 23, 58
Keegan, Patrick 117
Kelly, Elaine 223n
Kelly, George 152
Kerr, Peter 105
Klub Intelligencji Katolickiej 107–108
Knights of St Columba 145
Knox, Ronald 73

Ladies of Charity 25, 33–37

lapsed Catholics   75, 197
Larkin, Peter   206–207, 209n, 211n
Latin Mass Society   18
Latvia, Latvians   94, 97
Laughton Mathews, Vera   56
Lavelle, Paul   208n
Leeds   62, 66, 69, 70, 71, 135, 150, 165, 166, 192, 193
   university   188
Legion of Mary   11–12, 120
Leicester   64, 65, 70, 73
Leo XIII, Pope   29, 32, 35, 81; see also *Rerum Novarum*
libraries   63, 72, 89, 119, 141
Life in the Spirit seminars   182, 186, 188
listening
Lithuania   63, 90, 131, 207, 217, 221, 222
Liturgical Movement   180
liturgy   17, 33, 87, 132, 143, 150, 155, 194, 211–217; see also Eucharist; Mass
lived experience   204–207
Liverpool   23, 45n, 53, 59, 67, 69, 70, 72, 127, 135, 141, 144, 150, 155, 163n, 167, 175, 176, 177, 185
   Archdiocese   188; see also Downey, Richard; Keating, Frederick William
Loftus, Robert   225n
London   22, 25, 26, 33, 34, 38, 40, 55n, 56, 61, 66, 70, 72, 100, 101, 103, 104, 106, 107, 109, 110, 111, 117, 125, 135, 138, 141, 142, 143, 145, 147, 149, 160n, 165, 166, 167, 168, 172n, 173, 177–179, 183, 185, 188, 191, 209n, 211, 213, 220, 226
   university   106
Lopes, Michael   206
Lourdes   141, 148, 152, 154, 181
Lublin, Poland, see Catholic University of Lublin
Lumsden, Peter   173, 177, 178
Lynch, Bernard   225n

Lyons, Mary   113, 120, 127, 128

MacDonald, Andrew   86, 87, 89
McDonnnel, Kilian   181
McGlynn, Patrick   83–87 *passim*
McIntyre, John   58, 60, 61
McNabb, Vincent   65, 68
McNamara, Peggy   116
Maccagno, Dennis   118
Mackintosh, Donald   82, 84–86, 92
Maddison, Molly   118, 119, 125
magisterium   153, 191, 207, 215, 224
Manchester   2, 37–38, 60, 70, 72, 107, 135, 136n, 140, 142, 143, 147, 150, 166–167, 168, 177, 185, 187, 223, 226
Manning, Henry Edward   9, 20, 32, 163
Mansi, Dominic   213n
Marie-Salomé, see Roudaut, Marie-Renée
marriage   29, 34, 52–53, 55, 56n, 57, 106, 114, 116, 119–122, 127, 128, 151–152, 154, 156, 202n
marriage bar   47–48, 54
Martin, Carmel   174
Martin, Dan   174
Martin, Ralph   182
Martindale, Cyril Charlie   31, 43n
Mary, Blessed Virgin   5, 57n, 147, 154
Maryhill   176, 177n
masculinity   22, 132–158 *passim*
Mass   2, 17, 56–57, 63, 87, 100, 122, 146, 155, 157, 164, 165, 181, 197, 212–214, 216, 221; see also Eucharist; liturgy
Mathew, David   100
Maurin, Peter   160–162
Menevia, Diocese of   150, 187–188
Misner, Paul   130
Modernism (theological movement)   7, 30
Montessori, Maria   92
moral panic   201, 216, 217, 222

INDEX

Mother Marie-Salomé, *see* Roudaut, Marie-Renée
motherhood   29–31, 41, 52–53, 54, 58, 114, 116, 121, 128
muscular Christianity   133

National Catholic AIDS Network (NCAN)   206, 211
National Catholic Conference, Brighton (1906)   33
National Council of Women   49, 56
National Pastoral Congress (1980)   155
National Service Committee (NSC)   187–188, 193, 195, 196–197
National Union of Societies for Equal Citizenship   41, 55
National Union of Women's Suffrage Societies   41
Neville, Mildred   16–17
Newcastle   59, 66, 68, 70, 72, 135, 165, 167; *see also* Hexham and Newcastle, Diocese of
Newell, Martin   177
Newman Association   7, 9, 10, 94–112 *passim*
Newman Association Circles   97, 101, 104, 108
Newman Association International Centre   100–104, 111
Newman Association International Committee   102–104, 107–110 *passim*
Newman, John Henry   20, 96
Newman, Mary   23
Nichols, Vincent   179
nonviolence   159n, 161–162, 172–174, 178
Nottingham   65, 70
   Diocese   69
nuclear weapons   174, 176–177

Oberammergau   141
O'Connor, Francis   191

O'Connor, John   203, 204n
O'Hara, Gerald Patrick Aloysius   103
O'Reilly, Ciaron   175–177
Open Door Council   42, 47, 52
Order of Preachers, *see* Dominicans
Oriel College, Oxford   102, 105
orthodoxy   37, 215, 222
orthopraxis   224
Our Lady Guild of Ransom, *see* Guild of Ransom
Oxford   22, 26, 38, 70, 107, 150, 160n, 174, 175, 176, 177, 207n; *see also* Catholic Workers' College; Plater College
   University   30, 31, 108, 163; *see also* Blackfriars Hall; Oriel College

Pacifism   159n, 162, 167, 171, 173
Pakenham, Frank   150
Parr, Roy   225n
pastoral care   18, 187, 192, 198, 206, 209–211
PAX   18, 165n, 171, 172, 173
Pax Christi   18, 17In, 176, 178
Pax Romana   99, 100, 110–112
peace   18, 142, 164n, 167, 171–174, 176
Pendergast, Martin   204, 210, 211n, 212n, 218, 224n
pentecostalism   181–185
People of God   7, 132, 189
People of Praise   182, 190
personalism   161, 166
Petre, Maude   31, 38
philanthropy   20, 25, 30, 34, 39, 132; *see also* charitable works
Phillimore, John   80
pilgrimage   5, 9, 12, 57, 141, 146, 148, 152, 154, 155, 194
Pius X, Pope   29, 33, 35, 43
Pius XI, Pope   9, 43, 56n, 57, 77–79, 83–88 *passim*, 114, 123, 148; see also *Quadragesimo Anno*

Pius XII, Pope 58n, 84, 114, 128
Plater College 23; *see also* Catholic Workers' College
Ploughshares Movement 160, 175–178
Poland, Poles 3, 23, 94–112 *passim*
Polish Catholic Action 101, 107
Polish exiles 94–112 *passim*
Polish Red Cross 109
Polish University Catholic Association, *see* Veritas
Pope, Hugh 59–62, 64–65, 67–68, 70
Portlock, Stephen 225n
Positive Faith HIV Peer Support Ministry 225n, 226
Positively Catholic HIV Peer Support Group 211
prayer 13, 23, 43, 56, 57, 62, 63, 93, 126–127, 134, 143, 145–146, 147, 154–155, 181, 187, 194, 206, 208, 212–214, 217, 226
prayer groups 183–186, 188, 191–196
preaching 22n, 59–62, 65, 70, 104, 190, 192, 213n, 214–217, 222, 226n
prejudice 21n, 73, 201, 206, 208–209, 216–218, 222; *see also* anti-Catholicism; stigma
priesthood 156, 194
public health 55, 119, 198–200, 205, 207, 209n, 213n, 217

Quadragesimo Anno (1931) 10, 43, 114n, 123, 165
Quest 215n, 221

Radcliffe, Timothy 206n
Ranaghan, Dorothy and Kevin 182–183
Ratzinger, Joseph 204n
Rechowicz, Marian 103, 110
reform 9, 11, 16–17, 54, 84, 87, 90, 181
Reformation 153, 156

refugees 97n, 106n, 176–179
religious education 26n, 76–93 *passim*, 155
Religious Knowledge course books 89–93
religious orders, congregations 4–6, 18, 26n, 30, 37, 81, 86, 121, 123, 129, 180, 184, 185–186, 188, 195, 205
Rerum Novarum (1891) 10, 32, 35, 68, 165, 171n
retreats 61, 64, 65, 68, 125, 126, 146, 147, 151, 155, 174, 184, 211, 223, 225n, 226
Reynolds, Lisa 188, 189
Roche, Lawrence 110
Roche, Mary 85
rosary 23, 66, 146, 181
Rotary 142
Roudaut, Marie-Renée (Mother Marie-Salomé) 31
Runcie, Robert 202, 203n
Russia 104

Sacred Heart 78
saints, *see* Bernadette Soubirous; George; Joan of Arc; John Bosco; Mary; Therese of Lisieux; Thomas More
St Aloysius Church, East London 213
St Aloysius Church, Oxford 22, 24
Saint Joan's Social and Political Alliance 14, 40–58; *see also* Catholic Women's Suffrage Society
San Francisco, Archdiocese of 206
Sawicki, F. 107
Scottish Catholic Federation 82
Scottish Catholic Herald 69, 78, 83–84
scholarships 14, 105–106, 108, 111, 149
Second Vatican Council 1–2, 4, 7, 13, 16–18, 77, 93, 95, 116, 117n,

INDEX 251

132, 143, 152, 157, 180–181, 189, 196, 215
Second World War 2, 5, 12–13, 69, 81n, 92, 94, 111, 140, 147, 157, 162, 163n, 167, 172, 181, 200n
secularisation 154, 156, 181, 194
See-Judge-Act 121, 123–124, 169n
sermons, *see* preaching
Sex Qualification (Removal) Act of 1919 48, 52
sex workers 201
sexual intercourse 55, 137, 152–153, 215
sexuality 198, 202n, 212n, 219, 220
shame 210n, 217, 220
Sheed, Frank 64–66, 73–75
Sheffield 135
Shields, Thomas 92
Simon Community 172, 177n
sin 153n, 202–204, 219, 222, 225
Six Point Group 42, 47, 52
Skwarczyński, Paul 106
sociability 132–158 *passim*
socialisation 154, 156
Society of Jesus, *see* Jesuits
Society of St Vincent de Paul 18, 80, 176
South Africa 126
Southport 128, 141
Southwark 58, 67, 68
Southwark, Archdiocese of 58, 66, 69, 174, 209n
Spode Conference (1963) 173
Spode Conference (1986) 205–208, 210
Spode House 171, 173, 205
spirituality 11–12, 18, 95, 115, 126–127, 133, 146, 147, 155–156, 180–197 *passim*, 225–226
stigma, *see* HIV – stigma
Stigma of the Cross 222
Streeter, Ada 37
Student Christian Movement 173
students 28, 30, 95–96, 99, 102, 105–106, 108–109, 111, 118, 150, 167, 182, 193

Suenens, Leo Joseph 181, 191, 195
Swansea 104, 140n
Sword of the Spirit 12–13, 95

Talbot, Mary 21, 25, 34, 36, 37
Terrence Higgins Trust (THT) 205
Therese of Lisieux, Saint 126
Thomas More, Saint 154–155
three truths (Cardijn) 127
Tolkien, J. R. R. 150
Tomlin, Rene 120
Towey, Raymond 160n, 174
trade unions, trade unionists 11, 84n, 120, 137, 167n, 169, 171, 178
training for clergy 217, 218, 221
transnationalism 125–126, 133, 181–182
True House community 182
Tugwell, Simon 184

UNAIDS 198n
Union of Catholic Mothers 39, 140
Union of Catholic Students 101, 111
United States of America 25, 100, 101, 106, 167, 181–193 *passim*, 199, 204n
Universe 49, 50, 53
universities 24, 30–31, 49, 62, 72, 80, 83, 85, 95, 99, 103, 105–106, 150, 182, 190, 211n; *see also* Catholic University of Lublin; chaplaincy – universities; Leeds; London; Oxford
University Catholic Societies Federation 95, 101
Urquhart, Francis 31

Vatican 224
Vatican II, *see* Second Vatican Council
Vatican Conference on AIDS (1989) 206, 207n, 222
Vaughan, Bernard 26, 36–38
Vaughan House, Westminster 225

Veritas (Polish University Catholic Association)   104–109
vocations   30, 48, 74, 77, 119, 121–123, 128, 130–131, 156, 169n, 219

Wall, Barbara   163–165, 171
Wall, Bernard   163–165, 171
Walsh, Bob   166, 168–170, 172
Walsh, Michael   13
Walsh, Molly   169
Walsh, Thomas   36
Walsingham   57
Ward, Maisie   31, 63, 65–66, 73–75
Warner, Eleanor   30–31
Welby, Justin   179
welfare   5, 16, 41–42, 45, 52, 120, 139, 169
Western Evening Herald   72
Westminster   57, 60–61, 63–65, 68, 225
   Archbishop, *see* Bourne, Francis; Griffin, Bernard William; Hinsley, Arthur; Godfrey, William; Hume, Basil; Nichols, Vincent; Vaughan, Bernard
   Archdiocese   59, 68–69, 74, 167, 190, 209n, 211n, 213n
   Cathedral   57, 146, 155, 174n
Whately, Monica   47, 52
White, John   206–207, 211n
Whittaker, Edmund   80, 87
widows   141, 147
Willison, Mabel   29–30

Wilkinson, Sheila   121
Winston, Diane   204
women's employment   14, 42–58 *passim*, 84, 113–131 *passim*
women's rights   15, 21, 28–58 *passim*
Word of God community   182, 188, 190
workplace activism   115–120, 128
World War I, *see* First World War
World War II, *see* Second World War
World Youth Day   154
Wyatt-Papworth, Lucy   34, 37

Young Christian Students   118
Young Christian Workers   43, 113–131 *passim*, 148, 171
   chaplains   118, 119, 123, 125, 127, 129
   Girls' Movement   115, 117, 119, 125, 127n
   Gospel enquiries   121, 127
   organisers   116, 117–118, 121–129 *passim*
   sections   117–119, 122–123, 125, 127, 128, 129
   principle of like-to-like   123–124
   spirituality   115, 123, 126–127
   transnationalism   125–126
Young Worker newspaper   120, 129

Zanetti, Frances   38
Zwolski, Euegeniusz   109